PRAISE FOR THE

ALMANAC *of* ARCHITECTURE & DESIGN

"Indispensable for any public library, any design firm, and any school of architecture, landscape architecture, or interior design … solid, reliable, and remarkably complete."

Robert Campbell, Pulitzer Prize-winning Architecture Critic, *The Boston Globe*

———

"The Almanac of Architecture & Design *is more than a mere compilation of numbers and words and charts and graphs. … It is about ideas as well as information"*

Blair Kamin, Pulitzer Prize-winning Architecture Critic, *Chicago Tribune*

———

"No comparable resource exists."

Library Journal

———

"The reader who uses this book well will come away with a richer sense of the texture of the profession and of the architecture it produces."

Paul Goldberger, Pulitzer Prize-winning Architecture Critic, *The New Yorker*

———

"The definitive fact book on architecture and design."

The American Institute of Architects

———

"This is the book that informs decision makers like no other."

Society for Marketing Professional Services

———

"This almanac, filled with resources, can help all those involved in the building arts to better fulfill this unusual moment's potential."

Robert Ivy, Editor in Chief, *Architectural Record*

———

"A core reference title for personal, professional, and academic reference collections."

Midwest Book Review

———

"This is the comprehensive media guide to architecture and design's defining moments."

The Design Futures Council

DesignIntelligence®

ALMANAC of ARCHITECTURE & DESIGN 2011

12TH EDITION

DesignIntelligence®

ALMANAC *of*
ARCHITECTURE
& DESIGN 2011
12TH EDITION

FOUNDING EDITOR AND PUBLISHER
JAMES P. CRAMER

EDITOR
JANE PARADISE WOLFORD, PH.D.

östberg

Library of Design Management

Greenway Communications

Publisher and Founding Editor:	**James P. Cramer, Hon. AIA, Hon. IIDA, CAE**
Almanac Editor:	**Jane Paradise Wolford, Ph.D., LEED AP**
Art Director:	**Austin M. Cramer**
Graphic Design:	**Karen Berube**
Editorial Advisor:	**Jennifer Evans Yankopolus**
Market Data Consultant:	**Arol Wolford, Hon. AIA**
Research and Editorial Staff:	**Connie Brown, Lee Cuthbert, Mary Pereboom, Alexa Smith, Tonya Smith**
Indexer:	**Kay Wosewick**
Business Development Manager:	**Bill Brown**

Greenway Communications, LLC

Principal and President/CEO:	**James P. Cramer**
Principal for Research, Consulting, and Administration:	**Mary Pereboom**
Principal for Publishing and Editorial:	**Jane Gaboury**
Managing Director, Design Futures Council:	**Jonathan Bahe**
Art Director and Managing Editor, *DesignIntelligence*:	**Austin M. Cramer**
Manager, Östberg Library of Design Management:	**Tonya Smith**

Greenway Communications,
a division of The Greenway Group
25 Technology Parkway South, Suite 101
Atlanta, GA 30092
(800) 726-8603
www.greenway.us
www.di.net

Publisher's Cataloging-in-Publication
Almanac of architecture & design / James P. Cramer
and Jane Paradise Wolford, editors
   2011 ed.
   p. cm.
   Almanac of architecture and design
   Includes bibliographical references and index
   ISBN–13: 978-0-9846136-0-1
   ISBN–10: 0-9846136-0-9

   1. Architecture—Directories. 2. Architectural design. 3.
Architecture—United States. I. Title: Almanac of architecture
and design

NA9.A27 2011   720

Contents

5 OBITUARIES

6 BUILDINGS | Awards

7 BUILDING TYPES

8 OUTSIDE & INSIDE SPACES | Awards

9 SUSTAINABILITY | Green Design & Historic Preservation

10 MAKING A DIFFERENCE

11 DESIGN RESOURCES

Introduction

Architecture and design are never stagnant. Here in the 12th edition of the *Almanac of Architecture & Design* you will find stories of both growth and decline. As we enter the second decade of the 21st century, today's "best of times, worst of times" offers a great opportunity to consider what is important and what has been significant.

Our goal with the *Almanac* is to chronicle everything of importance in the designed environment. We document design authorship of significant buildings and we offer obituaries of leading designers who shaped our built environment. These have been our community's friends and teachers. Their work confirms the aspirations of the human spirit.

You will find dimensions of inspiration on many of the pages that follow. The directory and awards sections are overflowing with examples that showcase the increasing importance design.

In fact, we have assembled more information on change in the world of architecture and design than ever before. We believe that you will find value in a multitude of ways. Not only are there new statistics to consider, but you will also discover reinvention. Unfolding in these pages is the record of change in the design professions and the A/E/C industry. Despite the global economic slump, there are professional practices that are dominating their markets and earning awards in those realms. In fact, you'll find leadership examples of all shapes, sizes, and differentiated talents.

Billings of the top firms are in some cases up and in other down. Regardless, design isn't just about monetary growth and business; it is about planning the future and getting ready for what's next. The seeds for future success are being sown in innovative ways, and we have identified the movers and shakers in this sourcebook. For this reason, the *Almanac* serves as the primary media guide for architecture facts.

To be an architect or designer is an awesome responsibility. The end result is an outcome of teamwork. The owners, the designers, the contractors, and the engineers all work together to construct what will be used by groups as small as families and as large as nations. Architecture and design grabs us in ways we are often not conscious of, yet behavior, mood, and human activities are enriched by the success of the form and function of design. Human emotion resonates with the physical properties of a building to create an uplifting, energizing response that transcends expectations.

Here in the 12th edition of the *Almanac of Architecture & Design* you will find the charts, graphs, lists, and stories of progress and possibility. Thank you for joining us as we digest what's important today along with some hints of what is likely to come next.

James P. Cramer, Hon. AIA, Publisher and Founding Editor, jcramer@di.net
Jane Paradise Wolford, Ph.D., Editor, jwolford@di.net

DesignIntelligence 333 |

This chapter features a ranking of America's top 333 architecture firms, along with useful contact information and pertinent data.

DesignIntelligence 333

The *DesignIntelligence* 333 ranks the top 333 architecture and design firms in North America. To compile the most accurate and up-to-date information, the research staff of the *Almanac* surveyed firms throughout the United States and Canada during the spring and summer of 2010. Under the direction of the editors, extensive research was conducted by the *Almanac* staff and the research staff of *DesignIntelligence* to compile a comprehensive geographically and demographically diverse group of firms that would qualify for inclusion. Professional associations, media lists, client organizations, and conference registrations of the Design Futures Council were also studied to determine the most active leading firms in the US. The Greenway Group also researched additional media sources, such as leading professional and business publications read by clients in each of the areas of specialty.

The firms were mailed a letter inviting them to participate in the survey, along with a copy of the survey. The survey asked for information regarding their areas of specialty, employment counts, number of offices, fields of professional practice, 2009 gross professional fee revenues, leading officers of the firms, and other relevant information. The data collected was also used for the *Almanac*'s Directory of America's Leading Architecture and Design Firms.

Telephone calls and emails followed mailed surveys if additional information was needed. Each firm included in this *Almanac* was contacted a minimum of three times by mail, email, or telephone. When firms did not respond, estimates were made based on previous surveys completed by the firms for *DesignIntelligence*, listings in business media, Greenway's private research databases, reliable information on the Internet regarding employee counts, and other credible sources. At least three independent sources were used to estimate gross revenues when the firms did not supply these figures. Blank fields in the ranking section or missing profile information were due to the firm not returning its survey. Totals may not equal 100 percent due to rounding.

To fill out a survey for next year's *Almanac*, visit www.di.net, call *DesignIntelligence* at (678) 879-0929, or contact the editor at jwolford@di.net.

Note: n/p = not provided

Tim Griffith

William H. Hannon Library, Loyola Marymount University, Los Angeles, CA | AECOM

1 | AECOM (Architecture)

515 South Flower Street, Suite 3700
Los Angeles, CA 90071
(213) 593-8000
www.aecom.com
Jason Prior, CEO
Thomas K. Fridstein, Executive VP
Barbara Price, Executive VP
Rick Lincicome, Executive VP

WORLDWIDE REVENUE	$695,100,000
US REVENUE	$278,000,000
WORLDWIDE STAFF	4,369
HEADQUARTERS	Los Angeles, CA; 400+ offices
YEAR ESTABLISHED	1990

RECENT REPRESENTATIVE PROJECT

Blue Cross Blue Shield of Florida
Corporate Headquarters, Jacksonville, FL

GEOGRAPHIC ANALYSIS OF WORK IN THE US

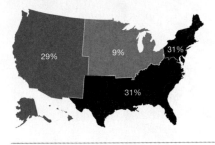

GEOGRAPHIC ANALYSIS OF WORK OUTSIDE THE US

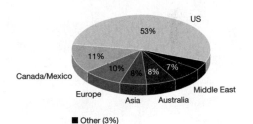

PRIMARY SERVICES OFFERED

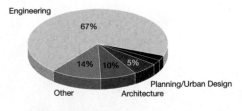

MARKET SEGMENTS

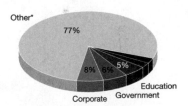

PHILOSOPHY

AECOM's purpose is to enhance and sustain the world's built, natural and social environments. We have come together as a global, integrated design platform with deep-seated connections to the adjacent fields of planning, engineering, and landscape architecture, suited to designing buildings that most of the world would experience. These buildings integrate with their natural and social contexts to help them become part of the solution to the world's greatest challenges.

AƎCOM

Benny Chan

Ritz-Carlton Hotel & Residences and JW Marriott at L.A. LIVE, Los Angeles, CA | Gensler

2 | Gensler

2 Harrison Street
San Francisco, CA 94105
(415) 433-3700
www.gensler.com
M. Arthur Gensler Jr., Chairman
Andy Cohen, Executive Director
Diane Hoskins, Executive Director

WORLDWIDE REVENUE	$550,000,000
US REVENUE	$418,000,000
WORLDWIDE STAFF	2,200
HEADQUARTERS	San Francisco, CA; 334 offices
YEAR ESTABLISHED	1965
RECENT REPRESENTATIVE PROJECT	

City Center
Las Vegas, NV

GEOGRAPHIC ANALYSIS OF WORK IN THE US

GEOGRAPHIC ANALYSIS OF WORK OUTSIDE THE US

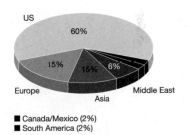

PRIMARY SERVICES OFFERED

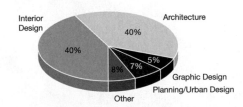

MARKET SEGMENTS

PHILOSOPHY

Redefining what's possible through the power of design is Gensler's global vision. Whether designing a small wine bottle label or a large new urban district, we strive to serve clients as trusted advisors, combining localized, real-time expertise with a global perspective. Our work reflects an enduring commitment to sustainability and the belief that design is one of the most powerful strategic tools for securing lasting competitive advantage.

Gensler

Jean Picoulet

King Abdullah University of Science and Technology, Thuwal, Saudi Arabia | HOK

3 | HOK

211 North Broadway, Suite 700	WORLDWIDE REVENUE	$473,000,000
St. Louis, MO 63102	US REVENUE	$276,000,000
(314) 421-2000	WORLDWIDE STAFF	1,874
www.hok.com	HEADQUARTERS	St. Louis, MO; 23 offices
William E. Valentine, Chairman	YEAR ESTABLISHED	1955
Bill Hellmuth, President	RECENT REPRESENTATIVE PROJECT	
Patrick MacLeamy, CEO	King Abdullah University of Science and Technology, Thuwal, Saudi Arabia	

GEOGRAPHIC ANALYSIS OF WORK IN THE US

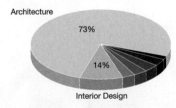

GEOGRAPHIC ANALYSIS OF WORK OUTSIDE THE US

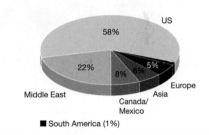

PRIMARY SERVICES OFFERED

■ Graphic Design (1%)   ■ Landscape Architecture (3%)
■ Engineering (3%)   ■ Planning/Urban Design (3%)
■ Other (3%)

MARKET SEGMENTS

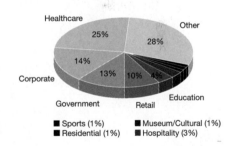

■ Sports (1%)   ■ Museum/Cultural (1%)
■ Residential (1%)   ■ Hospitality (3%)

PHILOSOPHY

HOK is committed to bringing ideas to life through creative, collaborative design solutions that meet our clients' needs while making the world a better place.

James Steinkamp

Chervon International Trading Company, Nanjing, China | Perkins+Will

Benjamin Benschneider

Center for Urban Waters, Tacoma, WA | Perkins+Will

4 | Perkins+Will

330 North Wabash Avenue, Suite 3600
Chicago, IL 60611
(312) 755-0770
www.perkinswill.com
Phil Harrison, President/CEO
Bill Viehman, VP

WORLDWIDE REVENUE	$406,900,000
US REVENUE	$291,200,000
WORLDWIDE STAFF	1,477
HEADQUARTERS	23 offices
YEAR ESTABLISHED	1935
RECENT REPRESENTATIVE PROJECT	

One Haworth Center
Holland, MI

GEOGRAPHIC ANALYSIS OF WORK IN THE US

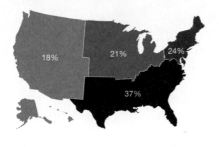

GEOGRAPHIC ANALYSIS OF WORK OUTSIDE THE US

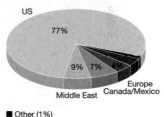

- Other (1%)
- Asia (2%)

PRIMARY SERVICES OFFERED

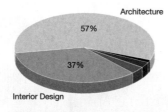

- Planning/Urban Design (1%)
- Other (2%)
- Landscape Architecture (3%)

MARKET SEGMENTS

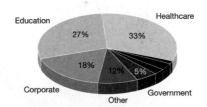

- Residential (1%)
- Hospitality (2%)
- Museum/Cultural (2%)

PHILOSOPHY

Perkins+Will adheres to the same design philosophy today that was crafted by its founders in 1935—"ideas + buildings that honor the broader goals of society." Sustainability plays an essential role in everything we do. It's our personal commitment to creating solutions that contribute to human well-being and enhance the long-term health of our planet. Although our designs may address many people, many places and many cultures, our work speaks to one human being at a time.

PERKINS
+ WILL

Nick Merrick © Hedrich Blessing

Burj Khalifa, Dubai, UAE | Skidmore, Owings & Merrill

5 | Skidmore, Owings & Merrill

224 South Michigan Avenue, Suite 1000
Chicago, IL 60604
(312) 554-9090
www.som.com
Gary Haney, Partner
Jeffrey J. McCarthy, Partner
Gene Schnair, Partner

WORLDWIDE REVENUE	$303,000,000
US REVENUE	$119,000,000
WORLDWIDE STAFF	908
HEADQUARTERS	10 offices
YEAR ESTABLISHED	1936
RECENT REPRESENTATIVE PROJECT	

Trump International Hotel and Tower
Chicago, IL

GEOGRAPHIC ANALYSIS OF WORK IN THE US

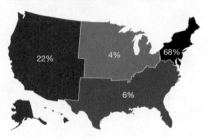

GEOGRAPHIC ANALYSIS OF WORK OUTSIDE THE US

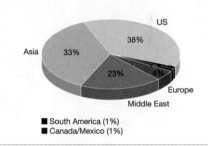

PRIMARY SERVICES OFFERED

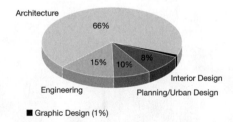

MARKET SEGMENTS

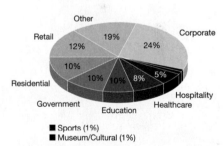

PHILOSOPHY

SOM's interdisciplinary practice composed of architecture, structural and MEP engineering, urban design, interior design, and environmental graphics, approaches each project from a holistic perspective. As a leader in the comprehensive integration of sustainable building ideas as well as intelligent building design using Building Information Modeling (BIM), advanced seismic engineering, and high-performance MEP systems, our buildings are socially and environmentally responsive, and perform functionally and aesthetically well into the future.

SOM

HDR Architecture, Inc.; © 2010 Creative Sources Photography

Parker H. Petit Science Center, Georgia State University, Atlanta, GA | HDR Architecture, Inc.

6 | HDR Architecture, Inc.

8404 Indian Hills Drive
Omaha, NE 68114
(402) 399-1000
www.hdrarchitecture.com
Merle Bachman, President
Michael Doiel, Senior VP
Doug Wignall, Senior VP

WORLDWIDE REVENUE	$286,540,295
US REVENUE	$258,541,678
WORLDWIDE STAFF	1,634
HEADQUARTERS	Omaha, NE; 40 offices
YEAR ESTABLISHED	1917
RECENT REPRESENTATIVE PROJECT	

US Centers for Disease Control
Atlanta, GA

GEOGRAPHIC ANALYSIS OF WORK IN THE US

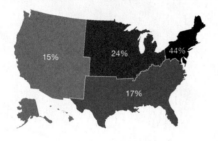

GEOGRAPHIC ANALYSIS OF WORK OUTSIDE THE US

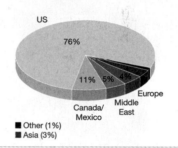

PRIMARY SERVICES OFFERED

MARKET SEGMENTS

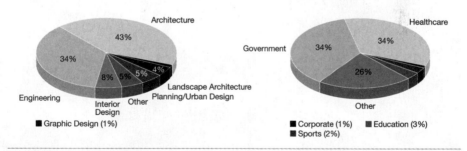

PHILOSOPHY

A dedication to establishing "clients for life" has always been one of HDR Architecture's foremost values. We are committed to creating rewarding and long-term relationships with our clients, as evidenced by our 80% repeat client base. As an employee-owned firm, each one of us feels a sense of accountability to our clients. Our culture of listening to our clients and acting on what they tell us is imperative to perpetuating our future success. Our clients inspire us.

HDR

Blake Marvin, HKS, Inc.

Cowboys Stadium, Arlington, TX | HKS, Inc.

7 | HKS, Inc.

1919 McKinney Avenue
Dallas, TX 75201
(214) 969-5599
www.hksinc.com
H. Ralph Hawkins, Chairman/CEO
J. Craig Beale, Executive VP
Nunzio M. DeSantis, Executive VP
Dan H. Noble, Executive VP

WORLDWIDE REVENUE	$262,000,000
US REVENUE	$242,000,000
WORLDWIDE STAFF	947
HEADQUARTERS	23 offices
YEAR ESTABLISHED	1939

RECENT REPRESENTATIVE PROJECT

Fort Hood Replacement Hospital
Fort Hood, TX

GEOGRAPHIC ANALYSIS OF WORK IN THE US

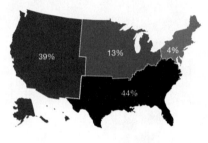

GEOGRAPHIC ANALYSIS OF WORK OUTSIDE THE US

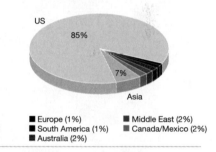

■ Europe (1%)   ■ Middle East (2%)
■ South America (1%)   ■ Canada/Mexico (2%)
■ Australia (2%)

PRIMARY SERVICES OFFERED

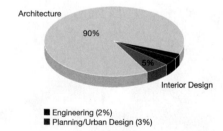

■ Engineering (2%)
■ Planning/Urban Design (3%)

MARKET SEGMENTS

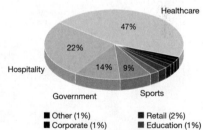

■ Other (1%)   ■ Retail (2%)
■ Corporate (1%)   ■ Education (1%)
■ Museum/Cultural (1%)   ■ Residential (2%)

PHILOSOPHY

HKS's vision is to be a global leader in professional design services—bringing value to clients through innovation while being committed to excellence, sustainability and sound business principles. We understand that our buildings will be in service to the public long after we have left our design posts. We strive to achieve enduring architecture that is individually responsive to each of our client's public forum needs.

City Crossing

City Crossing Grand Hyatt, Shenzhen, China | RTKL Associates Inc.

8 | RTKL Associates Inc.

901 South Bond Street

Baltimore, MD 21231

(410) 537-6000

www.rtkl.com

Lance K. Josal, President/CEO

Randall S. Pace, CFO

Allan M. Pinchoff, General Counsel

WORLDWIDE REVENUE	$205,959,000
US REVENUE	$147,504,000
WORLDWIDE STAFF	850
HEADQUARTERS	Baltimore, MD; 10 offices
YEAR ESTABLISHED	1946

RECENT REPRESENTATIVE PROJECT

L.A. Live

Los Angeles, CA

GEOGRAPHIC ANALYSIS OF WORK IN THE US

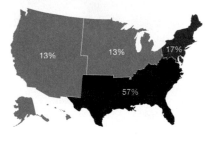

GEOGRAPHIC ANALYSIS OF WORK OUTSIDE THE US

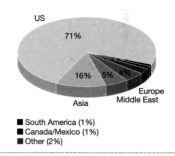

US 71%

16% Asia   5%   4%

Europe

Middle East

■ South America (1%)
■ Canada/Mexico (1%)
■ Other (2%)

PRIMARY SERVICES OFFERED

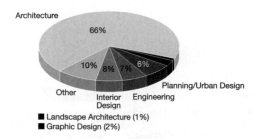

Architecture 66%

10%   8%   7%   6%

Other   Interior Design   Engineering   Planning/Urban Design

■ Landscape Architecture (1%)
■ Graphic Design (2%)

MARKET SEGMENTS

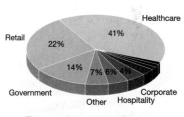

Retail 22%   Healthcare 41%

14%   7%   6%   4%

Government   Other   Hospitality   Corporate

■ Museum/Cultural (1%)   ■ Sports (1%)
■ Education (1%)   ■ Residential (3%)

PHILOSOPHY

RTKL is driven by a passion for great design, the creation of great places, and the creative process. Our firm is organized to encourage the creative process, to cross-pollinate ideas and talents across offices and deliver quality at all levels, in all places. Our passionate pursuit of excellence, the application of our creativity to solve our clients' challenges, our technical expertise, and our collaborative spirit are measures of our success. Creativity. Collaboration. Communication. These are our values.

RTKL

© lfang/NBBJ

Hangzhou Olympic Sports Center, Hangzhou, China | NBBJ in collaboration with CCDI

9 | NBBJ

223 Yale Avenue North
Seattle, WA 98109
(206) 223-5555
www.nbbj.com
Steve McConnell, Managing Partner/Design
Scott W. Wyatt, Managing Partner/Markets
John (Jay) F. Halleran, Managing Partner/
   Operations

WORLDWIDE REVENUE	$197,462,000
US REVENUE	$150,042,000
WORLDWIDE STAFF	702
HEADQUARTERS	Seattle, WA; 10 offices
YEAR ESTABLISHED	1943

RECENT REPRESENTATIVE PROJECT

Miller Family Pavilion, Cleveland Clinic
Cleveland, OH

GEOGRAPHIC ANALYSIS OF WORK IN THE US

GEOGRAPHIC ANALYSIS OF WORK OUTSIDE THE US

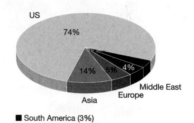

PRIMARY SERVICES OFFERED

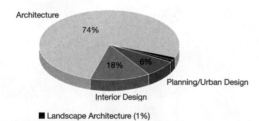

MARKET SEGMENTS

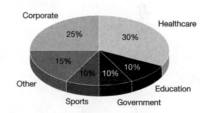

PHILOSOPHY

NBBJ fosters a creative culture that fuels passion and innovation along with a strong commitment to design excellence. The firm sees employees as its most valuable tool for continued success and is committed to providing comprehensive professional growth programs and mentoring. In addition, environmental and social sustainability are themes that touch every aspect of NBBJ, including enabling outlets for employees to give back to the community and providing healthy and sustainable working environments.

nbbj

LEO A DALY

East Bank of Yantai Outer Jia River Comprehensive Plan, Yantai, China | LEO A DALY

10 | LEO A DALY

8600 Indian Hills Drive
Omaha, NE 68114
(402) 391-8111
www.leodaly.com
Leo A. Daly III, Chairman/CEO
Charles D. Dalluge, Executive VP
Robert L. Luhrs, VP/CFO

WORLDWIDE REVENUE	$173,000,000
US REVENUE	$166,000,000
WORLDWIDE STAFF	1,000
HEADQUARTERS	Omaha, NE; 30 offices
YEAR ESTABLISHED	1915

RECENT REPRESENTATIVE PROJECT

Excellence Huanggang Century Center
Shenzhen, China

GEOGRAPHIC ANALYSIS OF WORK IN THE US

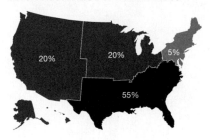

GEOGRAPHIC ANALYSIS OF WORK OUTSIDE THE US

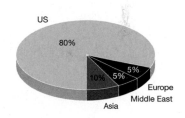

PRIMARY SERVICES OFFERED

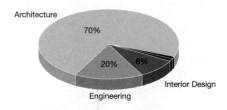

■ Planning/Urban Design (1%)
■ Graphic Design (1%)

MARKET SEGMENTS

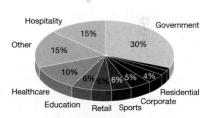

■ Religious (1%)
■ Museum/Cultural (2%)

PHILOSOPHY

LEO A DALY's design excellence philosophy revolves around our central goal—to create structures and environments of lasting aesthetic quality and functionality. We strive to design spaces that lift the spirit, move the emotions, and better our global surroundings. Our designs incorporate technological innovations while remaining responsive to their contexts—social, historical, and natural. Each project focuses on balancing contemporary design, trends and traditions, technology, and sustainability.

LEO A DALY

Cannon Design

King Faisal Specialist Hospital and Research Center, Riyadh, Saudi Arabia | Cannon Design

11 | Cannon Design

2170 Whitehaven Road
Grand Island, NY 14072
(716) 773-6800
www.cannondesign.com
Mark R. Mendell, Co-Chairman/President
Gary R. Miller, Co-Chairman/CEO
Kent Turner, President/ Cannon Design
   North America

WORLDWIDE REVENUE	$171,500,000
US REVENUE	$127,800,000
WORLDWIDE STAFF	1,016
HEADQUARTERS	17 offices
YEAR ESTABLISHED	1945
RECENT REPRESENTATIVE PROJECT	

Richmond Olympic Oval
Richmond, BC, Canada

GEOGRAPHIC ANALYSIS OF WORK IN THE US

GEOGRAPHIC ANALYSIS OF WORK OUTSIDE THE US

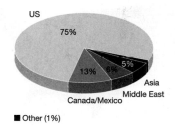

US 75%
Asia 5%
Middle East
Canada/Mexico
13% 6%
■ Other (1%)

PRIMARY SERVICES OFFERED

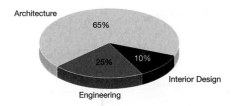

Architecture 65%
Engineering 25%
Interior Design 10%

MARKET SEGMENTS

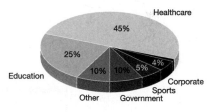

Healthcare 45%
Education 25%
Other 10%
Government 10%
Sports 5%
Corporate 4%
■ Retail (1%)

PHILOSOPHY

Cannon Design strives to create environments that are a thoughtful response to the program mission, physical setting, and functional purpose, reflecting the spirit and personality of each owner. The firm is focused on quality—with client satisfaction as the ultimate measurement. Cannon Design works continuously to advance the state of the art, contributing to the built environment and quality of life of the people for whom it creates living and working spaces.

CANNON DESIGN

12 | SmithGroup

500 Griswold Street, Suite 1700	WORLDWIDE REVENUE	$166,300,000
Detroit, MI 48226	US REVENUE	$166,200,000
(313) 983-3600	WORLDWIDE STAFF	800
www.smithgroup.com	HEADQUARTERS	11 offices
Carl Roehling, President	YEAR ESTABLISHED	1853
Mark Patterson, VP		

RECENT REPRESENTATIVE PROJECT

National Intrepid Center of Excellence
Bethesda, MD

GEOGRAPHIC ANALYSIS OF WORK IN THE US

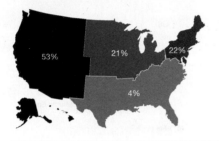

GEOGRAPHIC ANALYSIS OF WORK OUTSIDE THE US

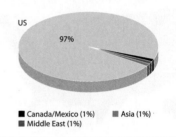

- Canada/Mexico (1%)   ■ Asia (1%)
- Middle East (1%)

PRIMARY SERVICES OFFERED

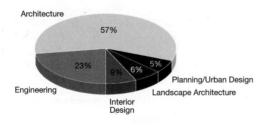

MARKET SEGMENTS

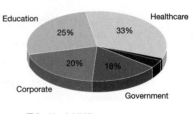

- Residential (1%)
- Museum/Cultural (3%)

PHILOSOPHY

At SmithGroup great design is about cultivating client relationships where creativity can flourish. It's about listening to and collaborating with clients to understand their needs and their objectives—and then coming up with design solutions backed up with empirical knowledge, solid engineering, and detailed execution that are unique, meaningful, and meet expectations every time.

13 | Stantec Architecture (US)

405 Howard Street
San Francisco, CA 94105
(415) 433-0120
www.stantec.com
F. Bradford (Rick) Drake, Principal
John (Jack) Cummiskey, Senior Principal
Joe Donovan, Senior Principal

WORLDWIDE REVENUE	$162,000,000
US REVENUE	$35,500,000
WORLDWIDE STAFF	850
HEADQUARTERS	San Francisco, CA; 17 offices
YEAR ESTABLISHED	1954

RECENT REPRESENTATIVE PROJECT

Peterborough Regional Health Center
Peterborough, ON, Canada

GEOGRAPHIC ANALYSIS OF WORK IN THE US

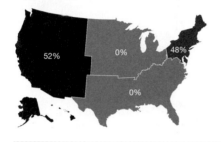

GEOGRAPHIC ANALYSIS OF WORK OUTSIDE THE US

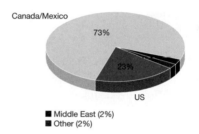

PRIMARY SERVICES OFFERED

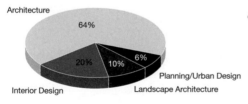

MARKET SEGMENTS

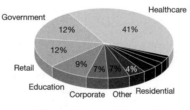

PHILOSOPHY

Stantec Architecture's integrated approach to design is characterized by clear ideas rooted in deep understanding of context, function, and best practices in pursuit of our clients' objectives. The result: designs that are timeless, intelligent, and sustainable.

14 | Burt Hill (in merger process with Stantec)

101 East Diamond Street
400 Morgan Center
Butler, PA 16001
(724) 285-4761
www.burthill.com
Harry Gordon, Chairman/COO
Peter H. Moriarty, President/CEO
Anton H. Germishuizen, Sr. VP/Design Dir.

WORLDWIDE REVENUE $128,100,000
US REVENUE $64,500,000
WORLDWIDE STAFF   656
HEADQUARTERS   Butler, PA; 13 offices
YEAR ESTABLISHED   1936
RECENT REPRESENTATIVE PROJECT
STEM Building, Delaware Community College, Media, PA

GEOGRAPHIC ANALYSIS OF WORK IN THE US

GEOGRAPHIC ANALYSIS OF WORK OUTSIDE THE US

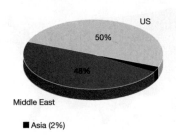

US 50%
Middle East 48%
■ Asia (2%)

PRIMARY SERVICES OFFERED

MARKET SEGMENTS

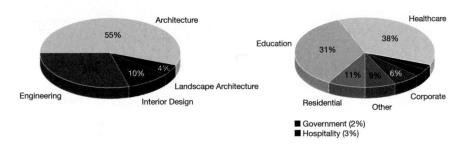

Architecture 55%
Engineering 10%
Interior Design 4%
Landscape Architecture
(Engineering)

Healthcare 38%
Education 31%
Residential 11%
Other 9%
Corporate 6%
■ Government (2%)
■ Hospitality (3%)

PHILOSOPHY

At Burt Hill we continually evaluate and assess what constitutes good design to create award-winning responsive and comprehensive built environments that challenge convention and evoke an emotional connection. Our integrated solutions and sustainable designs enable our clients' successes.

15 | SSOE Group

1001 Madison Avenue
Toledo, OH 43604
(419) 255-3830
www.ssoe.com
Tony Damon, CEO
David Verner, Senior VP
Lee Warnick, VP

WORLDWIDE REVENUE	$127,900,000
US REVENUE	$119,400,000
WORLDWIDE STAFF	876
HEADQUARTERS	Toledo, OH; 21 offices
YEAR ESTABLISHED	1948
RECENT REPRESENTATIVE PROJECT	

Volkswagen Assembly Plant
Chattanooga, TN

GEOGRAPHIC ANALYSIS OF WORK IN THE US

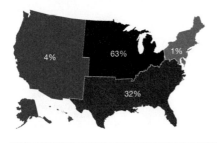

GEOGRAPHIC ANALYSIS OF WORK OUTSIDE THE US

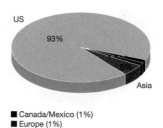

PRIMARY SERVICES OFFERED

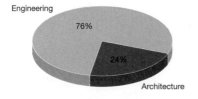

MARKET SEGMENTS

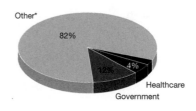

PHILOSOPHY

We make our clients successful by delivering the highest-value engineering, architectural, and project delivery services.

16 | Populous

300 Wyandotte Street
Kansas City, MO 64105
(816) 221-1500
www.populous.com
Earl Santee, Senior Principal
Rick Martin, Senior Principal
Ben Barnert, Senior Principal

WORLDWIDE REVENUE	$126,000,000
US REVENUE	$77,000,000
WORLDWIDE STAFF	428
HEADQUARTERS	Kansas City, MO; 10 offices
YEAR ESTABLISHED	1983
RECENT REPRESENTATIVE PROJECT	

Target Field
Minneapolis, MN

GEOGRAPHIC ANALYSIS OF WORK IN THE US

GEOGRAPHIC ANALYSIS OF WORK OUTSIDE THE US

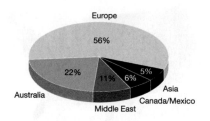

PRIMARY SERVICES OFFERED

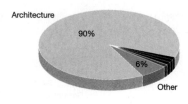

■ Graphic Design (1%)   ■ Interior Design (1%)
■ Landscape Architecture (1%)   ■ Planning/Urban Design (1%)

MARKET SEGMENTS

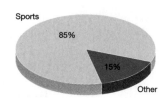

PHILOSOPHY

Populous is a global design practice specializing in environments that draw people and communities together for unforgettable experiences. We offer comprehensive design services, including sports architecture, conference and exhibition center architecture, master planning, events planning and overlay, interior design, sustainable design consulting, environmental graphics and way-finding, and facilities operations analysis. Our work is ultimately about and for the fans, the communities, and the people who gather in these places.

17 | Kohn Pedersen Fox

111 West 42nd Street
New York, NY 10036
(212) 977-6500
www.kpf.com
A. Eugene Kohn, Chairman
William Pedersen, Vice Chairman
William Louie, CEO

WORLDWIDE REVENUE	$123,563,000
US REVENUE	$72,777,936
WORLDWIDE STAFF	520
HEADQUARTERS	New York, NY; 18 offices
YEAR ESTABLISHED	1976
RECENT REPRESENTATIVE PROJECT	

Shanghai World Financial Center
Shanghai, China

GEOGRAPHIC ANALYSIS OF WORK IN THE US

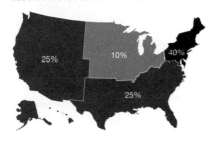

GEOGRAPHIC ANALYSIS OF WORK OUTSIDE THE US

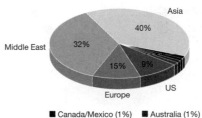

PRIMARY SERVICES OFFERED

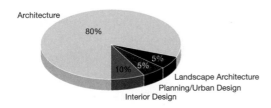

MARKET SEGMENTS

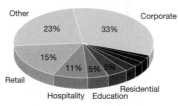

PHILOSOPHY

Kohn Pedersen Fox is committed to providing designs that create uplifting spaces for people, responding to community, context, and environment. The KPF creative process stresses an open exchange of ideas both within the firm and, more importantly, between the client and the firm throughout the development of a project.

18 | RMJM

275 7th Avenue, 24th Floor
New York, NY 10001
(212) 629-4100
www.rmjm.com
Sir Fraser Morrison, CEO/North America
Peter Schubert, Director of Design/NA
Philip Palmgren, Management Principal/
   Communications

WORLDWIDE REVENUE	$120,051,000
US REVENUE	$13,805,000
WORLDWIDE STAFF	1,281
HEADQUARTERS	New York, NY; 18 offices
YEAR ESTABLISHED	1956

RECENT REPRESENTATIVE PROJECT

Duke Univ./National Univ. of Singapore
Graduate Medical School, Singapore

GEOGRAPHIC ANALYSIS OF WORK IN THE US

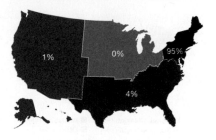

GEOGRAPHIC ANALYSIS OF WORK OUTSIDE THE US

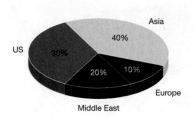

PRIMARY SERVICES OFFERED

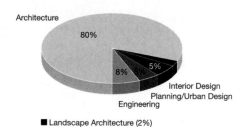

MARKET SEGMENTS

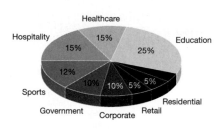

PHILOSOPHY

RMJM's architects place the client at the center of the creative process and unlock the potential of every opportunity through collaboration with our clients and other stakeholders. Our design approach results in sustainable architectural solutions based on first principles, and our workshop culture stimulates creative thinking and maintains the integrity of the design.

19 | Callison

1420 5th Avenue, Suite 2400
Seattle, WA 98101
(206) 623-4646
www.callison.com
Bob J. Tindal, Chairman
John T. Bierly, President
Steven E. Epple, Executive VP

WORLDWIDE REVENUE	$120,000,000
US REVENUE	$76,000,000
WORLDWIDE STAFF	550
HEADQUARTERS	Seattle, WA; 9 offices
YEAR ESTABLISHED	1975

RECENT REPRESENTATIVE PROJECT

The MIXc
Hangzhou, China

GEOGRAPHIC ANALYSIS OF WORK IN THE US

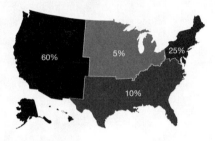

GEOGRAPHIC ANALYSIS OF WORK OUTSIDE THE US

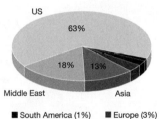

PRIMARY SERVICES OFFERED

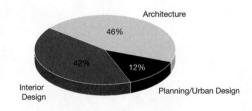

MARKET SEGMENTS

PHILOSOPHY

Our vision is to be a leader of change—expanding the traditional boundaries of design to embrace strategic thinking that fosters innovation. We create experiences where culture and commerce intersect, crafted with insightful design and an informed interpretation of the client's values.

Port of Portland Headquarters and Long-Term Parking Garage, Portland, OR | Zimmer Gunsul Frasca Architects

20 | Zimmer Gunsul Frasca Architects

1223 Southwest Washington Street
Suite 200
Portland, OR 97205
(503) 224-3860
www.zgf.com
Robert Packard, Managing Partner
Robert Frasca, Partner in Charge of Design

WORLDWIDE REVENUE	$113,473,189
US REVENUE	$110,012,452
WORLDWIDE STAFF	446
HEADQUARTERS	Portland, OR; 5 offices
YEAR ESTABLISHED	1959
RECENT REPRESENTATIVE PROJECT	

Twelve West
Portland, OR

GEOGRAPHIC ANALYSIS OF WORK IN THE US

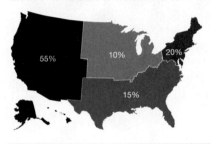

GEOGRAPHIC ANALYSIS OF WORK OUTSIDE THE US

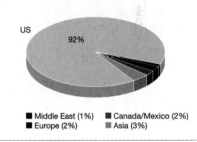

- Middle East (1%)   ■ Canada/Mexico (2%)
- Europe (2%)   ■ Asia (3%)

PRIMARY SERVICES OFFERED

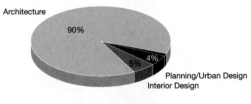

Architecture 90%
5%
4%
Planning/Urban Design
Interior Design

■ Landscape Architecture (1%)

MARKET SEGMENTS

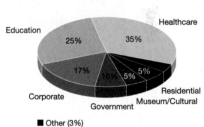

Education 25%   Healthcare 35%
17%
10% 5%
5%
Corporate   Residential
Government   Museum/Cultural

■ Other (3%)

PHILOSOPHY

Zimmer Gunsul Frasca Architects is focused on design quality. Design based on rigorous analytic processes and human understanding. Design that honors the unique qualities of its purpose and place and is environmentally responsible. Design that enriches and inspires people's lives.

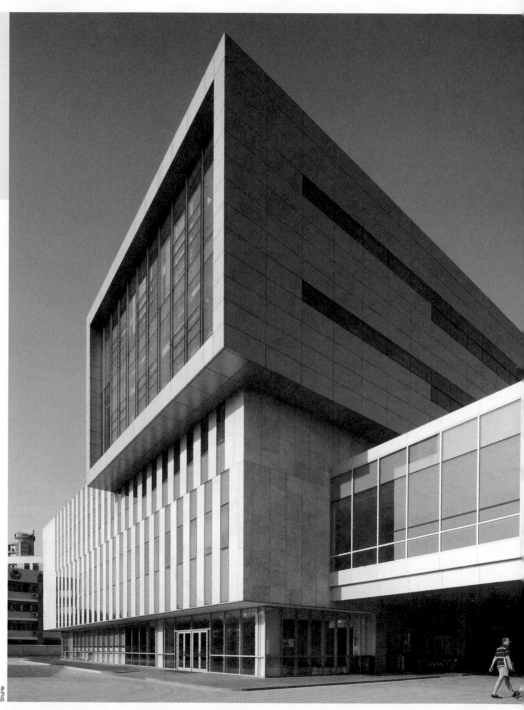

ShuHe

High School, Concordia International School Shanghai, Shanghai, China | Perkins Eastman

21 | Perkins Eastman

115 Fifth Avenue
New York, NY 10003
(212) 353-7200
www.perkinseastman.com
Bradford Perkins, Chairman/CEO

WORLDWIDE REVENUE	$110,000,000
US REVENUE	$88,000,000
WORLDWIDE STAFF	560
HEADQUARTERS	New York, NY; 13 offices
YEAR ESTABLISHED	1981

RECENT REPRESENTATIVE PROJECT

The Evelyn H. Lauder Breast Center, Sloan-Kettering Cancer Center, New York, NY

GEOGRAPHIC ANALYSIS OF WORK IN THE US

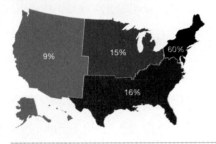

GEOGRAPHIC ANALYSIS OF WORK OUTSIDE THE US

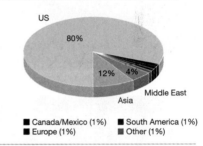

PRIMARY SERVICES OFFERED

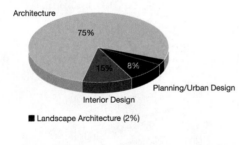

MARKET SEGMENTS

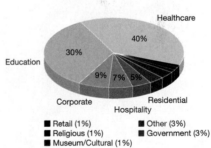

PHILOSOPHY

Perkins Eastman prides itself on progressive and inventive design that meets client goals and enhances the human experience. Underlying this philosophy is the conviction that with a thorough understanding of each building type's requirements, we could realize the true potential of any project and enrich the quality of life of its users as well as the communities in which it is located.

Perkins Eastman

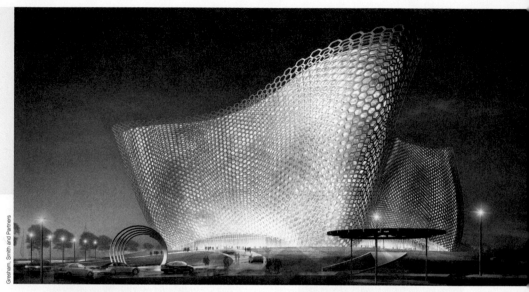

Gresham, Smith and Partners

Theatre Putuo Zhoushan Opera House, Zhoushan, China | Gresham, Smith and Partners

Gresham, Smith and Partners

Mercy Hospital, Miami, FL | Gresham, Smith and Partners

22 | Gresham, Smith and Partners

511 Union Street, Suite 1400
Nashville, TN 37219
(615) 770-8100
www.gspnet.com
James W. Bearden, CEO
Brackney J. Reed, Chairman/COO

WORLDWIDE REVENUE	$106,960,000
US REVENUE	$104,840,000
WORLDWIDE STAFF	653
HEADQUARTERS	Nashville, TN; 16 offices
YEAR ESTABLISHED	1967

RECENT REPRESENTATIVE PROJECT

Nissan Americas Corporate Facility
Franklin, TN

GEOGRAPHIC ANALYSIS OF WORK IN THE US

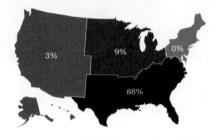

GEOGRAPHIC ANALYSIS OF WORK OUTSIDE THE US

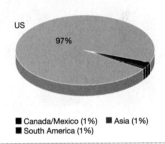

■ Canada/Mexico (1%) ■ Asia (1%)
■ South America (1%)

PRIMARY SERVICES OFFERED

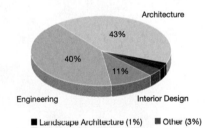

■ Landscape Architecture (1%)   ■ Other (3%)
■ Planning/Urban Design (2%)

MARKET SEGMENTS

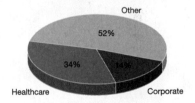

PHILOSOPHY

Clients choose Gresham, Smith and Partners because we are more than a design firm; we strive to be a true business partner and trusted advisor who shares the clients' vision and works with them to bring that vision to reality.

GRESHAM SMITH AND PARTNERS

Jason A. Knowles © Fentress Architects

Semper Fidelis Memorial Park Chapel, Quantico, VA | Fentress Architects

© Tim Hursley

National Cowboy & Western Heritage Museum, Oklahoma City, OK | Fentress Architects

23 | Fentress Architects

421 Broadway
Denver, CO 80203
(303) 722-5000
www.fentressarchitects.com
Curtis W. Fentress, President/Principal-
   in-Charge of Design
Agatha Kessler, CEO

WORLDWIDE REVENUE	$103,924,000
US REVENUE	$103,180,000
WORLDWIDE STAFF	155
HEADQUARTERS	Denver, CO; 4 offices
YEAR ESTABLISHED	1980
RECENT REPRESENTATIVE PROJECT	

LA Int'l Airport Master Plan & Int'l Terminal
Renovation, Los Angeles, CA

GEOGRAPHIC ANALYSIS OF WORK IN THE US

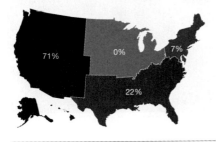

GEOGRAPHIC ANALYSIS OF WORK OUTSIDE THE US

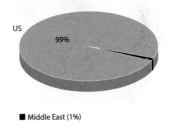

■ Middle East (1%)

PRIMARY SERVICES OFFERED

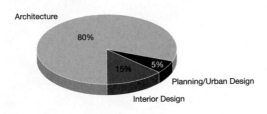

MARKET SEGMENTS

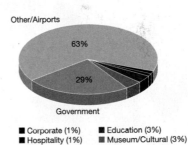

■ Corporate (1%)   ■ Education (3%)
■ Hospitality (1%)   ■ Museum/Cultural (3%)

PHILOSOPHY

Balancing creativity and discipline while focusing on people, Fentress Architects' Touch-
stones of Design create distinctive public architecture. This process of discovery leads to
a building's soul where community, context, and culture unite to bring design and function
in balance.

Metea Valley High School, Aurora, IL | DLR Group

Mall of America, Phase Two, Minneapolis, MN | DLR Group

24 | DLR Group

400 Essex Court
Omaha, NE 68114
(866) DLR-8600
www.dlrgroup.com
William G. (Griff) Davenport, Man. Principal
Jon Pettit, Managing Principal
Steven McKay, Sr. Principal/Design Leader

WORLDWIDE REVENUE	$94,600,000
US REVENUE	$94,600,000
WORLDWIDE STAFF	450
HEADQUARTERS	24 offices
YEAR ESTABLISHED	1966
RECENT REPRESENTATIVE PROJECT	

Marysville Getchell High School
Marysville, WA

GEOGRAPHIC ANALYSIS OF WORK IN THE US

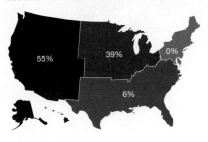

GEOGRAPHIC ANALYSIS OF WORK OUTSIDE THE US

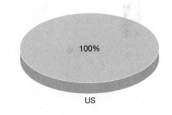

US

PRIMARY SERVICES OFFERED

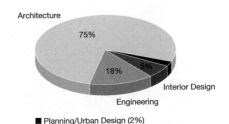

■ Planning/Urban Design (2%)

MARKET SEGMENTS

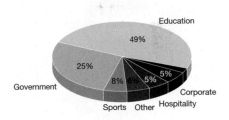

■ Retail (2%)

PHILOSOPHY

At DLR Goup, we believe that design fulfills and propels each client's goals and aspirations; that design articulates spaces to new levels of effectiveness; that design engages, inspires and fulfills: and that design elevates the human experience.

John Korom

Kerry Ingredients & Flavours, Innovation and Technical Center, Beloit, WI | HGA Architects and Engineers

25 | HGA Architects and Engineers

701 Washington Avenue North
Minneapolis, MN 55401
(612) 758-4000
www.hga.com
Daniel Avchen, Chairman/CEO
Stephen Fiskum, COO
Loren Ahles, VP

WORLDWIDE REVENUE	$90,000,000
US REVENUE	$88,000,000
WORLDWIDE STAFF	520
HEADQUARTERS	Minneapolis, MN; 6 offices
YEAR ESTABLISHED	1953
RECENT REPRESENTATIVE PROJECT	

SSM St. Clare Health Center
St. Louis, MO

GEOGRAPHIC ANALYSIS OF WORK IN THE US

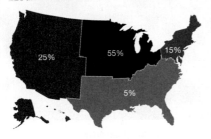

GEOGRAPHIC ANALYSIS OF WORK OUTSIDE THE US

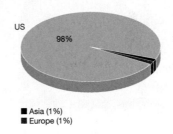

US 98%

■ Asia (1%)
■ Europe (1%)

PRIMARY SERVICES OFFERED

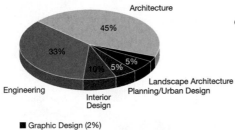

Architecture 45%
Engineering 33%
Interior Design 10%
5%
5%
Landscape Architecture
Planning/Urban Design

■ Graphic Design (2%)

MARKET SEGMENTS

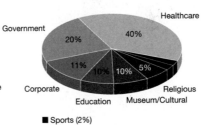

Government 20%
Healthcare 40%
Corporate 11%
10%
10%
5%
Religious
Education
Museum/Cultural

■ Sports (2%)
■ Hospitality (2%)

PHILOSOPHY

HGA will be known for the strength of our ideas and the quality of our solutions.

Ryan Beck

29 | Frontier Project, Cucamonga Valley Water District, Rancho Cucamonga, CA | HMC Architects

HMC Architects

29 | Malibu High School, Santa Monica-Malibu Unified School District, Malibu, CA | HMC Architects

26 | KlingStubbins

2301 Chestnut Street
Philadelphia, PA 19103
(215) 569-2900
www.klingstubbins.com
Mike Lorenz, National Managing Principal
Bradford Fiske, Senior Principal
Robert Hsu, Senior Principal

WORLDWIDE REVENUE	$87,000,000
WORLDWIDE STAFF	450
HEADQUARTERS	Philadelphia, PA
YEAR ESTABLISHED	1949

RECENT REPRESENTATIVE PROJECT

Autodesk Headquarters
Waltham, MA

27 | HNTB (Architecture)

715 Kirk Drive
Kansas City, MO 64105
(816) 472-1201
www.hntb.com
Terry Miller, CEO

WORLDWIDE REVENUE	$86,000,000
WORLDWIDE STAFF	101–450
HEADQUARTERS	Kansas City, MO
YEAR ESTABLISHED	1914

28 | Corgan Associates

401 North Houston Street
Dallas, TX 75202
(214) 748-2000
www.corgan.com
David Lind, Chairman
Bob Morris, President/CEO
John Holzheimer, COO/Managing Principal

WORLDWIDE REVENUE	$84,000,000
WORLDWIDE STAFF	296
HEADQUARTERS	Dallas, TX
YEAR ESTABLISHED	1938

RECENT REPRESENTATIVE PROJECT

One Arts Plaza
Dallas, TX

29 | HMC Architects

HMC Architects

633 West 5th Street, 3rd Floor
Los Angeles, CA 90071
(213) 542-8300
www.hmcarchitects.com
Randy Peterson, President/CEO
Lee Salin, Board Secretary
Chris Taylor, CMO

WORLDWIDE REVENUE	$83,403,495
WORLDWIDE STAFF	431
HEADQUARTERS	Los Angeles, CA
YEAR ESTABLISHED	1940

RECENT REPRESENTATIVE PROJECT

Frontier Project
Rancho Cucamonga, CA

© Eduard Hueber / archphoto.com

33 | Roberts Pavilion, Cooper University Hospital, Camden, NJ | EwingCole

30 | Rafael Viñoly Architects

50 Vandam Street
New York, NY 10013
(212) 924-5060
www.rvapc.com
Rafael Viñoly, President

WORLDWIDE REVENUE	$83,300,000
WORLDWIDE STAFF	510
HEADQUARTERS	New York, NY
YEAR ESTABLISHED	1983

31 | PageSoutherlandPage

3500 Maple Avenue, Suite 600
Dallas, TX 75219
(214) 522-3900
www.pspaec.com
Michael McCoy, VP
Mattia Flabiano, Principal
John N. Cryer, Principal

WORLDWIDE REVENUE	$75,000,000
WORLDWIDE STAFF	400
HEADQUARTERS	Dallas, TX
YEAR ESTABLISHED	1898

32 | PBK

11 Greenway Plaza
Houston, TX 77046
(713) 965-0608
www.pbk.com
Daniel L. Boggio, President/CEO
Ian Powell, Partner

WORLDWIDE REVENUE	$71,000,000
WORLDWIDE STAFF	300
HEADQUARTERS	Houston, TX
YEAR ESTABLISHED	1981

33 | EwingCole

EWING COLE

100 North 6th Street
Philadelphia, PA 19106
(215) 923-2020
www.ewingcole.com
John Gerbner, President
S. Mark Hebden, Executive VP
Donald Dissinger, Executive VP

WORLDWIDE REVENUE	$67,000,000
WORLDWIDE STAFF	360
HEADQUARTERS	Philadelphia, PA
YEAR ESTABLISHED	1961
RECENT REPRESENTATIVE PROJECT	

Cooper University Hospital Pavillion
Camden, NJ

KMD ARCHITECTS

36 | San Francisco Public Utilities Commission Headquarters, San Francisco, CA | KMD Architects

34 | EYP Architecture & Engineering

412 Broadway
Albany, NY 12207
(518) 431-3300
www.eypaedesign.com
Tom Birdsey, President/CEO
John Pocorobba, VP/Operations
Leila Kamal, VP/Design Expertise

WORLDWIDE REVENUE	$65,130,000
WORLDWIDE STAFF	325
HEADQUARTERS	Albany, NY
YEAR ESTABLISHED	1972
RECENT REPRESENTATIVE PROJECT	

New Integrated Science Complex, The
College of the Holy Cross, Worcester, MA

35 | SHW Group

5717 Legacy Drive, Suite 250
Plano, TX 75024
(888) SHW-1019
www.shwgroup.com
Gary Blanton, CEO
Kyle Bacon, COO
Matt Snider, CFO

WORLDWIDE REVENUE	$64,300,000
WORLDWIDE STAFF	334
HEADQUARTERS	Plano, TX
YEAR ESTABLISHED	1945
RECENT REPRESENTATIVE PROJECT	

Central Michigan University College
of Education, Mt. Pleasant, MI

36 | KMD Architects

KMDARCHITECTS

222 Vallejo Street
San Francisco, CA 94111
(415) 398-5191
www.kmdarchitects.com
Roy Latka, President
Robert Ludden, COO

WORLDWIDE REVENUE	$62,900,000
WORLDWIDE STAFF	195
HEADQUARTERS	San Francisco, CA
YEAR ESTABLISHED	1963
RECENT REPRESENTATIVE PROJECT	

El Camino Hospital
Mountain View, CA

37 | Anshen + Allen (Stantec)

901 Market Street, 6th Floor
San Francisco, CA 94103
(415) 882-9500
www.anshen.com
Roger Swanson, Chairman/CEO
Ann Killeen, Managing Principal
Jenifer Altenhoff, Principal

WORLDWIDE REVENUE	$62,854,000
WORLDWIDE STAFF	210
HEADQUARTERS	San Francisco, CA
YEAR ESTABLISHED	1940
RECENT REPRESENTATIVE PROJECT	

Stanford Medicine Outpatient Center
Redwood City, CA

Timmerman Photography

41 | Student Recreation Center Expansion, University of Arizona, Tucson, AZ | Sasaki Associates, Inc.

38 | Clark Nexsen

6160 Kempsville Circle, Suite 200 A
Norfolk, VA 23502
(757) 455-5800
www.clarknexsen.com
Chris Stone, President
Glenn E. McDowell, VP

WORLDWIDE REVENUE	$60,000,000
WORLDWIDE STAFF	450
HEADQUARTERS	Norfolk, VA
YEAR ESTABLISHED	1920

39 | NELSON

222-30 Walnut Street
Philadelphia, PA 19106
(215) 925-6562
www.nelsononline.com
John (Ozzie) Nelson, President/CEO
John J. Nelson Sr., Chairman
John A. Imbrogno, Senior VP

WORLDWIDE REVENUE	$57,311,250
WORLDWIDE STAFF	500
HEADQUARTERS	Philadelphia, PA
YEAR ESTABLISHED	1977
RECENT REPRESENTATIVE PROJECT	

Bank of America Infomart
Dallas, TX

40 | Teng & Associates

205 North Michigan Avenue
Chicago, IL 60601
(312) 616-0000
www.teng.com
Ivan J. Dvorak, President/CEO
Tim Neumann, Senior VP

WORLDWIDE REVENUE	$57,000,000
WORLDWIDE STAFF	400
HEADQUARTERS	Chicago, IL
YEAR ESTABLISHED	1959
RECENT REPRESENTATIVE PROJECT	

Warren E. Burger Federal Building and
US Courthouse, St. Paul, MN

41 | Sasaki Associates, Inc.   S A S A K I

64 Pleasant Street
Watertown, MA 02472
(617) 926-3300
www.sasaki.com
James A. Sukeforth, CEO
Dennis Pieprz, President
Pablo Savid-Buteler, Principal

WORLDWIDE REVENUE	$56,500,000
WORLDWIDE STAFF	270
HEADQUARTERS	Watertown, MA
YEAR ESTABLISHED	1953
RECENT REPRESENTATIVE PROJECT	

East Campus Athletic Village, Rensselaer
Polytechnic Institute, Troy, NY

Jim Steinkamp/Steinkamp Photography

43 | Prentice Women's Hospital, Chicago, IL | VOA Associates

42 | Heery International

999 Peachtree Street NE, Suite 300
Atlanta, GA 30309
(404) 881-9880
www.heery.com
Jim Moynihan, President/CEO
Michael Wass, Principal

WORLDWIDE REVENUE	$55,000,000
WORLDWIDE STAFF	350+
HEADQUARTERS	Atlanta, GA
YEAR ESTABLISHED	1952

43 | VOA Associates

VOA

224 South Michigan Avenue, Suite 1400
Chicago, IL 60604
(312) 554-1400
www.voa.com
Michael A. Toolis, Chairman/CEO
Percy E. Roberts, President/COO
Paul Hansen, Secretary

WORLDWIDE REVENUE	$54,800,000
WORLDWIDE STAFF	240
HEADQUARTERS	Chicago, IL
YEAR ESTABLISHED	1969
RECENT REPRESENTATIVE PROJECT	

Prentice Women's Hospital
Chicago, IL

44 | Wilson Associates

3811 Turtle Creek Boulevard, 15th Floor
Dallas, TX 75219
(214) 521-6753
www.wilsonassoc.com
Trisha Wilson, President/CEO
Cheryl Neumann, Executive VP/COO
James Rimelspach, EVP/Director of Design

WORLDWIDE REVENUE	$54,000,000
WORLDWIDE STAFF	316
HEADQUARTERS	Dallas, TX
YEAR ESTABLISHED	1971
RECENT REPRESENTATIVE PROJECT	

Atlantis, The Palm
The Palm Jumeirah, UAE

45 | Robert A.M. Stern Architects

460 West 34th Street
New York, NY 10001
(212) 967-5100
www.ramsa.com
Robert Stern, Senior Partner
Robert Buford Jr., Managing Partner

WORLDWIDE REVENUE	$53,469,000
WORLDWIDE STAFF	200
HEADQUARTERS	New York, NY
YEAR ESTABLISHED	1969
RECENT REPRESENTATIVE PROJECT	

Fifteen Central Park West
New York, NY

©2010 WHR Architects. Carlo Macalone photographer. Artwork by Dixie Friend Gay

49 | Ocean and Coastal Studies Building, Texas A&M University at Galveston, Galveston, TX | WHR Architects

©Aker Zvonkovic Photography, Houston, Texas

49 | Methodist Outpatient Center, Houston, TX | WHR Architects

46 | Payette

285 Summer Street
Boston, MA 02210
(617) 895-1000
www.payette.com
James H. Collins Jr., President
Roberta F. Haney, COO
J. Ian Adamson, Principal

WORLDWIDE REVENUE	$51,991,533
WORLDWIDE STAFF	137
HEADQUARTERS	Boston, MA
YEAR ESTABLISHED	1932

RECENT REPRESENTATIVE PROJECT

Comer Geochemistry Bldg., Lamont-
Doherty Earth Observatory, Palisades, NY

47 | Flad Architects

644 Science Drive
Madison, WI 53711
(608) 238-2661
www.flad.com
William (Bill) Bula, President/CEO
Jeffrey C. Zutz, Managing Principal
Laura Stillman, Principal

WORLDWIDE REVENUE	$51,000,000
WORLDWIDE STAFF	101–450
HEADQUARTERS	Madison, WI
YEAR ESTABLISHED	1927

48 | MulvannyG2 Architecture

1110 112th Avenue NE, Suite 500
Bellevue, WA 98004
(425) 463-2000
www.mulvannyg2.com
Ming Zhang, President
Mitch Smith, CEO
Brian Fleener, VP

WORLDWIDE REVENUE	$50,600,000
WORLDWIDE STAFF	302
HEADQUARTERS	Bellevue, WA
YEAR ESTABLISHED	1971

RECENT REPRESENTATIVE PROJECT

Bellevue Towers
Bellevue, WA

49 | WHR Architects

WHR ARCHITECTS

1111 Louisiana Street, 26th Floor
Houston, TX 77002
(713) 665-5665
www.whrarchitects.com
David H. Watkins, Chairman/President
Gailand Smith, Treasurer
Mary Le Johnson, Secretary

WORLDWIDE REVENUE	$50,355,658
WORLDWIDE STAFF	170
HEADQUARTERS	Houston, TX
YEAR ESTABLISHED	1979

RECENT REPRESENTATIVE PROJECT

Jersey Shore University Medical Center
Neptune, NJ

Costea Photography, Inc.

50 | NASA JPL Flight Projects Center, Pasadena, CA | LPA

Costea Photography, Inc.

50 | College of Education, California State University San Bernardino, San Bernardino, CA | LPA

50 | LPA

5161 California Avenue, Suite 100
Irvine, CA 92617
(949) 261-1001
www.lpainc.com
Dan Heinfeld, President
Robert O. Kupper, CEO
Charles Pruitt, CFO

LPA

WORLDWIDE REVENUE	$50,334,401
WORLDWIDE STAFF	214
HEADQUARTERS	Irvine, CA
YEAR ESTABLISHED	1965

RECENT REPRESENTATIVE PROJECT
NASA Jet Propulsion Laboratory
Pasadena, CA

51 | RSP Architects

1220 Marshall Street NE
Minneapolis, MN 55413
(612) 677-7100
www.rsparch.com
David C. Norback, President
Joseph J. Tyndall, Principal
Kristine Hargreaves, Principal

WORLDWIDE REVENUE	$46,000,000
WORLDWIDE STAFF	217
HEADQUARTERS	Minneapolis, MN
YEAR ESTABLISHED	1978

RECENT REPRESENTATIVE PROJECT
Musical Instrument Museum
Phoenix, AZ

52 | Ennead Architects

320 West 13th Street
New York, NY 10014
(212) 807-7171
www.ennead.com
Joseph Fleischer, Founding Partner
Timothy J. Hartung, Founding Partner
Duncan Hazard, Founding Partner

WORLDWIDE REVENUE	$44,611,000
WORLDWIDE STAFF	145
HEADQUARTERS	New York, NY
YEAR ESTABLISHED	1963

53 | LS3P Associates Ltd.

205 1/2 King Street
Charleston, SC 29401
(843) 577-4444
www.LS3P.com
Frank E. Lucas, Chairman
Michael Tribble, Vice Chairman
Thom Penney, President/CEO

WORLDWIDE REVENUE	$44,303,830
WORLDWIDE STAFF	207
HEADQUARTERS	Charleston, SC
YEAR ESTABLISHED	1963

RECENT REPRESENTATIVE PROJECT
Lowe's Corporate Headquarters
Mooresville, NC

54 | GHAFARI

17101 Michigan Avenue
Dearborn, MI 48126
(313) 441-3000
www.ghafari.com
Yousif Ghafari, Chairman
Kouhalia G. Hammer, President/CEO
Evangel Kokkino, President/Chicago Div.

WORLDWIDE REVENUE $44,232,932
WORLDWIDE STAFF   260
HEADQUARTERS   Dearborn, MI
YEAR ESTABLISHED   1982
RECENT REPRESENTATIVE PROJECT
New York Daily News Press Facility
Jersey City, NJ

55 | FKP Architects

8 Greenway, Suite 300
Houston, TX 77046
(713) 621-2178
www.fkp.com
John Crane, President/CEO
Edward Huckaby, Principal
Dan Killebrew, Principal

WORLDWIDE REVENUE $44,000,000
WORLDWIDE STAFF   128
HEADQUARTERS   Houston, TX
YEAR ESTABLISHED   1937

56 | BSA LifeStructures

9365 Counselors Row
Indianapolis, IN 46240
(317) 819-7878
www.bsalifestructures.com
Monte L. Hoover, Chairman
Samuel J. Reed, President
Donald B. Altemeyer, Vice Chairman

WORLDWIDE REVENUE $42,500,000
WORLDWIDE STAFF   242
HEADQUARTERS   Indianapolis, IN
YEAR ESTABLISHED   1975
RECENT REPRESENTATIVE PROJECT
Lakeland HealthCare/Regional Medical
Center Inpatient Pavilion, St. Joseph, MI

57 | Swanke Hayden Connell Architects

295 Lafayette Street
New York, NY 10025
(212) 226-9696
www.shca.com
Richard Hayden, Managing Principal

WORLDWIDE REVENUE $42,000,000
WORLDWIDE STAFF   235
HEADQUARTERS   New York, NY
YEAR ESTABLISHED   1906

58 | tvsdesign

1230 Peachtree Street NE, Suite 2700
Atlanta, GA 30309
(404) 888-6600
www.tvs-design.com
Roger L. Neuenschwander, President
Becky Ward, Managing Principal
Steve Clem, Principal

WORLDWIDE REVENUE	$41,810,966
WORLDWIDE STAFF	165
HEADQUARTERS	Atlanta, GA
YEAR ESTABLISHED	1968

RECENT REPRESENTATIVE PROJECT
Herman Miller Showroom
Los Angeles, CA

59 | Little

5815 Westpark Drive
Charlotte, NC 28217
(704) 525-6350
www.littleonline.com
Phil Kuttner, CEO
John Komisin, President/COO
James McGarry, CFO

WORLDWIDE REVENUE	$41,147,000
WORLDWIDE STAFF	290
HEADQUARTERS	Charlotte, NC
YEAR ESTABLISHED	1964

RECENT REPRESENTATIVE PROJECT
Food Lion Corporate Headquarters
Salisbury, NC

60 | Perkowitz+Ruth Architects

111 West Ocean Boulevard, 21st Floor
Long Beach, CA 90802
(562) 628-8000
www.prarchitects.com
Sy Perkowitz, President/CEO
Steven Ruth, Executive VP
Alan Pullman, Principal

WORLDWIDE REVENUE	$41,000,000
WORLDWIDE STAFF	225
HEADQUARTERS	Long Beach, CA
YEAR ESTABLISHED	1979

RECENT REPRESENTATIVE PROJECT
The Dalton
Pasadena, CA

61 | Fanning/Howey Associates

1200 Irmscher Boulevard
Celina, OH 45822
(888) 499-2292
www.fhai.com
Ronald H. Fanning, Chairman
Clair E. Howey, Vice Chairman
Daniel R. Mader, President/CEO

WORLDWIDE REVENUE	$40,538,509
WORLDWIDE STAFF	250
HEADQUARTERS	Celina, OH
YEAR ESTABLISHED	1961

RECENT REPRESENTATIVE PROJECT
Phelps Architecture, Construction and
Engineering High School, Washington, DC

Justin Maconochie

62 | Lobby/Administration Renovation, Mercedes Benz Research and Development North America, Detroit, MI |
Harley Ellis Devereaux

62 | Harley Ellis Devereaux

26913 Northwestern Highway, Suite 200
Southfield, MI 48033
(248) 262-1500
www.harleyellisdevereaux.com
Dennis M. King, Chairman
J. Peter Devereaux, President
Gary Skog, CEO

WORLDWIDE REVENUE	$39,500,000
WORLDWIDE STAFF	245
HEADQUARTERS	Southfield, MI
YEAR ESTABLISHED	1908
RECENT REPRESENTATIVE PROJECT	

San Diego Medical Examiners Building
San Diego, CA

63 | NTD Architecture

9655 Granite Ridge Drive, Suite 400
San Diego, CA 92123
(858) 569-3434
www.ntd.com
Jon Alan Baker, President/CEO
Jay Whisenant, Principal/COO
R. Todd Stichler, CFO/Partner

WORLDWIDE REVENUE	$38,000,000
WORLDWIDE STAFF	300
HEADQUARTERS	San Diego, CA
YEAR ESTABLISHED	1953
RECENT REPRESENTATIVE PROJECT	

North Tower Addition, Banner Thunderbird Medical Center, Glendale, AZ

64 | Cuningham Group Architecture

201 Main Street SE, Suite 325
Minneapolis, MN 55414
(612) 379-3400
www.cuningham.com
John Cuningham, Founder
John Quiter, Chairman
Timothy Dufault, President/CEO

WORLDWIDE REVENUE	$37,500,000
WORLDWIDE STAFF	163
HEADQUARTERS	Minneapolis, MN
YEAR ESTABLISHED	1968
RECENT REPRESENTATIVE PROJECT	

Epic Systems Corporation
Verona, WI

65 | Wimberly Allison Tong & Goo

8001 Irvine Center Drive, Suite 500
Irvine, CA 92618
(949) 574-8500
www.watg.com
Sidney Char, Senior VP
James Balding, Architect

WORLDWIDE REVENUE	$37,000,000
WORLDWIDE STAFF	101–450
HEADQUARTERS	Irvine, CA
YEAR ESTABLISHED	1945

Alan Karchmer

68 | School of Law, Camden, Rutgers University, Camden, NJ | Ayers/Saint/Gross

66 | gkkworks

2355 Main Street, Suite 220
Irvine, CA 92614
(949) 250-1500
www.gkkworks.com
Praful Kulkarni, President/CEO
David Hunt, VP/Architectural Services
Charlie Merrick, VP/Construction Services

WORLDWIDE REVENUE	$36,212,000
WORLDWIDE STAFF	99
HEADQUARTERS	Irvine, CA
YEAR ESTABLISHED	1991

RECENT REPRESENTATIVE PROJECT

Kohinoor Square Tower
Mumbai, India

67 | Beyer Blinder Belle

41 East 11th Street
New York, NY 10003
(212) 777-7800
www.beyerblinderbelle.com
John H. Beyer, Founding Partner
John Belle, Founding Partner
Frederick A. Bland, Managing Partner

WORLDWIDE REVENUE	$36,103,701
WORLDWIDE STAFF	122
HEADQUARTERS	New York, NY
YEAR ESTABLISHED	1968

RECENT REPRESENTATIVE PROJECT

Historic DC Courthouse
Washington, DC

68 | Ayers/Saint/Gross

AYERS
SAINT
GROSS

1040 Hull Street, Suite 100
Baltimore, MD 21230
(410) 347-8500
www.asg-architects.com
Richard Ayers, Chairman
James Wheeler, President
Adam Gross, Principal

WORLDWIDE REVENUE	$35,100,000
WORLDWIDE STAFF	110
HEADQUARTERS	Baltimore, MD
YEAR ESTABLISHED	1915

RECENT REPRESENTATIVE PROJECT

Johns Hopkins Eye Institute
Baltimore, MD

69 | CTA Architects

13 North 23rd Street
Billings, MT 59101
(406) 248-7455
www.ctagroup.com
Gene Kolstad, Chairman/Principal
Keith Rupert, CEO

WORLDWIDE REVENUE	$35,050,000
WORLDWIDE STAFF	275
HEADQUARTERS	Billings, MT
YEAR ESTABLISHED	1938

71 | 200 Fifth Avenue, New York, NY | STUDIOS Architecture

70 | Lord, Aeck & Sargent

1201 Peachtree Street NE, Suite 300
Atlanta, GA 30361
(404) 253-1400
www.lordaecksargent.com
Larry Lord, Founding Principal
Antonin Aeck, Founding Principal
Terry Sargent, Founding Principal

WORLDWIDE REVENUE	$35,010,000
WORLDWIDE STAFF	115
HEADQUARTERS	Atlanta, GA
YEAR ESTABLISHED	1942

71 | STUDIOS Architecture

STUDIOS
architecture

1625 M Street NW
Washington, DC 20036
(202) 736-5900
www.studiosarchitecture.com
Thomas Yee, Chairman
Todd DeGarmo, President/CEO

WORLDWIDE REVENUE	$35,000,000
WORLDWIDE STAFF	190
HEADQUARTERS	Washington, DC
YEAR ESTABLISHED	1985
RECENT REPRESENTATIVE PROJECT	

200 Fifth Avenue
New York, NY

72 | Pei Cobb Freed & Partners

88 Pine Street
New York, NY 10005
(212) 751-3122
www.pcf-p.com
Henry N. Cobb, Partner
Michael D. Flynn, Partner
George H. Miller, Partner

WORLDWIDE REVENUE	$34,500,000
WORLDWIDE STAFF	90
HEADQUARTERS	New York, NY
YEAR ESTABLISHED	1955
RECENT REPRESENTATIVE PROJECT	

Torre Espacio
Madrid, Spain

73 | TRO Jung | Brannen

22 Boston Wharf Road
Boston, MA 02210
(617) 502-3400
www.trojungbrannen.com
Robert W. Hoye, President/CEO
Mark Jussaume, COO
Bruce Johnson, CFO

WORLDWIDE REVENUE	$34,000,000
WORLDWIDE STAFF	212
HEADQUARTERS	Boston, MA
YEAR ESTABLISHED	1909
RECENT REPRESENTATIVE PROJECT	

Microsoft Startup Labs
Cambridge, MA

fotoworks - Benny Chan

75 | Westminster Rose Center, Westminster, CA | CO Architects

74 | Moseley Architects

3200 Norfolk Street
Richmond, VA 23230
(804) 794-7555
www.moseleyarchitects.com
Bob Mills, President

WORLDWIDE REVENUE	$33,900,000
WORLDWIDE STAFF	255
HEADQUARTERS	Richmond, VA
YEAR ESTABLISHED	1969

75 | CO Architects

CO ARCHITECTS

5055 Wilshire Boulevard, Suite 900
Los Angeles, CA 90036
(323) 525-0500
www.coarchitects.com
Scott P. Kelsey, Managing Principal
Thomas Chessum, Principal
Paul Zajfen, Principal

WORLDWIDE REVENUE	$32,640,400
WORLDWIDE STAFF	82
HEADQUARTERS	Los Angeles, CA
YEAR ESTABLISHED	2006
RECENT REPRESENTATIVE PROJECT	

Panorama City Medical Center
Panorama City, CA

76 | Roger Ferris + Partners

285 Riverside Avenue
Westport, CT 06880
(203) 222-4848
www.ferrisarch.com
Roger Ferris, Founding Partner
Dave Beem, Partner
Robert Marx, Partner

WORLDWIDE REVENUE	$32,300,000
WORLDWIDE STAFF	42
HEADQUARTERS	Westport, CT
YEAR ESTABLISHED	1986
RECENT REPRESENTATIVE PROJECT	

The Bridge Golf Clubhouse
Bridgehampton, NY

77 | Lionakis

1919 19th Street
Sacramento, CA 95811
(916) 558-1900
www.lionakis.com
Bruce Starkweather, President
Chuck Hack, Director of Business
   Development

WORLDWIDE REVENUE	$32,000,000
WORLDWIDE STAFF	200
HEADQUARTERS	Sacramento, CA
YEAR ESTABLISHED	1909

Steelman Partners

78 | Four Seasons Hotel, Macau, China | Steelman Partners

Steelman Partners

78 | Desert Butterfly, Dubai, UAE | Steelman Partners

78 | Steelman Partners

Steelman Partners

3330 West Desert Inn Road
Las Vegas, NV 89012
(702) 873-0221
www.paulsteelman.com
Paul Steelman, CEO
Ethan Nelson, President

WORLDWIDE REVENUE	$32,000,000
WORLDWIDE STAFF	175
HEADQUARTERS	Las Vegas, NV
YEAR ESTABLISHED	1987

RECENT REPRESENTATIVE PROJECT

Hard Rock Hotel - City of Dreams
Macau, China

79 | EDSA

1512 East Broward Boulevard, Suite 110
Fort Lauderdale, FL 33301
(954) 524-3330
www.edsaplan.com
Joseph J. Lalli, President/Managing
   Principal

WORLDWIDE REVENUE	$31,900,000
WORLDWIDE STAFF	215
HEADQUARTERS	Fort Lauderdale, FL
YEAR ESTABLISHED	1960

80 | Arquitectonica

801 Brickell Avenue, Suite 1100
Miami, FL 33131
(305) 372-1812
www.arquitectonica.com
Bernardo Fort-Brescia, CEO/Principal
Laurinda Spear, Founding Principal

WORLDWIDE REVENUE	$31,000,000
WORLDWIDE STAFF	360
HEADQUARTERS	Miami, FL
YEAR ESTABLISHED	1977

RECENT REPRESENTATIVE PROJECT

United States Federal Courthouse
Miami, FL

81 | SLAM Collaborative, The

80 Glastonbury Boulevard
Glastonbury, CT 06033
(860) 657-8077
www.slamcoll.com
James M. McManus, Chairman
Robert F. Pulito, President
Steven W. Ansel, Director of Design

WORLDWIDE REVENUE	$30,552,151
WORLDWIDE STAFF	159
HEADQUARTERS	Glastonbury, CT
YEAR ESTABLISHED	1976

RECENT REPRESENTATIVE PROJECT

Medical Education Building, Emory
University, Atlanta, GA

82 | HLW International

115 5th Avenue, 5th Floor
New York, NY 10003
(212) 353-4666
www.hlw.com
Theodore Hammer, Sr. Managing Partner
John Gering, Managing Partner
Susan Boyle, Managing Partner

WORLDWIDE REVENUE	$30,000,000
WORLDWIDE STAFF	157
HEADQUARTERS	New York, NY
YEAR ESTABLISHED	1885
RECENT REPRESENTATIVE PROJECT	

Hilton Hotels Grand Vacations Club
New York, NY

83 | Davis Brody Bond Aedas

315 Hudson Street
New York, NY 10013
(212) 633-4700
www.davisbrody.com
Steven Davis, Partner

WORLDWIDE REVENUE	$29,700,000
WORLDWIDE STAFF	n/p
HEADQUARTERS	New York, NY
YEAR ESTABLISHED	1952

84 | RNL

1050 17th Street, Suite A200
Denver, CO 80265
(303) 575-8589
www.rnldesign.com
H. Joshua Gould, Chairman/CEO
Richard L. von Luhrte, President
Michael Brendle, Design Principal

WORLDWIDE REVENUE	$29,600,000
WORLDWIDE STAFF	123
HEADQUARTERS	Denver, CO
YEAR ESTABLISHED	1956
RECENT REPRESENTATIVE PROJECT	

National Renewable Energy Laboratory
Research Support Facility, Golden, CO

85 | Shepley Bulfinch Richardson and Abbott

2 Seaport Lane
Boston, MA 02210
(617) 423-1700
www.sbra.com
Carole Wedge, President
Sidney Bowen, Managing Principal
Thomas Kearns, Principal

WORLDWIDE REVENUE	$29,200,000
WORLDWIDE STAFF	134
HEADQUARTERS	Boston, MA
YEAR ESTABLISHED	1874
RECENT REPRESENTATIVE PROJECT	

Smillow Cancer Hospital at Yale -
New Haven, New Haven, CT

86 | Murphy/Jahn

35 East Wacker Drive, Suite 300
Chicago, IL 60601
(312) 427-7300
www.murphyjahn.com
Helmut Jahn, President
Joseph Stypka, Director

WORLDWIDE REVENUE	$29,100,000
WORLDWIDE STAFF	85
HEADQUARTERS	Chicago, IL
YEAR ESTABLISHED	1937

87 | NAC|Architecture

1203 West Riverside Avenue
Spokane, WA 99201
(509) 838-8240
www.nacarchitecture.com
Bruce Blackmer, President/CEO
Gregory J. Stack, K-12 Knowledge Leader
Helena Jubany, Managing Principal

WORLDWIDE REVENUE	$29,000,000
WORLDWIDE STAFF	139
HEADQUARTERS	Spokane, WA
YEAR ESTABLISHED	1960
RECENT REPRESENTATIVE PROJECT	
Eastgate Elementary	
Bellevue, WA	

88 | FXFOWLE Architects

22 West 19th Street
New York, NY 10011
(212) 627-1700
www.fxfowle.com
Guy Geier, Senior Partner
Bruce Fowle, Senior Partner
Dan Kaplan, Senior Partner

WORLDWIDE REVENUE	$28,000,000
WORLDWIDE STAFF	125
HEADQUARTERS	New York, NY
YEAR ESTABLISHED	1978
RECENT REPRESENTATIVE PROJECT	
The Center for Global Conservation	
New York, NY	

89 | Lawrence Group

319 North 4th Street, Suite 1000
St. Louis, MO 63102
(314) 231-5700
www.thelawrencegroup.com
Steve Smith, CEO/Founding Principal
David Ohlemeyer, Founding Principal
Paul Doerner, Founding Principal

WORLDWIDE REVENUE	$27,400,188
WORLDWIDE STAFF	150
HEADQUARTERS	St. Louis, MO
YEAR ESTABLISHED	1983

90 | Mahlum

71 Columbia, Floor 4
Seattle, WA 98104
(206) 441-4151
www.mahlum.com
Gerald Reifert, Managing Partner
Anne Schopf, Design Partner
Robert Lober, Partner

WORLDWIDE REVENUE	$27,370,000
WORLDWIDE STAFF	85
HEADQUARTERS	Seattle, WA
YEAR ESTABLISHED	1938
RECENT REPRESENTATIVE PROJECT	

Clark Hall Restoration, University of
Washington, Seattle, WA

91 | Ballinger

833 Chestnut Street, Suite 1400
Philadelphia, PA 19107
(215) 446 0900
www.ballinger-ae.com
William Gustafson, Principal

WORLDWIDE REVENUE	$27,200,000
WORLDWIDE STAFF	130
HEADQUARTERS	Philadelphia, PA
YEAR ESTABLISHED	1878

92 | JCJ Architecture

38 Prospect Street
Hartford, CT 06103
(860) 247-9226
www.jcj.com
David G. Joslin, CEO
Peter M. Stevens, President
James E. LaPosta, Chief Arch. Officer

WORLDWIDE REVENUE	$27,100,000
WORLDWIDE STAFF	175
HEADQUARTERS	Hartford, CT
YEAR ESTABLISHED	1936
RECENT REPRESENTATIVE PROJECT	

New York State Theater
New York, NY

93 | Davis Partnership Architects

225 Main Street, Unit C101
Edwards, CO 81632
(970) 926-8960
www.davispartner.com
Gary M. Adams, Partner
Brit Probst, Principal

WORLDWIDE REVENUE	$26,911,000
WORLDWIDE STAFF	26–100
HEADQUARTERS	Edwards, CO
YEAR ESTABLISHED	1967

94 | RDG Planning & Design

301 Grand Avenue
Des Moines, IA 50309
(515) 288-3141
www.rdgusa.com
Philip A. Hodgin, CEO
John R. Birge, COO/Principal
John A. Sova, Principal

WORLDWIDE REVENUE	$26,700,000
WORLDWIDE STAFF	175
HEADQUARTERS	Des Moines, IA
YEAR ESTABLISHED	1966

RECENT REPRESENTATIVE PROJECT
Heavener Football Complex, University of Florida, Gainesville, FL

95 | WBCM

849 Fairmount Avenue, Suite 100
Baltimore, MD 21286
(410) 512-4500
www.wbcm.com
Doug Suess, Executive VP
Stephen Burdette, VP Architecture
Mike Bollinger, VP

WORLDWIDE REVENUE	$26,693,151
WORLDWIDE STAFF	181
HEADQUARTERS	Baltimore, MD
YEAR ESTABLISHED	1977

RECENT REPRESENTATIVE PROJECT
Lockheed Martin Center of Excellence Bethesda & Rockville, MD

96 | Morris Architects

1001 Fannin Street, Suite 300
Houston, TX 77002
(713) 622-1180
www.morrisarchitects.com
Chris Hudson, President/CEO
Gary Altergott, Secretary/Principal
Jim Pope, Treasurer/Principal

WORLDWIDE REVENUE	$26,111,668
WORLDWIDE STAFF	138
HEADQUARTERS	Houston, TX
YEAR ESTABLISHED	1938

RECENT REPRESENTATIVE PROJECT
CHRISTUS Moran Health Center Houston, TX

97 | KKE Architects (DLR) (acquired by DLR Group in July 2010)

300 1st Avenue North
Minneapolis, MN 55401
(612) 339-4200
www.kke.com
Gregory C. Hollenkamp, CEO
Todd Young, Principal
Greg Wollums, Principal

WORLDWIDE REVENUE	$26,000,000
WORLDWIDE STAFF	115
HEADQUARTERS	Minneapolis, MN
YEAR ESTABLISHED	1968

98 | SLCE Architects

841 Broadway, 7th Floor
New York, NY 10003
(212) 979-8400
www.slcearch.com
Peter Claman, Managing Partner

WORLDWIDE REVENUE	$25,900,000
WORLDWIDE STAFF	5–25
HEADQUARTERS	New York, NY
YEAR ESTABLISHED	1941

99 | Mancini - Duffy

39 West 13th Street
New York, NY 10011
(212) 938-1260
www.manciniduffy.com
Steve Bleiweiss, CMO
Ed Calabrese, Creative Director

WORLDWIDE REVENUE	$25,542,500
WORLDWIDE STAFF	65
HEADQUARTERS	New York, NY
YEAR ESTABLISHED	1920

100 | Arrowstreet

212 Elm Street
Somerville, MA 02144
(617) 623-5555
www.arrowstreet.com
Jim Batchelor, CEO

WORLDWIDE REVENUE	$25,160,000
WORLDWIDE STAFF	50
HEADQUARTERS	Somerville, MA
YEAR ESTABLISHED	1961

101 | Francis Cauffman

33 East 33rd Sreet, Suite 1201
New York, NY 10016
(646) 315-7000
www.franciscauffman.com
James T. Crispino, President

WORLDWIDE REVENUE	$25,050,000
WORLDWIDE STAFF	115
HEADQUARTERS	New York, NY
YEAR ESTABLISHED	1954
RECENT REPRESENTATIVE PROJECT	

Geisinger Critical Care Building
Wilkes-Barre, PA

102 | Durrant

400 Ice Harbor Drive

Dubuque, IA 52001

(563) 583-9131

www.durrant.com

Charles R. Marsden, President/CEO

WORLDWIDE REVENUE	$25,000,000
WORLDWIDE STAFF	114
HEADQUARTERS	Dubuque, IA
YEAR ESTABLISHED	1933

RECENT REPRESENTATIVE PROJECT

Israel Prison
Be'er Sheva, Israel

103 | Goody Clancy

420 Boylston Street

Boston, MA 02116

(617) 850-6516

www.goodyclancy.com

Roger N. Goldstein, Principal

Jean Carroon, Principal/Preservation

David Dixon, Principal/Planning & U.D.

WORLDWIDE REVENUE	$24,950,000
WORLDWIDE STAFF	105
HEADQUARTERS	Boston, MA
YEAR ESTABLISHED	1955

RECENT REPRESENTATIVE PROJECT

Hariri Building, McDonough Bus. School,
Georgetown University, Washington, DC

104 | GreenbergFarrow

1430 West Peachtree Street, Suite 200

Atlanta, GA 30309

(404) 601-4000

www.greenbergfarrow.com

Essie Ghadrdan, President/CEO

Hughes Thompson, Principal

Navid Magami, Principal

WORLDWIDE REVENUE	$24,800,000
WORLDWIDE STAFF	240
HEADQUARTERS	Atlanta, GA
YEAR ESTABLISHED	1974

RECENT REPRESENTATIVE PROJECT

Gateway Center, Bronx Terminal Market
New York, NY

105 | WD Partners

7007 Discovery Boulevard

Dublin, OH 43017

(614) 634-7000

www.wdpartners.com

Christopher Doerschlag, CEO

WORLDWIDE REVENUE	$24,769,000
WORLDWIDE STAFF	101–200
HEADQUARTERS	Dublin, OH
YEAR ESTABLISHED	1968

William Manning

107 | Southern State Community College, Washington Court House, OH | SHP Leading Design

106 | Adrian Smith + Gordon Gill Architecture

111 West Monroe, Suite 2300
Chicago, IL 60603
(312) 920-1888
www.smithgill.com
Adrian Smith, Partner
Gordon Gill, Partner
Robert Forest, Partner

WORLDWIDE REVENUE	$24,600,000
WORLDWIDE STAFF	100
HEADQUARTERS	Chicago, IL
YEAR ESTABLISHED	2006
RECENT REPRESENTATIVE PROJECT	

Masdar Headquarters
Abu Dhabi, UAE

107 | SHP Leading Design

SHP
LEADING DESIGN

4805 Montgomery Road
Cincinnati, OH 45212
(513) 381-2112
www.shp.com
Lauren B. Della Bella, President/CEO
Michael P. Dingeldein, VP/Secretary
Kevin E. Kreuz, VP/Treasurer

WORLDWIDE REVENUE	$24,566,800
WORLDWIDE STAFF	135
HEADQUARTERS	Cincinnati, OH
YEAR ESTABLISHED	1901
RECENT REPRESENTATIVE PROJECT	

Welcome Pavillion, Southern Baptist
Theological Seminary, Louisville, KY

108 | VLK Architects

2821 West 7th Street
Suite 300
Fort Worth, TX 76107
(817) 633-1600
www.vlkarchitects.com
Richard Jaynes, Principal

WORLDWIDE REVENUE	$24,480,000
WORLDWIDE STAFF	85
HEADQUARTERS	Fort Worth, TX
YEAR ESTABLISHED	1984

109 | Tsoi/Kobus & Associates

One Brattle Square
Cambridge, MA 02238
(617) 475-4000
www.tka-architects.com
Richard L. Kobus, Founding Principal
Ed Tsoi, Founding Principal
Mark Reed, VP

WORLDWIDE REVENUE	$24,200,000
WORLDWIDE STAFF	56
HEADQUARTERS	Cambridge, MA
YEAR ESTABLISHED	1983
RECENT REPRESENTATIVE PROJECT	

Center for Life Science
Boston, MA

110 | Devenney Group Architects

201 West Indian School Road
Phoenix, AZ 85013
(602) 943-8950
www.devenneygroup.com
Stephen Stack, President
James Mobley, VP/COO
Gary Goldberg, VP

WORLDWIDE REVENUE	$24,000,000
WORLDWIDE STAFF	70
HEADQUARTERS	Phoeniz, AZ
YEAR ESTABLISHED	1962
RECENT REPRESENTATIVE PROJECT	

Sutter Medical Center
Castro Valley, CA

111 | Kirksey

6909 Portwest Drive
Houston, TX 77024
(713) 850-9600
www.kirksey.com
Randall Walker, Executive VP
J. Scott Wilkinson, Executive VP/
    Commercial and Retail Team Leader

WORLDWIDE REVENUE	$23,900,000
WORLDWIDE STAFF	120
HEADQUARTERS	Houston, TX
YEAR ESTABLISHED	1971

112 | AC Martin

444 South Flower Street, Suite 1200
Los Angeles, CA 90071
(213) 683-1900
www.acmartin.com
Christopher C. Martin, Co-Chairman/CEO
David Martin, Co-Chair/Design Principal
Kenneth Lewis, President

WORLDWIDE REVENUE	$23,205,000
WORLDWIDE STAFF	101–150
HEADQUARTERS	Los Angeles, CA
YEAR ESTABLISHED	1906

113 | BWBR Architects

380 Saint Peter Street, Suite 600
St. Paul, MN 55102
(651) 222-3701
www.bwbr.com
Stephen Patrick, President/CEO
Peter Smith, Senior VP
Brian B. Buchholz, Senior VP

WORLDWIDE REVENUE	$23,200,000
WORLDWIDE STAFF	98
HEADQUARTERS	St. Paul, MN
YEAR ESTABLISHED	1922
RECENT REPRESENTATIVE PROJECT	

Maple Grove Hospital
Maple Grove, MN

114 | Kahler Slater

111 West Wisconsin Avenue
Milwaukee, WI 53203
(414) 272-2000
www.kahlerslater.com
George Meyer, Co-CEO
James Rasche, Co-CEO
Jill Morin, Co-CEO

WORLDWIDE REVENUE	$23,180,000
WORLDWIDE STAFF	130
HEADQUARTERS	Milwaukee, WI
YEAR ESTABLISHED	1908
RECENT REPRESENTATIVE PROJECT	

Martha Jefferson Hospital
Charlottesville, VA

115 | OZ Architecture

1805 29th Street, Suite 2054
Boulder, CO 80301
(303) 449-8900
www.ozarch.com
Jim Bershof, President
Bob West, Principal
Rick Petersen, Principal

WORLDWIDE REVENUE	$23,100,000
WORLDWIDE STAFF	175
HEADQUARTERS	Boulder, CO
YEAR ESTABLISHED	1964

116 | Helman Hurley Charvat Peacock/Architects

222 West Maitland Boulevard
Maitland, FL 32751
(407) 644-2656
www.hhcp.com
William C. Charvat, Executive VP/COO
Gregory Dungan, Managing Partner

WORLDWIDE REVENUE	$23,077,500
WORLDWIDE STAFF	21–100
HEADQUARTERS	Maitland, FL
YEAR ESTABLISHED	1975

117 | Costas Kondylis Design

31 West 27th Street
New York, NY 10001
(212) 725-4655
www.kondylisdesign.com
Costas Kondylis, CEO

WORLDWIDE REVENUE	$23,035,000
WORLDWIDE STAFF	21–100
HEADQUARTERS	New York, NY
YEAR ESTABLISHED	2009

118 | GBBN Architects

332 East 8th Street
Cincinnati, OH 45202
(513) 241-8700
www.gbbn.com
Robert Gramann, President/CEO
Joseph Schwab, VP/Partner
Greg Otis, Partner/Secretary

WORLDWIDE REVENUE	$23,000,000
WORLDWIDE STAFF	105
HEADQUARTERS	Cincinnati, OH
YEAR ESTABLISHED	1958

RECENT REPRESENTATIVE PROJECT
Ascent Condominiums
Covington, KY

119 | FreemanWhite

8845 Red Oak Boulevard
Charlotte, NC 28217
(704) 523-2230
www.freemanwhite.com
Franklin H. Brooks, CEO

WORLDWIDE REVENUE	$22,500,000
WORLDWIDE STAFF	118
HEADQUARTERS	Charlotte, NC
YEAR ESTABLISHED	1892

RECENT REPRESENTATIVE PROJECT
Doylestown Hospital Emergency
Department, Doylestown, PA

120 | FGM Architects

1211 West 22nd Street, Suite 705
Oak Brook, IL 60523
(630) 574-8300
www.fgmarchitects.com
John Ochoa, President/CEO
August Battaglia, VP/Director of Design
James G. Woods, VP

WORLDWIDE REVENUE	$22,300,000
WORLDWIDE STAFF	85
HEADQUARTERS	Oak Brook, IL
YEAR ESTABLISHED	1945

RECENT REPRESENTATIVE PROJECT
Hickory Creek Middle School
Frankfort, IL

121 | Gould Evans

4041 Mill Street
Kansas City, MO 64111
(816) 931-6655
www.gouldevans.com
Bob Gould, Partner
Trudi Hummel, Partner
Tony Rohr, Business Manager

WORLDWIDE REVENUE	$22,200,000
WORLDWIDE STAFF	101–150
HEADQUARTERS	Kansas City, MO
YEAR ESTABLISHED	1974

122 | Karlsberger

99 East Main Street
Columbus, OH 43215
(614) 461-9500
www.karlsberger.com
Michael D. Tyne, Chairman

WORLDWIDE REVENUE	$22,100,000
WORLDWIDE STAFF	75
HEADQUARTERS	Columbus, OH
YEAR ESTABLISHED	1928

123 | RBB Architects

10980 Wilshire Boulevard
Los Angeles, CA 90024
(310) 473-3555
www.rbbinc.com
Joseph Balbona, CEO
Deneys Purcell, President
Art Border, Senior VP

WORLDWIDE REVENUE	$22,000,000
WORLDWIDE STAFF	55
HEADQUARTERS	Los Angeles, CA
YEAR ESTABLISHED	1952
RECENT REPRESENTATIVE PROJECT	

Acute Care Tower, Mission Hospital
Mission Viejo, CA

124 | SchenkelShultz

200 East Robinson Street, Suite 300
Orlando, FL 32801
(407) 872-3322
www.schenkelshultz.com
J. Thomas Chandler, President/COO
Michael Gouloff, CEO

WORLDWIDE REVENUE	$21,950,000
WORLDWIDE STAFF	21–100
HEADQUARTERS	Fort Wayne, IN
YEAR ESTABLISHED	1958

125 | Opsis Architecture

920 Northwest 17th Avenue
Portland, OR 97209
(503) 525-9511
www.opsisarch.com
Alec Holser, Principal
James Meyer, Principal
Jim Kalvelage, Principal

WORLDWIDE REVENUE	$21,930,000
WORLDWIDE STAFF	1–20
HEADQUARTERS	Portland, OR
YEAR ESTABLISHED	1999

1st image

127 | China Diamond Exchange Center, Shanghai, China | Goettsch Partners

126 | Ratcliff

5856 Doyle Street
Emeryville, CA 94608
(510) 899-6400
www.ratcliffarch.com
Christopher (Kit) Ratcliff, President/CEO
Dan Wetherell, COO/Principal
David Dersch, CFO

WORLDWIDE REVENUE	$21,800,000
WORLDWIDE STAFF	75
HEADQUARTERS	Emeryville, CA
YEAR ESTABLISHED	1906

RECENT REPRESENTATIVE PROJECT
Doe Library Annex, University of California
Berkeley, CA

127 | Goettsch Partners

goettschpartners

224 South Michigan Avenue, 17th Floor
Chicago, IL 60604
(312) 356-0600
www.gpchicago.com
James Goettsch, President
Steven M. Nilles, Partner
James Zheng, Partner

WORLDWIDE REVENUE	$21,756,000
WORLDWIDE STAFF	85
HEADQUARTERS	Chicago, IL
YEAR ESTABLISHED	1938

RECENT REPRESENTATIVE PROJECT
300 East Randolph Expansion
Chicago, IL

128 | Westlake Reed Leskosky

925 Euclid Avenue, Suite 1900
Cleveland, OH 44115
(216) 522-1350
www.wrldesign.com
Paul E. Westlake Jr., Managing Principal
Ronald A. Reed, Principal
Vince Leskosky, Principal

WORLDWIDE REVENUE	$21,675,000
WORLDWIDE STAFF	115
HEADQUARTERS	Cleveland, OH
YEAR ESTABLISHED	1905

RECENT REPRESENTATIVE PROJECT
Bethel Woods Center for the Arts
Bethel, NY

129 | Moody - Nolan

300 Spruce Street, Suite 300
Columbus, OH 43215
(877) 530-4984
www.moodynolan.com
Curtis Moody, President

WORLDWIDE REVENUE	$21,200,000
WORLDWIDE STAFF	21–100
HEADQUARTERS	Columbus, OH
YEAR ESTABLISHED	1982

130 | Harvard Jolly Architecture

5201 West Kennedy Boulevard, Suite 515
Tampa, FL 33609
(813) 286-8206
www.harvardjolly.com
John Clees, Principal
Jeff Cobble, Executive VP

WORLDWIDE REVENUE	$21,037,500
WORLDWIDE STAFF	101–150
HEADQUARTERS	Tampa, FL
YEAR ESTABLISHED	1938

131 | Cooper Carry

191 Peachtree Street NE, Suite 2400
Atlanta, GA 30303
(404) 237-2000
www.coopercarry.com
Kevin Cantley, President/CEO
Jerome Cooper, Founding Principal
Pope Bulloch, Principal

WORLDWIDE REVENUE	$21,000,000
WORLDWIDE STAFF	175–225
HEADQUARTERS	Atlanta, GA
YEAR ESTABLISHED	1960

132 | Symmes Maini & McKee Associates

1000 Massachusetts Avenue
Cambridge, MA 02138
(617) 547-5400
www.smma.com
Michael K. Powers, CEO

WORLDWIDE REVENUE	$20,900,000
WORLDWIDE STAFF	140
HEADQUARTERS	Cambridge, MA
YEAR ESTABLISHED	1955

133 | Solomon Cordwell Buenz

625 North Michigan Avenue, Suite 800
Chicago, IL 60611
(312) 896-1100
www.scb.com
John C. Lahey, Chairman/President/CEO
Martin F. Wolf, Principal
Gary Kohn, Principal

WORLDWIDE REVENUE	$20,800,000
WORLDWIDE STAFF	92
HEADQUARTERS	Chicago, IL
YEAR ESTABLISHED	1931
RECENT REPRESENTATIVE PROJECT	
	The Legacy at Millennium Park
	Chicago, IL

134 | Hanbury Evans Wright Vlattas + Company

120 Atlantic Street	WORLDWIDE REVENUE	$20,500,000
Norfolk, VA 23510	WORLDWIDE STAFF	75
(757) 321-9600	HEADQUARTERS	Norfolk, VA
www.hewv.com	YEAR ESTABLISHED	1985
Jane Cady Wright, President/CEO	RECENT REPRESENTATIVE PROJECT	
S. Michael Evans, VP	Ferguson Center for the Arts, Christopher	
Nicholas E. Vlattas, COO/CFO	Newport University, Newport News, VA	

135 | ARC/Architectural Resources Cambridge

Five Cambridge Center	WORLDWIDE REVENUE	$20,200,000
Cambridge, MA 02142	WORLDWIDE STAFF	68
(617) 547-2200	HEADQUARTERS	Cambridge, MA
www.arcusa.com	YEAR ESTABLISHED	1969
Henry Reeder, Chair/Founding Principal	RECENT REPRESENTATIVE PROJECT	
Arthur Cohen, Founding Principal	Genzyme Science Center	
Philip Laird, President	Framingham, MA	

136 | CBT

110 Canal Street	WORLDWIDE REVENUE	$20,000,000
Boston, MA 02114	WORLDWIDE STAFF	225
(617) 262-4354	HEADQUARTERS	Boston, MA
www.cbtarchitects.com	YEAR ESTABLISHED	1967
Richard Bertman, Principal	RECENT REPRESENTATIVE PROJECT	
Charles Tseckares, Principal	Mandarin Oriental Hotel	
Robert Brown, Principal	Boston, MA	

137 | RATIO Architects

107 South Pennsylvania Street, Suite 100	WORLDWIDE REVENUE	$19,925,000
Indianapolis, IN 46204	WORLDWIDE STAFF	75
(317) 633-4040	HEADQUARTERS	Indianapolis, IN
www.ratioarchitects.com	YEAR ESTABLISHED	1982
William Browne Jr., President/Principal	RECENT REPRESENTATIVE PROJECT	
R. Tim Barrick, Principal	North/Endzone Addition, Indiana Univer-	
N. Anthony Steinhardt, Principal	sity Memorial Stadium, Bloomington, IN	

138 | Steffian Bradley Architects

100 Summer Street
Boston, MA 02110
(617) 305-7100
www.steffian.com
Kurt A. Rockstroh, President/CEO
Peter Steffian, Principal

WORLDWIDE REVENUE	$19,847,500
WORLDWIDE STAFF	150
HEADQUARTERS	Boston, MA
YEAR ESTABLISHED	1932

139 | Cromwell Architects Engineers

101 South Spring Street
Cromwell Building
Little Rock, AR 72201
(501) 372-2900
www.cromwell.com
Charlie Penix, President

WORLDWIDE REVENUE	$19,600,000
WORLDWIDE STAFF	105
HEADQUARTERS	Little Rock, AR
YEAR ESTABLISHED	1885

140 | BRPH

3670 Maguire Boulevard, Suite 300
Orlando, FL 32803
(407) 896-9301
www.brph.com
Brad Harmsen, Chairman/CEO

WORLDWIDE REVENUE	$19,500,000
WORLDWIDE STAFF	215
HEADQUARTERS	Orlando, FL
YEAR ESTABLISHED	1964

141 | Dattner Architects

130 West 57th Street
New York, NY 10019
(212) 247-2660
www.dattner.com
William Stein, Principal
Beth Greenberg, Principal
Daniel R. Heuberger, Principal

WORLDWIDE REVENUE	$19,400,000
WORLDWIDE STAFF	74
HEADQUARTERS	New York, NY
YEAR ESTABLISHED	1964
RECENT REPRESENTATIVE PROJECT	
Schomberg Center for Research	
New York, NY	

142 | Dekker/Perich/Sabatini

7601 Jefferson Northeast, Suite 100
Albuquerque, NM 87109
(505) 761-9700
www.dpsdesign.org
Steve Perich, Managing Partner

WORLDWIDE REVENUE	$19,300,000
WORLDWIDE STAFF	155
HEADQUARTERS	Albuquerque, NM
YEAR ESTABLISHED	1998

143 | Rosser International

524 West Peachtree Street
Atlanta, GA 30308
(404) 876-3800
www.rosser.com
William Griffin, Chairman
Wiliam Golson, VP
Fred Krenson, VP

WORLDWIDE REVENUE	$19,000,000
WORLDWIDE STAFF	115
HEADQUARTERS	Atlanta, GA
YEAR ESTABLISHED	1947
RECENT REPRESENTATIVE PROJECT	

University of West Georgia Coliseum
Carrollton, GA

144 | McKissack & McKissack

1401 New York Avenue NW, Suite 900
Washington, DC 20005
(202) 347-1446
www.mckissackdc.com
Deryl McKissack, President/CEO

WORLDWIDE REVENUE	$18,900,000
WORLDWIDE STAFF	110
HEADQUARTERS	Washington, DC
YEAR ESTABLISHED	1990

145 | Rees Associates

1801 North Lamar Street
Suite 600
Dallas, TX 75202
(214) 522-7337
www.rees.com
Frank W. Rees, President/CEO

WORLDWIDE REVENUE	$18,870,000
WORLDWIDE STAFF	100
HEADQUARTERS	Oklahoma City, OK
YEAR ESTABLISHED	1975

Warren Jagger Photography

146 | Waterplace, Providence, RI | ADD Inc

146 | ADD Inc

311 Summer Street
Boston, MA 02210
(617) 234-3100
www.addinc.com
Fred Kramer, President

ADD Inc

WORLDWIDE REVENUE	$18,785,000
WORLDWIDE STAFF	130
HEADQUARTERS	Boston, MA
YEAR ESTABLISHED	1971
RECENT REPRESENTATIVE PROJECT	

Waterplace
Providence, RI

147 | MCG

1055 East Colorado Boulevard
Suite 400
Pasadena, CA 91106
(626) 793-9119
www.mcgarchitecture.com
Rick Gaylord, Chairman
Brian Tiedge, President

WORLDWIDE REVENUE	$18,700,000
WORLDWIDE STAFF	100
HEADQUARTERS	Pasadena, CA
YEAR ESTABLISHED	1927

148 | Hord Coplan Macht

750 East Pratt Street, Suite 1100
Baltimore, MD 21202
(410) 837-7311
www.hcm2.com
Edward M. Hord, Senior Principal
Lee Coplan, Senior Principal
Carol Macht, Senior Principal

WORLDWIDE REVENUE	$18,600,000
WORLDWIDE STAFF	80
HEADQUARTERS	Baltimore, MD
YEAR ESTABLISHED	1977

149 | BBG-BBGM

350 5th Avenue
Empire State Building
New York, NY 10118
(212) 888-7667
www.bbg-bbgm.com
Christina Hart, Partner

WORLDWIDE REVENUE	$18,500,000
WORLDWIDE STAFF	120
HEADQUARTERS	New York, NY
YEAR ESTABLISHED	1984

Barbara Karant, Karant + Associates

151 | Education Center, College of DuPage Technology, Glen Ellyn, IL | DeStefano Partners

150 | Gehry Partners

12541 Beatrice Street
Los Angeles, CA 90066
(310) 482-3000
www.foga.com
Frank Gehry, Architect

WORLDWIDE REVENUE	$18,360,000
WORLDWIDE STAFF	135
HEADQUARTERS	Los Angeles, CA
YEAR ESTABLISHED	1962

151 | DeStefano Partners

DE STEFANO PARTNERS

330 North Wabash Avenue, Suite 3200
Chicago, IL 60611
(312) 836-4321
www.dpdesigns.com
James R. DeStefano, Founding Principal
Scott S. Sarver, Chairman/Design Principal
Duane L. Sohl, President

WORLDWIDE REVENUE	$18,300,000
WORLDWIDE STAFF	95
HEADQUARTERS	Chicago, IL
YEAR ESTABLISHED	1988
RECENT REPRESENTATIVE PROJECT	
Doosan Haeundae Zenith	
Busan, South Korea	

152 | Highland Associates

228 East 45th Street, 7th Floor
New York, NY 10017
(212) 681-0200
www.highlandassociates.com
Michael Dench, Managing Partner
Jeffrey Pencek, Principal
Gil Ben-Ami, Principal

WORLDWIDE REVENUE	$18,200,000
WORLDWIDE STAFF	21–100
HEADQUARTERS	Clarks Summit, PA
YEAR ESTABLISHED	1988

153 | WDG Architecture

1025 Connecticut Avenue NW, Suite 300
Washington, DC 20036
(202) 857-8300
www.wdgarch.com
George Dove, Managing Principal

WORLDWIDE REVENUE	$18,100,000
WORLDWIDE STAFF	21–100
HEADQUARTERS	Washington, DC
YEAR ESTABLISHED	1938

D. A. Horchner/Design Workshop

154 | Northwest Campus, Pima Community College, Tucson, AZ | Design Workshop

154 | Design Workshop

1390 Lawrence Street, Suite 200
Denver, CO 80204
(303) 623-5186
www.designworkshop.com
Kurt Culbertson, Chairman
Rebecca Zimmerman, President
Todd Johnson, Chief Design Officer

DESIGNWORKSHOP

WORLDWIDE REVENUE	$17,935,000
WORLDWIDE STAFF	120
HEADQUARTERS	Denver, CO
YEAR ESTABLISHED	1969

RECENT REPRESENTATIVE PROJECT
Riverfront Commons
Denver, CO

155 | Ware Malcomb

10 Edelman
Irvine, CA 92618
(949) 660-9128
www.waremalcomb.com
Lawrence Armstrong, CEO
Kenneth Wink, VP
Jay Todisco, VP

WORLDWIDE REVENUE	$17,700,000
WORLDWIDE STAFF	21–100
HEADQUARTERS	Irvine, CA
YEAR ESTABLISHED	1972

156 | BLT Architects

1216 Arch Street. 8th Floor
Philadelphia, PA 19107
(215) 563-3900
www.blta.com
Michael L. Prifti, Managing Principal

WORLDWIDE REVENUE	$17,500,000
WORLDWIDE STAFF	21–100
HEADQUARTERS	Philadelphia, PA
YEAR ESTABLISHED	1961

157 | EDI Architecture

2800 Post Oak Boulevard, Suite 3800
Houston, TX 77056
(877) 375-1401
www.ediarchitecture.com
Victor A. Mirontschuk, President
Brit L. Perkins, Senior VP
Dennis Thompson, Senior VP

WORLDWIDE REVENUE	$17,255,000
WORLDWIDE STAFF	70
HEADQUARTERS	Houston, TX
YEAR ESTABLISHED	1976

RECENT REPRESENTATIVE PROJECT
Dana Hotel and Spa
Chicago, IL

158 | Elkus Manfredi Architects

300 A Street
Boston, MA 02210
(617) 426-1300
www.elkus-manfredi.com
Howard F. Elkus, Principal
David P. Manfredi, Principal
Elizabeth O. Lowrey, Principal

WORLDWIDE REVENUE $17,231,592
WORLDWIDE STAFF 96
HEADQUARTERS Boston, MA
YEAR ESTABLISHED 1988
RECENT REPRESENTATIVE PROJECT
Emerson College Paramount Center
Boston, MA

159 | Davis Carter Scott

1676 International Drive, Suite 500
McLean, VA 22102
(703) 556-9275
www.dcsdesign.com
Doug Carter, President

WORLDWIDE REVENUE $17,161,500
WORLDWIDE STAFF 21–100
HEADQUARTERS McLean, VA
YEAR ESTABLISHED 1968

160 | L. Robert Kimball & Associates (Architecture)

615 West Highland Avenue
Ebensburg, PA 15931
(814) 472-7700
www.lrkimball.com
R. Jeffrey Kimball, President/CEO
Ann K. Balazs, Senior VP
Csaba S. Balazs, Senior VP

WORLDWIDE REVENUE $17,150,000
WORLDWIDE STAFF 115
HEADQUARTERS Edensburg, PA
YEAR ESTABLISHED 1953
RECENT REPRESENTATIVE PROJECT
Altoona Area Junior/Senior High School
Altoona, PA

161 | BHDP

302 West 3rd Street, Suite 500
Cincinnati, OH 45202
(513) 271-1634
www.bhdp.com
Michael J. Habel, President

WORLDWIDE REVENUE $17,100,000
WORLDWIDE STAFF 101–450
HEADQUARTERS Cincinnati, OH
YEAR ESTABLISHED 1937

162 | Fletcher Thompson

3 Corporate Drive, Suite 500
Shelton, CT 06484
(203) 225-6500
www.fletcherthompson.com
Jim Beaudin, President
Jim Boughton, Principal

WORLDWIDE REVENUE	$17,050,000
WORLDWIDE STAFF	101–450
HEADQUARTERS	Shelton, CT
YEAR ESTABLISHED	1910

163 | Omniplan

1845 Woodall Rodgers Freeway, Suite 1500
Dallas, TX 75201
(214) 826-7080
www.omniplan.com
Michael Hellinghausen, COO/Principal
Mark Dilworth, Principal
Tipton Housewright, Principal

WORLDWIDE REVENUE	$16,900,000
WORLDWIDE STAFF	50
HEADQUARTERS	Dallas, TX
YEAR ESTABLISHED	1953

164 | Shalom Baranes Associates

3299 K Street Northwest
Suite 400
Washington, DC 20007
(202) 342-2200
www.sbaranes.com
Shalom Baranes, Principal

WORLDWIDE REVENUE	$16,800,000
WORLDWIDE STAFF	21–100
HEADQUARTERS	Washington, DC
YEAR ESTABLISHED	1981

165 | BOORA Architects

720 Southwest Washington Street
Suite 800
Portland, OR 97205
(503) 226-1575
www.boora.com
Patrick Harrington, Managing Principal
Tom Pene, Principal

WORLDWIDE REVENUE	$16,750,000
WORLDWIDE STAFF	21–100
HEADQUARTERS	Portland, OR
YEAR ESTABLISHED	1958

166 | Wisnewski Blair & Associates

44 Canal Center Plaza
Suite 100
Alexandria, VA 22314
(703) 836-7766
www.wba-arch.com
Joseph Wisnewski, President
Luther C. Blair Jr., VP

WORLDWIDE REVENUE $16,700,000
WORLDWIDE STAFF 61
HEADQUARTERS Alexandria, VA
YEAR ESTABLISHED 1976
RECENT REPRESENTATIVE PROJECT
1.3 Million Square Feet Government
Campus, Undisclosed Location

167 | Facility Design Group

2233 Lake Park Drive
Smyrna, GA 30080
(770) 437-2700
www.facilitygroup.com
Paul Grupe, Principal

WORLDWIDE REVENUE $16,500,000
WORLDWIDE STAFF 76–125
HEADQUARTERS Smyrna, GA
YEAR ESTABLISHED 1986

168 | Stevens & Wilkinson

100 Peachtree Street NW, Suite 2500
Atlanta, GA 30303
(404) 522-8888
www.stevenswilkinson.com
Ron Stang, CEO
Mark Newdow, Principal

WORLDWIDE REVENUE $16,235,000
WORLDWIDE STAFF 76–125
HEADQUARTERS Atlanta, GA
YEAR ESTABLISHED 1919

169 | Hickok Cole Architects

1023 31st Street NW
Washington, DC 20007
(202) 667-9776
www.hickokcole.com
Michael Hickok, Principal

WORLDWIDE REVENUE $16,056,500
WORLDWIDE STAFF 26–75
HEADQUARTERS Washington, DC
YEAR ESTABLISHED 1987

170 | H+L Architecture

1755 Blake Street, Suite 400
Denver, CO 80202
(303) 298-4700
www.hlarch.com
Rob Davidson, Partner
Scott S. Kuehn, Principal
Patrick Johnson, Principal

WORLDWIDE REVENUE	$16,000,000
WORLDWIDE STAFF	76
HEADQUARTERS	Denver, CO
YEAR ESTABLISHED	1963

RECENT REPRESENTATIVE PROJECT
Adams City High School
Commerce City, CO

171 | Carrier Johnson + CULTURE

1301 3rd Avenue
San Diego, CA 92101
(619) 239-2353
www.carrierjohnson.com
Gordon R. Carrier, Principal
Michael C. Johnson, Principal

WORLDWIDE REVENUE	$15,980,000
WORLDWIDE STAFF	40
HEADQUARTERS	San Diego, CA
YEAR ESTABLISHED	1977

172 | Orcutt | Winslow

3003 North Central, 16th Floor
Phoenix, AZ 85012
(602) 257-1764
www.owp.com
Paul Winslow, Founding Partner
Bill Sheely, Partner
Neil Terry, Partner

WORLDWIDE REVENUE	$15,909,450
WORLDWIDE STAFF	82
HEADQUARTERS	Phoenix, AZ
YEAR ESTABLISHED	1971

RECENT REPRESENTATIVE PROJECT
Beatitudes Campus
Phoenix, AZ

173 | Hixson

659 Van Meter Street
Cincinnati, OH 45202
(513) 241-1230
www.hixson-inc.com
J. Wickliffe Ach, President/CEO
Michael D. Follmer, VP
Thomas J. Hellmann, Senior VP

WORLDWIDE REVENUE	$15,800,000
WORLDWIDE STAFF	115
HEADQUARTERS	Cincinnati, OH
YEAR ESTABLISHED	1948

RECENT REPRESENTATIVE PROJECT
Kitchens of Sara Lee, Sara Lee
Headquarters, Downers Grove, IL

174 | Hobbs+Black Architects

100 North State Street
Ann Arbor, MI 48104
(734) 663-4189
www.hobbs-black.com
William Hobbs, President
John Hinkley, Executive VP
John Barker, Executive VP

WORLDWIDE REVENUE	$15,647,000
WORLDWIDE STAFF	90
HEADQUARTERS	Ann Arbor, MI
YEAR ESTABLISHED	1965

RECENT REPRESENTATIVE PROJECT
City Creek Center
Salt Lake City, UT

175 | ka

1468 West 9th Street, Suite 600
Cleveland, OH 44113
(216) 781-9144
www.kainc.com
James B. Heller, President
John Burk, COO
Darrell K. Pattison, Chief Strategic Officer

WORLDWIDE REVENUE	$15,385,000
WORLDWIDE STAFF	55
HEADQUARTERS	Cleveland, OH
YEAR ESTABLISHED	1960

RECENT REPRESENTATIVE PROJECT
Annapolis Towne Centre@Parole
Annapolis, MD

176 | Lee, Burkhart, Liu

13335 Maxella Avenue
Marina del Rey, CA 90292
(310) 829-2249
www.lblarch.com
Kenneth Lee, Principal
Erich Burkhart, Principal
Ken Liu, Principal

WORLDWIDE REVENUE	$15,300,000
WORLDWIDE STAFF	58
HEADQUARTERS	Marina Del Rey, CA
YEAR ESTABLISHED	1986

177 | RMW Architecture & Interiors

160 Pine Street
San Francisco, CA 94111
(415) 781-9800
www.rmw.com
Thomas B. Gerfen, Chairman/CEO
Glenn E. Bauer, Vice Chairman
Russ Nichols, Executive VP

WORLDWIDE REVENUE	$15,177,584
WORLDWIDE STAFF	66
HEADQUARTERS	San Francisco, CA
YEAR ESTABLISHED	1970

RECENT REPRESENTATIVE PROJECT
Marin County Health and Wellness
Campus, San Rafael, CA

178 | Nadel

1990 South Bundy Drive, 4th Floor
Los Angeles, CA 90025
(310) 826-2100
www.nadelarc.com
Herbert Nadel, Chairman/CEO
Richard Hampel, VP

WORLDWIDE REVENUE	$15,000,000
WORLDWIDE STAFF	100
HEADQUARTERS	Los Angeles, CA
YEAR ESTABLISHED	1973
RECENT REPRESENTATIVE PROJECT	

Futian Mixed-Use Sports Center
Shezhen, China

179 | Niles Bolton Associates

3060 Peachtree Road, Suite 600
Atlanta, GA 30305
(404) 365-7600
www.nilesbolton.com
G. Niles Bolton, Chairman/CEO

WORLDWIDE REVENUE	$14,800,000
WORLDWIDE STAFF	101–200
HEADQUARTERS	Atlanta, GA
YEAR ESTABLISHED	1975

180 | Humphreys & Partners Architects

5339 Alpha Road
Dallas, TX 75240
(972) 701-9636
www.humphreys.com
Mark Humphreys, CEO

WORLDWIDE REVENUE	$14,790,000
WORLDWIDE STAFF	76–100
HEADQUARTERS	Dallas, TX
YEAR ESTABLISHED	1991

181 | Arcturis

720 Olive Street, Suite 200
St. Louis, MO 63101
(314) 206-7100
www.arcturis.com
Patricia Whitaker, President/CEO

WORLDWIDE REVENUE	$14,343,750
WORLDWIDE STAFF	90
HEADQUARTERS	St. Louis, MO
YEAR ESTABLISHED	1977

182 | Johnson Fain

1201 North Broadway
Los Angeles, CA 90012
(323) 224-6000
www.johnsonfain.com
Scott Johnson, Principal

WORLDWIDE REVENUE	$14,025,000
WORLDWIDE STAFF	21–100
HEADQUARTERS	Los Angeles, CA
YEAR ESTABLISHED	1931

183 | TSP

1112 North West Avenue
Sioux Falls, SD 57104
(605) 336-1160
www.teamtsp.com
Richard Gustaf, CEO
Gary Sabart, Business Development

WORLDWIDE REVENUE	$13,900,000
WORLDWIDE STAFF	101–450
HEADQUARTERS	Sioux Falls, SD
YEAR ESTABLISHED	1930

184 | Odell

800 West Hill Street, 3rd Floor
Charlotte, NC 28208
(704) 414-1000
www.odell.com
James Snyder, Chairman/CEO
Roger M. Soto, President/Director of Design
J. Michael Woollen, Managing Principal

WORLDWIDE REVENUE	$13,800,000
WORLDWIDE STAFF	21–100
HEADQUARTERS	Charlotte, NC
YEAR ESTABLISHED	1940

185 | Friedmutter Group

4022 Dean Martin Drive
Las Vegas, NV 89103
(702) 736-7477
www.friedmuttergroup.com
Brad Friedmutter, Founder/CEO
Chuck Jones, VP
Douglas Friedmutter, Principal

WORLDWIDE REVENUE	$13,770,000
WORLDWIDE STAFF	70
HEADQUARTERS	Las Vegas, NV
YEAR ESTABLISHED	1992

186 | Gruen Associates

6330 San Vicente Boulevard
Suite 200
Los Angeles, CA 90048
(323) 937-4270
www.gruenassociates.com
Ki Suh Park, Managing Partner

WORLDWIDE REVENUE	$13,604,250
WORLDWIDE STAFF	21–100
HEADQUARTERS	Los Angeles, CA
YEAR ESTABLISHED	1946

187 | Bay Architects

18201 Gulf Freeway
Webster, TX 77598
(281) 286-6605
www.bayarchitects.com
Calvin E. Powitzky, Senior Principal

WORLDWIDE REVENUE	$13,591,500
WORLDWIDE STAFF	21–100
HEADQUARTERS	Webster, TX
YEAR ESTABLISHED	1995

188 | Pieper O'Brien Herr Architects

3000 Royal Boulevard South
Alpharetta, GA 30022
(770) 569-1706
www.poharchitects.com
Charles J. O'Brien, President
Jeff Pieper, Partner

WORLDWIDE REVENUE	$13,430,000
WORLDWIDE STAFF	21–100
HEADQUARTERS	Alpharetta, GA
YEAR ESTABLISHED	1971

189 | Good Fulton & Farrell

2808 Fairmont Street, Suite 300
Dallas, TX 75201
(214) 303-1500
www.gff.com
Larry Good, President
Duncan T. Fulton, Managing Principal
David M. Farrell, Design Principal

WORLDWIDE REVENUE	$13,390,000
WORLDWIDE STAFF	68
HEADQUARTERS	Dallas, TX
YEAR ESTABLISHED	1982
RECENT REPRESENTATIVE PROJECT	
Crow Holdings at Old Parkland	
Dallas, TX	

Brian Robbins

190 | Navy Federal Credit Union, Brian L. McDonnell Center at Heritage Oaks, Pensacola, FL | ASD

190 | ASD

55 Ivan Allen Junior Boulevard, Suite 100
Atlanta, GA 30308
(404) 688-3318
www.asdnet.com
Thom Williams, President
Michael Neiswander, VP
Roberto Paredes, VP

WORLDWIDE REVENUE	$13,200,000
WORLDWIDE STAFF	86
HEADQUARTERS	Atlanta, GA
YEAR ESTABLISHED	1963

RECENT REPRESENTATIVE PROJECT
Navy Federal Heritage Oaks Campus,
Phase II, Pensacola, FL

191 | DES Architects + Engineers

399 Bradford Street
Redwood City, CA 94063
(650) 364-6453
www.des-ae.com
Stephen Mincey, CEO

WORLDWIDE REVENUE	$13,196,250
WORLDWIDE STAFF	101–450
HEADQUARTERS	Redwood City, CA
YEAR ESTABLISHED	1973

192 | THW Design

2100 RiverEdge Parkway, Suite 900
Atlanta, GA 30328
(404) 252-8040
www.thw.com
Bill Witte, CEO

WORLDWIDE REVENUE	$13,175,000
WORLDWIDE STAFF	45
HEADQUARTERS	Atlanta, GA
YEAR ESTABLISHED	1957

193 | BOKA Powell

8070 Park Lane, Suite 300
Dallas, TX 75231
(972) 701-9000
www.bokapowell.com
Chris W. Barnes, Principal
Donald R. Powell, Principal

WORLDWIDE REVENUE	$13,166,500
WORLDWIDE STAFF	80
HEADQUARTERS	Dallas, TX
YEAR ESTABLISHED	1975

194 | Architects Design Group

333 North Knowles Avenue
Winter Park, FL 32789
(407) 647-1706
www.adgusa.org
Keith Reeves, Managing Principal

WORLDWIDE REVENUE	$13,090,000
WORLDWIDE STAFF	21–100
HEADQUARTERS	Winter Park, FL
YEAR ESTABLISHED	1971

195 | Goodwyn, Mills & Cawood

2660 EastChase Lane, Suite 200
Montgomery, AL 36117
(334) 271-3200
www.gmcnetwork.com
Steve Cawood, President

WORLDWIDE REVENUE	$12,850,000
WORLDWIDE STAFF	101–450
HEADQUARTERS	Montgomery, AL
YEAR ESTABLISHED	1975

196 | CR Architecture + Design

600 Vine Street, Suite 2210
Cincinnati, OH 45202
(513) 721-8080
www.colerussell.com
David Arends, CEO

WORLDWIDE REVENUE	$12,843,500
WORLDWIDE STAFF	21–100
HEADQUARTERS	Cincinnati, OH
YEAR ESTABLISHED	1982

197 | Gwathmey Siegel & Associates Architects

475 10th Avenue
New York, NY 10018
(212) 947-1240
www.gwathmey-siegel.com
Robert Siegel, Principal/Founding Partner

WORLDWIDE REVENUE	$12,835,850
WORLDWIDE STAFF	21–100
HEADQUARTERS	New York, NY
YEAR ESTABLISHED	1968

198 | TAYLOR

2220 North University Drive
Newport Beach, CA 92660
(949) 574-1325
www.taa1.com
Neal Rinella, Principal

WORLDWIDE REVENUE	$12,835,000
WORLDWIDE STAFF	21–100
HEADQUARTERS	Newport Beach, CA
YEAR ESTABLISHED	1979

199 | Mithun

1201 Alaskan Way, Suite 200
Seattle, WA 98101
(206) 623-3344
www.mithun.com
Bert Gregory, President/CEO
Bruce Williams, VP/Managing Principal
David Goldberg, Managing Principal

WORLDWIDE REVENUE	$12,800,000
WORLDWIDE STAFF	143
HEADQUARTERS	Seattle, WA
YEAR ESTABLISHED	1949
RECENT REPRESENTATIVE PROJECT	

Puyallup City Hall
Puyallup, WA

200 | Legat Architects

651 West Washington Boulevard
Suite 1
Chicago, IL 60661
(312) 258-9595
www.legat.com
Patrick Brosnan, President

WORLDWIDE REVENUE	$12,792,500
WORLDWIDE STAFF	21–100
HEADQUARTERS	Chicago, IL
YEAR ESTABLISHED	1964

201 | Jerde Partnership, The

913 Ocean Front Walk
Venice, CA 90291
(310) 399-1987
www.jerde.com
Jon Jerde, Chairman
Rick Poulos, Executive VP
John Simones, Director of Design

WORLDWIDE REVENUE	$12,500,000
WORLDWIDE STAFF	70
HEADQUARTERS	Venice, CA
YEAR ESTABLISHED	1977
RECENT REPRESENTATIVE PROJECT	

Santa Monica Place
Santa Monica, CA

Allen T. Jones, VCU

204 | Brandcenter, Virginia Commonwealth University, Richmond, VA | Baskervill

202 | Wakefield Beasley & Associates

5155 Peachtree Parkway, Suite 3220
Norcross, GA 30092
(770) 209-9393
www.wakefieldbeasley.com
John Beasley, Managing Principal

WORLDWIDE REVENUE	$12,300,000
WORLDWIDE STAFF	85
HEADQUARTERS	Norcross, GA
YEAR ESTABLISHED	1980

203 | Baker Barrios Architects

189 South Orange Avenue, Suite 1700
Orlando, FL 32801
(407) 926-3000
www.bakerbarrios.com
Timothy R. Baker, Principal
Robert Ledford, Principal

WORLDWIDE REVENUE	$12,155,000
WORLDWIDE STAFF	76–125
HEADQUARTERS	Orlando, FL
YEAR ESTABLISHED	1993

204 | Baskervill

101 South 15th Street, Suite 200
Richmond, VA 23219
(804) 343-1010
www.baskervill.com
Brent G. Farmer, Chairman
Robert J. Clark, President
Bruce Tyler, Principal

WORLDWIDE REVENUE	$12,131,000
WORLDWIDE STAFF	61
HEADQUARTERS	Richmond, VA
YEAR ESTABLISHED	1897
RECENT REPRESENTATIVE PROJECT	Brandcenter, Virginia Commonwealth University, Richmond, VA

205 | Bermello Ajamil & Partners

2601 South Bayshore Drive, Suite 1000
Miami, FL 33133
(305) 859-2050
www.bamiami.com
Willy A. Bermello, Partner
Luis Ajamil, President

WORLDWIDE REVENUE	$12,002,000
WORLDWIDE STAFF	21–100
HEADQUARTERS	Miami, FL
YEAR ESTABLISHED	1939

206 | Environetics

8530 Venice Boulevard
Los Angeles, CA 90034
(310) 287-2180
www.environetics.com
Rodney Stone, President
David Rush, Managing Principal
Hans Erdenberger, Managing Principal

WORLDWIDE REVENUE	$12,000,000
WORLDWIDE STAFF	73
HEADQUARTERS	Los Angeles, CA
YEAR ESTABLISHED	1947

RECENT REPRESENTATIVE PROJECT
Brown Place Charter School
New York, NY

207 | VITETTA

4747 South Broad Street
Philadelphia, PA 19112
(215) 218-4747
www.vitetta.com
Alan P. Hoffman, President

WORLDWIDE REVENUE	$11,950,000
WORLDWIDE STAFF	101–200
HEADQUARTERS	Philadelphia, PA
YEAR ESTABLISHED	1967

208 | Cooper, Robertson & Partners

311 West 43rd Street
New York, NY 10036
(212) 247-1717
www.cooperrobertson.com
Alexander Cooper, Founding Partner
Jaquelin T. Robertson, Founding Partner

WORLDWIDE REVENUE	$11,900,000
WORLDWIDE STAFF	21–100
HEADQUARTERS	New York, NY
YEAR ESTABLISHED	1979

209 | Altoon + Porter Architects

444 South Flower Street, 48th Floor
Los Angeles, CA 90071
(213) 225-1900
www.altoonporter.com
Ronald A. Altoon, Partner
James F. Porter, Partner
Gary K. Dempster, Partner

WORLDWIDE REVENUE	$11,815,000
WORLDWIDE STAFF	48
HEADQUARTERS	Los Angeles, CA
YEAR ESTABLISHED	1984

RECENT REPRESENTATIVE PROJECT
Fashion World
Las Vegas, NV

210 | Overland Partners Architects

5101 Broadway Street	WORLDWIDE REVENUE	$11,500,000
San Antonio, TX 78209	WORLDWIDE STAFF	58
(210) 829-7003	HEADQUARTERS	San Antonio, TX
www.overlandpartners.com	YEAR ESTABLISHED	1987
Richard M. Archer, Principal	RECENT REPRESENTATIVE PROJECT	
Timothy B. Blonkvist, Principal	Haven for Hope Homeless Center	
Robert L. Shemwell, Principal	San Antonio, TX	

211 | DiMella Shaffer

281 Summer Street	WORLDWIDE REVENUE	$11,475,000
Boston, MA 02210	WORLDWIDE STAFF	80
(617) 426-5004	HEADQUARTERS	Boston, MA
www.dimellashaffer.com	YEAR ESTABLISHED	1965
Frank DiMella, Senior Principal		

212 | Handel Architects

150 Varick Street	WORLDWIDE REVENUE	$11,390,000
New York, NY 10013	WORLDWIDE STAFF	76–125
(212) 595-4112	HEADQUARTERS	New York, NY
www.handelarchitects.com	YEAR ESTABLISHED	1995
Gary Handel, President/Founding Partner		

213 | Opus Architects & Engineers

10350 Bren Road West	WORLDWIDE REVENUE	$11,300,000
Minnetonka, MN 55343	WORLDWIDE STAFF	75
(952) 656-4464	HEADQUARTERS	Minneapolis, MN
www.opuscorp.com	YEAR ESTABLISHED	1991
Edward Gschneidner, VP/Architecture	RECENT REPRESENTATIVE PROJECT	
Grant Peterson, VP/Architecture	Anderson Student Center, University of	
Michael Lederle, VP/Engineering	St. Thomas, St. Paul, MN	

214 | Miller Hull Partnership, The

71 Columbia Street, Polson Bldg., 6th Fl.
Seattle, WA 98104
(206) 682-6837
www.millerhull.com
Ronald O. Rochon, Managing Partner
Craig Curtis, Partner
Norman Strong, Partner

WORLDWIDE REVENUE	$11,268,000
WORLDWIDE STAFF	67
HEADQUARTERS	Seattle, WA
YEAR ESTABLISHED	1977

RECENT REPRESENTATIVE PROJECT
156 West Superior
Chicago, IL

215 | Ascension Group Architects

1250 East Copeland Road, Suite 500
Arlington, TX 76011
(817) 226-1917
www.ascensiongroup.biz
Rod L. Booze, Managing Principal
David Tooley, Principal
Erick Westerholm, Principal

WORLDWIDE REVENUE	$11,200,000
WORLDWIDE STAFF	35
HEADQUARTERS	Arlington, TX
YEAR ESTABLISHED	2001

RECENT REPRESENTATIVE PROJECT
Forest Park Medical Center
Dallas, TX

216 | Hart | Howerton

One Union Street
San Francisco, CA 94111
(415) 439-2200
www.harthowerton.com
Robert Lamb Hart, Charman Emeritus
David P. Howerton, Chairman
Jim Tinson, CEO

WORLDWIDE REVENUE	$11,135,000
WORLDWIDE STAFF	95
HEADQUARTERS	New York, NY
YEAR ESTABLISHED	1967

217 | MBH Architects

2470 Mariner Square Loop
Alameda, CA 94501
(510) 865-8663
www.mbharch.com
John McNulty, Founding Principal
Dennis Heath, Founding Principal
F. Clay Fry, Principal

WORLDWIDE REVENUE	$11,127,000
WORLDWIDE STAFF	65
HEADQUARTERS	Alameda, CA
YEAR ESTABLISHED	1989

RECENT REPRESENTATIVE PROJECT
Ashton Apartments
San Francisco, CA

218 | Cambridge Seven Associates

1050 Massachusetts Avenue
Cambridge, MA 02138
(617) 492-7000
www.c7a.com
Peter G. Kuttner, President

WORLDWIDE REVENUE	$11,115,000
WORLDWIDE STAFF	45
HEADQUARTERS	Cambridge, MA
YEAR ESTABLISHED	1962

219 | Van Tilburg, Banvard & Soderbergh

1738 Berkeley Street
Santa Monica, CA 90404
(310) 394-0273
www.vtbs.com
Johannes Van Tilburg, Founding Principal
Navy F. Banvard, Principal
Gustaf Soderbergh, Principal

WORLDWIDE REVENUE	$10,965,000
WORLDWIDE STAFF	76–125
HEADQUARTERS	Santa Monica, CA
YEAR ESTABLISHED	1971

220 | Marshall Craft Associates

6112 York Road
Baltimore, MD 21212
(410) 532-3131
www.marshallcraft.com
Linton S. (Buck) Marshall, President
Michael S. Craft, Founding Principal

WORLDWIDE REVENUE	$10,900,000
WORLDWIDE STAFF	35
HEADQUARTERS	Baltimore, MD
YEAR ESTABLISHED	1986

221 | Gromatzky Dupree & Associates

3090 Olive Street, Suite 500
Dallas, TX 75219
(214) 871-9078
www.gdainet.com
Charles Gromatzky, Founding Partner
Robert B. Dupree, Founding Partner

WORLDWIDE REVENUE	$10,880,000
WORLDWIDE STAFF	21–100
HEADQUARTERS	Dallas, TX
YEAR ESTABLISHED	1984

Eric Kreher, AIA

225 | The Heights, The Beck Group Tampa Regional Office, Tampa, FL | The Beck Group

The Beck Group

225 | Children's Lobby, Shinkwang Church, Iksan, South Korea | The Beck Group

222 | Ehrenkrantz Eckstut & Kuhn Architects

161 Avenue of the Americas
3rd Floor
New York, NY 10013
(212) 353-0400
www.eekarchitects.com
Stanton Eckstut, Founding Principal

WORLDWIDE REVENUE	$10,795,000
WORLDWIDE STAFF	21–100
HEADQUARTERS	New York, NY
YEAR ESTABLISHED	1972

223 | Hollis + Miller

8205 West 108th Terrace, Suite 200
Overland Park, KS 66210
(913) 451-8886
www.hollisandmiller.com
John Wisniewski, President
Kirk Horner, VP
John Southard, VP

WORLDWIDE REVENUE	$10,721,050
WORLDWIDE STAFF	55
HEADQUARTERS	Overland Park, KS
YEAR ESTABLISHED	1950
RECENT REPRESENTATIVE PROJECT	

Staley High School
Kansas City, KS

224 | Bostwick Design Partnership

2729 Prospect Avenue
Cleveland, OH 44115
(216) 621-7900
www.bostwickdesign.com
Robert Bostwick, President

WORLDWIDE REVENUE	$10,625,000
WORLDWIDE STAFF	35
HEADQUARTERS	Cleveland, OH
YEAR ESTABLISHED	1962

225 | Beck Group, The (Architecture)   BECK

1807 Ross Avenue, Suite 500
Dallas, TX 75201
(214) 303-6200
www.beckgroup.com
Henry C. Beck III, CEO
Rick del Monte, Managing Director
Kip Daniel, Managing Director

WORLDWIDE REVENUE	$10,600,000
WORLDWIDE STAFF	73
HEADQUARTERS	Dallas, TX
YEAR ESTABLISHED	1912
RECENT REPRESENTATIVE PROJECT	

Hunt Oil Company Headquarters
Dallas, TX

226 | Robertson Loia Roof

3460 Preston Ridge Road, Suite 275
Alpharetta, GA 30005
(770) 674-2600
www.rlrpc.com
L. Taylor Robertson, Principal
Michael Loia, Principal

WORLDWIDE REVENUE	$10,574,000
WORLDWIDE STAFF	90
HEADQUARTERS	Alpharetta, GA
YEAR ESTABLISHED	1980

227 | JHP Architecture/Urban Design

8340 Meadow Road, Suite 150
Dallas, TX 75231
(214) 363-5687
www.jhparch.com
Mike Arbour, President
Ron Harwick, VP

WORLDWIDE REVENUE	$10,548,500
WORLDWIDE STAFF	21–100
HEADQUARTERS	Dallas, TX
YEAR ESTABLISHED	1979

228 | Smallwood, Reynolds, Stewart, Stewart & Assoc.

3565 Piedmont Road NE
One Piedmont Center, Suite 303
Atlanta, GA 30305
(404) 233-5453
www.srssa.com
Howard H. Stewart, President
William D. Reynolds, VP

WORLDWIDE REVENUE	$10,430,000
WORLDWIDE STAFF	67
HEADQUARTERS	Atlanta, GA
YEAR ESTABLISHED	1979
RECENT REPRESENTATIVE PROJECT	

3344 Peachtree Street
Atlanta, GA

229 | GUND Partnership

47 Thorndike Street
Cambridge, MA 02141
(617) 250-6800
www.gundpartnership.com
Graham Gund, President
John Prokos, Managing Principal
Youngmin Jahan, Principal

WORLDWIDE REVENUE	$10,412,500
WORLDWIDE STAFF	21–100
HEADQUARTERS	Cambridge, MA
YEAR ESTABLISHED	1971

230 | Group 70 International

925 Bethel Street
Honolulu, HI 96813
(808) 523-5866
www.group70int.com
Francis S. Oda, Chairman/CEO

WORLDWIDE REVENUE	$10,400,000
WORLDWIDE STAFF	21–100
HEADQUARTERS	Honolulu, HI
YEAR ESTABLISHED	1971

231 | BAR Architects

543 Howard Street
San Francisco, CA 94105
(415) 293-5700
www.bararch.com
Guy Chambers, Principal

WORLDWIDE REVENUE	$10,327,500
WORLDWIDE STAFF	21–100
HEADQUARTERS	San Francisco, CA
YEAR ESTABLISHED	1966

232 | Centerbrook Architects and Planners

67 Main Street
Centerbrook, CT 06409
(860) 767-0175
www.centerbrook.com
William H. Grover, Partner
Chris Hill, Director of Business Development

WORLDWIDE REVENUE	$10,285,000
WORLDWIDE STAFF	21–100
HEADQUARTERS	Centerbrook, CT
YEAR ESTABLISHED	1970

233 | Forum Studio

2199 Innerbelt Business Center Drive
St. Louis, MO 63114
(314) 429-1010
www.forumstudio.com
Christopher Cedergreen, President/
    Principal-in-Charge

WORLDWIDE REVENUE	$10,242,500
WORLDWIDE STAFF	70
HEADQUARTERS	St. Louis, MO
YEAR ESTABLISHED	1999

234 | Development Design Group

3700 O'Donnell Street
Baltimore, MD 21224
(410) 962-0505
www.ddg-usa.com
Roy H. Higgs, CEO/Principal-in-Charge
Ahsin Rasheed, Senior Partner
Guillermo Lopez, Senior Partner

WORLDWIDE REVENUE	$10,200,000
WORLDWIDE STAFF	89
HEADQUARTERS	Baltimore, MD
YEAR ESTABLISHED	1979
RECENT REPRESENTATIVE PROJECT	

Istinye Park Shopping & Residential
Istanbul, Turkey

235 | Thalden-Boyd-Emery Architects

1133 Olivette Executive Parkway
Olivette, MO 63132
(314) 727-7000
www.thaldenboyd.com
Rich Emery, Partner
Barry Thalden, Partner
Chief Boyd, Partner

WORLDWIDE REVENUE	$10,150,000
WORLDWIDE STAFF	10–25
HEADQUARTERS	Olivette, MO
YEAR ESTABLISHED	1962

236 | Charlan Brock & Associates

1770 Fennell Street
Maitland, FL 32751
(407) 660-8900
www.cbaarchitects.com
Butch Charlan, Principal
Gary Brock, Principal

WORLDWIDE REVENUE	$10,115,000
WORLDWIDE STAFF	21–100
HEADQUARTERS	Maitland, FL
YEAR ESTABLISHED	1981

237 | Torti Gallas and Partners

1300 Spring Street
Silver Spring, MD 20910
(301) 588-4800
www.tortigallas.com
John Torti, President

WORLDWIDE REVENUE	$10,050,000
WORLDWIDE STAFF	90
HEADQUARTERS	Silver Spring, MD
YEAR ESTABLISHED	1953

238 | Sherlock Smith & Adams

3047 Carter Hill Road
Montgomery, AL 36111
(334) 263-6481
www.ssainc.com
Robert Snider, Chairman/President

WORLDWIDE REVENUE	$10,025,000
WORLDWIDE STAFF	21–100
HEADQUARTERS	Montgomery, AL
YEAR ESTABLISHED	1946

239 | Astorino

227 Fort Pitt Boulevard
Pittsburgh, PA 15222
(412) 765-1700
www.astorino.com
Louis D. Astorino, Chairman/CEO
Louis P. Astorino, Senior Principal

WORLDWIDE REVENUE	$10,010,000
WORLDWIDE STAFF	115
HEADQUARTERS	Pittsburgh, PA
YEAR ESTABLISHED	1972
RECENT REPRESENTATIVE PROJECT	

Children's Hospital
Pittsburgh, PA

240 | JBHM Architects

308 East Pearl Street, Suite 300
Jackson, MS 39201
(601) 352-2699
www.jbhm.com
Richard McNeel, President
Joseph S. Henderson, VP

WORLDWIDE REVENUE	$10,000,000
WORLDWIDE STAFF	52
HEADQUARTERS	Jackson, MS
YEAR ESTABLISHED	1970
RECENT REPRESENTATIVE PROJECT	

Boys & Girls Club of the Gulf Coast
Pass Christian, MS

241 | DTJ Design

3101 Iris Avenue, Suite 130
Boulder, CO 80301
(303) 443-7533
www.dtjdesign.com
Mike Beitzel, President

WORLDWIDE REVENUE	$9,945,000
WORLDWIDE STAFF	21–100
HEADQUARTERS	Boulder, CO
YEAR ESTABLISHED	1988

242 | Engberg Anderson

320 East Buffalo Street
Milwaukee, WI 53202
(414) 944-9000
www.engberganderson.com
Keith Anderson, Partner
Charles Engberg, Partner

WORLDWIDE REVENUE	$9,775,000
WORLDWIDE STAFF	50
HEADQUARTERS	Milwaukee, WI
YEAR ESTABLISHED	1988

243 | DWL Architects + Planners

2333 North Central Avenue
Phoenix, AZ 85004
(602) 264-9731
www.dwlarchitects.com
Michael Haake, Chairman
Stephen Rao, President
Mark Dee, Executive VP

WORLDWIDE REVENUE	$9,731,340
WORLDWIDE STAFF	32
HEADQUARTERS	Phoenix, AZ
YEAR ESTABLISHED	1949
RECENT REPRESENTATIVE PROJECT	

Appaloosa Library
Scottsdale, AZ

244 | Shremshock Architects & Engineers

6130 South Sunbury Road
Westerville, OH 43081
(614) 545-4550
www.shremshock.com
Gerald Shremshock, Principal
Scott Shremshock, Director

WORLDWIDE REVENUE	$9,690,000
WORLDWIDE STAFF	45
HEADQUARTERS	Westerville, OH
YEAR ESTABLISHED	1976

245 | GGLO

1301 1st Street, Suite 301
Seattle, WA 98101
(206) 467-5828
www.gglo.com
Will Castillo, Managing Principal
Bill Gaylord, Principal/Dir. of Bus. Dev.
Alan Grainger, Principal

WORLDWIDE REVENUE	$9,664,444
WORLDWIDE STAFF	57
HEADQUARTERS	Seattle, WA
YEAR ESTABLISHED	1986
RECENT REPRESENTATIVE PROJECT	

Allison Inn and Spa
Newberg, OR

246 | MAI design group

383 Inverness Parkway, Suite 190
Englewood, CO 80112
(720) 266-2582
www.mai-architects.com
Michael Marsh, Principal
Bryan Webb, Principal

WORLDWIDE REVENUE	$9,647,500
WORLDWIDE STAFF	6–25
HEADQUARTERS	Englewood, CO
YEAR ESTABLISHED	1996

247 | Elness Swenson Graham Architects

500 Washington Avenue South
Suite 1080
Minneapolis, MN 55438
(612) 339-5508
www.esgarch.com
Mark Swenson, President
David Graham, Founding Principal

WORLDWIDE REVENUE	$9,639,000
WORLDWIDE STAFF	50
HEADQUARTERS	Minneapolis, MN
YEAR ESTABLISHED	1982
RECENT REPRESENTATIVE PROJECT	

Forshay Hotel/W Minneapolis
Minneapolis, MN

248 | Aguirre Roden

10670 N. Central Expressway, 6th Floor
Dallas, TX 75231
(972) 788-1508
www.aguirreroden.com
Pedro Aguirre, President/CEO
Gary Roden, Executive VP/COO
Frost Gardner, VP/Engineering

WORLDWIDE REVENUE	$9,620,000
WORLDWIDE STAFF	90
HEADQUARTERS	Dallas, TX
YEAR ESTABLISHED	1960
RECENT REPRESENTATIVE PROJECT	

WinStar World Casino
Thackerville, OK

249 | KPS Group

2101 1st Avenue North
Birmingham, AL 35203
(205) 458-3217
www.kpsgroup.com
G. Gray Plosser Jr., President
Donald Simpson, Senior VP
Hugh B. Thorton Jr., Senior VP

WORLDWIDE REVENUE	$9,600,000
WORLDWIDE STAFF	38
HEADQUARTERS	Birmingham, AL
YEAR ESTABLISHED	1965
RECENT REPRESENTATIVE PROJECT	

Ruffner Mountain Nature Center
Birmingham, AL

250 | SLATERPAULL Architects

1515 Arapahoe Street
One Park Central, Suite 400
Denver, CO 80202
(303) 607-0977
www.slaterpaull.com
James C. Pedler, President
Clayton Cole, VP

WORLDWIDE REVENUE	$9,550,000
WORLDWIDE STAFF	45
HEADQUARTERS	Denver, CO
YEAR ESTABLISHED	1972

RECENT REPRESENTATIVE PROJECT

Valor High School
Highlands Ranch, CO

251 | Merriman Associates/Architects

300 North Field Street
Dallas, TX 75202
(214) 987-1299
www.merriman-maa.com
Jerald Merriman, President

WORLDWIDE REVENUE	$9,435,000
WORLDWIDE STAFF	21–100
HEADQUARTERS	Dallas, TX
YEAR ESTABLISHED	1987

252 | Anderson Mason Dale Architects

3198 Speer Boulevard
Denver, CO 80211
(303) 294-9448
www.amdarchitects.com
Paul S. Haack, President
Andrew G. Nielsen, VP/Treasurer
David C. Pfeifer, VP/Secretary

WORLDWIDE REVENUE	$9,350,000
WORLDWIDE STAFF	40
HEADQUARTERS	Denver, CO
YEAR ESTABLISHED	1960

RECENT REPRESENTATIVE PROJECT

Educ. Facility #2, Anschutz Med. Campus,
University of Colorado, Aurora, CO

253 | William Rawn Associates, Architects, Inc.

10 Post Office Square, Suite 1010
Boston, MA 02109
(617) 423-3470
www.rawnarch.com
William Rawn III, Founding Principal
Douglas Johnston, Principal

WORLDWIDE REVENUE	$9,222,550
WORLDWIDE STAFF	21–100
HEADQUARTERS	Boston, MA
YEAR ESTABLISHED	1983

254 | CMA

1300 Summit Avenue, Suite 300
Fort Worth, TX 76102
(817) 877-0044
www.cmarch.com
Patrick Blees, Principal

WORLDWIDE REVENUE	$9,171,500
WORLDWIDE STAFF	85
HEADQUARTERS	Fort Worth, TX
YEAR ESTABLISHED	1990

255 | H3 Hardy Collaboration Architecture

902 Broadway, 19th Floor
New York, NY 10010
(212) 677-6030
www.h3hc.com
Hugh Hardy, Senior Partner
Jack Martin, Partner
John Fontillas, Partner

WORLDWIDE REVENUE	$9,100,000
WORLDWIDE STAFF	32
HEADQUARTERS	New York, NY
YEAR ESTABLISHED	1962
RECENT REPRESENTATIVE PROJECT	

US Federal Courthouse
Jackson, MS

256 | klipp

201 Broadway
Denver, CO 80203
(303) 893-1990
www.klipparch.com
Brian Klipp, CEO

WORLDWIDE REVENUE	$9,052,500
WORLDWIDE STAFF	50
HEADQUARTERS	Denver, CO
YEAR ESTABLISHED	1979

257 | Lehman Smith McLeish

1212 Bank Street Northwest
Suite 350
Washington, DC 20007
(202) 295-4800
www.lsm.com
Debra Lehman-Smith, Partner
James Black McLeish, Partner

WORLDWIDE REVENUE	$9,000,000
WORLDWIDE STAFF	35
HEADQUARTERS	Washington, DC
YEAR ESTABLISHED	1991
RECENT REPRESENTATIVE PROJECT	

K & L Gates Center
Pittsburgh, PA

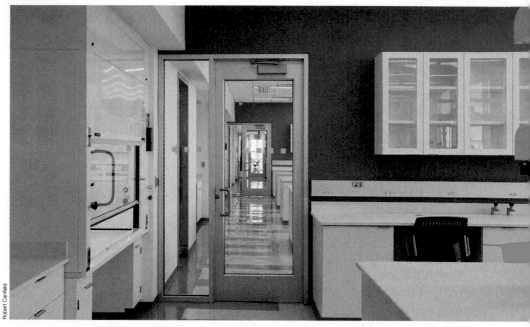

Robert Canfield

260 | Zilkha Neurogenetic Institute, University of Southern California, Los Angeles, CA | Research Facilities Design

Woodruff/Brown Architectural Photography

260 | Johnson Hall of Science, St. Lawrence University, Canton, NY | Research Facilities Design

258 | Lantz-Boggio Architects

5650 DTC Parkway, Suite 200
Greenwood Village, CO 80111
(303) 773-0436
www.lantz-boggio.com
Dennis R. Boggio, President/Director of
   Development Services

WORLDWIDE REVENUE	$8,967,500
WORLDWIDE STAFF	40
HEADQUARTERS	Greenwood Village, CO
YEAR ESTABLISHED	1946

259 | Tower Pinkster

242 East Kalamazoo Avenue
Kalamazoo, MI 49007
(269) 343-6133
www.towerpinkster.com
Arnold Mikon, CEO
Tom Mathison, Chairman
Richard Bromfield, Director

WORLDWIDE REVENUE	$8,925,000
WORLDWIDE STAFF	60
HEADQUARTERS	Kalamazoo, MI
YEAR ESTABLISHED	1953
RECENT REPRESENTATIVE PROJECT	
Civic Theater Renovations	
Grand Rapids, MI	

260 | Research Facilities Design   **RFD**

3965 5th Avenue, Suite 400
San Diego, CA 92103
(619) 297-0159
www.rfd.com
W. Malcolm Barksdale, President
Richard M. Heinz, VP
Sean Towne, Principal

WORLDWIDE REVENUE	$8,900,000
WORLDWIDE STAFF	33
HEADQUARTERS	San Diego, CA
YEAR ESTABLISHED	1984
RECENT REPRESENTATIVE PROJECT	
Masdar Institute of Science, Phase IA	
Abu Dhabi, UAE	

261 | Wald, Ruhnke & Dost Architects

2340 Garden Road, Suite 100
Monterey, CA 93940
(831) 649-4642
www.wrdarch.com
Frank Dost, Principal
Henry Ruhnke, Principal

WORLDWIDE REVENUE	$8,840,000
WORLDWIDE STAFF	40
HEADQUARTERS	Monterey, CA
YEAR ESTABLISHED	1990

262 | CDH Partners

675 Tower Road
Marietta, GA 30060
(770) 423-0016
www.cdhpartners.com
William E. Chegwidden, President
Tom Smith, Principal
Tim Parham, Principal

WORLDWIDE REVENUE	$8,820,000
WORLDWIDE STAFF	51
HEADQUARTERS	Marietta, GA
YEAR ESTABLISHED	1977
RECENT REPRESENTATIVE PROJECT	

Holy Spirit Catholic Church
Atlanta, GA

263 | Huntsman Architectural Group

50 California Street, 7th Floor
San Francisco, CA 94111
(415) 394-1212
www.huntsmanag.com
Dan Huntsman, President
Susan Williams, Senior VP/Principal
Mark Harbick, VP/Director of Design

WORLDWIDE REVENUE	$8,800,000
WORLDWIDE STAFF	65
HEADQUARTERS	San Francisco, CA
YEAR ESTABLISHED	1981
RECENT REPRESENTATIVE PROJECT	

Dutch Consulate
San Francisco, CA

264 | Bergmeyer Associates

51 Sleeper Street, 6th Floor
Boston, MA 02210
(617) 542-1025
www.bergmeyer.com
David Tubridy, President/CEO
Michael Davis, VP

WORLDWIDE REVENUE	$8,797,500
WORLDWIDE STAFF	48
HEADQUARTERS	Boston, MA
YEAR ESTABLISHED	1973

265 | Bignell Watkins Hasser Architects

One Park Place, Suite 250
Annapolis, MD 21401
(301) 224-2727
www.bigwaha.com
Frank Watkins, President/CEO
George Hasser, Principal

WORLDWIDE REVENUE	$8,670,000
WORLDWIDE STAFF	50–100
HEADQUARTERS	Annapolis, MD
YEAR ESTABLISHED	1977

266 | Hornberger + Worstell

170 Maiden Lane
San Francisco, CA 94108
(415) 391-1080
www.hornbergerworstell.com
Mark Hornberger, Founding Principal
Christian Low, Sr. VP/Managing Principal
Jack Worstell, Founding Partner

WORLDWIDE REVENUE	$8,600,000
WORLDWIDE STAFF	40
HEADQUARTERS	San Francisco, CA
YEAR ESTABLISHED	1980

RECENT REPRESENTATIVE PROJECT
Ghirardelli Square
San Francisco, CA

267 | Morphosis

2041 Colorado Avenue
Santa Monica, CA 90404
(310) 453-2247
www.morphosis.com
Thom Mayne, Founder/Design Director

WORLDWIDE REVENUE	$8,585,000
WORLDWIDE STAFF	21–100
HEADQUARTERS	Santa Monica, CA
YEAR ESTABLISHED	1972

268 | Meyer, Scherer & Rockcastle

710 South 2nd Street, 8th Floor
Minneapolis, MN 55401
(612) 375-0336
www.msrltd.com
Jeffrey Scherer, CEO
Jack Poling, President
Tom Meyer, VP

WORLDWIDE REVENUE	$8,562,900
WORLDWIDE STAFF	45
HEADQUARTERS	Minneapolis,MN
YEAR ESTABLISHED	1981

RECENT REPRESENTATIVE PROJECT
St. Cloud Public Library
St. Cloud, MN

269 | SHoP Architects

11 Park Place
New York, NY 10007
(212) 889 9005
www.shoparc.com
Christopher Sharples, Partner

WORLDWIDE REVENUE	$8,500,000
WORLDWIDE STAFF	21–100
HEADQUARTERS	New York, NY
YEAR ESTABLISHED	1996

270 | BJAC

811 West Hargett Street
Raleigh, NC 27603
(919) 833-8818
www.bjac.com
Mary Louise Jurkowski, CEO
Jennifer Amster, Dir. of Higher Educ.
Leo Sagasti, Dir. of Const. Mgmt.

WORLDWIDE REVENUE	$8,447,096
WORLDWIDE STAFF	31
HEADQUARTERS	Raleigh, NC
YEAR ESTABLISHED	1994
RECENT REPRESENTATIVE PROJECT	

Randolph Hospital Outpatient & Cancer
Center, Asheboro, NC

271 | DesignGroup

515 East Main Street
Columbus, OH 43215
(614) 255-0515
www.dgcolumbus.com
Robert Vennemeyer, President/CEO

WORLDWIDE REVENUE	$8,287,500
WORLDWIDE STAFF	20–100
HEADQUARTERS	Columbus, OH
YEAR ESTABLISHED	1972

272 | Mackey Mitchell Architects

401 South 18th Street
St. Louis, MO 63103
(314) 421-1815
www.mackeymitchell.com
Eugene J. Mackey, Chairman
Dan S. Mitchell, President
Richard B. Kirschner, Partner

WORLDWIDE REVENUE	$8,259,400
WORLDWIDE STAFF	41
HEADQUARTERS	St. Louis, MO
YEAR ESTABLISHED	1968
RECENT REPRESENTATIVE PROJECT	

Wohl Center, Washington University in St.
Louis, St. Louis, MO

273 | Pope Associates

1255 Energy Park Drive
St. Paul, MN 55108
(651) 642-9200
www.popearch.com
Jon R. Pope, President/Principal

WORLDWIDE REVENUE	$8,245,000
WORLDWIDE STAFF	21–100
HEADQUARTERS	St. Paul, MN
YEAR ESTABLISHED	1974

274 | Rogers Marvel Architects

145 Hudson Street, 3rd Floor
New York, NY 10013
(212) 941-6718
www.rogersmarvel.com
Robert M. Rogers, Principal
Jonathan J. Marvel, Principal
Jennifer Ganley, Dir. of Bus. Dev.

WORLDWIDE REVENUE	$8,200,000
WORLDWIDE STAFF	44
HEADQUARTERS	New York, NY
YEAR ESTABLISHED	1998
RECENT REPRESENTATIVE PROJECT	

State Street Townhouses
Brooklyn, NY

275 | MSTSD

1776 Peachtree Road NW, Suite 180
Atlanta, GA 30309
(404) 962-9680
www.mstsd.com
W. Grant Moseley, President

WORLDWIDE REVENUE	$8,160,000
WORLDWIDE STAFF	20
HEADQUARTERS	Atlanta, GA
YEAR ESTABLISHED	1989

276 | Hunton Brady Architects

800 North Magnolia Avenue
Suite 600
Orlando, FL 32803
(407) 839-0886
www.huntonbrady.com
Chuck Cole, President

WORLDWIDE REVENUE	$8,113,250
WORLDWIDE STAFF	21–100
HEADQUARTERS	Orlando, FL
YEAR ESTABLISHED	1947

277 | Cetra Ruddy

584 Broadway, Suite 401
New York, NY 10012
(212) 941-9801
www.cetraruddy.com
Nancy J. Ruddy, President
John Cetra, Executive VP

WORLDWIDE REVENUE	$8,100,000
WORLDWIDE STAFF	59
HEADQUARTERS	New York, NY
YEAR ESTABLISHED	1987
RECENT REPRESENTATIVE PROJECT	

77 Hudson & 70 Green Street
Jersey City, NJ

278 | Richard Meier & Partners Architects

475 10th Avenue, 6th Floor
New York, NY 10018
(212) 967-6060
www.richardmeier.com
Richard Meier, President
Michael Palladino, Partner

WORLDWIDE REVENUE	$8,000,000
WORLDWIDE STAFF	100
HEADQUARTERS	New York, NY
YEAR ESTABLISHED	1963
RECENT REPRESENTATIVE PROJECT	

Jesolo Lido Condominium
Jesolo, Italy

279 | Bargmann Hendrie & Archetype

300 A Street
Boston, MA 02210
(617) 350-0450
www.bhplus.com
Carolyn Hendrie, Founding Principal
Joel Bargmann, Founding Principal

WORLDWIDE REVENUE	$7,990,000
WORLDWIDE STAFF	32
HEADQUARTERS	Boston, MA
YEAR ESTABLISHED	1981

280 | Staffelbach

2525 McKinnon, Suite 800
Dallas, TX 75201
(214) 747-2511
www.staffelbach.com
Jo Staffelbach Heinz, President/CEO
Andre Staffelfach, Creative Principal
Cynthia Byars, VP

WORLDWIDE REVENUE	$7,900,000
WORLDWIDE STAFF	70
HEADQUARTERS	Dallas, TX
YEAR ESTABLISHED	1966
RECENT REPRESENTATIVE PROJECT	

Kosmos Energy
Dallas, TX

281 | BNIM Architects

106 West 14th Street, Suite 200
Kansas City, MO 64105
(816) 783-1500
www.bnim.com
Steve McDowell, President
Casey Cassias, Director of Practice
Robert Berkebile, Founding Principal

WORLDWIDE REVENUE	$7,888,822
WORLDWIDE STAFF	85
HEADQUARTERS	Kansas City, MO
YEAR ESTABLISHED	1970
RECENT REPRESENTATIVE PROJECT	

Omega Institute for Sustainable Living
Rhinebeck, NY

282 | CASCO

10877 Watson Road
St. Louis, MO 63127
(314) 821-1100
www.cascocorp.com
James Alberts, President
Paul Huber, Managing Principal

WORLDWIDE REVENUE	$7,862,500
WORLDWIDE STAFF	95
HEADQUARTERS	St. Louis, MO
YEAR ESTABLISHED	1959

283 | Bennett Wagner & Grody Architects

1301 Wazee Street, Suite 100
Denver, CO 80204
(303) 623-7323
www.bwgarchitects.com
Martha L. Bennett, Principal

WORLDWIDE REVENUE	$7,848,050
WORLDWIDE STAFF	30
HEADQUARTERS	Denver, CO
YEAR ESTABLISHED	1989
RECENT REPRESENTATIVE PROJECT	

Academic Instruction Building, Colorado
State University, Fort Collins, CO

284 | Field Paoli Architects

150 California Street, 7th Floor
San Francisco, CA 94111
(415) 788-6606
www.fieldpaoli.com
Rob Anderson, President/Principal
Raul Anziani, Principal

WORLDWIDE REVENUE	$7,828,500
WORLDWIDE STAFF	25
HEADQUARTERS	San Francisco, CA
YEAR ESTABLISHED	1986

285 | Design Collective

601 East Pratt Street, Suite 300
Baltimore, MD 21202
(410) 685-6655
www.designcollective.com
Dennis R. Jankiewicz, President

WORLDWIDE REVENUE	$7,803,000
WORLDWIDE STAFF	75
HEADQUARTERS	Baltimore, MD
YEAR ESTABLISHED	1978

Ed LaCasse

287 | Carey S. Thomas Library, Denver Seminary, Littleton, CO | MOA Architecture

286 | Cook + Fox Architects

641 Avenue of the Americas, 8th Floor
New York, NY 10011
(212) 477-0287
www.cookplusfox.com
Richard A. Cook, Partner

WORLDWIDE REVENUE	$7,735,000
WORLDWIDE STAFF	21–100
HEADQUARTERS	New York, NY
YEAR ESTABLISHED	2003

287 | MOA Architecture

821 17th Street, Suite 400
Denver, CO 80202
(303) 308-1190
www.moaarch.com
Robert Outland, Chairman
Barry Koury, President
Jack Mousseau, Director of Design

WORLDWIDE REVENUE	$7,548,000
WORLDWIDE STAFF	32
HEADQUARTERS	Denver, CO
YEAR ESTABLISHED	1981
RECENT REPRESENTATIVE PROJECT	

Aurora High School Addition and
Renovation, Aurora, CO

288 | Hawley Peterson & Snyder Architects

444 Castro Street, Suite 1000
Mountain View, CA 94041
(650) 968-2944
www.hpsarch.com
Curtis Snyder, Principal
Richard Kirchner, Principal
Alan Turner, Principal

WORLDWIDE REVENUE	$7,522,500
WORLDWIDE STAFF	39
HEADQUARTERS	Mountain View, CA
YEAR ESTABLISHED	1957

289 | Canin Associates

500 Delaney Avenue, Suite 404
Orlando, FL 32801
(407) 422-4040
www.canin.com
Myrna Canin, VP

WORLDWIDE REVENUE	$7,458,750
WORLDWIDE STAFF	55
HEADQUARTERS	Orlando, FL
YEAR ESTABLISHED	1983

290 | Hamilton Anderson Associates

1435 Randolph Street, Suite 200
Detroit, MI 48226
(313) 964-0270
www.hamilton-anderson.com
Rainy Hamilton Jr., President
Kent Anderson, Principal
Thomas Sherry, Principal

WORLDWIDE REVENUE	$7,400,000
WORLDWIDE STAFF	70
HEADQUARTERS	Detroit, MI
YEAR ESTABLISHED	1994

RECENT REPRESENTATIVE PROJECT
City Center
Las Vegas, NV

291 | Yost Grube Hall Architecture

1211 Southwest 5th Avenue, Suite 2700
Portland, OR 97204
(503) 221-0150
www.ygh.com
Joachim Grube, Principal
Nels Hall, Principal
John Blumthal, Principal

WORLDWIDE REVENUE	$7,395,000
WORLDWIDE STAFF	61
HEADQUARTERS	Portland, OR
YEAR ESTABLISHED	1964

292 | Portico Group, The

1500 4th Avenue, 3rd Floor
Seattle, WA 98101
(206) 621-2196
www.porticogroup.com
Michael Hamm, President/CEO
Charles Mayes, Principal
Tim Nicoulin, CFO

WORLDWIDE REVENUE	$7,299,816
WORLDWIDE STAFF	37
HEADQUARTERS	Seattle, WA
YEAR ESTABLISHED	1984

RECENT REPRESENTATIVE PROJECT
Happy Hollow Park and Zoo
San Jose, CA

293 | Hodges & Associates Architects

13642 Omega Road
Dallas, TX 75244
(972) 387-1000
www.hodgesusa.com
Charles M. Hodges, Principal

WORLDWIDE REVENUE	$7,233,500
WORLDWIDE STAFF	33
HEADQUARTERS	Dallas, TX
YEAR ESTABLISHED	1977

294 | 4240 Architecture

3003 Larimer Street
Denver, CO 80205
(303) 292-3388
www.4240architecture.com
E. Randal Johnson, President
Thomas R. Brauer, Principal

WORLDWIDE REVENUE	$7,200,000
WORLDWIDE STAFF	21–100
HEADQUARTERS	Denver, CO
YEAR ESTABLISHED	2003

295 | Bullock Tice Associates

909 E Cervantes, Suite B
Pensacola, FL 32501
(850) 434-5444
www.bullocktice.com
John P. Tice Jr., President/CEO
Mike Richardson, Senior VP
John Molloy, VP

WORLDWIDE REVENUE	$7,098,709
WORLDWIDE STAFF	44
HEADQUARTERS	Pensacola, FL
YEAR ESTABLISHED	1958
RECENT REPRESENTATIVE PROJECT	

7th Special Forces Group Facilities
Eglin Air Force Base, FL

296 | Crawford Archtitects

1801 McGee, Suite 200
Kansas City, MO 64108
(816) 421-2640
www.crawfordarch.com
David Murphy, Partner
Stacey Jones, Partner

WORLDWIDE REVENUE	$7,055,000
WORLDWIDE STAFF	1–25
HEADQUARTERS	Kansas City, MO
YEAR ESTABLISHED	2001

297 | Machado and Silvetti Associates

560 Harrison Avenue, Suite 301
Boston, MA 02118
(617) 426-7070
www.machado-silvetti.com
Rodolfo Machado, Partner
Jorge Silvetti, Partner

WORLDWIDE REVENUE	$7,000,000
WORLDWIDE STAFF	55
HEADQUARTERS	Boston, MA
YEAR ESTABLISHED	1985
RECENT REPRESENTATIVE PROJECT	

Olayan School of Business, American
University of Beirut, Beirut, Lebanon

298 | Ellenzweig

1280 Massachusetts Avenue
Cambridge, MA 02138
(617) 491-5575
www.ellenzweig.com
Michael Lauber, President

WORLDWIDE REVENUE	$6,999,750
WORLDWIDE STAFF	55
HEADQUARTERS	Cambridge, MA
YEAR ESTABLISHED	1965

299 | Loebl Schlossman & Hackl

233 North Michigan Avenue, Suite 3000
Chicago, IL 60601
(312) 565-1800
www.lshdesign.com
Donald J. Hackl, President
Robert K. Clough, Principal
James B. Pritchett, Principal

WORLDWIDE REVENUE	$6,935,000
WORLDWIDE STAFF	35
HEADQUARTERS	Chicago, IL
YEAR ESTABLISHED	1925

300 | BKV Group

222 North 2nd Street
Minneapolis, MN 55401
(612) 339-3752
www.bkvgroup.com
Jack Boarman, Principal
David Kroos, Principal
Gary Vogel, Principal

WORLDWIDE REVENUE	$6,885,000
WORLDWIDE STAFF	65
HEADQUARTERS	Minneapolis, MN
YEAR ESTABLISHED	1978

301 | MKC Associates

40 West 4th Street
Mansfield, OH 44902
(877) 652-1102
www.mkcinc.com
Alvin Berger, President
Jim Schmidt, VP

WORLDWIDE REVENUE	$6,842,500
WORLDWIDE STAFF	21–100
HEADQUARTERS	Mansfield, OH
YEAR ESTABLISHED	1924

302 | BCA

210 Hammond Avenue
Fremont, CA 94539
(510) 445-1000
www.bcainconline.com
Paul Bunton, President
James E. Moore, Studio Principal

WORLDWIDE REVENUE	$6,800,000
WORLDWIDE STAFF	5–20
HEADQUARTERS	Fremont, CA
YEAR ESTABLISHED	1989

303 | Marks, Thomas Architects

1414 Key Highway
Baltimore, MD 21230
(410) 539-4300
www.marks-thomas.com
Paul Marks, Founding Principal Emeritus
Gilbert Thomas, Principal Emeritus
Magda Westerhout, Principal

WORLDWIDE REVENUE	$6,715,000
WORLDWIDE STAFF	45
HEADQUARTERS	Baltimore, MD
YEAR ESTABLISHED	1967

304 | Margulies Perruzzi Architects

308 Congress Street
Boston, MA 02210
(617) 482-3232
www.mp-architects.com
Marc Margulies, Principal
Daniel P. Perruzzi Jr., Principal
Janet Morra, Principal

WORLDWIDE REVENUE	$6,700,000
WORLDWIDE STAFF	32
HEADQUARTERS	Boston, MA
YEAR ESTABLISHED	1988
RECENT REPRESENTATIVE PROJECT	
175/185 Wyman Street	
Waltham, MA	

305 | ICON Architecture

38 Chauncy Street, Suite 1401
Boston, MA 02111
(617) 451-3333
www.iconarch.com
Nancy Ludwig, President
Steven A. Heikin, VP/Senior Principal
Richard O'Dwyer, VP/Senior Principal

WORLDWIDE REVENUE	$6,600,900
WORLDWIDE STAFF	32
HEADQUARTERS	Boston, MA
YEAR ESTABLISHED	1996
RECENT REPRESENTATIVE PROJECT	
Avenir	
Boston, MA	

306 | Urban Design Associates

707 Grant Street
Gulf Tower, 31st Floor
Pittsburgh, PA 15219
(412) 263-5200
www.urbandesignassociates.com
Barry Long Jr., CEO

WORLDWIDE REVENUE	$6,600,000
WORLDWIDE STAFF	5–20
HEADQUARTERS	Pittsburgh, PA
YEAR ESTABLISHED	1964

307 | TR,i Architects

9812 Manchester Road
St. Louis, MO 63119
(314) 395-9750
www.triarchitects.com
Thomas Roof, President

WORLDWIDE REVENUE	$6,587,500
WORLDWIDE STAFF	18
HEADQUARTERS	St. Louis, MO
YEAR ESTABLISHED	1989

308 | Beame Architectural Partnership

116 Alhambra Circle, Suite J
Coral Gables, FL 33134
(305) 444-7100
www.bapdesign.com
Lawrence Beame, President
David Herbert, VP

WORLDWIDE REVENUE	$6,580,000
WORLDWIDE STAFF	30
HEADQUARTERS	Miami, FL
YEAR ESTABLISHED	1984
RECENT REPRESENTATIVE PROJECT	
Oceanside at Pompano Beach Pompano Beach, FL	

309 | Holzman Moss Bottino Architecture

214 West 29th Street, 17th Floor
New York, NY 10001
(212) 465-0808
www.holzmanmoss.com
Malcolm Holzman, Partner
Douglas Moss, Partner
Nestor Bottino, Partner

WORLDWIDE REVENUE	$6,540,000
WORLDWIDE STAFF	28
HEADQUARTERS	New York, NY
YEAR ESTABLISHED	2004
RECENT REPRESENTATIVE PROJECT	
Hylton Performing Arts Center, George Mason University, Manassas, VA	

310 | Stephen B. Jacobs Group/Andi Pepper Designs

281 Park Avenue South
New York, NY 10016
(212) 421-3712
www.sbjgroup.com
Stephen B. Jacobs, President
Andi Pepper, President/AP Designs
Herbert Weber, VP

WORLDWIDE REVENUE	$6,500,000
WORLDWIDE STAFF	50
HEADQUARTERS	New York, NY
YEAR ESTABLISHED	1967
RECENT REPRESENTATIVE PROJECT	

Gansevoort South
Miami Beach, FL

311 | Lindsay, Pope, Brayfield & Associates

344 West Pike Street
Lawrenceville, GA 30046
(770) 963-8989
www.lpbatlanta.com
Buck Lindsay, President

WORLDWIDE REVENUE	$6,464,250
WORLDWIDE STAFF	5–20
HEADQUARTERS	Lawrenceville, GA
YEAR ESTABLISHED	1975

312 | DiGiorgio Associates

225 Friend Street
Boston, MA 02114
(617) 723-7100
www.dai-boston.com
Domenic DiGiorgio, President/Founder

WORLDWIDE REVENUE	$6,460,000
WORLDWIDE STAFF	21–100
HEADQUARTERS	Boston, MA
YEAR ESTABLISHED	1984

313 | Architects Delawie Wilkes Rodrigues Barker

2265 India Street
San Diego, CA 92101
(619) 299-6690
www.a-dwrb.com
Michael B. Wilkes, CEO
Paul Schroeder, Principal

WORLDWIDE REVENUE	$6,426,000
WORLDWIDE STAFF	21–100
HEADQUARTERS	San Diego, CA
YEAR ESTABLISHED	1961

Peter Carpi

317 | 45 Province Street, Boston, MA | Bruner/Cott & Associates

314 | GSR Andrade Architects

4121 Commerce Street, Suite One
Dallas, TX 75226
(214) 824-7040
www.gsr-andrade.com
Fernando Andrade, Principal
Gary Staiger, Principal
Jason Russell, Principal

WORLDWIDE REVENUE	$6,417,500
WORLDWIDE STAFF	27
HEADQUARTERS	Dallas, TX
YEAR ESTABLISHED	1984

315 | Newport Collaborative

38 Washington Square
Newport, RI 02840
(401) 846-9583
www.ncarchitects.com
John Grosvenor, President

WORLDWIDE REVENUE	$6,311,250
WORLDWIDE STAFF	25
HEADQUARTERS	Newport, RI
YEAR ESTABLISHED	1981

316 | Davis

60 East Rio Salado Parkway, Suite 118
Tempe, AZ 85281
(480) 638-1100
www.thedavisexperience.com
Michael R. Davis, CEO/Director of Design
R. Nicholas Loope, President/COO

WORLDWIDE REVENUE	$6,306,000
WORLDWIDE STAFF	18
HEADQUARTERS	Tempe, AZ
YEAR ESTABLISHED	1975
RECENT REPRESENTATIVE PROJECT	

Classic Residence at Silverstone
Scottsdale, AZ

317 | Bruner/Cott & Associates

Bruner/Cott
architects and planners

130 Prospect Street
Cambridge, MA 02139
(617) 492-8400
www.brunercott.com
Simeon Bruner, Founding Principal
Leland D. Cott, Founding Principal

WORLDWIDE REVENUE	$6,303,000
WORLDWIDE STAFF	52
HEADQUARTERS	Cambridge, MA
YEAR ESTABLISHED	1972
RECENT REPRESENTATIVE PROJECT	

45 Province Street
Boston, MA

318 | Humphries Poli Architects

2100 Downing Street
Denver, CO 80205
(303) 607-0040
www.hparch.com
Dennis R. Humphries, Principal
Joe Poli, Principal
Adam Ambro, Associate Principal

WORLDWIDE REVENUE	$6,300,000
WORLDWIDE STAFF	37
HEADQUARTERS	Denver, CO
YEAR ESTABLISHED	1994
RECENT REPRESENTATIVE PROJECT	

North Creek Mixed Use Facility
Denver, CO

319 | Fox Architects

8444 Westpark Drive, Suite 120
McLean, VA 22102
(703) 821-7990
www.fox-architects.com
Robert D. Fox, Principal
Sabret Flocos, Principal
Jim Allegro, Principal

WORLDWIDE REVENUE	$6,200,000
WORLDWIDE STAFF	51
HEADQUARTERS	McLean, VA
YEAR ESTABLISHED	2003
RECENT REPRESENTATIVE PROJECT	

BP America, Inc.
Washington, DC

320 | M & A Architects

6161 Riverside Drive, Suite A
Dublin, OH 43017
(614) 764-0407
www.meachamapel.com
Mark Daniels, President
John Eymann, Secretary/Treasurer

WORLDWIDE REVENUE	$6,135,300
WORLDWIDE STAFF	21–100
HEADQUARTERS	Dublin, OH
YEAR ESTABLISHED	1980

321 | Hardy McCullah/MLM Architects

12221 Merit Drive, Suite 280
Dallas, TX 75251
(972) 385-1900
www.hmmlmarchitects.com
Hardy McCullah, Principal

WORLDWIDE REVENUE	$6,077,500
WORLDWIDE STAFF	5–20
HEADQUARTERS	Dallas, TX
YEAR ESTABLISHED	1967

322 | Dougherty + Dougherty Architects

3194D Airport Loop Drive
Costa Mesa, CA 92626
(714) 427-0277
www.ddarchitecture.com
Brian Dougherty, Partner
Betsey Olenick Dougherty, Partner
Lai-Yin Cheah, Partner

WORLDWIDE REVENUE	$6,050,000
WORLDWIDE STAFF	35
HEADQUARTERS	Costa Mesa, CA
YEAR ESTABLISHED	1979

RECENT REPRESENTATIVE PROJECT
Newport Coast Community Center
Newport Beach, CA

323 | Robert M. Swedroe Architects & Planners

12000 Biscayne Boulevard, Suite 602
Miami, FL 33181
(305) 758-1200
www.swedroe.com
Robert M. Swedroe, Founding Partner
Joseph J. Swedroe, Partner
Michael Agnoli, Director of Design

WORLDWIDE REVENUE	$6,025,000
WORLDWIDE STAFF	20
HEADQUARTERS	Miami, FL
YEAR ESTABLISHED	1974

RECENT REPRESENTATIVE PROJECT
Trump Hollywood
Hollywood, FL

324 | Rubeling & Associates

1104 Kenilworth Drive, Suite 500
Towson, MD 21204
(410) 337-2886
www.rubeling.com
Albert W. Rubeling, President
John J. DiMenna, Executive VP
David P. Recchia, VP

WORLDWIDE REVENUE	$6,010,000
WORLDWIDE STAFF	27
HEADQUARTERS	Baltimore, MD
YEAR ESTABLISHED	1981

RECENT REPRESENTATIVE PROJECT
Randallstown Community Center
Baltimore County, MD

325 | Swaback Partners

7550 East McDonald Drive
Scottsdale, AZ 85250
(480) 367-2100
www.swabackpartners.com
Vernon Swaback, Managing Partner
Jon C. Bernhard, Partner
John E. Sather, Partner

WORLDWIDE REVENUE	$6,000,000
WORLDWIDE STAFF	25
HEADQUARTERS	Scottsdale, AZ
YEAR ESTABLISHED	1978

RECENT REPRESENTATIVE PROJECT
Curci Residence
Paradise Valley, AZ

326 | Flansburgh Architects

77 North Washington Street
Boston, MA 02114
(617) 367 3970
www.faiarchitects.com
David A. Croteau, President
Alan S. Ross, Principal
Duncan McClelland, Principal

WORLDWIDE REVENUE	$5,910,000
WORLDWIDE STAFF	21–100
HEADQUARTERS	Boston, MA
YEAR ESTABLISHED	1963

327 | Kann Partners

33 South Gay Street, Suite 400
Baltimore, MD 21202
(410) 234-0900
www.kannpartners.com
Donald R. Kann, President
Jonathan McGowan, Partner
Cass Gottlieb, Partner

WORLDWIDE REVENUE	$5,907,500
WORLDWIDE STAFF	35
HEADQUARTERS	Baltimore, MD
YEAR ESTABLISHED	1974

328 | Crabtree, Rohrbaugh & Associates

401 East Winding Hill Road
Mechanicsburg, PA 17055
(717) 458-0272
www.cra-architects.com
Tom Crabtree, Co-Founder
Doug Rohrbaugh, Co-Founder

WORLDWIDE REVENUE	$5,805,000
WORLDWIDE STAFF	80
HEADQUARTERS	Mechanicsburg, PA
YEAR ESTABLISHED	1984

329 | Domenech Hicks & Krockmalnic Architects

54 Canal Street, Suite 200
Boston, MA 02114
(617) 267-6408
www.dhkinc.com
Fernando Domenech, President
Alberto Cardenas, VP

WORLDWIDE REVENUE	$5,788,500
WORLDWIDE STAFF	5–20
HEADQUARTERS	Boston, MA
YEAR ESTABLISHED	1985

330 | JPC Architects

601 108th Avenue NE, Suite 2250
Bellevue, WA 98004
(425) 641-9200
www.jpc-inc.com
Dan Butler, Principal
Ann Derr, Principal
Dennis Dieni, Principal

WORLDWIDE REVENUE	$5,780,000
WORLDWIDE STAFF	45
HEADQUARTERS	Bellevue, WA
YEAR ESTABLISHED	1986

331 | Bohlin Cywinski Jackson

8 West Market Street, Suite 1200
Wilkes-Barre, PA 18701
(507) 825-8756
www.bcj.com
Jon C. Jackson, Principal

WORLDWIDE REVENUE	$5,694,150
WORLDWIDE STAFF	185
HEADQUARTERS	N/A
YEAR ESTABLISHED	1965

332 | SB Architects

1 Beach Street, Suite 301
San Francisco, CA 94133
(415) 673-8990
www.sb-architects.com
Scott A. Lee, President
Joseph A. Andriola, Senior VP
John Cisco, CFO

WORLDWIDE REVENUE	$5,687,000
WORLDWIDE STAFF	65
HEADQUARTERS	San Francisco, CA
YEAR ESTABLISHED	1960
RECENT REPRESENTATIVE PROJECT	

Bahia Beach Resort & Golf Club
Rio Grande, Puerto Rico

333 | Design Partnership of Cambridge

500 Rutherford Avenue
Hood Business Park
Charlestown, MA 02129
(617) 241-9800
www.design-partnership.com
David R. Finney, President

WORLDWIDE REVENUE	$5,686,500
WORLDWIDE STAFF	21–100
HEADQUARTERS	Charleston, MA
YEAR ESTABLISHED	1981

2

AMERICA'S LEADING
ARCHITECTURE & DESIGN FIRMS |

This chapter features an alphabetical listing
of leading North American architecture and
design firms with data about the type of
services they offer; their size, headquarters,
and geography; the market segments they
work in; and metrics from the *DI Index*.

America's Leading Architecture & Design Firms 2011

This section of the *Almanac* features an alphabetical listing of leading North American design and engineering firms selected by the editors. Each year, *DesignIntelligence* polls architects and designers in North America regarding their firms' officers, firm size, primary services offered, market segments and geographical locations served, and the nature of their practices. The firms are invited to participate in additional research underwritten by the Design Futures Council, which includes surveys about trends and market shifts, compensation and fees, technology, mergers and acquisitions, and management strategies.

The key to interpreting the tables is featured below. Firm size, headquarters (HQ), firm type, and markets are determined by *DesignIntelligence* surveys or from record files. Although the concept of headquarters might be less normative than in the past, this convention is still often used for diagnostic purposes in many market-data studies. If your firm has no headquarters and we have listed one, please make sure to complete a survey next year at di.net. The list of services includes market segments and specific professional specializations. The DI Index was determined by survey responses, with further research conducted by *DesignIntelligence* and Greenway Group analysts. The criteria include geographic service coverage and reputation (awards as listed in the *Almanac of Architecture & Design* and recognition in professional and business publications). Of the five tiers, only firms in the top three (as represented by 3–5 stars) are included due to space considerations. Abbreviations were used in some firm names due to space constraints: architecture = Arch.; architects = Archts.; associates = Assoc.; construction = Const.; engineers = Engrs.

Principals of firms who want to be included in our next *Almanac* can obtain and/or fill in a survey at di.net; email the editor, Jane Wolford, at jwolford@di.net for a copy; or call *DesignIntelligence* at (678) 879-0929. Firms appearing in this *Almanac* can expect to receive a copy of next year's survey in the mail soon or can request a survey by contacting DI or the editor.

KEY

Size

🀆	Small	20 employees or less
🀆🀆	Medium	21–100 employees
🀆🀆🀆	Large	101–450 employees
🀆🀆🀆🀆	Extra Large	451+ employees
🀆	N/A	Not available

HQ

Listed by state, Canada (CAN) or Mexico (MEX).

Regions Served

E	East		C	Canada
M	Midwest		G	Global
S	South			
W	West			

Services Offered

A	Architecture		I	Interior Design
E	Engineering		L	Landscape Architecture
G	Graphic Design		P	Planning/Urban Design
O	Other (including industrial design)			

Market Segments

C	Corporate		M	Museum/Cultural
E	Education		RI	Religious
G	Government		R	Residential
Hc	Healthcare		Re	Retail
H	Hospitality		S	Sports
I	Industrial		O	Other

DI Brand Recognition Index

★★★★★ Top tier global and categorical leader recognition
★★★★ Exceptional national and categorical leader recognition
★★★ Strong regional and categorical leader recognition
★★ Notable and growing with emerging categorical recognition
★ Professional practice notable in city and region

Don Pearse Photographers, Inc.

Stafford Hospital Center, Stafford, VA | Ellerbe Becket, an AECOM Company

	Size	HQ	Regions	Services	Markets	DI Index
4240 Architecture www.4240architecture.com	👥	CO	E M S W C G	A E G I L P O	C E G Hc H I M RI R Re S O	★★★
505 Design www.505design.com	👤	CO	E M S W C G	A E G I L P O	C E G Hc H I M RI R Re S O	★★★
A 4 Architecture www.a4arch.com	👤	RI	E M S W C G	A E G I L P O	C E G Hc H I M RI R Re S O	★★★
A. Morton Thomas & Associates www.amtengineering.com	👥👥	MD	E M S W C G	A E G I L P O	C E G Hc H I M RI R Re S O	★★★
Abell & Associates Architects www.jamesabell.com	👤	AZ	E M S W C G	A E G I L P O	C E G Hc H I M RI R Re S O	★★★
AC Martin www.acmartin.com	👥👥	CA	E M S W C G	A E G I L P O	C E G Hc H I M RI R Re S O	★★★★
Acai Associates www.acaiworld.com	👥👥👥	FL	E M S W C G	A E G I L P O	C E G Hc H I M RI R Re S O	★★★
ACI/Boland www.aci-boland.com	👥	MO	E M S W C G	A E G I L P O	C E G Hc H I M RI R Re S O	★★★
Adache Group Architects www.adache.com	👥	FL	E M S W C G	A E G I L P O	C E G Hc H I M RI R Re S O	★★★
Adamson Associates Architects www.adamson-associates.com	👤	CAN	E M S W C G	A E G I L P O	C E G Hc H I M RI R Re S O	★★★
ADD Inc www.addinc.com	👥👥	MA	E M S W C G	A E G I L P O	C E G Hc H I M RI R Re S O	★★★★
Adrian Smith + Gordon Gill Architecture www.smithgill.com	👥👥	IL	E M S W C G	A E G I L P O	C E G Hc H I M RI R Re S O	★★★★★
AE Design www.ae-design.com	👤	GA	E M S W C G	A E G I L P O	C E G Hc H I M RI R Re S O	★★★
AECOM (Architecture) www.aecom.com	👥👥👥	CA	E M S W C G	A E G I L P O	C E G Hc H I M RI R Re S O	★★★★★
AEDIS Architecture & Planning www.aedisgroup.com	👥	CA	E M S W C G	A E G I L P O	C E G Hc H I M RI R Re S O	★★★★★
Affiniti Architects www.affinitiarchitects.com	👥	FL	E M S W C G	A E G I L P O	C E G Hc H I M RI R Re S O	★★★
Aguirre Roden www.aguirreroden.com	👥	TX	E M S W C G	A E G I L P O	C E G Hc H I M RI R Re S O	★★★

REGIONS: East (E), Midwest (M), South (S), West (W), Canada (C), Global (G)

SERVICES: Architecture (A), Engineering (E), Graphic Design (G), Interior Design (I), Landscape Architecture (L), Planning/Urban Design (P), Other-including Industrial Design (O)

MARKETS: Corporate (C), Education (E), Government (G), Healthcare (Hc), Hospitality (H), Industrial (I), Museum/Cultural (M), Religious (RI), Residential (R), Retail (Re), Sports (S), Other (O)

	Size	HQ	Regions	Services	Markets	DI Index
Albert Kahn Associates www.albertkahn.com	👤👤👤	MI	E M S W C G	A E G I L P O	C E G Hc H I M RI R Re S O	★★★★
Alliance Architects www.alliancearch.com	👤	TX	E M S W C G	A E G I L P O	C E G Hc H I M RI R Re S O	★★★
Allied Works Architecture www.alliedworks.com	👤👤	OR	E M S W C G	A E G I L P O	C E G Hc H I M RI R Re S O	★★★★
Altoon + Porter Architects www.altoonporter.com	👤👤	CA	E M S W C G	A E G I L P O	C E G Hc H I M RI R Re S O	★★★★
AM Partners www.ampartners.com	👤👤	HI	E M S W C G	A E G I L P O	C E G Hc H I M RI R Re S O	★★★
Ambia www.ambia-inc.com	👤	WA	E M S W C G	A E G I L P O	C E G Hc H I M RI R Re S O	★★★
Ammon Heisler Sachs Architects www.ahsarch.com	👤	MD	E M S W C G	A E G I L P O	C E G Hc H I M RI R Re S O	★★★
Anderson Brule Architects www.aba-arch.com	👤	CA	E M S W C G	A E G I L P O	C E G Hc H I M RI R Re S O	★★★
Anderson Mason Dale Architects www.amdarchitects.com	👤👤	CO	E M S W C G	A E G I L P O	C E G Hc H I M RI R Re S O	★★★★
Ankrom Moisan Associated Architects www.amaa.com	👤👤	OR	E M S W C G	A E G I L P O	C E G Hc H I M RI R Re S O	★★★
Ann Beha Architects www.annbeha.com	👤👤	MA	E M S W C G	A E G I L P O	C E G Hc H I M RI R Re S O	★★★★
Anova Architects www.anovaarchitects.com	👤👤	CA	E M S W C G	A E G I L P O	C E G Hc H I M RI R Re S O	★★★
Anshen + Allen (Stantec) www.anshen.com	👤👤👤	CA	E M S W C G	A E G I L P O	C E G Hc H I M RI R Re S O	★★★★★
Antinozzi Associates www.antinozzi.com	👤	CT	E M S W C G	A E G I L P O	C E G Hc H I M RI R Re S O	★★★
Apostolou Associates www.apostolouassociates.com	👤	PA	E M S W C G	A E G I L P O	C E G Hc H I M RI R Re S O	★★★
App Architecture www.app-arch.com	👤👤	OH	E M S W C G	A E G I L P O	C E G Hc H I M RI R Re S O	★★★
ARC/Architectural Resources Cambridge www.arcusa.com	👤👤	MA	E M S W C G	A E G I L P O	C E G Hc H I M RI R Re S O	★★★

REGIONS: East (E), Midwest (M), South (S), West (W), Canada (C), Global (G)

SERVICES: Architecture (A), Engineering (E), Graphic Design (G), Interior Design (I), Landscape Architecture (L), Planning/Urban Design (P), Other-including Industrial Design (O)

MARKETS: Corporate (C), Education (E), Government (G), Healthcare (Hc), Hospitality (H), Industrial (I), Museum/Cultural (M), Religious (RI), Residential (R), Retail (Re), Sports (S), Other (O)

	Size	HQ	Regions	Services	Markets	DI Index
ARCADIS www.arcadis-us.com	👤👤👤👤	CO	E M S W C G	A E G I L P O	C E G Hc H I M RI R Re S O	★★★★★
Archicon www.archicon.com	👤👤	AZ	E M S W C G	A E G I L P O	C E G Hc H I M RI R Re S O	★★★
Architects Barrentine.Bates.Lee www.archbbl.com	👤👤	OR	E M S W C G	A E G I L P O	C E G Hc H I M RI R Re S O	★★★
Architects BCRA www.bcradesign.com	👤👤👤	WA	E M S W C G	A E G I L P O	C E G Hc H I M RI R Re S O	★★★
Architects Delawie Wilkes Rodrigues Barker www.a-dwrb.com	👤👤	CA	E M S W C G	A E G I L P O	C E G Hc H I M RI R Re S O	★★★
Architects Design Group www.adgusa.org	👤👤	FL	E M S W C G	A E G I L P O	C E G Hc H I M RI R Re S O	★★★
Architects In Partnership www.aipdesign.com	👤	FL	E M S W C G	A E G I L P O	C E G Hc H I M RI R Re S O	★★★
Architects Pacific www.architectspacificinc.com	👤	HI	E M S W C G	A E G I L P O	C E G Hc H I M RI R Re S O	★★★
Architects Studio www.architectsstudio.us	👤	HI	E M S W C G	A E G I L P O	C E G Hc H I M RI R Re S O	★★★
Architectural Alliance www.archalliance.com	👤👤	MN	E M S W C G	A E G I L P O	C E G Hc H I M RI R Re S O	★★★
Architectural Concepts www.arconcepts.com	👤👤	PA	E M S W C G	A E G I L P O	C E G Hc H I M RI R Re S O	★★★
Architectural Resource Team www.art-team.com	👤	AZ	E M S W C G	A E G I L P O	C E G Hc H I M RI R Re S O	★★★
Architectural Resources www.archres.com	👤👤	NY	E M S W C G	A E G I L P O	C E G Hc H I M RI R Re S O	★★★
Architectural Resources Group www.argsf.com	👤👤	CA	E M S W C G	A E G I L P O	C E G Hc H I M RI R Re S O	★★★
Architectural Resources Inc. www.arimn.com	👤	MN	E M S W C G	A E G I L P O	C E G Hc H I M RI R Re S O	★★★
Architecture Incorporated www.architectureinc.com	👤👤	SD	E M S W C G	A E G I L P O	C E G Hc H I M RI R Re S O	★★★
Architecture PML www.archpml.com	👤	CO	E M S W C G	A E G I L P O	C E G Hc H I M RI R Re S O	★★★★

REGIONS: East (E), Midwest (M), South (S), West (W), Canada (C), Global (G)

SERVICES: Architecture (A), Engineering (E), Graphic Design (G), Interior Design (I),
Landscape Architecture (L), Planning/Urban Design (P), Other-including Industrial Design (O)

MARKETS: Corporate (C), Education (E), Government (G), Healthcare (Hc), Hospitality (H), Industrial (I)
Museum/Cultural (M), Religious (RI), Residential (R), Retail (Re), Sports (S), Other (O)

	Size	HQ	Regions	Services	Markets	DI Index
Architecture, Inc. www.archinc.com	👤	VA	E M S W C G	A E G I L P O	C E G Hc H I M RI R Re S O	★★★
ArchitectureIsFun www.architectureisfun.com	👤	IL	E M S W C G	A E G I L P O	C E G Hc H I M RI R Re S O	★★★
Architekton www.architekton.com	👥	AZ	E M S W C G	A E G I L P O	C E G Hc H I M RI R Re S O	★★★★
Arcturis www.arcturis.com	👥👥	MO	E M S W C G	A E G I L P O	C E G Hc H I M RI R Re S O	★★★
ARIUMae www.ariumae.com	👤	MD	E M S W C G	A E G I L P O	C E G Hc H I M RI R Re S O	★★★
Arquitectonica www.arquitectonica.com	👥👥	FL	E M S W C G	A E G I L P O	C E G Hc H I M RI R Re S O	★★★★★
Arrington Watkins Architects www.awarch.com	👥	AZ	E M S W C G	A E G I L P O	C E G Hc H I M RI R Re S O	★★★
Arrowstreet www.arrowstreet.com	👥👥	MA	E M S W C G	A E G I L P O	C E G Hc H I M RI R Re S O	★★★
Ascension Group Architects www.ascensiongroup.biz	👥	TX	E M S W C G	A E G I L P O	C E G Hc H I M RI R Re S O	★★★
ASD www.asdnet.com	👥	GA	E M S W C G	A E G I L P O	C E G Hc H I M RI R Re S O	★★★★
Astorino www.astorino.com	👥👥	PA	E M S W C G	A E G I L P O	C E G Hc H I M RI R Re S O	★★★★
ATI Architects & Engineers www.atiae.com	👥	CA	E M S W C G	A E G I L P O	C E G Hc H I M RI R Re S O	★★★
Austin Company, The www.theaustin.com	👥👥👥	OH	E M S W C G	A E G I L P O	C E G Hc H I M RI R Re S O	★★★★
Austin Kuester www.austinkuester.com	👤	VA	E M S W C G	A E G I L P O	C E G Hc H I M RI R Re S O	★★★
Ayers/Saint/Gross www.asg-architects.com	👥👥	MD	E M S W C G	A E G I L P O	C E G Hc H I M RI R Re S O	★★★★★
Baird Sampson Neuert Architects www.bsnarchitects.com	👤	CAN	E M S W C G	A E G I L P O	C E G Hc H I M RI R Re S O	★★★
Baker Barrios Architects www.bakerbarrios.com	👥👥	FL	E M S W C G	A E G I L P O	C E G Hc H I M RI R Re S O	★★★

B

REGIONS: East (E), Midwest (M), South (S), West (W), Canada (C), Global (G)

SERVICES: Architecture (A), Engineering (E), Graphic Design (G), Interior Design (I), Landscape Architecture (L), Planning/Urban Design (P), Other-including Industrial Design (O)

MARKETS: Corporate (C), Education (E), Government (G), Healthcare (Hc), Hospitality (H), Industrial (I), Museum/Cultural (M), Religious (RI), Residential (R), Retail (Re), Sports (S), Other (O)

	Size	HQ	Regions	Services	Markets	DI Index
Ballinger www.ballinger-ae.com	👤👤👤	PA	E M S W C G	A E G I L P O	C E G Hc H I M RI R Re S O	★★★★
BAR Architects www.bararch.com	👤👤	CA	E M S W C G	A E G I L P O	C E G Hc H I M RI R Re S O	★★★
Bargmann Hendrie & Archetype www.bhplus.com	👤👤	MA	E M S W C G	A E G I L P O	C E G Hc H I M RI R Re S O	★★★
Barker Rinker Seacat Architecture www.brsarch.com	👤👤	CO	E M S W C G	A E G I L P O	C E G Hc H I M RI R Re S O	★★★★
Barry Bebart Architecture www.bebartarchitecture.com	👤	IL	E M S W C G	A E G I L P O	C E G Hc H I M RI R Re S O	★★★
BartonPartners www.bartonpartners.com	👤👤	PA	E M S W C G	A E G I L P O	C E G Hc H I M RI R Re S O	★★★
Baskervill www.baskervill.com	👤👤	VA	E M S W C G	A E G I L P O	C E G Hc H I M RI R Re S O	★★★
Bassetti Architects www.bassettiarch.com	👤	WA	E M S W C G	A E G I L P O	C E G Hc H I M RI R Re S O	★★★
Bauer and Wiley Architects www.bauerandwiley.com	👤	CA	E M S W C G	A E G I L P O	C E G Hc H I M RI R Re S O	★★★
Bay Architects www.bayarchitects.com	👤👤	TX	E M S W C G	A E G I L P O	C E G Hc H I M RI R Re S O	★★★
BBG-BBGM www.bbg-bbgm.com	👤👤👤	NY	E M S W C G	A E G I L P O	C E G Hc H I M RI R Re S O	★★★★★
BC Architects www.bcarchitects.com	👤	FL	E M S W C G	A E G I L P O	C E G Hc H I M RI R Re S O	★★★
BCA www.bcainconline.com	👤	CA	E M S W C G	A E G I L P O	C E G Hc H I M RI R Re S O	★★★
BEA International www.beai.com	👤👤	FL	E M S W C G	A E G I L P O	C E G Hc H I M RI R Re S O	★★★
Beame Architectural Partnership www.bapdesign.com	👤👤	FL	E M S W C G	A E G I L P O	C E G Hc H I M RI R Re S O	★★★
Bearsch Compeau Knudson Architects & Engineers www.bckpc.com	👤👤	NY	E M S W C G	A E G I L P O	C E G Hc H I M RI R Re S O	★★★
Beatty, Harvey, Coco Architects www.bhc-architects.com	👤👤	NY	E M S W C G	A E G I L P O	C E G Hc H I M RI R Re S O	★★★

REGIONS: East (E), Midwest (M), South (S), West (W), Canada (C), Global (G)

SERVICES: Architecture (A), Engineering (E), Graphic Design (G), Interior Design (I),
Landscape Architecture (L), Planning/Urban Design (P), Other-including Industrial Design (O)

MARKETS: Corporate (C), Education (E), Government (G), Healthcare (Hc), Hospitality (H), Industrial (I)
Museum/Cultural (M), Religious (RI), Residential (R), Retail (Re), Sports (S), Other (O)

	Size	HQ	Regions	Services	Markets	DI Index
Beck Group, The (Architecture) www.beckgroup.com	👥	TX	E M S W C G	A E G I L P O	C E G Hc H I M RI R Re S O	★★★★
Becker & Becker Associates www.beckerandbecker.com	👤	CT	E M S W C G	A E G I L P O	C E G Hc H I M RI R Re S O	★★★
BEI Associates www.beiassociates.com	👥	MI	E M S W C G	A E G I L P O	C E G Hc H I M RI R Re S O	★★★
Benham Companies, The www.benham.com	👥👥	OK	E M S W C G	A E G I L P O	C E G Hc H I M RI R R Re S O	★★★
Benjamin Woo Architects www.benwooarchitects.com	👤	HI	E M S W C G	A E G I L P O	C E G Hc H I M RI R Re S O	★★★
Bennett Wagner & Grody Archt. www.bwgarchitects.com	👥	CO	E M S W C G	A E G I L P O	C E G Hc H I M RI R Re S O	★★★
Bentel & Bentel Architects/ Planners www.bentelandbentel.com	👤	NY	E M S W C G	A E G I L P O	C E G Hc H I M RI R Re S O	★★★
Bergmann Associates www.bergmannpc.com	👥👥	NY	E M S W C G	A E G I L P O	C E G Hc H I M RI R Re S O	★★★
Bergmeyer Associates www.bergmeyer.com	👥👥	MA	E M S W C G	A E G I L P O	C E G Hc H I M RI R Re S O	★★★★
Bermello Ajamil & Partners www.bamiami.com	👥	FL	E M S W C G	A E G I L P O	C E G Hc H I M RI R Re S O	★★★
Bernardon Haber Holloway www.bernardon.com	👥	PA	E M S W C G	A E G I L P O	C E G Hc H I M RI R Re S O	★★★
Beyer Blinder Belle www.beyerblinderbelle.com	👥	NY	E M S W C G	A E G I L P O	C E G Hc H I M RI R Re S O	★★★★★
BHDP www.bhdp.com	👥👥	OH	E M S W C G	A E G I L P O	C E G Hc H I M RI R Re S O	★★★
Bialosky & Partners Architects www.bialosky.com	👥	OH	E M S W C G	A E G I L P O	C E G Hc H I M RI R Re S O	★★★
Bignell Watkins Hasser Architects www.bigwaha.com	👥	MD	E M S W C G	A E G I L P O	C E G Hc H I M RI R Re S O	★★★
Bing Thom Architects www.bingthomarchitects.com	👥	CAN	E M S W C G	A E G I L P O	C E G Hc H I M RI R Re S O	★★★★
BJAC www.bjac.com	👥	NC	E M S W C G	A E G I L P O	C E G Hc H I M RI R Re S O	★★★

REGIONS: East (E), Midwest (M), South (S), West (W), Canada (C), Global (G)

SERVICES: Architecture (A), Engineering (E), Graphic Design (G), Interior Design (I), Landscape Architecture (L), Planning/Urban Design (P), Other-including Industrial Design (O)

MARKETS: Corporate (C), Education (E), Government (G), Healthcare (Hc), Hospitality (H), Industrial (I), Museum/Cultural (M), Religious (RI), Residential (R), Retail (Re), Sports (S), Other (O)

	Size	HQ	Regions	Services	Markets	DI Index
BKV Group www.bkvgroup.com	👥	MN	E M S W C G	A E G I L P O	C E G Hc H I M RI R Re S O	★★★
Blackburn Architects www.blackburnarchitects.com	👤	IN	E M S W C G	A E G I L P O	C E G Hc H I M RI R Re S O	★★★
Blackney Hayes Architects www.blackneyhayes.com	👥	PA	E M S W C G	A E G I L P O	C E G Hc H I M RI R Re S O	★★★
Blankstudio Architecture www.blankspaces.net	👤	AZ	E M S W C G	A E G I L P O	C E G Hc H I M RI R Re S O	★★★
BLT Architects www.blta.com	👥	PA	E M S W C G	A E G I L P O	C E G Hc H I M RI R Re S O	★★★
BNIM Architects www.bnim.com	👥👤	MO	E M S W C G	A E G I L P O	C E G Hc H I M RI R Re S O	★★★★★
Boggs & Partners Architects www.boggspartners.com	👤	MD	E M S W C G	A E G I L P O	C E G Hc H I M RI R Re S O	★★★
Bohlin Cywinski Jackson www.bcj.com	👥	N/A	E M S W C G	A E G I L P O	C E G Hc H I M RI R Re S O	★★★★★
BOKA Powell www.bokapowell.com	👥	TX	E M S W C G	A E G I L P O	C E G Hc H I M RI R Re S O	★★★
BOORA Architects www.boora.com	👥	OR	E M S W C G	A E G I L P O	C E G Hc H I M RI R Re S O	★★★★
Booth Hansen Associates www.boothansen.com	👤	IL	E M S W C G	A E G I L P O	C E G Hc H I M RI R Re S O	★★★★
Borrelli + Partners www.borrelliarchitects.com	👤	FL	E M S W C G	A E G I L P O	C E G Hc H I M RI R Re S O	★★★
Bostwick Design Partnership www.bostwickdesign.com	👥	OH	E M S W C G	A E G I L P O	C E G Hc H I M RI R Re S O	★★★
Boulder Associates www.boulderassociates.com	👥	CO	E M S W C G	A E G I L P O	C E G Ho H I M RI R Re S O	★★★
Brand + Allen Architects www.brandallen.com	👥	TX	E M S W C G	A E G I L P O	C E G Hc H I M RI R Re S O	★★★
Brasher Design www.brasherdesign.com	👤	MD	E M S W C G	A E G I L P O	C E G Hc H I M RI R Re S O	★★★
Braun & Steidl Architects www.bsa-net.com	👥	OH	E M S W C G	A E G I L P O	C E G Hc H I M RI R Re S O	★★★

REGIONS: East (E), Midwest (M), South (S), West (W), Canada (C), Global (G)

SERVICES: Architecture (A), Engineering (E), Graphic Design (G), Interior Design (I),
Landscape Architecture (L), Planning/Urban Design (P), Other-including Industrial Design (O)

MARKETS: Corporate (C), Education (E), Government (G), Healthcare (Hc), Hospitality (H), Industrial (I)
Museum/Cultural (M), Religious (RI), Residential (R), Retail (Re), Sports (S), Other (O)

	Size	HQ	Regions	Services	Markets	DI Index
Brininstool, Kerwin & Lynch www.bklarch.com		IL	E M S W C G	A E G I L P O	C E G Hc H I M RI R Re S O	★★★★
Brown Craig Turner www.brownandcraig.com		MD	E M S W C G	A E G I L P O	C E G Hc H I M RI R Re S O	★★★
Browning Day Mullins Dierdorf Architects www.bdmd.com		IN	E M S W C G	A E G I L P O	C E G Hc H I M RI R Re S O	★★★
BRPH www.brph.com		FL	E M S W C G	A E G I L P O	C E G H I M RI R Re S O	★★★
Bruce Mau Design www.brucemaudesign.com		CAN	E M S W C G	A E G I L P O	C E G Hc H I M RI R Re S O	★★★★★
Bruner/Cott & Associates www.brunercott.com		MA	E M S W C G	A E G I L P O	C E G Hc H I M RI R Re S O	★★★★
BSA Architects www.bsaarchitects.com		CA	E M S W C G	A E G I L P O	C E G Hc H I M RI R Re S O	★★★
BSA LifeStructures www.bsalifestructures.com		IN	E M S W C G	A E G I L P O	C E G Hc H I M RI R Re S O	★★★★
Buchart-Horn www.bh-ba.com		PA	E M S W C G	A E G I L P O	C E G Hc H I M RI R Re S O	★★★
Bullock Tice Associates www.bullocktice.com		FL	E M S W C G	A E G I L P O	C E G Hc H I M RI R Re S O	★★★
Bumpus & Associates www.bumpusandassociates.com		FL	E M S W C G	A E G I L P O	C E G Hc H I M RI R Re S O	★★★
Burke Hogue Mills www.bhm.us.com		FL	E M S W C G	A E G I L P O	C E G Hc H I M RI R Re S O	★★★
Burkett Design www.burkettdesign.com		CO	E M S W C G	A E G I L P O	C E G Hc H I M RI R Re S O	★★★
Burns & McDonnell www.burnsmcd.com		MO	E M S W C G	A E G I L P O	C E G Hc H I M RI R Re S O	★★★
Burt Hill (in merger process with Stantec) www.burthill.com		PA	E M S W C G	A E G I L P O	C E G Hc H I M RI R Re S O	★★★★★
Busby Perkins+Will www.busby.ca		CAN	E M S W C G	A E G I L P O	C E G Hc H I M RI R Re S O	★★★★★
Butler Design Group www.butlerdesigngroup.com		AZ	E M S W C G	A E G I L P O	C E G Hc H I M RI R Re S O	★★★

REGIONS: East (E), Midwest (M), South (S), West (W), Canada (C), Global (G)

SERVICES: Architecture (A), Engineering (E), Graphic Design (G), Interior Design (I), Landscape Architecture (L), Planning/Urban Design (P), Other-including Industrial Design (O)

MARKETS: Corporate (C), Education (E), Government (G), Healthcare (Hc), Hospitality (H), Industrial (I) Museum/Cultural (M), Religious (RI), Residential (R), Retail (Re), Sports (S), Other (O)

	Size	HQ	Regions	Services	Markets	DI Index
Butler Rogers Baskett Architects www.brb.com		NY	E M S W C G	A E G I L P O	C E G Hc H I M RI R Re S O	★★★
BWBR Architects www.bwbr.com		MN	E M S W C G	A E G I L P O	C E G Hc H I M RI R Re S O	★★★★
C.N. Carley Associates www.cncarley.com		NH	E M S W C G	A E G I L P O	C E G Hc H I M RI R Re S O	★★★
C.T. Hsu + Associates www.cthsu.com		FL	E M S W C G	A E G I L P O	C E G Hc H I M RI R Re S O	★★★
CADM Architectecture www.cadmarchitects.com		AR	E M S W C G	A E G I L P O	C E G Hc H I M RI R Re S O	★★★
Callison www.callison.com		WA	E M S W C G	A E G I L P O	C E G Hc H I M RI R Re S O	★★★★★
CAMA www.camainc.com		CT	E M S W C G	A E G I L P O	C E G Hc H I M RI R Re S O	★★★★
Cambridge Seven Associates www.c7a.com		MA	E M S W C G	A E G I L P O	C E G Hc H I M RI R Re S O	★★★★
Canin Associates www.canin.com		FL	E M S W C G	A E G I L P O	C E G Hc H I M RI R Re S O	★★★
Cannon Design www.cannondesign.com		N/A	E M S W C G	A E G I L P O	C E G Hc H I M RI R Re S O	★★★★★
Carde Ten Architects www.cardeten.com		CA	E M S W C G	A E G I L P O	C E G Hc H I M RI R Re S O	★★★
Carrier Johnson + CULTURE www.carrierjohnson.com		CA	E M S W C G	A E G I L P O	C E G Hc H I M RI R Re S O	★★★★
Cascade Design Collaborative www.cascadedesigncollab.com		WA	E M S W C G	A E G I L P O	C E G Hc H I M RI R Re S O	★★★
CASCO www.cascocorp.com		MO	E M S W C G	A E G I L P O	C E G Hc H I M RI R Re S O	★★★
Cass I Sowatsky I Chapman + Associates www.csc-a.com		CA	E M S W C G	A E G I L P O	C E G Hc H I M RI R Re S O	★★★
CBLH Design www.cblhdesign.com		OH	E M S W C G	A E G I L P O	C E G Hc H I M RI R Re S O	★★★
CBT www.cbtarchitects.com		MA	E M S W C G	A E G I L P O	C E G Hc H I M RI R Re S O	★★★

REGIONS: East (E), Midwest (M), South (S), West (W), Canada (C), Global (G)

SERVICES: Architecture (A), Engineering (E), Graphic Design (G), Interior Design (I),
Landscape Architecture (L), Planning/Urban Design (P), Other-including Industrial Design (O)

MARKETS: Corporate (C), Education (E), Government (G), Healthcare (Hc), Hospitality (H), Industrial (I)
Museum/Cultural (M), Religious (RI), Residential (R), Retail (Re), Sports (S), Other (O)

Sabrina A. Carpenter, CDH Partners

CDH Partners' Offices, Marietta, GA | CDH Partners

	Size	HQ	Regions	Services	Markets	DI Index
CCBG Architects www.ccbg-arch.com	👤	AZ	E M S W C G	A E G I L P O	C E G Hc H I M Rl R Re S O	★★★
CDH Partners www.cdhpartners.com	👥	GA	E M S W C G	A E G I L P O	C E G Hc H I M Rl R Re S O	★★★
CDI Corp. www.cdicorp.com	👥	PA	E M S W C G	A E G I L P O	C E G Hc H I M Rl R Re S O	★★★
CDS International www.cdsintl.com	👤	HI	E M S W C G	A E G I L P O	C E G Hc H I M Rl R Re S O	★★★
Cecil Baker + Partners www.cbaarch.com	👥	PA	E M S W C G	A E G I L P O	C E G Hc H I M Rl R Re S O	★★★
Celli-Flynn Brennan Architects & Planners www.cfbarchitects.com	👤	PA	E M S W C G	A E G I L P O	C E G Hc H I M Rl R Re S O	★★★
Centerbrook Architects and Planners www.centerbrook.com	👥	CT	E M S W C G	A E G I L P O	C E G Hc H I M Rl R Re S O	★★★
Cetra Ruddy www.cetraruddy.com	👥	NY	E M S W C G	A E G I L P O	C E G Hc H I M Rl R Re S O	★★★
Chambers, Murphy & Burge Architects www.cmbarchitects.com	👤	OH	E M S W C G	A E G I L P O	C E G Hc H I M Rl R Re S O	★★★
Champalimaud www.champalimauddesign.com	👥	NY	E M S W C G	A E G I L P O	C E G Hc H I M Rl R Re S O	★★★★★
Champlin Architecture www.charchitects.com	👤	OH	E M S W C G	A E G I L P O	C E G Hc H I M Rl R Re S O	★★★
Charlan Brock & Associates www.cbaarchitects.com	👤	FL	E M S W C G	A E G I L P O	C E G Hc H I M Rl R Re S O	★★★
Childs Mascari Warner Architects www.childsmascariwarner.com	👥	CA	E M S W C G	A E G I L P O	C E G Hc H I M Rl R Re S O	★★★
Chiodini Associates www.chiodini.com	👤	MO	E M S W C G	A E G I L P O	C E G Hc H I M Rl R Re S O	★★★
Chipman Adams Architects www.chipmanadams.com	👥	IL	E M S W C G	A E G I L P O	C E G Hc H I M Rl R Re S O	★★★
Cho Benn Holback + Associates www.cbhassociates.com	👥	MD	E M S W C G	A E G I L P O	C E G Hc H I M Rl R Re S O	★★★
Christner www.christnerinc.com	👥	MO	E M S W C G	A E G I L P O	C E G Hc H I M Rl R Re S O	★★★

REGIONS: East (E), Midwest (M), South (S), West (W), Canada (C), Global (G)

SERVICES: Architecture (A), Engineering (E), Graphic Design (G), Interior Design (I),
Landscape Architecture (L), Planning/Urban Design (P), Other-including Industrial Design (O)

MARKETS: Corporate (C), Education (E), Government (G), Healthcare (Hc), Hospitality (H), Industrial (I)
Museum/Cultural (M), Religious (Rl), Residential (R), Retail (Re), Sports (S), Other (O)

	Size	HQ	Regions	Services	Markets	DI Index
City Architecture www.cityarch.com	👥	OH	E M S W C G	A E G I L P O	C E G Hc H I M RI R Re S O	★★★
CJS Group Architects www.cjsgrouparchitects.com	👤	HI	E M S W C G	A E G I L P O	C E G Hc H I M RI R Re S O	★★★
Clark Nexsen www.clarknexsen.com	👥	VA	E M S W C G	A E G I L P O	C E G Hc H I M RI R Re S O	★★★★
CLC Associates www.clcassoc.com	👥	CO	E M S W C G	A E G I L P O	C E G Hc H I M RI R Re S O	★★★
CMA www.cmarch.com	👥	TX	E M S W C G	A E G I L P O	C E G Hc H I M RI R Re S O	★★★
CMSS Architects www.cmssarchitects.com	👥	VA	E M S W C G	A E G I L P O	C E G Hc H I M RI R Re S O	★★★
CO Architects www.coarchitects.com	👥	CA	E M S W C G	A E G I L P O	C E G Hc H I M RI R Re S O	★★★
Cohos Evamy Partners www.cohos-evamy.com	👥👥	CAN	E M S W C G	A E G I L P O	C E G Hc H I M RI R Re S O	★★★★
Colimore Thoemke Architects www.colimorethoemke.com	👤	MD	E M S W C G	A E G I L P O	C E G Hc H I M RI R Re S O	★★★
Collaborative Design Group www.collaborativedesigngroup.com	👥	MN	E M S W C G	A E G I L P O	C E G Hc H I M RI R Re S O	★★★
Collective Invention www.collectiveinvention.com	👤	CA	E M S W C G	A E G I L P O	C E G Hc H I M RI R Re S O	★★★
CollinsWoerman www.collinswoerman.com	👥	WA	E M S W C G	A E G I L P O	C E G Hc H I M RI R Re S O	★★★
Colorado Architecture Partnership www.cyberarchitects.com	👤	CO	E M S W C G	A E G I L P O	C E G Hc H I M RI R Re S O	★★★
Communication Arts (Stantec) www.commartsdesign.com	👥	CO	E M S W C G	A E G I L P O	C E G Hc H I M RI R Re S O	★★★★
Cook + Fox Architects www.cookplusfox.com	👥	NY	E M S W C G	A E G I L P O	C E G Hc H I M RI R Re S O	★★★★
Cooper Carry www.coopercarry.com	👥👥	GA	E M S W C G	A E G I L P O	C E G Hc H I M RI R Re S O	★★★★
Cooper, Robertson & Partners www.cooperrobertson.com	👥	NY	E M S W C G	A E G I L P O	C E G Hc H I M RI R Re S O	★★★★★

REGIONS: East (E), Midwest (M), South (S), West (W), Canada (C), Global (G)

SERVICES: Architecture (A), Engineering (E), Graphic Design (G), Interior Design (I),
Landscape Architecture (L), Planning/Urban Design (P), Other-including Industrial Design (O)

MARKETS: Corporate (C), Education (E), Government (G), Healthcare (Hc), Hospitality (H), Industrial (I)
Museum/Cultural (M), Religious (RI), Residential (R), Retail (Re), Sports (S), Other (O)

	Size	HQ	Regions		Services		Markets		DI Index
Corbet Cibinel Architects www.cibinel.com	👤	CAN	E M S W C G	A E G I L P O		C E G Hc H I M RI R Re S O		★★★
Corbin Design www.corbindesign.com	👤	MI	E M S W C G	A E G I L P O		C E G Hc H I M RI R Re S O		★★★★
Cordogan, Clark and Associates www.cordoganclark.com	👥	IL	E M S W C G	A E G I L P O		C E G Hc H I M RI R Re S O		★★★
CORE Architecture + Design www.coredc.com	👥	DC	E M S W C G	A E G I L P O		C E G Hc H I M RI R Re S O		★★★
Corgan Associates www.corgan.com	👥👥	TX	E M S W C G	A E G I L P O		C E G Hc H I M RI R Re S O		★★★★
Costas Kondylis Design www.kondylisdesign.com	👥	NY	E M S W C G	A E G I L P O		C E G Hc H I M RI R Re S O		★★★★
CR Architecture + Design www.colerussell.com	👥	OH	E M S W C G	A E G I L P O		C E G Hc H I M RI R Re S O		★★★
Crabtree, Rohrbaugh & Assoc. www.cra-architects.com	👥	PA	E M S W C G	A E G I L P O		C E G Hc H I M RI R Re S O		★★★
Crafton Tull Sparks www.craftontullsparks.com	👥👥	AR	E M S W C G	A E G I L P O		C E G Hc H I M RI R Re S O		★★★
Craig Gaulden Davis www.cgdarch.com	👥	SC	E M S W C G	A E G I L P O		C E G Hc H I M RI R Re S O		★★★
Crawford Archtitects www.crawfordarch.com	👤	MO	E M S W C G	A E G I L P O		C E G Hc H I M RI R Re S O		★★★
Cromwell Architects Engineers www.cromwell.com	👥👥	AR	E M S W C G	A E G I L P O		C E G Hc H I M RI R Re S O		★★★
CSA Group www.csagroup.com	👥👥👥	PR	E M S W C G	A E G I L P O		C E G Hc H I M RI R Re S O		★★★
CSO Architects www.csoinc.net	👥	IN	E M S W C G	A E G I L P O		C E G Hc H I M RI R Re S O		★★★
CTA Architects www.ctagroup.com	👥👥	MT	E M S W C G	A E G I L P O		C E G Hc H I M RI R Re S O		★★★★
Cuhaci & Peterson www.c-p.com	👥	FL	E M S W C G	A E G I L P O		C E G Hc H I M RI R Re S O		★★★
Cuningham Group Architecture www.cuningham.com	👥👥	MN	E M S W C G	A E G I L P O		C E G Hc H I M RI R Re S O		★★★★

REGIONS: East (E), Midwest (M), South (S), West (W), Canada (C), Global (G)
SERVICES: Architecture (A), Engineering (E), Graphic Design (G), Interior Design (I),
Landscape Architecture (L), Planning/Urban Design (P), Other-including Industrial Design (O)
MARKETS: Corporate (C), Education (E), Government (G), Healthcare (Hc), Hospitality (H), Industrial (I)
Museum/Cultural (M), Religious (RI), Residential (R), Retail (Re), Sports (S), Other (O)

	Size	HQ	Regions	Services	Markets	DI Index
Cunningham I Quill Architects www.cunninghamquill.com	👥👥	DC	E M S W C G	A E G I L P O	C E G Hc I M RI R Re S O	★★★
Cutler Associates www.cutlerassociatesinc.com	👥👥👥	MA	E M S W C G	A E G I L P O	C E G Hc H I M RI R Re S O	★★★
D2CA Architects www.d2ca.com	👤	PA	E M S W C G	A E G I L P O	C E G Hc H I M RI R Re S O	★★★
DAG Architects www.dagarchitects.com	👥👥	FL	E M S W C G	A E G I L P O	C E G Hc H I M RI R Re S O	★★★
Dahlin Group www.dahlingroup.com	👥👥👥	CA	E M S W C G	A E G I L P O	C E G Hc H I M RI R Re S O	★★★
Daniel P. Coffey & Associates www.dpcalto.com	👤	IL	E M S W C G	A E G I L P O	C E G Hc H I M RI R Re S O	★★★
Daniel Smith & Associates www.dsaarch.com	👤	CA	E M S W C G	A E G I L P O	C E G Hc H I M RI R Re S O	★★★
Danielian Assoicates www.danielian.com	👥👥	CA	E M S W C G	A E G I L P O	C E G Hc H I M RI R Re S O	★★★
Dattner Architects www.dattner.com	👥👥	NY	E M S W C G	A E G I L P O	C E G Hc H I M RI R Re S O	★★★
David M. Schwarz Architects www.dmsas.com	👥👥	DC	E M S W C G	A E G I L P O	C E G Hc H I M RI R Re S O	★★★★
David Oakey Designs www.davidoakeydesigns.com	👤	GA	E M S W C G	A E G I L P O	C E G Hc H I M RI R Re S O	★★★★
Davis www.thedavisexperience.com	👥👥	AZ	E M S W C G	A E G I L P O	C E G Hc H I M RI R Re S O	★★★
Davis Brody Bond Aedas www.davisbrody.com	👥👥👥	NY	E M S W C G	A E G I L P O	C E G Hc H I M RI R Re S O	★★★★
Davis Carter Scott www.dcsdesign.com	👥👥	VA	E M S W C G	A E G I L P O	C E G Hc H I M RI R Re S O	★★★
Davis Partnership Architects www.davispartner.com	👥👥	CO	E M S W C G	A E G I L P O	C E G Hc H I M RI R Re S O	★★★
Dekker/Perich/Sabatini www.dpsdesign.org	👥👥👥	NM	E M S W C G	A E G I L P O	C E G Hc H I M RI R Re S O	★★★
DES Architects + Engineers www.des-ae.com	👥👥👥	CA	E M S W C G	A E G I L P O	C E G Hc H I M RI R Re S O	★★★

REGIONS: East (E), Midwest (M), South (S), West (W), Canada (C), Global (G)

SERVICES: Architecture (A), Engineering (E), Graphic Design (G), Interior Design (I),
Landscape Architecture (L), Planning/Urban Design (P), Other-including Industrial Design (O)

MARKETS: Corporate (C), Education (E), Government (G), Healthcare (Hc), Hospitality (H), Industrial (I)
Museum/Cultural (M), Religious (RI), Residential (R), Retail (Re), Sports (S), Other (O)

	Size	HQ	Regions	Services	Markets	DI Index
Design Alliance Architects, The www.tda-architects.com		PA	E M S W C G	A E G I L P O	C E G Hc H I M Rl R Re S O	★★★
Design Collective www.designcollective.com		MD	E M S W C G	A E G I L P O	C E G Hc H I M Rl R Re S O	★★★
Design Partners www.designpartnersinc.com		HI	E M S W C G	A E G I L P O	C E G Hc H I M Rl R Re S O	★★★
Design Partnership of Cambridge www.design-partnership.com		MA	E M S W C G	A E G I L P O	C E G Hc H I M Rl R Re S O	★★★
Design Workshop www.designworkshop.com		CO	E M S W C G	A E G I L P O	C E G Hc H I M Rl R Re S O	★★★★★
DesignGroup www.dgcolumbus.com		OH	E M S W C G	A E G I L P O	C E G Hc H I M Rl R Re S O	★★★
DeStefano Partners www.dpdesigns.com		IL	E M S W C G	A E G I L P O	C E G Hc H I M Rl R Re S O	★★★★
Development Design Group www.ddg-usa.com		MD	E M S W C G	A E G I L P O	C E G Hc H I M Rl R Re S O	★★★
Devenney Group Architects www.devenneygroup.com		AZ	E M S W C G	A E G I L P O	C E G Hc H I M Rl R Re S O	★★★★
Devrouax & Purnell Architects www.dp-architects.com		DC	E M S W C G	A E G I L P O	C E G Hc H I M Rl R Re S O	★★★
Diamond + Schmitt www.dsai.ca		CAN	E M S W C G	A E G I L P O	C E G Hc H I M Rl R Re S O	★★★★★
Dick & Fritsche Design Group www.dfdg.com		AZ	E M S W C G	A E G I L P O	C E G Hc H I M Rl R Re S O	★★★★
DiClemente Siegel Design www.dsdonline.com		MI	E M S W C G	A E G I L P O	C E G Hc H I M Rl R Re S O	★★★★
Diedrich www.diedrichllc.com		GA	E M S W C G	A E G I L P O	C F G Hc H I M Rl R Re S O	★★★
Diekema Hamann Architecture + Engineering www.dhae.com		MI	E M S W C G	A E G I L P O	C E G Hc H I M Rl R Re S O	★★★
DiGiorgio Associates www.dai-boston.com		MA	E M S W C G	A E G I L P O	C E G Hc H I M Rl R Re S O	★★★
DiMella Shaffer www.dimellashaffer.com		MA	E M S W C G	A E G I L P O	C E G Hc H I M Rl R Re S O	★★★

REGIONS: East (E), Midwest (M), South (S), West (W), Canada (C), Global (G)

SERVICES: Architecture (A), Engineering (E), Graphic Design (G), Interior Design (I), Landscape Architecture (L), Planning/Urban Design (P), Other-including Industrial Design (O)

MARKETS: Corporate (C), Education (E), Government (G), Healthcare (Hc), Hospitality (H), Industrial (I) Museum/Cultural (M), Religious (Rl), Residential (R), Retail (Re), Sports (S), Other (O)

Phoenix College, Phoenix, AZ | DLR Group

Los Angeles Southwest College, Los Angeles, CA | DLR Group

	Size	HQ	Regions	Services	Markets	DI Index
Dinmore and Cisco Architects www.konaarchitects.com	👤	HI	E M S W C G	A E G I L P O	C E G Hc H I M RI R Re S O	★★★
DLR Group www.dlrgroup.com	👥👥👥	N/A	E M S W C G	A E G I L P O	C E G Hc H I M RI R Re S O	★★★★★
DMR www.dmrarchitects.com	👤	NJ	E M S W C G	A E G I L P O	C E G Hc H I M RI R Re S O	★★★
DNK Architects www.dnkarchitects.com	👤	OH	E M S W C G	A E G I L P O	C E G Hc H I M RI R Re S O	★★★
Domenech Hicks & Krockmalnic Architects www.dhkinc.com	👤	MA	E M S W C G	A E G I L P O	C E G Hc H I M RI R Re S O	★★★
Dominy + Associates Architects www.domusstudio.com	👤	CA	E M S W C G	A E G I L P O	C E G Hc H I M RI R Re S O	★★★
Domokur Architects www.domokur.com	👤	OH	E M S W C G	A E G I L P O	C E G Hc H I M RI R Re S O	★★★
Dorsky Hodgson Parrish Yue Architects www.dorskyhodgson.com	👥	OH	E M S W C G	A E G I L P O	C E G Hc H I M RI R Re S O	★★★★★
Dougherty + Dougherty Architects www.ddarchitecture.com	👥	CA	E M S W C G	A E G I L P O	C E G Hc H I M RI R Re S O	★★★
Douglas Cardinal Architect www.djcarchitect.com	👤	CAN	E M S W C G	A E G I L P O	C E G Hc H I M RI R Re S O	★★★★★
Dowler-Gruman Architects www.dga-mv.com	👤	CA	E M S W C G	A E G I L P O	C E G Hc H I M RI R Re S O	★★★
DRS Architects www.drsarchitects.com	👥	PA	E M S W C G	A E G I L P O	C E G Hc H I M RI R Re S O	★★★
Drummey Rosane Anderson www.draarchitects.com	👥	MA	E M S W C G	A E G I L P O	C E G Hc H I M RI R Re S O	★★★
DTJ Design www.dtjdesign.com	👥	CO	E M S W C G	A E G I L P O	C E G Hc H I M RI R Re S O	★★★
Duany Plater-Zyberk & Company www.dpz.com	👥	FL	E M S W C G	A E G I L P O	C E G Hc H I M RI R Re S O	★★★★★
Dujardin Design Associates www.dujardindesign.com	👤	CT	E M S W C G	A E G I L P O	C E G Hc H I M RI R Re S O	★★★★
Dull Olson Weekes Architects www.dowa.com	👥	OR	E M S W C G	A E G I L P O	C E G Hc H I M RI R Re S O	★★★

REGIONS: East (E), Midwest (M), South (S), West (W), Canada (C), Global (G)

SERVICES: Architecture (A), Engineering (E), Graphic Design (G), Interior Design (I), Landscape Architecture (L), Planning/Urban Design (P), Other-including Industrial Design (O)

MARKETS: Corporate (C), Education (E), Government (G), Healthcare (Hc), Hospitality (H), Industrial (I), Museum/Cultural (M), Religious (RI), Residential (R), Retail (Re), Sports (S), Other (O)

	Size	HQ	Regions	Services	Markets	DI Index
Durrant www.durrant.com	👤👤👤	IA	E M S W C G	A E G I L P O	C E G Hc H I M RI R Re S O	★★★
DWL Architects + Planners www.dwlarchitects.com	👤👤	AZ	E M S W C G	A E G I L P O	C E G Hc H I M RI R Re S O	★★★
Dykeman Architects www.dykeman.net	👤👤	WA	E M S W C G	A E G I L P O	C E G Hc H I M RI R Re S O	★★★
Eckert Wordell www.eckert-wordell.com	👤👤	MI	E M S W C G	A E G I L P O	C E G Hc H I M RI R Re S O	★★★
Edge & Tinney Architects www.edge-tinney.com	👤	OH	E M S W C G	A E G I L P O	C E G Hc H I M RI R Re S O	★★★
EDI Architecture www.ediarchitecture.com	👤👤👤	TX	E M S W C G	A E G I L P O	C E G Hc H I M RI R Re S O	★★★
EDSA www.edsaplan.com	👤👤👤	FL	E M S W C G	A E G I L P O	C E G Hc H I M RI R Re S O	★★★★★
Edwards + Hotchkiss Architects www.eandharch.com	👤	TN	E M S W C G	A E G I L P O	C E G Hc H I M RI R Re S O	★★★
EHDD www.ehdd.com	👤👤	CA	E M S W C G	A E G I L P O	C E G Hc H I M RI R Re S O	★★★
Ehrenkrantz Eckstut & Kuhn Architects www.eekarchitects.com	👤👤	NY	E M S W C G	A E G I L P O	C E G Hc H I M RI R Re S O	★★★★
Eight, Inc. www.eightinc.com	👤👤👤	CA	E M S W C G	A E G I L P O	C E G Hc H I M RI R Re S O	★★★
Eisenman Architects www.eisenmanarchitects.com	👤👤	NY	E M S W C G	A E G I L P O	C E G Hc H I M RI R Re S O	★★★★★
Elkus Manfredi Architects www.elkus-manfredi.com	👤👤👤	MA	E M S W C G	A E G I L P O	C E G Hc H I M RI R Re S O	★★★
Ellenzweig www.ellenzweig.com	👤👤	MA	E M S W C G	A E G I L P O	C E G Hc H I M RI R Re S O	★★★
Elness Swenson Graham Archts. www.esgarch.com	👤👤	MN	E M S W C G	A E G I L P O	C E G Hc H I M RI R Re S O	★★★★
Emc2 GROUP Architects www.emc2architects.com	👤	AZ	E M S W C G	A E G I L P O	C E G Hc H I M RI R Re S O	★★★
Engberg Anderson www.engberganderson.com	👤👤	WI	E M S W C G	A E G I L P O	C E G Hc H I M RI R Re S O	★★★

REGIONS: East (E), Midwest (M), South (S), West (W), Canada (C), Global (G)

SERVICES: Architecture (A), Engineering (E), Graphic Design (G), Interior Design (I),
Landscape Architecture (L), Planning/Urban Design (P), Other-including Industrial Design (O)

MARKETS: Corporate (C), Education (E), Government (G), Healthcare (Hc), Hospitality (H), Industrial (I)
Museum/Cultural (M), Religious (RI), Residential (R), Retail (Re), Sports (S), Other (O)

	Size	HQ	Regions	Services	Markets	DI Index
Engstrom Design Group www.engstromdesign.com	👥	CA	E M S W C G	A E G I L P O	C E G Hc H I M RI R Re S O	★★★
Ennead Architects www.ennead.com	👥	NY	E M S W C G	A E G I L P O	C E G Hc H I M RI R Re S O	★★★★
ENTOS Design www.entosdesign.com	👤	TX	E M S W C G	A E G I L P O	C E G Hc H I M RI R Re S O	★★★
Environetics www.environetics.com	👥	CA	E M S W C G	A E G I L P O	C E G Hc H I M RI R Re S O	★★★
Envision Design www.envisionsite.com	👤	DC	E M S W C G	A E G I L P O	C E G Hc H I M RI R Re S O	★★★★
Eppstein Uhen Architects www.eua.com	👥	WI	E M S W C G	A E G I L P O	C E G Hc H I M RI R Re S O	★★★
Epstein www.epsteinglobal.com	👥	IL	E M S W C G	A E G I L P O	C E G Hc H I M RI R Re S O	★★★★
Eskew + Dumez + Ripple www.eskewdumezripple.com	👥	LA	E M S W C G	A E G I L P O	C E G Hc H I M RI R Re S O	★★★★
ESP Associates www.espassociates.com	👥	NC	E M S W C G	A E G I L P O	C E G Hc H I M RI R Re S O	★★★
Evans Group, The www.theevansgroup.com	👥	FL	E M S W C G	A E G I L P O	C E G Hc H I M RI R Re S O	★★★
EwingCole www.ewingcole.com	👥	PA	E M S W C G	A E G I L P O	C E G Hc H I M RI R Re S O	★★★★
EYP Architecture & Engineering www.eypaedesign.com	👥	NY	E M S W C G	A E G I L P O	C E G Hc H I M RI R Re S O	★★★★
Facility Design Group www.facilitygroup.com	👥	GA	E M S W C G	A E G I L P O	C E G Hc H I M RI R Re S O	★★★
Fanning/Howey Associates www.fhai.com	👥	OH	E M S W C G	A E G I L P O	C E G Hc H I M RI R Re S O	★★★★
Fathom www.gofathom.com	👤	PA	E M S W C G	A E G I L P O	C E G Hc H I M RI R Re S O	★★★
Fentress Architects www.fentressarchitects.com	👥	CO	E M S W C G	A E G I L P O	C E G Hc H I M RI R Re S O	★★★★★
Fergus Garber Group www.fgg-arch.com	👤	CA	E M S W C G	A E G I L P O	C E G Hc H I M RI R Re S O	★★★

REGIONS: East (E), Midwest (M), South (S), West (W), Canada (C), Global (G)

SERVICES: Architecture (A), Engineering (E), Graphic Design (G), Interior Design (I),
Landscape Architecture (L), Planning/Urban Design (P), Other-including Industrial Design (O)

MARKETS: Corporate (C), Education (E), Government (G), Healthcare (Hc), Hospitality (H), Industrial (I)
Museum/Cultural (M), Religious (RI), Residential (R), Retail (Re), Sports (S), Other (O)

	Size	HQ	Regions		Services		Markets		DI Index
Ferguson & Shamamian Architects www.fergusonshamamian.com	👥	NY	E M S W C G	A E G I L P O	C E G Hc H I M RI R Re S O				★★★
Ferguson Pape Baldwin Architects www.mbarch.com	👥	CA	E M S W C G	A E G I L P O	C E G Hc H I M RI R Re S O				★★★
Ferraro Choi and Associates www.ferrarochoi.com	👤	HI	E M S W C G	A E G I L P O	C E G Hc H I M RI R Re S O				★★★
FGM Architects www.fgmarchitects.com	👥	IL	E M S W C G	A E G I L P O	C E G Hc H I M RI R Re S O				★★★
Field Paoli Architects www.fieldpaoli.com	👥	CA	E M S W C G	A E G I L P O	C E G Hc H I M RI R Re S O				★★★
Finegold Alexander + Associates www.faainc.com	👥	MA	E M S W C G	A E G I L P O	C E G Hc H I M RI R Re S O				★★★
FitzGerald Associates Architects www.fitzgeraldassociates.net	👥	IL	E M S W C G	A E G I L P O	C E G Hc H I M RI R Re S O				★★★
FKP Architects www.fkp.com	👥👥	TX	E M S W C G	A E G I L P O	C E G Hc H I M RI R Re S O				★★★★
Flad Architects www.flad.com	👥👥	WI	E M S W C G	A E G I L P O	C E G Hc H I M RI R Re S O				★★★★
Flansburgh Architects www.faiarchitects.com	👥	MA	E M S W C G	A E G I L P O	C E G Hc H I M RI R Re S O				★★★
Fletcher Farr Ayotte www.ffadesign.com	👥	OR	E M S W C G	A E G I L P O	C E G Hc H I M RI R Re S O				★★★
Fletcher Thompson www.fletcherthompson.com	👥👥	CT	E M S W C G	A E G I L P O	C E G Hc H I M RI R Re S O				★★★
Flewelling & Moody www.flewelling-moody.com	👥	CA	E M S W C G	A E G I L P O	C E G Hc H I M RI R Re S O				★★★
Ford Powell & Carson www.fpcarch.com	👥	TX	E M S W C G	A E G I L P O	C E G Hc H I M RI R Re S O				★★★★
Foreman Architects Engineers www.foremangroup.com	👥	PA	E M S W C G	A E G I L P O	C E G Hc H I M RI R Re S O				★★★
Forum Architecture & Interior Design www.forumarchitecture.com	👤	FL	E M S W C G	A E G I L P O	C E G Hc H I M RI R Re S O				★★★
Forum Studio www.forumstudio.com	👥	MO	E M S W C G	A E G I L P O	C E G Hc H I M RI R Re S O				★★★★

REGIONS: East (E), Midwest (M), South (S), West (W), Canada (C), Global (G)

SERVICES: Architecture (A), Engineering (E), Graphic Design (G), Interior Design (I),
Landscape Architecture (L), Planning/Urban Design (P), Other-including Industrial Design (O)

MARKETS: Corporate (C), Education (E), Government (G), Healthcare (Hc), Hospitality (H), Industrial (I)
Museum/Cultural (M), Religious (RI), Residential (R), Retail (Re), Sports (S), Other (O)

	Size	HQ	Regions	Services	Markets	DI Index
Foss Architecture & Interiors www.fossarch.com		ND	E M S W C G	A E G I L P O	C E G Hc H I M RI R Re S O	★★★
Fox Architects www.fox-architects.com		VA	E M S W C G	A E G I L P O	C E G Hc H I M RI R Re S O	★★★★
Francis Cauffman www.franciscauffman.com		NY	E M S W C G	A E G I L P O	C E G Hc H I M RI R Re S O	★★★★
Frankel + Coleman (312) 697-1620		IL	E M S W C G	A E G I L P O	C E G Hc H I M RI R Re S O	★★★★★
Franklin Associates Architects www.franklinarch.com		TN	E M S W C G	A E G I L P O	C E G Hc H I M RI R Re S O	★★★
FRCH Design Worldwide www.frch.com		OH	E M S W C G	A E G I L P O	C E G Hc H I M RI R Re S O	★★★★★
Freelon Group, The www.freelon.com		NC	E M S W C G	A E G I L P O	C E G Hc H I M RI R Re S O	★★★★
FreemanWhite www.freemanwhite.com		NC	E M S W C G	A E G I L P O	C E G Hc H I M RI R Re S O	★★★★
Freiheit & Ho Architects www.fhoarch.com		WA	E M S W C G	A E G I L P O	C E G Hc H I M RI R Re S O	★★★
French + Ryan www.frenchryan.com		DE	E M S W C G	A E G I L P O	C E G Hc H I M RI R Re S O	★★★
French Associates www.frenchaia.com		MI	E M S W C G	A E G I L P O	C E G Hc H I M RI R Re S O	★★★
Friedmutter Group www.friedmuttergroup.com		NV	E M S W C G	A E G I L P O	C E G Hc H I M RI R Re S O	★★★
Fugleberg Koch www.fuglebergkoch.com		FL	E M S W C G	A E G I L P O	C E G Hc H I M RI R Re S O	★★★
FXFOWLE Architects www.fxfowle.com		NY	E M S W C G	A E G I L P O	C E G Hc H I M RI R Re S O	★★★★★
G **Gantt Huberman Architects** www.gantthuberman.com		NC	E M S W C G	A E G I L P O	C E G Hc H I M RI R Re S O	★★★★
Garcia Stromberg www.garciastromberg.com		FL	E M S W C G	A E G I L P O	C E G Hc H I M RI R Re S O	★★★
Gaudreau www.gaudreauinc.com		MD	E M S W C G	A E G I L P O	C E G Hc H I M RI R Re S O	★★★

REGIONS: East (E), Midwest (M), South (S), West (W), Canada (C), Global (G)

SERVICES: Architecture (A), Engineering (E), Graphic Design (G), Interior Design (I), Landscape Architecture (L), Planning/Urban Design (P), Other-including Industrial Design (O)

MARKETS: Corporate (C), Education (E), Government (G), Healthcare (Hc), Hospitality (H), Industrial (I), Museum/Cultural (M), Religious (RI), Residential (R), Retail (Re), Sports (S), Other (O)

David Joseph

Warburg Pincus, New York, NY | Gensler

	Size	HQ	Regions	Services	Markets	DI Index
Gauthier, Alvarado & Associates www.gaa-ae.com	👥	VA	E M S W C G	A E G I L P O	C E G Hc H I M RI R Re S O	★★★
GBBN Architects www.gbbn.com	👥	OH	E M S W C G	A E G I L P O	C E G Hc H I M RI R Re S O	★★★★
GBD Architects www.gbdarchitects.com	👥	OR	E M S W C G	A E G I L P O	C E G Hc H I M RI R Re S O	★★★
Gehry Partners www.foga.com	👥	CA	E M S W C G	A E G I L P O	C E G Hc H I M RI R Re S O	★★★★★
Gensler www.gensler.com	👥👥	CA	E M S W C G	A E G I L P O	C E G Hc H I M RI R Re S O	★★★★★
GGLO www.gglo.com	👥	WA	E M S W C G	A E G I L P O	C E G Hc H I M RI R Re S O	★★★
GH2 Architects www.gh2architects.com	👤	OK	E M S W C G	A E G I L P O	C E G Hc H I M RI R Re S O	★★★
GHAFARI www.ghafari.com	👥	MI	E M S W C G	A E G I L P O	C E G Hc H I M RI R Re S O	★★★★★
Gibbs Gage Architects www.gibbspage.com	👥	CAN	E M S W C G	A E G I L P O	C E G Hc H I M RI R Re S O	★★★★
Giffin Bolte Jurgens www.gbjarch.com	👤	OR	E M S W C G	A E G I L P O	C E G Hc H I M RI R Re S O	★★★
Gilbert, Van H., Architect www.vhgarchitect.com	👥	NM	E M S W C G	A E G I L P O	C E G Hc H I M RI R Re S O	★★★
Gilmore Group www.gilmoregroup.com	👤	NY	E M S W C G	A E G I L P O	C E G Hc H I M RI R Re S O	★★★
gkkworks www.gkkworks.com	👥	CA	E M S W C G	A E G I L P O	C E G Hc H I M RI R Re S O	★★★★
Glidden Spina & Partners www.gsp-architects.com	👤	FL	E M S W C G	A E G I L P O	C E G Hc H I M RI R Re S O	★★★
Godsey Associates www.godseyassociates.com	👤	KY	E M S W C G	A E G I L P O	C E G Hc H I M RI R Re S O	★★★
Goettsch Partners www.gpchicago.com	👥	IL	E M S W C G	A E G I L P O	C E G Hc H I M RI R Re S O	★★★★★
Good Fulton & Farrell www.gff.com	👥	TX	E M S W C G	A E G I L P O	C E G Hc H I M RI R Re S O	★★★★

REGIONS: East (E), Midwest (M), South (S), West (W), Canada (C), Global (G)

SERVICES: Architecture (A), Engineering (E), Graphic Design (G), Interior Design (I),
Landscape Architecture (L), Planning/Urban Design (P), Other-including Industrial Design (O)

MARKETS: Corporate (C), Education (E), Government (G), Healthcare (Hc), Hospitality (H), Industrial (I)
Museum/Cultural (M), Religious (RI), Residential (R), Retail (Re), Sports (S), Other (O)

	Size	HQ	Regions	Services	Markets	DI Index
Goodwyn, Mills & Cawood www.gmcnetwork.com	👤👤👤	AL	E M S W C G	A E G I L P O	C E G Hc H I M RI R Re S O	★★★★
Goody Clancy www.goodyclancy.com	👤👤👤	MA	E M S W C G	A E G I L P O	C E G Hc H I M RI R Re S O	★★★★
Goshow Architects www.goshow.com	👤👤	NY	E M S W C G	A E G I L P O	C E G Hc H I M RI R Re S O	★★★
Gould Evans www.gouldevans.com	👤👤👤	MO	E M S W C G	A E G I L P O	C E G Hc H I M RI R Re S O	★★★★
Grant & Sinclair Architects www.grantandsinclair.com	👤👤	CAN	E M S W C G	A E G I L P O	C E G Hc H I M RI R Re S O	★★★★
GREC Architects www.grecstudio.com	👤	IL	E M S W C G	A E G I L P O	C E G Hc H I M RI R Re S O	★★★
GreenbergFarrow www.greenbergfarrow.com	👤👤👤	GA	E M S W C G	A E G I L P O	C E G Hc H I M RI R Re S O	★★★★
Gresham, Smith and Partners www.gspnet.com	👤👤👤👤	TN	E M S W C G	A E G I L P O	C E G Hc H I M RI R Re S O	★★★★★
Griffiths Rankin Cook Architects www.grcarchitects.com	👤	CAN	E M S W C G	A E G I L P O	C E G Hc H I M RI R Re S O	★★★
Grimm + Parker Architects www.grimmandparker.com	👤👤	MD	E M S W C G	A E G I L P O	C E G Hc H I M RI R Re S O	★★★
Gromatzky Dupree & Associates www.gdainet.com	👤👤	TX	E M S W C G	A E G I L P O	C E G Hc H I M RI R Re S O	★★★
Group 70 International www.group70int.com	👤👤	HI	E M S W C G	A E G I L P O	C E G Hc H I M RI R Re S O	★★★
Group Mackenzie www.groupmackenzie.com	👤👤	OR	E M S W C G	A E G I L P O	C E G Hc H I M RI R Re S O	★★★
Groupe Cardinal Hardy www.cardinal-hardy.ca	👤	CAN	E M S W C G	A E G I L P O	C E G Hc H I M RI R Re S O	★★★
Gruen Associates www.gruenassociates.com	👤👤	CA	E M S W C G	A E G I L P O	C E G Hc H I M RI R Re S O	★★★★
Gruzen Samton www.gruzensamton.com	👤👤	NY	E M S W C G	A E G I L P O	C E G Hc H I M RI R Re S O	★★★
GSR Andrade Architects www.gsr-andrade.com	👤	TX	E M S W C G	A E G I L P O	C E G Hc H I M RI R Re S O	★★★

REGIONS: East (E), Midwest (M), South (S), West (W), Canada (C), Global (G)

SERVICES: Architecture (A), Engineering (E), Graphic Design (G), Interior Design (I), Landscape Architecture (L), Planning/Urban Design (P), Other-including Industrial Design (O)

MARKETS: Corporate (C), Education (E), Government (G), Healthcare (Hc), Hospitality (H), Industrial (I) Museum/Cultural (M), Religious (RI), Residential (R), Retail (Re), Sports (S), Other (O)

	Size	HQ	Regions	Services	Markets	DI Index
GUND Partnership www.gundpartnership.com	👥	MA	E M S W C G	A E G I L P O	C E G Hc H I M RI R Re S O	★★★★
Gwathmey Siegel & Associates Architects www.gwathmey-siegel.com	👥	NY	E M S W C G	A E G I L P O	C E G Hc H I M RI R Re S O	★★★★★
GWWO www.gwwoinc.com	👥	MD	E M S W C G	A E G I L P O	C E G Hc H I M RI R Re S O	★★★
GYA Architects www.gyaarchitects.com	👤	PA	E M S W C G	A E G I L P O	C E G Hc H I M RI R Re S O	★★★
H+L Architecture www.hlarch.com	👥	CO	E M S W C G	A E G I L P O	C E G Hc H I M RI R Re S O	★★★
H2L2 www.h2l2.com	👥	PA	E M S W C G	A E G I L P O	C E G Hc H I M RI R Re S O	★★★
H3 Hardy Collaboration Archt. www.h3hc.com	👥	NY	E M S W C G	A E G I L P O	C E G Hc H I M RI R Re S O	★★★★
Hamilton Anderson Associates www.hamilton-anderson.com	👥	MI	E M S W C G	A E G I L P O	C E G Hc H I M RI R Re S O	★★★
Hanbury Evans Wright Vlattas + Company www.hewv.com	👥	VA	E M S W C G	A E G I L P O	C E G Hc H I M RI R Re S O	★★★★★
Handel Architects www.handelarchitects.com	👥	NY	E M S W C G	A E G I L P O	C E G Hc H I M RI R Re S O	★★★
Hardison Komatsu Ivelich & Tucker www.hkit.com	👥	CA	E M S W C G	A E G I L P O	C E G Hc H I M RI R Re S O	★★★
Hardy McCullah/MLM Architects www.hmmlmarchitects.com	👤	TX	E M S W C G	A E G I L P O	C E G Hc H I M RI R Re S O	★★★
Hargreaves Associates www.hargreaves.com	👥	CA	E M S W C G	A E G I L P O	C E G Hc H I M RI R Re S O	★★★★★
Harley Ellis Devereaux www.harleyellisdevereaux.com	👥	MI	E M S W C G	A E G I L P O	C E G Hc H I M RI R Re S O	★★★★
Hart I Howerton www.harthowerton.com	👥	NY	E M S W C G	A E G I L P O	C E G Hc H I M RI R Re S O	★★★★
Hart Freeland Roberts www.hfrdesign.com	👥	TN	E M S W C G	A E G I L P O	C E G Hc H I M RI R Re S O	★★★
Hartman Design Group www.hartmandesigngroup.com	👤	MD	E M S W C G	A E G I L P O	C E G Hc H I M RI R Re S O	★★★

REGIONS:　East (E), Midwest (M), South (S), West (W), Canada (C), Global (G)

SERVICES:　Architecture (A), Engineering (E), Graphic Design (G), Interior Design (I), Landscape Architecture (L), Planning/Urban Design (P), Other-including Industrial Design (O)

MARKETS:　Corporate (C), Education (E), Government (G), Healthcare (Hc), Hospitality (H), Industrial (I), Museum/Cultural (M), Religious (RI), Residential (R), Retail (Re), Sports (S), Other (O)

HDR Architecture, Inc.; © 2010 Farshid Assassi

Bellevue Medical Center, Bellevue, NE | HDR Architecture, Inc.

	Size	HQ	Regions	Services	Markets	DI Index
Harvard Jolly Architecture www.harvardjolly.com	👤👤👤	FL	E M S W C G	A E G I L P O	C E G Hc H I M Rl R Re S O	★★★
Hasenstab Architects www.hainc.cc	👤👤	OH	E M S W C G	A E G I L P O	C E G Hc H I M Rl R Re S O	★★★
Hastings & Chivetta Architects www.hastingschivetta.com	👤👤	MO	E M S W C G	A E G I L P O	C E G Hc H I M Rl R Re S O	★★★★
Hawley Peterson & Snyder www.hpsarch.com	👤👤	CA	E M S W C G	A E G I L P O	C E G Hc H I M Rl R Re S O	★★★
Hayes Architecture/Interiors www.hayesstudio.com	👤	AZ	E M S W C G	A E G I L P O	C E G Hc H I M Rl R Re S O	★★★
HBE www.hbecorp.com	👤👤👤	MO	E M S W C G	A E G I L P O	C E G Hc H I M Rl R Re S O	★★★
HBT Architects www.hbtarchitects.com	👤	NY	E M S W C G	A E G I L P O	C E G Hc H I M Rl R Re S O	★★★
HDA Architects www.hd-architects.com	👤	AZ	E M S W C G	A E G I L P O	C E G Hc H I M Rl R Re S O	★★★
HDR Architecture, Inc. www.hdrarchitecture.com	👤👤👤👤	NE	E M S W C G	A E G I L P O	C E G Hc H I M Rl R Re S O	★★★★★
Heery International www.heery.com	👤👤👤	GA	E M S W C G	A E G I L P O	C E G Hc H I M Rl R Re S O	★★★★
Helix Architecture + Design www.helixkc.com	👤👤	MO	E M S W C G	A E G I L P O	C E G Hc H I M Rl R Re S O	★★★
Heller and Metzger www.hellerandmetzger.com	👤	DC	E M S W C G	A E G I L P O	C E G Hc H I M Rl R Re S O	★★★
Heller Manus Architects www.hellermanus.com	👤	CA	E M S W C G	A E G I L P O	C E G Hc H I M Rl R Re S O	★★★
Helman Hurley Charvat Peacock/ Architects www.hhcp.com	👤👤	FL	E M S W C G	A E G I L P O	C E G Hc H I M Rl R Re S O	★★★
Helpern Architects www.helpern.com	👤	NY	E M S W C G	A E G I L P O	C E G Hc H I M Rl R Re S O	★★★
Herbert I Lewis I Kruse I Blunck Architecture www.hlkb.com	👤👤	IA	E M S W C G	A E G I L P O	C E G Hc H I M Rl R Re S O	★★★
Herman Gibans Fodor www.hgfarchitects.com	👤	OH	E M S W C G	A E G I L P O	C E G Hc H I M Rl R Re S O	★★★

REGIONS: East (E), Midwest (M), South (S), West (W), Canada (C), Global (G)

SERVICES: Architecture (A), Engineering (E), Graphic Design (G), Interior Design (I), Landscape Architecture (L), Planning/Urban Design (P), Other-including Industrial Design (O)

MARKETS: Corporate (C), Education (E), Government (G), Healthcare (Hc), Hospitality (H), Industrial (I) Museum/Cultural (M), Religious (Rl), Residential (R), Retail (Re), Sports (S), Other (O)

	Size	HQ	Regions	Services	Markets	DI Index
Hermes Architects www.hermesarchitects.com		TX	E M S W C G	A E G I L P O	C E G Hc H I M Rl R Re S O	★★★
HGA Architects and Engineers www.hga.com		MN	E M S W C G	A E G I L P O	C E G Hc H I M Rl R Re S O	★★★★★
HH Architects www.hharchitects.com		TX	E M S W C G	A E G I L P O	C E G Hc H I M Rl R Re S O	★★★
Hickok Cole Architects www.hickokcole.com		DC	E M S W C G	A E G I L P O	C E G Hc H I M Rl R Re S O	★★★
Highland Associates www.highlandassociates.com		PA	E M S W C G	A E G I L P O	C E G Hc H I M Rl R Re S O	★★★
Hixson www.hixson-inc.com		OH	E M S W C G	A E G I L P O	C E G Hc H I M Rl R Re S O	★★★
HKS, Inc. www.hksinc.com		N/A	E M S W C G	A E G I L P O	C E G Hc H I M Rl R Re S O	★★★★★
HLW International www.hlw.com		NY	E M S W C G	A E G I L P O	C E G Hc H I M Rl R Re S O	★★★★
HMC Architects www.hmcarchitects.com		CA	E M S W C G	A E G I L P O	C E G Hc H I M Rl R Re S O	★★★★★
HMFH Architects www.hmfh.com		MA	E M S W C G	A E G I L P O	C E G Hc H I M Rl R Re S O	★★★
Hnedak Bobo Group www.hbginc.com		TN	E M S W C G	A E G I L P O	C E G Hc H I M Rl R Re S O	★★★
HNTB (Architecture) www.hntb.com		MO	E M S W C G	A E G I L P O	C E G Hc H I M Rl R Re S O	★★★★
Hobbs+Black Architects www.hobbs-black.com		MI	E M S W C G	A E G I L P O	C E G Hc H I M Rl R Re S O	★★★
Hodges & Associates Architects www.hodgesusa.com		TX	E M S W C G	A E G I L P O	C E G Hc H I M Rl R Re S O	★★★
Hoerr Schaudt Landscape Archts. www.hoerrschaudt.com		IL	E M S W C G	A E G I L P O	C E G Hc H I M Rl R Re S O	★★★
HOK www.hok.com		MO	E M S W C G	A E G I L P O	C E G Hc H I M Rl R Re S O	★★★★★
Holabird & Root www.holabird.com		IL	E M S W C G	A E G I L P O	C E G Hc H I M Rl R Re S O	★★★★

REGIONS: East (E), Midwest (M), South (S), West (W), Canada (C), Global (G)

SERVICES: Architecture (A), Engineering (E), Graphic Design (G), Interior Design (I), Landscape Architecture (L), Planning/Urban Design (P), Other-including Industrial Design (O)

MARKETS: Corporate (C), Education (E), Government (G), Healthcare (Hc), Hospitality (H), Industrial (I), Museum/Cultural (M), Religious (Rl), Residential (R), Retail (Re), Sports (S), Other (O)

	Size	HQ	Regions		Services		Markets		DI Index
Holleran Duitsman Architects www.hdai.com	👤	MO	E M S W C G	A E G I L P O		C E G Hc H I M RI R Re S O		★★★
Hollis + Miller www.hollisandmiller.com	👥	KS	E M S W C G	A E G I L P O		C E G Hc H I M RI R Re S O		★★★
Holzman Moss Bottino Archt. www.holzmanmoss.com	👥	NY	E M S W C G	A E G I L P O		C E G Hc H I M RI R Re S O		★★★★
Hord Coplan Macht www.hcm2.com	👥	MD	E M S W C G	A E G I L P O		C E G Hc H I M RI R Re S O		★★★
Hornberger + Worstell www.hornbergerworstell.com	👥	CA	E M S W C G	A E G I L P O		C E G Hc H I M RI R Re S O		★★★
Horty Elving & Associates www.hortyelving.com	👥	MN	E M S W C G	A E G I L P O		C E G Hc H I M RI R Re S O		★★★
Humphreys & Partners Archts. www.humphreys.com	👥👥	TX	E M S W C G	A E G I L P O		C E G Hc H I M RI R Re S O		★★★
Humphries Poli Architects www.hparch.com	👥	CO	E M S W C G	A E G I L P O		C E G Hc H I M RI R Re S O		★★★
Hunton Brady Architects www.huntonbrady.com	👤	FL	E M S W C G	A E G I L P O		C E G Hc H I M RI R Re S O		★★★
Huntsman Architectural Group www.huntsmanag.com	👥	NY	E M S W C G	A E G I L P O		C E G Hc H I M RI R Re S O		★★★
Hutker Architects www.hutkerarchitects.com	👥	MA	E M S W C G	A E G I L P O		C E G Hc H I M RI R Re S O		★★★
HWH Architects Engineers Planners www.hwhaep.com	👤	OH	E M S W C G	A E G I L P O		C E G Hc H I M RI R Re S O		★★★
IA Interior Architects www.interiorarchitects.com	👥👥	CA	E M S W C G	A E G I L P O		C E G Hc H I M RI R Re S O		★★★★
IBI Group www.ibigroup.com	👥👥	CAN	E M S W C G	A E G I L P O		C E G Hc H I M RI R Re S O		★★★
ICON Architecture www.iconarch.com	👥	MA	E M S W C G	A E G I L P O		C E G Hc H I M RI R Re S O		★★★
IDC Architects (a division of CH2M Hill) www.idcarchitects.com	👥	OR	E M S W C G	A E G I L P O		C E G Hc H I M RI R Re S O		★★★
IKM www.ikminc.com	👤	PA	E M S W C G	A E G I L P O		C E G Hc H I M RI R Re S O		★★★

REGIONS: East (E), Midwest (M), South (S), West (W), Canada (C), Global (G)

SERVICES: Architecture (A), Engineering (E), Graphic Design (G), Interior Design (I), Landscape Architecture (L), Planning/Urban Design (P), Other-including Industrial Design (O)

MARKETS: Corporate (C), Education (E), Government (G), Healthcare (Hc), Hospitality (H), Industrial (I), Museum/Cultural (M), Religious (RI), Residential (R), Retail (Re), Sports (S), Other (O)

	Size	HQ	Regions		Services		Markets		DI Index
Indovina Associates Architects www.indovina.net	👤	PA	E M S W C G		A E G I L P O		C E G Hc H I M RI R Re S O		★★★
Integrated Design Solutions www.ids-troy.com	👤👤👤	MI	E M S W C G		A E G I L P O		C E G Hc H I M RI R Re S O		★★★
Interplan www.interplanorlando.com	👤👤👤	FL	E M S W C G		A E G I L P O		C E G Hc H I M RI R Re S O		★★★
IR2 Interior Resource www.ir2.com	👤	CA	E M S W C G		A E G I L P O		C E G Hc H I M RI R Re S O		★★★
Ittner Architects www.ittnerarchitects.com	👤	MO	E M S W C G		A E G I L P O		C E G Hc H I M RI R Re S O		★★★
Jackson & Ryan Architects www.jacksonryan.com	👤	TX	E M S W C G		A E G I L P O		C E G Hc H I M RI R Re S O		★★★
Janson Goldstein www.jansongoldstein.com	👤	NY	E M S W C G		A E G I L P O		C E G Hc H I M RI R Re S O		★★★
JBHM Architects www.jbhm.com	👤👤	MS	E M S W C G		A E G I L P O		C E G Hc H I M RI R Re S O		★★★
JCJ Architecture www.jcj.com	👤👤👤	CT	E M S W C G		A E G I L P O		C E G Hc H I M RI R Re S O		★★★★
Jerde Partnership, The www.jerde.com	👤👤	CA	E M S W C G		A E G I L P O		C E G Hc H I M RI R Re S O		★★★★★
JG Johnson Architects www.jgjohnson.com	👤	CO	E M S W C G		A E G I L P O		C E G Hc H I M RI R Re S O		★★★
JHP Architecture/Urban Design www.jhparch.com	👤👤	TX	E M S W C G		A E G I L P O		C E G Hc H I M RI R Re S O		★★★
JKR Partners www.jkrpartners.com	👤	PA	E M S W C G		A E G I L P O		C E G Hc H I M RI R Re S O		★★★
JLG Architects www.jlgarchitects.com	👤👤	MN	E M S W C G		A E G I L P O		C E G Hc H I M RI R Re S O		★★★
JMA www.jmaarch.com	👤👤	NV	E M S W C G		A E G I L P O		C E G Hc H I M RI R Re S O		★★★
JMZ Architects and Planners www.jmzarchitects.com	👤	NY	E M S W C G		A E G I L P O		C E G Hc H I M RI R Re S O		★★★
John Ciardullo Associates www.jca-ny.com	👤	NY	E M S W C G		A E G I L P O		C E G Hc H I M RI R Re S O		★★★

REGIONS: East (E), Midwest (M), South (S), West (W), Canada (C), Global (G)

SERVICES: Architecture (A), Engineering (E), Graphic Design (G), Interior Design (I), Landscape Architecture (L), Planning/Urban Design (P), Other-including Industrial Design (O)

MARKETS: Corporate (C), Education (E), Government (G), Healthcare (Hc), Hospitality (H), Industrial (I) Museum/Cultural (M), Religious (RI), Residential (R), Retail (Re), Sports (S), Other (O)

	Size	HQ	Regions		Services		Markets		DI Index
John Poe Architects www.johnpoe.com	👤	OH	E M S W C G		A E G I L P O		C E G Hc H I M RI R Re S O		★★★
John Portman & Associates www.portmanusa.com	👥	GA	E M S W C G		A E G I L P O		C E G Hc H I M RI R Re S O		★★★★★
John Snyder Architects www.js-architects.com	👤	NY	E M S W C G		A E G I L P O		C E G Hc H I M RI R Re S O		★★★
Johnsen Schmaling Architects www.johnsenschmaling.com	👤	WI	E M S W C G		A E G I L P O		C E G Hc H I M RI R Re S O		★★★
Johnson Fain www.johnsonfain.com	👥	CA	E M S W C G		A E G I L P O		C E G Hc H I M RI R Re S O		★★★★
Joseph Wong Design Assoc. www.jwdainc.com	👥	CA	E M S W C G		A E G I L P O		C E G Hc H I M RI R Re S O		★★★
Jova/Daniels/Busby www.jova.com	👤	GA	E M S W C G		A E G I L P O		C E G Hc H I M RI R Re S O		★★★
JPC Architects www.jpc-inc.com	👤	WA	E M S W C G		A E G I L P O		C E G Hc H I M RI R Re S O		★★★
JRB Group Architects, The www.jrbgroup.com	👤	IL	E M S W C G		A E G I L P O		C E G Hc H I M RI R Re S O		★★★
JSA www.jsainc.com	👥	NH	E M S W C G		A E G I L P O		C E G Hc H I M RI R Re S O		★★★★
JSA Architecture Planning Engineering Interior Design www.jsa-architects.com	👤	PA	E M S W C G		A E G I L P O		C E G Hc H I M RI R Re S O		★★★
JZMK Partners www.jzmkpartners.com	👤	CA	E M S W C G		A E G I L P O		C E G Hc H I M RI R Re S O		★★★
K **ka** www.kainc.com	👥	OH	E M S W C G		A E G I L P O		C E G Hc H I M RI R Re S O		★★★
Kahler Slater www.kahlerslater.com	👥👤	WI	E M S W C G		A E G I L P O		C E G Hc H I M RI R Re S O		★★★★★
KAI Design & Build www.kai-db.com	👥	MO	E M S W C G		A E G I L P O		C E G Hc H I M RI R Re S O		★★★
Kallmann McKinnell & Wood Architects www.kmwarch.com	👥	MA	E M S W C G		A E G I L P O		C E G Hc H I M RI R Re S O		★★★★★
Kann Partners www.kannpartners.com	👥	MD	E M S W C G		A E G I L P O		C E G Hc H I M RI R Re S O		★★★

REGIONS: East (E), Midwest (M), South (S), West (W), Canada (C), Global (G)

SERVICES: Architecture (A), Engineering (E), Graphic Design (G), Interior Design (I), Landscape Architecture (L), Planning/Urban Design (P), Other-including Industrial Design (O)

MARKETS: Corporate (C), Education (E), Government (G), Healthcare (Hc), Hospitality (H), Industrial (I) Museum/Cultural (M), Religious (RI), Residential (R), Retail (Re), Sports (S), Other (O)

Nic Lehoux

British Columbia Institute of Technology Aerospace Technology Campus, Richmond, BC, Canada | Kasian Architecture Interior Design & Planning

	Size	HQ	Regions	Services	Markets	DI Index
Kanner Architects www.kannerarch.com	👥	CA	E M S W C G	A E G I L P O	C E G Hc H I M RI R Re S O	★★★
Karlsberger www.karlsberger.com	👥	OH	E M S W C G	A E G I L P O	C E G Hc H I M RI R Re S O	★★★
Kasian Architecture Interior Design and Planning www.kasian.com	👥	CAN	E M S W C G	A E G I L P O	C E G Hc H I M RI R Re S O	★★★★★
KBJ Architects www.kbj.com	👥	FL	E M S W C G	A E G I L P O	C E G Hc H I M RI R Re S O	★★★
KCBA Architects www.kcba-architects.com	👥	PA	E M S W C G	A E G I L P O	C E G Hc H I M RI R Re S O	★★★
KDF Architecture www.kdfarchitecture.com	👤	WA	E M S W C G	A E G I L P O	C E G Hc H I M RI R Re S O	★★★
Kell Munoz Architects www.kellmunoz.com	👥	TX	E M S W C G	A E G I L P O	C E G Hc H I M RI R Re S O	★★★
Kerns Group Architects www.kernsgroup.com	👤	VA	E M S W C G	A E G I L P O	C E G Hc H I M RI R Re S O	★★★
Kevin Roche John Dinkeloo & Associates www.krjda.com	👤	CT	E M S W C G	A E G I L P O	C E G Hc H I M RI R Re S O	★★★★★
KieranTimberlake www.kierantimberlake.com	👥	PA	E M S W C G	A E G I L P O	C E G Hc H I M RI R Re S O	★★★★★
Kiku Obata & Company www.kikuobata.com	👤	MO	E M S W C G	A E G I L P O	C E G Hc H I M RI R Re S O	★★★
Killefer Flammang Architects www.kfarchitects.com	👤	CA	E M S W C G	A E G I L P O	C E G Hc H I M RI R Re S O	★★★
Kirksey www.kirksey.com	👥👥	TX	E M S W C G	A E G I L P O	C E G Hc H I M RI R Re S O	★★★★
Kitchen & Associates Architectural Services www.kitchenandassociates.com	👤	NJ	E M S W C G	A E G I L P O	C E G Hc H I M RI R Re S O	★★★
KKE Architects (DLR Group) www.kke.com	👥👥	MN	E M S W C G	A E G I L P O	C E G Hc H I M RI R Re S O	★★★★★
KlingStubbins www.klingstubbins.com	👥👥	PA	E M S W C G	A E G I L P O	C E G Hc H I M RI R Re S O	★★★★★
klipp www.klipparch.com	👥	CO	E M S W C G	A E G I L P O	C E G Hc H I M RI R Re S O	★★★★

REGIONS: East (E), Midwest (M), South (S), West (W), Canada (C), Global (G)

SERVICES: Architecture (A), Engineering (E), Graphic Design (G), Interior Design (I), Landscape Architecture (L), Planning/Urban Design (P), Other-including Industrial Design (O)

MARKETS: Corporate (C), Education (E), Government (G), Healthcare (Hc), Hospitality (H), Industrial (I), Museum/Cultural (M), Religious (RI), Residential (R), Retail (Re), Sports (S), Other (O)

	Size	HQ	Regions	Services	Markets	DI Index
KMA Architecture & Engineering www.kma-ae.com	👥👥	CA	E M S W C G	A E G I L P O	C E G Hc H I M RI R Re S O	★★★
KMD Architects www.kmdarchitects.com	👥👥👥	CA	E M S W C G	A E G I L P O	C E G Hc H I M RI R Re S O	★★★★
Kodet Architectural Group www.kodet.com	👤	MN	E M S W C G	A E G I L P O	C E G Hc H I M RI R Re S O	★★★★
Kohl Gramigna & Associates www.kgmarchitects.com	👤	GA	E M S W C G	A E G I L P O	C E G Hc H I M RI R Re S O	★★★
Kohn Pedersen Fox www.kpf.com	👥👥👥	NY	E M S W C G	A E G I L P O	C E G Hc H I M RI R Re S O	★★★★★
Koning Eizenberg Architecture www.kearch.com	👤	CA	E M S W C G	A E G I L P O	C E G Hc H I M RI R Re S O	★★★
KPS Group www.kpsgroup.com	👥👥	AL	E M S W C G	A E G I L P O	C E G Hc H I M RI R Re S O	★★★
Krei Architecture (division of Parametrix) www.parametrix.com	👤	WA	E M S W C G	A E G I L P O	C E G Hc H I M RI R Re S O	★★★
Kromm Rikimaru and Johansen www.krjarch.com	👤	MO	E M S W C G	A E G I L P O	C E G Hc H I M RI R Re S O	★★★
KTGY Group www.ktgy.com	👤	CA	E M S W C G	A E G I L P O	C E G Hc H I M RI R Re S O	★★★
Kubala Washatko Architects www.tkwa.com	👤	WI	E M S W C G	A E G I L P O	C E G Hc H I M RI R Re S O	★★★
Kuhlman Design Group www.kdginc.com	👥👥👥	MO	E M S W C G	A E G I L P O	C E G Hc H I M RI R Re S O	★★★
Kurtz Associates Architects www.kurtzarch.com	👤	IL	E M S W C G	A E G I L P O	C E G Hc H I M RI R Re S O	★★★
Kwan Henmi www.kwanhenmi.com	👥👥	CA	E M S W C G	A E G I L P O	C E G Hc H I M RI R Re S O	★★★
KYA Design Group www.kyadesigngroup.com	👤	HI	E M S W C G	A E G I L P O	C E G Hc H I M RI R Re S O	★★★
KZF Design www.kzf.com	👥👥	OH	E M S W C G	A E G I L P O	C E G Hc H I M RI R Re S O	★★★
L. Robert Kimball & Associates (Architecture) www.lrkimball.com	👥👥👥	PA	E M S W C G	A E G I L P O	C E G Hc H I M RI R Re S O	★★★

REGIONS: East (E), Midwest (M), South (S), West (W), Canada (C), Global (G)

SERVICES: Architecture (A), Engineering (E), Graphic Design (G), Interior Design (I),
Landscape Architecture (L), Planning/Urban Design (P), Other-including Industrial Design (O)

MARKETS: Corporate (C), Education (E), Government (G), Healthcare (Hc), Hospitality (H), Industrial (I)
Museum/Cultural (M), Religious (RI), Residential (R), Retail (Re), Sports (S), Other (O)

	Size	HQ	Regions	Services	Markets	DI Index
Laguarda Low Architects www.laguardalow.com	👤	TX	E M S W C G	A E G I L P O	C E G Hc H I M RI R Re S O	★★★
LAI Design Group www.landarchitects.net	👤	CO	E M S W C G	A E G I L P O	C E G Hc H I M RI R Re S O	★★★
Lake/Flato Architects www.lakeflato.com	👥	TX	E M S W C G	A E G I L P O	C E G Hc H I M RI R Re S O	★★★★★
Lami Grubb Architects www.lamigrubb.com	👥	PA	E M S W C G	A E G I L P O	C E G Hc H I M RI R Re S O	★★★
Langdon Wilson Architecture Planning Interiors www.langdonwilson.com	👥👥	CA	E M S W C G	A E G I L P O	C E G Hc H I M RI R Re S O	★★★
Lantz-Boggio Architects www.lantz-boggio.com	👥	CO	E M S W C G	A E G I L P O	C E G Hc H I M RI R Re S O	★★★
Lawrence Group www.thelawrencegroup.com	👥👥	MO	E M S W C G	A E G I L P O	C E G Hc H I M RI R Re S O	★★★
LCA Architects www.lca-architects.com	👥	CA	E M S W C G	A E G I L P O	C E G Hc H I M RI R Re S O	★★★
Lee Harris Pomeroy Architects www.lhparch.com	👥	NY	E M S W C G	A E G I L P O	C E G Hc H I M RI R Re S O	★★★
Lee, Burkhart, Liu www.lblarch.com	👥	CA	E M S W C G	A E G I L P O	C E G Hc H I M RI R Re S O	★★★★
Legat Architects www.legat.com	👥	IL	E M S W C G	A E G I L P O	C E G Hc H I M RI R Re S O	★★★★
Legorreta + Legorreta www.legorretalegorreta.com	👥	MEX	E M S W C G	A E G I L P O	C E G Hc H I M RI R Re S O	★★★★★
Lehman Smith McLeish www.lsm.com	👥	DC	E M S W C G	A E G I L P O	C E G Hc H I M RI R Re S O	★★★★★
LEO A DALY www.leodaly.com	👥👥	NE	E M S W C G	A E G I L P O	C E G Hc H I M RI R Re S O	★★★★★
Leotta Designers www.leottadesigners.com	👤	FL	E M S W C G	A E G I L P O	C E G Hc H I M RI R Re S O	★★★
Levi + Wong Design Associates www.lwda.com	👤	MA	E M S W C G	A E G I L P O	C E G Hc H I M RI R Re S O	★★★
Levin Porter Associates www.levin-porter.com	👤	OH	E M S W C G	A E G I L P O	C E G Hc H I M RI R Re S O	★★★

REGIONS: East (E), Midwest (M), South (S), West (W), Canada (C), Global (G)

SERVICES: Architecture (A), Engineering (E), Graphic Design (G), Interior Design (I), Landscape Architecture (L), Planning/Urban Design (P), Other-including Industrial Design (O)

MARKETS: Corporate (C), Education (E), Government (G), Healthcare (Hc), Hospitality (H), Industrial (I), Museum/Cultural (M), Religious (RI), Residential (R), Retail (Re), Sports (S), Other (O)

	Size	HQ	Regions		Services		Markets		DI Index
Levinson Alcoser Associates www.levinsonalcoser.com	♦	TX	E M S W C G		A E G I L P O		C E G Hc H I M RI R Re S O		★★★
LHB Engineers & Architects www.lhbcorp.com	♦♦	MN	E M S W C G		A E G I L P O		C E G Hc H I M RI R Re S O		★★★
Lindsay Newman Architecture & Design www.lnarchitecture.com	♦	NY	E M S W C G		A E G I L P O		C E G Hc H I M RI R Re S O		★★★
Lindsay, Pope, Brayfield & Assoc. www.lpbatlanta.com	♦	GA	E M S W C G		A E G I L P O		C E G Hc H I M RI R Re S O		★★★
Lionakis www.lionakis.com	♦♦	CA	E M S W C G		A E G I L P O		C E G Hc H I M RI R Re S O		★★★
Little www.littleonline.com	♦♦♦	NC	E M S W C G		A E G I L P O		C E G Hc H I M RI R Re S O		★★★★
LMN Architects www.lmnarchitects.com	♦♦♦	WA	E M S W C G		A E G I L P O		C E G Hc H I M RI R Re S O		★★★★★
Loebl Schlossman & Hackl www.lshdesign.com	♦♦	IL	E M S W C G		A E G I L P O		C E G Hc H I M RI R Re S O		★★★
Lohan Anderson www.lohananderson.com	♦	IL	E M S W C G		A E G I L P O		C E G Hc H I M RI R Re S O		★★★
Lord, Aeck & Sargent www.lordaecksargent.com	♦♦♦	GA	E M S W C G		A E G I L P O		C E G Hc H I M RI R Re S O		★★★★★
Lorenz + Williams www.lorenzwilliams.com	♦♦	OH	E M S W C G		A E G I L P O		C E G Hc H I M RI R Re S O		★★★
LPA www.lpainc.com	♦♦♦	CA	E M S W C G		A E G I L P O		C E G Hc H I M RI R Re S O		★★★★
LPK www.lpkarchitects.com	♦	MS	E M S W C G		A E G I L P O		C E G Hc H I M RI R Re S O		★★★
LRS Architects www.lrsarchitects.com	♦♦	OR	E M S W C G		A E G I L P O		C E G Hc H I M RI R Re S O		★★★
LS3P Associates Ltd. www.LS3P.com	♦♦♦	SC	E M S W C G		A E G I L P O		C E G Hc H I M RI R Re S O		★★★★★
LSW Architects www.lsw-architects.com	♦	WA	E M S W C G		A E G I L P O		C E G Hc H I M RI R Re S O		★★★
Lucas Schwering Architects www.lsarc.net	♦	KY	E M S W C G		A E G I L P O		C E G Hc H I M RI R Re S O		★★★

REGIONS: East (E), Midwest (M), South (S), West (W), Canada (C), Global (G)

SERVICES: Architecture (A), Engineering (E), Graphic Design (G), Interior Design (I),
         Landscape Architecture (L), Planning/Urban Design (P), Other-including Industrial Design (O)

MARKETS: Corporate (C), Education (E), Government (G), Healthcare (Hc), Hospitality (H), Industrial (I)
         Museum/Cultural (M), Religious (RI), Residential (R), Retail (Re), Sports (S), Other (O)

	Size	HQ	Regions	Services	Markets	DI Index
Lucchesi Galati Architects www.lgainc.com	🧍	NV	E M S W C G	A E G I L P O	C E G Hc H I M Rl R Re S O	★★★
Lyman Davidson Dooley www.lddi-architects.com	🧍	GA	E M S W C G	A E G I L P O	C E G Hc H I M Rl R Re S O	★★★
M & A Architects www.meachamapel.com	🧍	OH	E M S W C G	A E G I L P O	C E G Hc H I M Rl R Re S O	★★★
Macgregor Associates Architects www.macgregorassoc.com	🧍	GA	E M S W C G	A E G I L P O	C E G Hc H I M Rl R Re S O	★★★
Machado and Silvetti Associates www.machado-silvetti.com	🧍🧍	MA	E M S W C G	A E G I L P O	C E G Hc H I M Rl R Re S O	★★★★★
Mackey Mitchell Architects www.mackeymitchell.com	🧍🧍	MO	E M S W C G	A E G I L P O	C E G Hc H I M Rl R Re S O	★★★★
MacLachlan, Cornelius & Filoni Architects www.mcfarchitects.com	🧍	PA	E M S W C G	A E G I L P O	C E G Hc H I M Rl R Re S O	★★★
Maguire Group www.maguiregroup.com	🧍🧍	MA	E M S W C G	A E G I L P O	C E G Hc H I M Rl R Re S O	★★★
Mahlum www.mahlum.com	🧍🧍🧍	WA	E M S W C G	A E G I L P O	C E G Hc H I M Rl R Re S O	★★★
MAI design group www.mai-architects.com	🧍	CO	E M S W C G	A E G I L P O	C E G Hc H I M Rl R Re S O	★★★
Mancini - Duffy www.manciniduffy.com	🧍🧍	NY	E M S W C G	A E G I L P O	C E G Hc H I M Rl R Re S O	★★★
Manning Architects www.manningarchitects.com	🧍🧍	LA	E M S W C G	A E G I L P O	C E G Hc H I M Rl R Re S O	★★★★
Mansac Isaac Architects www.miarch.com	🧍🧍	CAN	E M S W C G	A E G I L P O	C E G Hc H I M Rl R Re S O	★★★★
Maregatti Interiors (part of BSA LifeStructures) www.maregattiinteriors.com	🧍	IN	E M S W C G	A E G I L P O	C E G Hc H I M Rl R Re S O	★★★★
Margulies Peruzzi Architects www.mp-architects.com	🧍🧍	MA	E M S W C G	A E G I L P O	C E G Hc H I M Rl R Re S O	★★★
Mark Cavagnero Associates www.cavagnero.com	🧍🧍	CA	E M S W C G	A E G I L P O	C E G Hc H I M Rl R Re S O	★★★★
Marks, Thomas Architects www.marks-thomas.com	🧍🧍	MD	E M S W C G	A E G I L P O	C E G Hc H I M Rl R Re S O	★★★

REGIONS: East (E), Midwest (M), South (S), West (W), Canada (C), Global (G)

SERVICES: Architecture (A), Engineering (E), Graphic Design (G), Interior Design (I), Landscape Architecture (L), Planning/Urban Design (P), Other-including Industrial Design (O)

MARKETS: Corporate (C), Education (E), Government (G), Healthcare (Hc), Hospitality (H), Industrial (I), Museum/Cultural (M), Religious (Rl), Residential (R), Retail (Re), Sports (S), Other (O)

	Size	HQ	Regions	Services	Markets	DI Index
Marmol Radziner www.marmol-radziner.com	👥	CA	E M S W C G	A E G I L P O	C E G Hc H I M RI R Re S O	★★★
Marnell Corrao Associates www.marnellcorrao.com	👤	NV	E M S W C G	A E G I L P O	C E G Hc H I M RI R Re S O	★★★
Marshall Craft Associates www.marshallcraft.com	👥	MD	E M S W C G	A E G I L P O	C E G Hc H I M RI R Re S O	★★★
Marshall Tittemore Architects www.mtalink.com	👤	CAN	E M S W C G	A E G I L P O	C E G Hc H I M RI R Re S O	★★★★
Martin Holub Architects & Planners www.mharchitects.com	👤	NY	E M S W C G	A E G I L P O	C E G Hc H I M RI R Re S O	★★★
Martinez + Cutri Architects www.mc-architects.com	👤	CA	E M S W C G	A E G I L P O	C E G Hc H I M RI R Re S O	★★★
Mason Architects www.masonarch.com	👤	HI	E M S W C G	A E G I L P O	C E G Hc H I M RI R Re S O	★★★
Matrix Spencer www.matrixdesigncompanies.com	👥	TX	E M S W C G	A E G I L P O	C E G Hc H I M RI R Re S O	★★★
MBH Architects www.mbharch.com	👥	CA	E M S W C G	A E G I L P O	C E G Hc H I M RI R Re S O	★★★
MC Harry & Associates www.mcharry.com	👤	FL	E M S W C G	A E G I L P O	C E G Hc H I M RI R Re S O	★★★
MCA Architects www.mca-architects.com	👤	OR	E M S W C G	A E G I L P O	C E G Hc H I M RI R Re S O	★★★
McCall Design Group www.mccalldesign.com	👥	CA	E M S W C G	A E G I L P O	C E G Hc H I M RI R Re S O	★★★
McCarty Holsaple McCarty www.mhminc.com	👤	TN	E M S W C G	A E G I L P O	C E G Hc H I M RI R Re S O	★★★
MCG www.mcgarchitecture.com	👥👥	CA	E M S W C G	A E G I L P O	C E G Hc H I M RI R Re S O	★★★
McGranahan Architects www.mcgranahan.com	👥	WA	E M S W C G	A E G I L P O	C E G Hc H I M RI R Re S O	★★★
McKissack & McKissack www.mckissackdc.com	👥👥	DC	E M S W C G	A E G I L P O	C E G Hc H I M RI R Re S O	★★★★
McLarand Vasquez Emsiek & Partners www.mve-architects.com	👥	CA	E M S W C G	A E G I L P O	C E G Hc H I M RI R Re S O	★★★

REGIONS: East (E), Midwest (M), South (S), West (W), Canada (C), Global (G)

SERVICES: Architecture (A), Engineering (E), Graphic Design (G), Interior Design (I), Landscape Architecture (L), Planning/Urban Design (P), Other-including Industrial Design (O)

MARKETS: Corporate (C), Education (E), Government (G), Healthcare (Hc), Hospitality (H), Industrial (I) Museum/Cultural (M), Religious (RI), Residential (R), Retail (Re), Sports (S), Other (O)

	Size	HQ	Regions	Services	Markets	DI Index
MCM Architects www.mcmarchitects.com		OR	E M S W / C G	A E G I / L P O	C E G Hc H I / M RI R Re S O	★★★
McMonigal Architects www.mcmonigal.com		MN	E **M** S W / C G	A E G I / L P O	C E G Hc H I / **M** RI R Re S O	★★★
Mead & Hunt www.meadhunt.com		WI	E M S W / C G	A E G I / L P O	C E G Hc H I / M RI R Re S O	★★★
Meeks + Partners www.meekspartners.com		TX	E M S W / C G	A E G I / L P O	C E G Hc H I / M RI R Re S O	★★★
Mekus Tanager www.mekustanager.com		IL	E M S W / C G	A E G I / L P O	C E G Hc H I / M RI R Re S O	★★★
Merrick & Company www.merrick.com		CO	E M S W / C G	A E G I / L P O	C E G Hc H I / M RI R Re S O	★★★
Merriman Associates/Architects www.merriman-maa.com		TX	E M S W / C G	A E G I / L P O	C E G Hc H I / M RI R Re S O	★★★
Meyer, Scherer & Rockcastle www.msrltd.com		MN	E M S W / C G	A E G I / L P O	C E G Hc H I / M RI R Re S O	★★★★★
MGA Architecture www.mgahawaii.com		HI	E M S W / C G	A E G I / L P O	C E G Hc H I / M RI R Re S O	★★★
MGA Partners www.mgapartners.com		PA	E M S W / C G	A E G I / L P O	C E G Hc H I / M RI R Re S O	★★★
MGE Architects www.mgearchitects.com		FL	E M S W / C G	A E G I / L P O	C E G Hc H I / M RI R Re S O	★★★
MHTN Architects www.mhtn.com		UT	E M S W / C G	A E G I / L P O	C E G Hc H I / M RI R Re S O	★★★
Michael Graves & Associates www.michaelgraves.com		NJ	E M S W / C G	A E G I / L P O	C E G Hc H I / M RI R Re S O	★★★★★
Michael Schuster Associates www.msaarch.com		OH	E M S W / C G	A E G I / L P O	C E G Hc H I / M RI R Re S O	★★★
Michael Van Valkenburgh Assoc. www.mvvainc.com		NY	E M S W / C G	A E G I / L P O	C E G Hc H I / M RI R Re S O	★★★★★
Michael Willis Architects www.mwaarchitects.com		CA	E M S W / C G	A E G I / L P O	C E G Hc H I / M RI R Re S O	★★★
Middough Consulting www.middough.com		OH	E M S W / C G	A E G I / L P O	C E G Hc H I / M RI R Re S O	★★★

REGIONS: East (E), Midwest (M), South (S), West (W), Canada (C), Global (G)

SERVICES: Architecture (A), Engineering (E), Graphic Design (G), Interior Design (I), Landscape Architecture (L), Planning/Urban Design (P), Other-including Industrial Design (O)

MARKETS: Corporate (C), Education (E), Government (G), Healthcare (Hc), Hospitality (H), Industrial (I), Museum/Cultural (M), Religious (RI), Residential (R), Retail (Re), Sports (S), Other (O)

	Size	HQ	Regions		Services		Markets		DI Index
Miller Dunwiddie Architects www.millerdunwiddie.com	👥	MN	E M S W C G	A E G I L P O		C E G Hc H I M RI R Re S O		★★★★
Miller Hull Partnership, The www.millerhull.com	👥	WA	E M S W C G	A E G I L P O		C E G Hc H I M RI R Re S O		★★★★★
Milton Glaser www.miltonglaser.com	👤	NY	E M S W C G	A E G I L P O		C E G Hc H I M RI R Re S O		★★★★★
Mitchell Associates www.mitchellai.com	👥	DE	E M S W C G	A E G I L P O		C E G Hc H I M RI R Re S O		★★★
Mitchell I Giurgola Architects www.mitchellgiurgola.com	👤	NY	E M S W C G	A E G I L P O		C E G Hc H I M RI R Re S O		★★★★
Mithun www.mithun.com	👥👥	WA	E M S W C G	A E G I L P O		C E G Hc H I M RI R Re S O		★★★★★
MKC Associates www.mkcinc.com	👥	OH	E M S W C G	A E G I L P O		C E G Hc H I M RI R Re S O		★★★
MKTHINK www.mkthink.com	👤	CA	E M S W C G	A E G I L P O		C E G Hc H I M RI R Re S O		★★★
MOA Architecture www.moaarch.com	👥	CO	E M S W C G	A E G I L P O		C E G Hc H I M RI R Re S O		★★★
Moeckel Carbonell Associates www.architectsde.com	👤	DE	E M S W C G	A E G I L P O		C E G Hc H I M RI R Re S O		★★★
Mojo Stumer Architects www.mojostumer.com	👥	NY	E M S W C G	A E G I L P O		C E G Hc H I M RI R Re S O		★★★
Montalba Architects www.montalbaarchitects.com	👤	CA	E M S W C G	A E G I L P O		C E G Hc H I M RI R Re S O		★★★
Moody - Nolan www.moodynolan.com	👥	OH	E M S W C G	A E G I L P O		C E G Hc H I M RI R Re S O		★★★
Moon Mayoras Architects www.moonmayoras.com	👤	CA	E M S W C G	A E G I L P O		C E G Hc H I M RI R Re S O		★★★
Moore Planning Group www.mooreplanninggroup.com	👤	LA	E M S W C G	A E G I L P O		C E G Hc H I M RI R Re S O		★★★
Moore Ruble Yudell Architects & Planners www.moorerubleyudell.com	👥	CA	E M S W C G	A E G I L P O		C E G Hc H I M RI R Re S O		★★★★★
Moriyama & Teshima Architects www.mtarch.com	👤	CAN	E M S W C G	A E G I L P O		C E G Hc H I M RI R Re S O		★★★★

REGIONS: East (E), Midwest (M), South (S), West (W), Canada (C), Global (G)

SERVICES: Architecture (A), Engineering (E), Graphic Design (G), Interior Design (I),
Landscape Architecture (L), Planning/Urban Design (P), Other-including Industrial Design (O)

MARKETS: Corporate (C), Education (E), Government (G), Healthcare (Hc), Hospitality (H), Industrial (I)
Museum/Cultural (M), Religious (RI), Residential (R), Retail (Re), Sports (S), Other (O)

	Size	HQ	Regions	Services	Markets	DI Index
Morphosis www.morphosis.com		CA	E M S W C G	A E G I L P O	C E G Hc H I M RI R Re S O	★★★★★
Morris Architects www.morrisarchitects.com		TX	E M S W C G	A E G I L P O	C E G Hc H I M RI R Re S O	★★★★
Moseley Architects www.moseleyarchitects.com		VA	E M S W C G	A E G I L P O	C E G Hc H I M RI R Re S O	★★★
Moshe Safdie and Associates www.msafdie.com		MA	E M S W C G	A E G I L P O	C E G Hc H I M RI R Re S O	★★★★★
Mount Vernon Group Architects www.mvgarchitects.com		MA	E M S W C G	A E G I L P O	C E G Hc H I M RI R Re S O	★★★
MRI Architectural Group www.mriarchitects.com		FL	E M S W C G	A E G I L P O	C E G Hc H I M RI R Re S O	★★★
MSTSD www.mstsd.com		GA	E M S W C G	A E G I L P O	C E G Hc H I M RI R Re S O	★★★
MulvannyG2 Architecture www.mulvannyg2.com		WA	E M S W C G	A E G I L P O	C E G Hc H I M RI R Re S O	★★★★
Munger Munger + Associates www.mungermunger.com		OH	E M S W C G	A E G I L P O	C E G Hc H I M RI R Re S O	★★★
Murphy and Dittenhafer www.murphdittarch.com		MD	E M S W C G	A E G I L P O	C E G Hc H I M RI R Re S O	★★★
Murphy/Jahn www.murphyjahn.com		IL	E M S W C G	A E G I L P O	C E G Hc H I M RI R Re S O	★★★★★
MW Steele Group www.mwsteele.com		CA	E M S W C G	A E G I L P O	C E G Hc H I M RI R Re S O	★★★
NAC | Architecture www.nacarchitecture.com		WA	E M S W C G	A E G I L P O	C E G Hc H I M RI R Re S O	★★★
Nacht & Lewis Architects www.nlarch.com		CA	E M S W C G	A E G I L P O	C E G Hc H I M RI R Re S O	★★★
Nadel www.nadelarc.com		CA	E M S W C G	A E G I L P O	C E G Hc H I M RI R Re S O	★★★
Nagle Hartray Danker Kagan McKay Penny www.nhdkmp.com		IL	E M S W C G	A E G I L P O	C E G Hc H I M RI R Re S O	★★★
NBBJ www.nbbj.com		WA	E M S W C G	A E G I L P O	C E G Hc H I M RI R Re S O	★★★★★

REGIONS: East (E), Midwest (M), South (S), West (W), Canada (C), Global (G)

SERVICES: Architecture (A), Engineering (E), Graphic Design (G), Interior Design (I), Landscape Architecture (L), Planning/Urban Design (P), Other-including Industrial Design (O)

MARKETS: Corporate (C), Education (E), Government (G), Healthcare (Hc), Hospitality (H), Industrial (I) Museum/Cultural (M), Religious (RI), Residential (R), Retail (Re), Sports (S), Other (O)

	Size	HQ	Regions		Services		Markets		DI Index
NELSON www.nelsononline.com		PA	E M S W C G		A E G I L P O		C E G Hc H I M RI R Re S O		★★★★
Neumann Smith & Associates www.neumannsmith.com		MI	E M S W C G		A E G I L P O		C E G Hc H I M RI R Re S O		★★★
Newport Collaborative www.ncarchitects.com		RI	E M S W C G		A E G I L P O		C E G Hc H I M RI R Re S O		★★★
Niles Bolton Associates www.nilesbolton.com		GA	E M S W C G		A E G I L P O		C E G Hc H I M RI R Re S O		★★★★
NORR Architects Planners www.norr.com		CAN	E M S W C G		A E G I L P O		C E G Hc H I M RI R Re S O		★★★
Norris Design www.norris-design.com		CO	E M S W C G		A E G I L P O		C E G Hc H I M RI R Re S O		★★★
NTD Architecture www.ntd.com		CA	E M S W C G		A E G I L P O		C E G Hc H I M RI R Re S O		★★★★
Nudell Architects www.jhn.com		MI	E M S W C G		A E G I L P O		C E G Hc H I M RI R Re S O		★★★
O'Brien/Atkins Associates www.obrienatkins.com		NC	E M S W C G		A E G I L P O		C E G Hc H I M RI R Re S O		★★★
O'Connell Robertson & Assoc. www.oconnellrobertson.com		TX	E M S W C G		A E G I L P O		C E G Hc H I M RI R Re S O		★★★
OBM International www.obmi.com		FL	E M S W C G		A E G I L P O		C E G Hc H I M RI R Re S O		★★★
Odell www.odell.com		NC	E M S W C G		A E G I L P O		C E G Hc H I M RI R Re S O		★★★
Ohlson Lavoie Collaborative www.olcdesigns.com		CO	E M S W C G		A E G I L P O		C E G Hc H I M RI R Re S O		★★★
OLIN www.theolinstudio.com		PA	E M S W C G		A E G I L P O		C E G Hc H I M RI R Re S O		★★★★★
Oliver Design Group www.odg-architects.com		FL	E M S W C G		A E G I L P O		C E G Hc H I M RI R Re S O		★★★
Olivieri, Shousky & Kiss www.olivieriarchitects.com		NJ	E M S W C G		A E G I L P O		C E G Hc H I M RI R Re S O		★★★
Olson Kundig Architects www.olsonkundigarchitects.com		WA	E M S W C G		A E G I L P O		C E G Hc H I M RI R Re S O		★★★★★

REGIONS: East (E), Midwest (M), South (S), West (W), Canada (C), Global (G)

SERVICES: Architecture (A), Engineering (E), Graphic Design (G), Interior Design (I), Landscape Architecture (L), Planning/Urban Design (P), Other-including Industrial Design (O)

MARKETS: Corporate (C), Education (E), Government (G), Healthcare (Hc), Hospitality (H), Industrial (I), Museum/Cultural (M), Religious (RI), Residential (R), Retail (Re), Sports (S), Other (O)

	Size	HQ	Regions		Services		Markets		DI Index
Omniplan www.omniplan.com	👥	TX	E M S W C G	A E G I L P O		C E G Hc H I M RI R Re S O		★★★
Opsis Architecture www.opsisarch.com	👤	OR	E M S W C G	A E G I L P O		C E G Hc H I M RI R Re S O		★★★
Opus Architects & Engineers www.opuscorp.com	👥	MN	E M S W C G	A E G I L P O		C E G Hc H I M RI R Re S O		★★★
Orcutt I Winslow www.owp.com	👥	AZ	E M S W C G	A E G I L P O		C E G Hc H I M RI R Re S O		★★★★
Otis Koglin Wilson Architects www.okwarchitects.com	👥👥	OR	E M S W C G	A E G I L P O		C E G Hc H I M RI R Re S O		★★★
Oudens Knoop Knoop + Sachs Architects www.okarch.com	👥	MD	E M S W C G	A E G I L P O		C E G Hc H I M RI R Re S O		★★★
Overland Partners Architects www.overlandpartners.com	👥	TX	E M S W C G	A E G I L P O		C E G Hc H I M RI R Re S O		★★★★
OZ Architecture www.ozarch.com	👥👥	CO	E M S W C G	A E G I L P O		C E G Hc H I M RI R Re S O		★★★
Pacific Architects www.pacarchitects.com	👥	HI	E M S W C G	A E G I L P O		C E G Hc H I M RI R Re S O		★★★
PageSoutherlandPage www.pspaec.com	👥👥	TX	E M S W C G	A E G I L P O		C E G Hc H I M RI R Re S O		★★★★★
Parker Scaggiari www.psvegas.com	👤	NV	E M S W C G	A E G I L P O		C E G Hc H I M RI R Re S O		★★★
Partners & Sirny Architects www.partnersandsirny.com	👤	MN	E M S W C G	A E G I L P O		C E G Hc H I M RI R Re S O		★★★
Partridge Architects www.partridgearch.com	👤	PA	E M S W C G	A E G I L P O		C E G Hc H I M RI R Re S O		★★★
Paul Segal Associates www.paulsegalassociates.com	👤	NY	E M S W C G	A E G I L P O		C E G Hc H I M RI R Re S O		★★★
Paulsen Architectural Design www.paulsenarchitects.com	👤	MN	E M S W C G	A E G I L P O		C E G Hc H I M RI R Re S O		★★★
Payette www.payette.com	👥👥	MA	E M S W C G	A E G I L P O		C E G Hc H I M RI R Re S O		★★★★★
pb2 Architecture & Engineering www.pb2ae.com	👤	AR	E M S W C G	A E G I L P O		C E G Hc H I M RI R Re S O		★★★

REGIONS: East (E), Midwest (M), South (S), West (W), Canada (C), Global (G)

SERVICES: Architecture (A), Engineering (E), Graphic Design (G), Interior Design (I), Landscape Architecture (L), Planning/Urban Design (P), Other-including Industrial Design (O)

MARKETS: Corporate (C), Education (E), Government (G), Healthcare (Hc), Hospitality (H), Industrial (I) Museum/Cultural (M), Religious (RI), Residential (R), Retail (Re), Sports (S), Other (O)

Chris Cooper

Evelyn H. Lauder Breast Center, Memorial Sloan-Kettering Cancer Center (MSKCC) and MSKCC Imaging Center, New York, NY | Perkins Eastman

	Size	HQ	Regions	Services	Markets	DI Index
PBK www.pbk.com	†††	TX	E M S W / C G	A E G I / L P O	C E G Hc H I / M RI R Re S O	★★★★
PBR Hawaii www.pbrhawaii.com	††	HI	E M S W / C G	A E G I / L P O	C E G Hc H I / M RI R Re S O	★★★
Peckham & Wright Architects www.pwarchitects.com	†	MO	E M S W / C G	A E G I / L P O	C E G Hc H I / M RI R Re S O	★★★
Peckham Guyton Albers & Viets www.pgav.com	†††	MO	E M S W / C G	A E G I / L P O	C E G Hc H I / M RI R Re S O	★★★
Pei Cobb Freed & Partners www.pcf-p.com	†††	NY	E M S W / C G	A E G I / L P O	C E G Hc H I / M RI R Re S O	★★★★★
Pelli Clarke Pelli Architects www.pcparch.com	††	CT	E M S W / C G	A E G I / L P O	C E G Hc H I / M RI R Re S O	★★★★★
Pellow Architects www.pellowarchitects.com	††	CAN	E M S W / C G	A E G I / L P O	C E G Hc H I / M RI R Re S O	★★★
Perfido Weiskopf Wagstaff + Goettel www.pwwgarch.com	†	PA	E M S W / C G	A E G I / L P O	C E G Hc H I / M RI R Re S O	★★★
Perkins+Will www.perkinswill.com	††††	N/A	E M S W / C G	A E G I / L P O	C E G Hc H I / M RI R Re S O	★★★★★
Perkins Eastman www.perkinseastman.com	††††	NY	E M S W / C G	A E G I / L P O	C E G Hc H I / M RI R Re S O	★★★★★
Perkowitz+Ruth Architects www.prarchitects.com	†††	CA	E M S W / C G	A E G I / L P O	C E G Hc H I / M RI R Re S O	★★★★
Perry Dean Rogers I Partners Architects www.perrydean.com	†	MA	E M S W / C G	A E G I / L P O	C E G Hc H I / M RI R Re S O	★★★★
Peter Chermayeff www.peterchermayeff.com	†	MA	E M S W / C G	A E G I / L P O	C E G Hc H I / M RI R Re S O	★★★★
Peter Henry Architects www.chebucto.ns.ca/Business/PHARCH	††	CAN	E M S W / C G	A E G I / L P O	C E G Hc H I / M RI R Re S O	★★★
Peter Marino Architect www.petermarinoarchitect.com	†††	NY	E M S W / C G	A E G I / L P O	C E G Hc H I / M RI R Re S O	★★★★
Peter Vincent Architects www.pva.com	†	HI	E M S W / C G	A E G I / L P O	C E G Hc H I / M RI R Re S O	★★★
PGAL www.pgal.com	††	TX	E M S W / C G	A E G I / L P O	C E G Hc H I / M RI R Re S O	★★★

REGIONS: East (E), Midwest (M), South (S), West (W), Canada (C), Global (G)

SERVICES: Architecture (A), Engineering (E), Graphic Design (G), Interior Design (I), Landscape Architecture (L), Planning/Urban Design (P), Other-including Industrial Design (O)

MARKETS: Corporate (C), Education (E), Government (G), Healthcare (Hc), Hospitality (H), Industrial (I), Museum/Cultural (M), Religious (RI), Residential (R), Retail (Re), Sports (S), Other (O)

Scott McDonald, Hendrich Blessing

300 North LaSalle, Chicago, IL | Pickard Chilton

	Size	HQ	Regions	Services	Markets	DI Index
Phillips Partnership www.phillipspart.com		GA	E M S W C G	A E G I L P O	C E G Hc H I M RI R Re S O	★★★★
Philo Wilke Partnership www.pwarch.com		TX	E M S W C G	A E G I L P O	C E G Hc H I M RI R Re S O	★★★
Pica + Sullivan Architects www.picasullivan.com		CA	E M S W C G	A E G I L P O	C E G Hc H I M RI R Re S O	★★★
Pickard Chilton www.pickardchilton.com		CT	E M S W C G	A E G I L P O	C E G Hc H I M RI R Re S O	★★★★★
Pieper O'Brien Herr Architects www.poharchitects.com		GA	E M S W C G	A E G I L P O	C E G Hc H I M RI R Re S O	★★★
Pinnacle Architects www.pinnaclearchitects.com		OH	E M S W C G	A E G I L P O	C E G Hc H I M RI R Re S O	★★★
Plant Architect www.branchplant.com		CAN	E M S W C G	A E G I L P O	C E G Hc H I M RI R Re S O	★★★
Platt Byard Dovell White Archts. www.pbdw.com		NY	E M S W C G	A E G I L P O	C E G Hc H I M RI R Re S O	★★★
Poggemeyer Design Group www.poggemeyer.com		OH	E M S W C G	A E G I L P O	C E G Hc H I M RI R Re S O	★★★
Polk Stanley Wilcox www.polkstanleywilcox.com		AR	E M S W C G	A E G I L P O	C E G Hc H I M RI R Re S O	★★★
POLLACK Architecture www.pollackarch.com		CA	E M S W C G	A E G I L P O	C E G Hc H I M RI R Re S O	★★★
Pope Associates www.popearch.com		MN	E M S W C G	A E G I L P O	C E G Hc H I M RI R Re S O	★★★
Populous www.populous.com		MO	US n/p C G	A E G I L P O	C E G Hc H I M RI R Re S O	★★★★★
Portico Group, The www.porticogroup.com		WA	E M S W C G	A F G I L P O	C E G Hc H I M RI R Re S O	★★★
PositivEnergy Practice www.pepractice.com		IL	E M S W C G	A E G I L P O	C E G Hc H I M RI R Re S O	★★★
Preston Partnership, The www.theprestonpartnership.com		GA	E M S W C G	A E G I L P O	C E G Hc H I M RI R Re S O	★★★
PSA-Dewberry www.dewberry.com		VA	E M S W C G	A E G I L P O	C E G Hc H I M RI R Re S O	★★★

REGIONS:　East (E), Midwest (M), South (S), West (W), Canada (C), Global (G)

SERVICES:　Architecture (A), Engineering (E), Graphic Design (G), Interior Design (I),
Landscape Architecture (L), Planning/Urban Design (P), Other-including Industrial Design (O)

MARKETS:　Corporate (C), Education (E), Government (G), Healthcare (Hc), Hospitality (H), Industrial (I)
Museum/Cultural (M), Religious (RI), Residential (R), Retail (Re), Sports (S), Other (O)

	Size	HQ	Regions	Services	Markets	DI Index
Pugh + Scarpa www.pugh-scarpa.com		CA	E M S W C G	A E G I L P O	C E G Hc H I M RI R Re S O	★★★★★
Pyatok Architects www.pyatok.com		CA	E M S W C G	A E G I L P O	C E G Hc H I M RI R Re S O	★★★
Q **Quinn Evan Architects** www.quinnevans.com		DC	E M S W C G	A E G I L P O	C E G Hc H I M RI R Re S O	★★★
Quorum Architects www.quorumarchitects.com		WI	E M S W C G	A E G I L P O	C E G Hc H I M RI R Re S O	★★★
R **Rafael Viñoly Architects** www.rvapc.com		NY	E M S W C G	A E G I L P O	C E G Hc H I M RI R Re S O	★★★★★
Randall Stout Architects www.stoutarc.com		CA	E M S W C G	A E G I L P O	C E G Hc H I M RI R Re S O	★★★
Randy Brown Architects www.randybrownarchitects.com		NE	E M S W C G	A E G I L P O	C E G Hc H I M RI R Re S O	★★★★★
Ratcliff www.ratcliffarch.com		CA	E M S W C G	A E G I L P O	C E G Hc H I M RI R Re S O	★★★★
RATIO Architects www.ratioarchitects.com		IN	E M S W C G	A E G I L P O	C E G Hc H I M RI R Re S O	★★★★
RBB Architects www.rbbinc.com		CA	E M S W C G	A E G I L P O	C E G Hc H I M RI R Re S O	★★★
RDG Planning & Design www.rdgusa.com		IA	E M S W C G	A E G I L P O	C E G Hc H I M RI R Re S O	★★★★
Rees Associates www.rees.com		TX	E M S W C G	A E G I L P O	C E G Hc H I M RI R Re S O	★★★
Renaissance 3 Architects www.r3a.com		PA	E M S W C G	A E G I L P O	C E G Hc H I M RI R Re S O	★★★
Research Facilities Design www.rfd.com		CA	E M S W C G	A E G I L P O	C E G Hc H I M RI R Re S O	★★★
richärd+bauer www.richard-bauer.com		AZ	E M S W C G	A E G I L P O	C E G Hc H I M RI R Re S O	★★★
Richard Fleischman Architects www.studiorfa.com		OH	E M S W C G	A E G I L P O	C E G Hc H I M RI R Re S O	★★★
Richard Matsunaga & Associates Architects www.rmaia-architects.com		HI	E M S W C G	A E G I L P O	C E G Hc H I M RI R Re S O	★★★

REGIONS: East (E), Midwest (M), South (S), West (W), Canada (C), Global (G)

SERVICES: Architecture (A), Engineering (E), Graphic Design (G), Interior Design (I), Landscape Architecture (L), Planning/Urban Design (P), Other-including Industrial Design (O)

MARKETS: Corporate (C), Education (E), Government (G), Healthcare (Hc), Hospitality (H), Industrial (I) Museum/Cultural (M), Religious (RI), Residential (R), Retail (Re), Sports (S), Other (O)

	Size	HQ	Regions	Services	Markets	DI Index
Richard Meier & Partners Archts. www.richardmeier.com		NY	E M S W C G	A E G I L P O	C E G Hc H I M RI R Re S O	★★★★★
Rick Ryniak Architects www.ryniak.com		HI	E M S W C G	A E G I L P O	C E G Hc H I M RI R Re S O	★★★★★
Riecke Sunnland Kono Architects www.rskarchitects.com		HI	E M S W C G	A E G I L P O	C E G Hc H I M RI R Re S O	★★★
RJC Architects www.rjcarch.com		CA	E M S W C G	A E G I L P O	C E G Hc H I M RI R Re S O	★★★
RMJM www.rmjm.com		NY	E M S W C G	A E G I L P O	C E G Hc H I M RI R Re S O	★★★★★
RMW Architecture & Interiors www.rmw.com		CA	E M S W C G	A E G I L P O	C E G Hc H I M RI R Re S O	★★★
RNL www.rnldesign.com		CO	E M S W C G	A E G I L P O	C E G Hc H I M RI R Re S O	★★★★★
Rob Wellington Quigley www.robquigley.com		CA	E M S W C G	A E G I L P O	C E G Hc H I M RI R Re S O	★★★★
Robert A.M. Stern Architects www.ramsa.com		NY	E M S W C G	A E G I L P O	C E G Hc H I M RI R Re S O	★★★★★
Robert Kubicek Architects & Associates www.rkaa.com		AZ	E M S W C G	A E G I L P O	C E G Hc H I M RI R Re S O	★★★★
Robert M. Swedroe Architects & Planners www.swedroe.com		FL	E M S W C G	A E G I L P O	C E G Hc H I M RI R Re S O	★★★
Robert P. Madison International www.rpmadison.com		OH	E M S W C G	A E G I L P O	C E G Hc H I M RI R Re S O	★★★
Robertson Loia Roof www.rlrpc.com		GA	E M S W C G	A E G I L P O	C E G Hc H I M RI R Re S O	★★★
Rockwell Group www.rockwellgroup.com		NY	E M S W C G	A E G I L P O	C E G Hc H I M RI R Re S O	★★★★★
Rodriguez and Quiroga Architects Chartered www.rodriguezquiroga.com		FL	E M S W C G	A E G I L P O	C E G Hc H I M RI R Re S O	★★★
Roesling Nakamura Terada Archts. www.rntarchitects.com		CA	E M S W C G	A E G I L P O	C E G Hc H I M RI R Re S O	★★★
Roger Ferris + Partners www.ferrisarch.com		CT	E M S W C G	A E G I L P O	C E G Hc H I M RI R Re S O	★★★

REGIONS: East (E), Midwest (M), South (S), West (W), Canada (C), Global (G)

SERVICES: Architecture (A), Engineering (E), Graphic Design (G), Interior Design (I),
Landscape Architecture (L), Planning/Urban Design (P), Other-including Industrial Design (O)

MARKETS: Corporate (C), Education (E), Government (G), Healthcare (Hc), Hospitality (H), Industrial (I)
Museum/Cultural (M), Religious (RI), Residential (R), Retail (Re), Sports (S), Other (O)

© RTKL.com/David Whitcomb

1225 Connecticut Avenue, Washington, DC | RTKL Associates Inc.

	Size	HQ	Regions	Services	Markets	DI Index
Rogers Marvel Architects www.rogersmarvel.com	👥	NY	E M S W C G	A E G I L P O	C E G Hc H I M RI R Re S O	★★★★★
Ross Schonder Sterzinger Cupcheck www.rsscarch.com	👤	PA	E M S W C G	A E G I L P O	C E G Hc H I M RI R Re S O	★★★
Rosser International www.rosser.com	👥👥	GA	E M S W C G	A E G I L P O	C E G Hc H I M RI R Re S O	★★★
Rossetti www.rossetti.com	👥👥	MI	E M S W C G	A E G I I P O	C E G Hc H I M RI R Re S O	★★★★
RSP Architects www.rsparch.com	👥👥	MN	E M S W C G	A E G I L P O	C E G Hc H I M RI R Re S O	★★★★
RTKL Associates Inc. www.rtkl.com	👥👥👥	MD	E M S W C G	A E G I L P O	C E G Hc H I M RI R Re S O	★★★★★
Rubeling & Associates www.rubeling.com	👥	MD	E M S W C G	A E G I L P O	C E G Hc H I M RI R Re S O	★★★
RWA Architects www.rwaarchitects.com	👤	OH	E M S W C G	A E G I L P O	C E G Hc H I M RI R Re S O	★★★
Salerno/Livingston Architects www.slarchitects.com	👤	CA	E M S W C G	A E G I L P O	C E G Hc H I M RI R Re S O	★★★
Salmela Architects www.salmelaarchitect.com	👤	MN	E M S W C G	A E G I L P O	C E G Hc H I M RI R Re S O	★★★★★
Sandvick Architects www.sandvickarchitects.com	👥	OH	E M S W C G	A E G I L P O	C E G Hc H I M RI R Re S O	★★★
Sarah Nettleton Architects www.sarah-architects.com	👤	MN	E M S W C G	A E G I L P O	C E G Hc H I M RI R Re S O	★★★
Sasaki Associates, Inc. www.sasaki.com	👥👥	MA	E M S W C G	A E G I L P O	C E G Hc H I M RI R Re S O	★★★★★
Saucier & Flynn www.saucierflynn.com	👤	NH	E M S W C G	A E G I L P O	C E G Hc H I M RI R Re S O	★★★
Saucier and Perrotte Architects www.saucierperrotte.com	👤	CAN	E M S W C G	A E G I L P O	C E G Hc H I M RI R Re S O	★★★
SaylorGregg Architects www.saylorgregg.com	👤	PA	E M S W C G	A E G I L P O	C E G Hc H I M RI R Re S O	★★★
SB Architects www.sb-architects.com	👥	CA	E M S W C G	A E G I L P O	C E G Hc H I M RI R Re S O	★★★

REGIONS:　East (E), Midwest (M), South (S), West (W), Canada (C), Global (G)

SERVICES:　Architecture (A), Engineering (E), Graphic Design (G), Interior Design (I),
Landscape Architecture (L), Planning/Urban Design (P), Other-including Industrial Design (O)

MARKETS:　Corporate (C), Education (E), Government (G), Healthcare (Hc), Hospitality (H), Industrial (I)
Museum/Cultural (M), Religious (RI), Residential (R), Retail (Re), Sports (S), Other (O)

Hornsilver Residence, Vail, CO | Shepherd Resources/Douglas Miller DeChant Architects

Watersong Lane, Rocky Mountain Region, CO | Shepherd Resources/Douglas Miller DeChant Architects

	Size	HQ	Regions	Services	Markets	DI Index
SchenkelShultz www.schenkelshultz.com		IN	**E** **M** **S** W / C **G**	**A** E G I / L P O	**C** **E** **G** Hc H I / **M** **RI** R Re S O	★★★
Schoenhardt Architecture www.schoenhardt.com		CT	**E** M S W / C **G**	**A** E G **I** / L P O	**C** **E** **G** Hc **H** I / **M** **RI** **R** Re S O	★★★
Schooley Caldwell Associates www.sca-ae.com		OH	E **M** S W / C **G**	**A** E G I / **L** P O	**C** **E** **G** Hc H I / **M** **RI** R Re S O	★★★
Schroeder Slater www.schroederslater.com		GA	**E** M **S** W / C **G**	**A** E G I / L P O	C **E** G Hc H I / M **RI** **R** Re **S** O	★★★
Schwartz/Silver Architects www.schwartzsilver.com		MA	**E** M S W / C **G**	**A** E G **I** / L P O	**C** **E** **G** Hc H I / **M** **RI** R Re S O	★★★
Scott Blakeslee Disher & Assoc. www.sbdassociates.com		FL	E M **S** W / C **G**	**A** E G I / L **P** O	C **E** G Hc H I / M **RI** **R** **Re** **S** O	★★★
Scott Partnership Architecture, The www.scottarchitects.com		FL	E M **S** W / C **G**	**A** E G **I** / L P O	**C** E **G** Hc **H** I / M **RI** **R** **Re** S O	★★★
Seaver Franks Architects www.seaverfranks.com		AZ	E M S **W** / C **G**	**A** E G **I** / L P O	**C** **E** **G** Hc H I / **M** **RI** **R** **Re** **S** O	★★★
SEM Architects www.semarchitects.com		CO	E M S **W** / C **G**	**A** E G **I** / L P O	**C** **E** **G** Hc **H** I / M **RI** **R** **Re** S O	★★★
Semple Brown Design www.sbdesign-pc.com		CO	E M S **W** / C **G**	**A** E G **I** / L P O	**C** **E** **G** Hc H I / **M** **RI** **R** **Re** S O	★★★
SGPA Architecture and Planning www.sgpa.com		CA	E M S **W** / C **G**	**A** E G **I** / **L** **P** O	**C** **E** **G** Hc H I / M **RI** **R** **Re** S O	★★★
SH Architecture www.sh-architecture.com		NV	E M S **W** / C **G**	**A** E G **I** / L **P** O	**C** **E** **G** Hc H I / M **RI** R Re **S** **O**	★★★
Shalom Baranes Associates www.sbaranes.com		DC	**E** M S W / C **G**	**A** E G **I** / L **P** O	C E **G** Hc H I / M **RI** **R** **Re** S O	★★★
Shea Architects www.shealink.com		MN	E **M** S W / C **G**	**A** E **G** **I** / L P O	**C** E G Hc **H** I / M **RI** **R** Re S O	★★★★
Shepherd Resources/Douglas Miller DeChant Architects www.sriarchitect.com		CO	E M S **W** / C **G**	**A** E G **I** / L P O	C E G Hc H I / M **RI** **R** Re S **O**	★★★★
Shepley Bulfinch Richardson and Abbott www.sbra.com		MA	**E** **M** **S** **W** / C **G**	**A** E G **I** / L **P** O	**C** E **G** Hc H I / M **RI** R Re S O	★★★★★
Sherlock Smith & Adams www.ssainc.com		AL	**E** M **S** W / C **G**	**A** E **G** **I** / L **P** O	**C** **E** **G** Hc **H** I / **M** **RI** **R** Re S O	★★★

REGIONS: East (E), Midwest (M), South (S), West (W), Canada (C), Global (G)

SERVICES: Architecture (A), Engineering (E), Graphic Design (G), Interior Design (I),
Landscape Architecture (L), Planning/Urban Design (P), Other-including Industrial Design (O)

MARKETS: Corporate (C), Education (E), Government (G), Healthcare (Hc), Hospitality (H), Industrial (I)
Museum/Cultural (M), Religious (RI), Residential (R), Retail (Re), Sports (S), Other (O)

	Size	HQ	Regions	Services	Markets	DI Index
Sheward Partnership, The www.theshewardpartnership.com	👤	PA	E M S W C G	A E G I L P O	C E G Hc H I M RI R Re S O	★★★
Shive-Hattery www.shive-hattery.com	👥👥	IA	E M S W C G	A E G I L P O	C E G Hc H I M RI R Re S O	★★★
Shlemmer+Algaze+Associates www.saaia.com	👥👥	CA	E M S W C G	A E G I L P O	C E G Hc H I M RI R Re S O	★★★
Sholar Architecture and Const. www.sholarco.com	👤	CO	E M S W C G	A E G I L P O	C E G Hc H I M RI R Re S O	★★★
SHoP Architects www.shoparc.com	👥👥	NY	E M S W C G	A E G I L P O	C E G Hc H I M RI R Re S O	★★★★
Shore Point Architecture www.shorepointarch.com	👤	NJ	E M S W C G	A E G I L P O	C E G Hc H I M RI R Re S O	★★★
Short Elliott Hendrickson www.sehinc.com	👥👥👥	MN	E M S W C G	A E G I L P O	C E G Hc H I M RI R Re S O	★★★
SHP Leading Design www.shp.com	👥👥	OH	E M S W C G	A E G I L P O	C E G Hc H I M RI R Re S O	★★★★
Shremshock Architects & Engrs. www.shremshock.com	👥👥	OH	E M S W C G	A E G I L P O	C E G Hc H I M RI R Re S O	★★★
Shultz & Associates www.thearchitectfirm.com	👤	ND	E M S W C G	A E G I L P O	C E G Hc H I M RI R Re S O	★★★
SHW Group www.shwgroup.com	👥👥	TX	E M S W C G	A E G I L P O	C E G Hc H I M RI R Re S O	★★★★
Sink Combs Dethlefs www.sinkcombs.com	👤	CO	E M S W C G	A E G I L P O	C E G Hc H I M RI R Re S O	★★★
Sizemore Group www.sizemoregroup.com	👥	GA	E M S W C G	A E G I L P O	C E G Hc H I M RI R Re S O	★★★
Skidmore, Owings & Merrill www.som.com	👥👥👥	N/A	E M S W C G	A E G I L P O	C E G Hc H I M RI R Re S O	★★★★★
Slack Alost Architecture www.samassoc.com	👥	LA	E M S W C G	A E G I L P O	C E G Hc H I M RI R Re S O	★★★
SLAM Collaborative, The www.slamcoll.com	👥👥👥	CT	E M S W C G	A E G I L P O	C E G Hc H I M RI R Re S O	★★★★
SLATERPAULL Architects www.slaterpaull.com	👥	CO	E M S W C G	A E G I L P O	C E G Hc H I M RI R Re S O	★★★★

REGIONS: East (E), Midwest (M), South (S), West (W), Canada (C), Global (G)

SERVICES: Architecture (A), Engineering (E), Graphic Design (G), Interior Design (I), Landscape Architecture (L), Planning/Urban Design (P), Other-including Industrial Design (O)

MARKETS: Corporate (C), Education (E), Government (G), Healthcare (Hc), Hospitality (H), Industrial (I) Museum/Cultural (M), Religious (RI), Residential (R), Retail (Re), Sports (S), Other (O)

	Size	HQ	Regions	Services	Markets	DI Index
SLCE Architects www.slcearch.com	👤	NY	E M S W C G	A E G I L P O	C E G Hc H I M RI R Re S O	★★★
Slifer Designs www.sliferdesigns.com	👤	CO	E M S W C G	A E G I L P O	C E G Hc H I M RI R Re S O	★★★
Slocum Platts Architects Design Studio www.slocumplatts.com	👤	FL	E M S W C G	A E G I L P O	C E G Hc H I M RI R Re S O	★★★
Smallwood, Reynolds, Stewart, Stewart & Associates www.srssa.com	👤👤👤	GA	E M S W C G	A E G I L P O	C E G Hc H I M RI R Re S O	★★★
Smith Carter www.smithcarter.com	👤👤👤	CAN	E M S W C G	A E G I L P O	C E G Hc H I M RI R Re S O	★★★★★
Smith Consulting Architects www.sca-sd.com	👤👤	CA	E M S W C G	A E G I L P O	C E G Hc H I M RI R Re S O	★★★
SmithGroup www.smithgroup.com	👤👤👤👤	N/A	E M S W C G	A E G I L P O	C E G Hc H I M RI R Re S O	★★★★★
Soderstrom Architects www.sdra.com	👤	OR	E M S W C G	A E G I L P O	C E G Hc H I M RI R Re S O	★★★
Solomon Cordwell Buenz www.scb.com	👤👤👤	IL	E M S W C G	A E G I L P O	C E G Hc H I M RI R Re S O	★★★★
Southern A&E www.southernae.com	👤	GA	E M S W C G	A E G I L P O	C E G Hc H I M RI R Re S O	★★★
Sowinski Sullivan Architects www.sowinskisullivan.com	👤👤	NJ	E M S W C G	A E G I L P O	C E G Hc H I M RI R Re S O	★★★
SpaceSmith www.spacesmith.net	👤	NY	E M S W C G	A E G I L P O	C E G Hc H I M RI R Re S O	★★★
Spector Group Architects www.spectorgroup.com	👤	NY	E M S W C G	A E G I L P O	C E G Hc H I M RI R Re S O	★★★
spg3 www.spg3.com	👤	PA	E M S W C G	A E G I L P O	C E G Hc H I M RI R Re S O	★★★
SRG Partnership www.srgpartnership.com	👤👤	WA	E M S W C G	A E G I L P O	C E G Hc H I M RI R Re S O	★★★
SSOE Group www.ssoe.com	👤👤👤	OH	E M S W C G	A E G I L P O	C E G Hc H M RI R Re S O	★★★★
Staffelbach www.staffelbach.com	👤👤	TX	E M S W C G	A E G I L P O	C E G Hc H I M RI R Re S O	★★★★★

REGIONS: East (E), Midwest (M), South (S), West (W), Canada (C), Global (G)

SERVICES: Architecture (A), Engineering (E), Graphic Design (G), Interior Design (I), Landscape Architecture (L), Planning/Urban Design (P), Other-including Industrial Design (O)

MARKETS: Corporate (C), Education (E), Government (G), Healthcare (Hc), Hospitality (H), Industrial (I), Museum/Cultural (M), Religious (RI), Residential (R), Retail (Re), Sports (S), Other (O)

	Size	HQ	Regions	Services	Markets	DI Index
Stanley Love-Stanley www.stanleylove-stanleypc.com	♦	GA	E M S W C G	A E G I L P O	C E G Hc H I M RI R Re S O	★★★
Stantec Architecture (US) www.stantec.com	♦♦♦♦	CA	E M S W C G	A E G I L P O	C E G Hc H I M RI R Re S O	★★★★★
Steelman Partners www.paulsteelman.com	♦♦♦	NV	E M S W C G	A E G I L P O	C E G Hc H I M RI R Re S O	★★★★
Steffian Bradley Architects www.steffian.com	♦♦♦	MA	E M S W C G	A E G I L P O	C E G Hc H I M RI R Re S O	★★★★
Steinberg Architects www.steinbergarchitects.com	♦♦♦	CA	E M S W C G	A E G I L P O	C E G Hc H I M RI R Re S O	★★★
Stephen B. Jacobs Group/ Andi Pepper Designs www.sbjgroup.com	♦♦	NY	E M S W C G	A E G I L P O	C E G Hc H I M RI R Re S O	★★★
Steven Holl Architects www.stevenholl.com	♦	NY	E M S W C G	A E G I L P O	C E G Hc H I M RI R Re S O	★★★★★
Stevens & Wilkinson www.stevenswilkinson.com	♦♦♦	GA	E M S W C G	A E G I L P O	C E G Hc H I M RI R Re S O	★★★
STG Design www.stgdesign.com	♦♦	TX	E M S W C G	A E G I L P O	C E G Hc H I M RI R Re S O	★★★
Strada Architecture www.stradallc.com	♦	PA	E M S W C G	A E G I L P O	C E G Hc H I M RI R Re S O	★★★
Strekalovsky Architecture www.strekalovskyarchitecture.com	♦	MA	E M S W C G	A E G I L P O	C E G Hc H I M RI R Re S O	★★★
Studio 2030 www.studio2030.com	♦	MN	E M S W C G	A E G I L P O	C E G Hc H I M RI R Re S O	★★★
Studio Meng Strazzara www.studioms.com	♦	WA	E M S W C G	A E G I L P O	C E G Hc H I M RI R Re S O	★★★
STUDIOS Architecture www.studiosarchitecture.com	♦♦♦	DC	E M S W C G	A E G I L P O	C E G Hc H I M RI R Re S O	★★★★★
STV Group www.stvinc.com	♦♦♦♦	NY	E M S W C G	A E G I L P O	C E G Hc H I M RI R Re S O	★★★★
Susanka Studios www.susanka.com	♦	MN	E M S W C G	A E G I L P O	C E G Hc H I M RI R Re S O	★★★★★
Swaback Partners www.swabackpartners.com	♦♦	AZ	E M S W C G	A E G I L P O	C E G Hc H I M RI R Re S O	★★★★

REGIONS: East (E), Midwest (M), South (S), West (W), Canada (C), Global (G)

SERVICES: Architecture (A), Engineering (E), Graphic Design (G), Interior Design (I),
Landscape Architecture (L), Planning/Urban Design (P), Other-including Industrial Design (O)

MARKETS: Corporate (C), Education (E), Government (G), Healthcare (Hc), Hospitality (H), Industrial (I)
Museum/Cultural (M), Religious (RI), Residential (R), Retail (Re), Sports (S), Other (O)

	Size	HQ	Regions	Services	Markets	DI Index
Swanke Hayden Connell Archts. www.shca.com	👤👤👤	NY	E M S W C G	A E G I L P O	C E G Hc H I M RI R Re S O	★★★★
Symmes Maini & McKee Assoc. www.smma.com	👤👤👤	MA	E M S W C G	A E G I L P O	C E G Hc H I M RI R Re S O	★★★
TAYLOR www.taa1.com	👤👤	CA	E M S W C G	A E G I L P O	C E G Hc H I M RI R Re S O	★★★
TCF Architecture www.tcfarchitecture.com	👤	WA	E M S W C G	A E G I L P O	C E G Hc H I M RI R Re S O	★★★
TDA Architecture www.thendesign.com	👤	OH	E M S W C G	A E G I L P O	C E G Hc H I M RI R Re S O	★★★
TEN Arquitectos www.ten-arquitectos.com	👤👤	MEX	E M S W C G	A E G I L P O	C E G Hc H I M RI R Re S O	★★★★★
Teng & Associates www.teng.com	👤👤👤	IL	E M S W C G	A E G I L P O	C E G Hc H I M RI R Re S O	★★★★
Terence Williams Architect www.twarchitect.ca	👤	CAN	E M S W C G	A E G I L P O	C E G Hc H I M RI R Re S O	★★★
Tessier Associates www.tessierarchitects.com	👤	MA	E M S W C G	A E G I L P O	C E G Hc H I M RI R Re S O	★★★
Thalden-Boyd-Emery Architects www.thaldenboyd.com	👤	MO	E M S W C G	A E G I L P O	C E G Hc H I M RI R Re S O	★★★
Thomas Biro Associates www.thomasbiro.com	👤	NJ	E M S W C G	A E G I L P O	C E G Hc H I M RI R Re S O	★★★
Thompson & Litton www.t-l.com	👤👤👤	VA	E M S W C G	A E G I L P O	C E G Hc H I M RI R Re S O	★★★
Threshold Acoustics www.thresholdacoustics.com	👤	IL	E M S W C G	A E G I L P O	C E G Hc H I M RI R Re S O	★★★
THW Design www.thw.com	👤👤	GA	E M S W C G	A E G I L P O	C E G Hc H I M RI R Re S O	★★★
Tigerman McCurry Architects www.tigerman-mccurry.com	👤	IL	E M S W C G	A E G I L P O	C E G Hc H I M RI R Re S O	★★★★★
TMP Associates www.tmp-architecture.com	👤👤👤	MI	E M S W C G	A E G I L P O	C E G Hc H I M RI R Re S O	★★★
Tod Williams Billie Tsien Archts. www.twbta.com	👤👤	NY	E M S W C G	A E G I L P O	C E G Hc H I M RI R Re S O	★★★★★

REGIONS: East (E), Midwest (M), South (S), West (W), Canada (C), Global (G)

SERVICES: Architecture (A), Engineering (E), Graphic Design (G), Interior Design (I), Landscape Architecture (L), Planning/Urban Design (P), Other-including Industrial Design (O)

MARKETS: Corporate (C), Education (E), Government (G), Healthcare (Hc), Hospitality (H), Industrial (I) Museum/Cultural (M), Religious (RI), Residential (R), Retail (Re), Sports (S), Other (O)

	Size	HQ	Regions		Services		Markets		DI Index
Todd & Associates www.toddassoc.com	👤	AZ	E M S W C G	A E G I L P O		C E G Hc H I M RI R Re S O		★★★
Torti Gallas and Partners www.tortigallas.com	👥	MD	E M S W C G	A E G I L P O		C E G Hc H I M RI R Re S O		★★★★
Tower Design Group www.towerhawaii.com	👤	HI	E M S W C G	A E G I L P O		C E G Hc H I M RI R Re S O		★★★
Tower Pinkster www.towerpinkster.com	👥	MI	E M S W C G	A E G I L P O		C E G Hc H I M RI R Re S O		★★★
TR,i Architects www.triarchitects.com	👤	MO	E M S W C G	A E G I L P O		C E G Hc H I M RI R Re S O		★★★
TRA Architects www.traarchitects.com	👤	FL	E M S W C G	A E G I L P O		C E G Hc H I M RI R Re S O		★★★
Trivers Associates www.trivers.com	👤	MO	E M S W C G	A E G I L P O		C E G Hc H I M RI R Re S O		★★★
TRO Jung I Brannen www.trojungbrannen.com	👥👥	MA	E M S W C G	A E G I L P O		C E G Hc H I M RI R Re S O		★★★★
TruexCullins www.truexcullins.com	👥	VT	E M S W C G	A E G I L P O		C E G Hc H I M RI R Re S O		★★★
Tryba Architects www.dota.com	👤	CO	E M S W C G	A E G I L P O		C E G Hc H I M RI R Re S O		★★★
Tsao & McKown Architects www.tsao-mckown.com	👤	NY	E M S W C G	A E G I L P O		C E G Hc H I M RI R Re S O		★★★
Tsoi/Kobus & Associates www.tka-architects.com	👥👥	MA	E M S W C G	A E G I L P O		C E G Hc H I M RI R Re S O		★★★★
TSP www.teamtsp.com	👥👥	SD	E M S W C G	A E G I L P O		C E G Hc H I M RI R Re S O		★★★
Tucker Sadler Architects www.tuckersadler.com	👥	CA	E M S W C G	A E G I L P O		C E G Hc H I M RI R Re S O		★★★
Tushie Montgomery Architects www.tmiarchitects.com	👤	MN	E M S W C G	A E G I L P O		C E G Hc H I M RI R Re S O		★★★
TVA Architects www.tvaarchitects.com	👥	OR	E M S W C G	A E G I L P O		C E G Hc H I M RI R Re S O		★★★
tvsdesign www.tvs-design.com	👥👥	GA	E M S W C G	A E G I L P O		C E G Hc H I M RI R Re S O		★★★★★

REGIONS: East (E), Midwest (M), South (S), West (W), Canada (C), Global (G)

SERVICES: Architecture (A), Engineering (E), Graphic Design (G), Interior Design (I),
Landscape Architecture (L), Planning/Urban Design (P), Other-including Industrial Design (O)

MARKETS: Corporate (C), Education (E), Government (G), Healthcare (Hc), Hospitality (H), Industrial (I)
Museum/Cultural (M), Religious (RI), Residential (R), Retail (Re), Sports (S), Other (O)

		Size	HQ	Geography	Type	Markets	DI Index
U	Urbahn Architects www.urbahn.com	👤	NY	E M S W C G	A E G I L P O	C E G Hc H I M RI R Re S O	★★★
	Urban Design Associates www.urbandesignassociates.com	👤	PA	E M S W C G	A E G I L P O	C E G Hc H I M RI R Re S O	★★★★★
	USKH www.uskh.com	👥	AK	E M S W C G	A E G I L P O	C E G Hc H I M RI R Re S O	★★★
V	Van Tilburg, Banvard & Soderbergh www.vtbs.com	👥👥	CA	E M S W C G	A E G I L P O	C E G Hc H I M RI R Ro S O	★★★
	Vasquez + Marshall & Associates www.vmarch.net	👤	CA	E M S W C G	A E G I L P O	C E G Hc H I M RI R Re S O	★★★
	VBN Architects www.vbnarch.com	👤	CA	E M S W C G	A E G I L P O	C E G Hc H I M RI R Re S O	★★★
	VEBH Architects www.vebh.com	👤	PA	E M S W C G	A E G I L P O	C E G Hc H I M RI R Re S O	★★★
	Venturi, Scott, Brown and Assoc. www.vsba.com	👤	PA	E M S W C G	A E G I L P O	C E G Hc H I M RI R Re S O	★★★★★
	Vision 3 Architects www.vision3architects.com	👤	RI	E M S W C G	A E G I L P O	C E G Hc H I M RI R Re S O	★★★
	VITETTA www.vitetta.com	👥👥	PA	E M S W C G	A E G I L P O	C E G Hc H I M RI R Re S O	★★★★
	VJAA www.vjaa.com	👥	MN	E M S W C G	A E G I L P O	C E G Hc H I M RI R Re S O	★★★★★
	VLK Architects www.vlkarchitects.com	👤	TX	E M S W C G	A E G I L P O	C E G Hc H I M RI R Re S O	★★★
	VOA Associates www.voa.com	👥👥	IL	E M S W C G	A E G I L P O	C E G Hc H I M RI R Re S O	★★★★
	VPS Architecture www.vpsarch.com	👤	IN	E M S W C G	A E G I L P O	C E G Hc H I M RI R Re S O	★★★
W	W Architecture & Landscape Architecture www.w-architecture.com	👤	NY	E M S W C G	A E G I L P O	C E G Hc H I M RI R Re S O	★★★
	Wakefield Beasley & Associates www.wakefieldbeasley.com	👥👥	GA	E M S W C G	A E G I L P O	C E G Hc H I M RI R Re S O	★★★
	Wald, Ruhnke & Dost Architects www.wrdarch.com	👥👥	CA	E M S W C G	A E G I L P O	C E G Hc H I M RI R Re S O	★★★

REGIONS: East (E), Midwest (M), South (S), West (W), Canada (C), Global (G)

SERVICES: Architecture (A), Engineering (E), Graphic Design (G), Interior Design (I), Landscape Architecture (L), Planning/Urban Design (P), Other-including Industrial Design (O)

MARKETS: Corporate (C), Education (E), Government (G), Healthcare (Hc), Hospitality (H), Industrial (I) Museum/Cultural (M), Religious (RI), Residential (R), Retail (Re), Sports (S), Other (O)

	Size	HQ	Regions	Services	Markets	DI Index
Walsh Bishop Associates www.walshbishop.com	👤	MN	E M S W C G	A E G I L P O	C E G Hc H I M RI R Re S O	★★★
Wank Adams Slavin Associates www.wasallp.com	👥👥👥	NY	E M S W C G	A E G I L P O	C E G Hc H I M RI R Re S O	★★★★
Ware Malcomb www.waremalcomb.com	👥👥	CA	E M S W C G	A E G I L P O	C E G Hc H I M RI R Re S O	★★★
Waterleaf Architecture & Interiors www.waterleaf-ai.com	👤	OR	E M S W C G	A E G I L P O	C E G Hc H I M RI R Re S O	★★★
WBCM www.wbcm.com	👥👥👥	MD	E M S W C G	A E G I L P O	C E G Hc H I M RI R Re S O	★★★
WD Partners www.wdpartners.com	👥👥	OH	E M S W C G	A E G I L P O	C E G Hc H I M RI R Re S O	★★★★
WDG Architecture www.wdgarch.com	👥👥	DC	E M S W C G	A E G I L P O	C E G Hc H I M RI R Re S O	★★★
Weiss/Manfredi Architects www.weissmanfredi.com	👥👥	NY	E M S W C G	A E G I L P O	C E G Hc H I M RI R Re S O	★★★★
Westlake Reed Leskosky www.wrldesign.com	👥👥👥	OH	E M S W C G	A E G I L P O	C E G Hc H I M RI R Re S O	★★★★
WHR Architects www.whrarchitects.com	👥👥👥	TX	E M S W C G	A E G I L P O	C E G Hc H I M RI R Re S O	★★★★
Widseth Smith Nolting & Assoc. www.wsn-mn.com	👥👥👥	MN	E M S W C G	A E G I L P O	C E G Hc H I M RI R Re S O	★★★
William McDonough + Partners www.mcdonoughpartners.com	👥👥	VA	E M S W C G	A E G I L P O	C E G Hc H I M RI R Re S O	★★★★★
William Nicholas Bodouva + Associates www.bodouva.com	👥👥👥	NY	E M S W C G	A E G I L P O	C E G Hc H I M RI R Re S O	★★★
William Rawn Associates, Architects, Inc. www.rawnarch.com	👤	MA	E M S W C G	A E G I L P O	C E G Hc H I M RI R Re S O	★★★★★
Williams Blackstock Architects www.wba-architects.com	👤	AL	E M S W C G	A E G I L P O	C E G Hc H I M RI R Re S O	★★★
Wilson Architectural Group www.wilsonargroup.com	👤	TX	E M S W C G	A E G I L P O	C E G Hc H I M RI R Re S O	★★★
Wilson Associates www.wilsonassoc.com	👥👥👥	TX	E M S W C G	A E G I L P O	C E G Hc H I M RI R Re S O	★★★★★

GEOGRAPHY: East (E), Midwest (M), South (S), West (W), Canada (C), Global (G)

TYPE: Architecture (A), Engineering (E), Graphic Design (G), Interior Design (I), Landscape Architecture (L), Planning/Urban Design (P), Other-including Industrial Design (O)

MARKETS: Corporate (C), Education (E), Government (G), Healthcare (Hc), Hospitality (H), Industrial (I) Museum/cultural (M), Religious (RI), Residential (R), Retail (Re), Sports (S), Other (O)

	Size	HQ	Regions	Services	Markets	DI Index
Wimberly Allison Tong & Goo www.watg.com	👤👤👤	CA	E M S W C G	A E G I L P O	C E G Hc H I M RI R Re S O	★★★★★
Wisnewski Blair & Associates www.wba-arch.com	👤👤	VA	E M S W C G	A E G I L P O	C E G Hc H I M RI R Re S O	★★★
Wiss, Janney, Elstner Assoc. www.wje.com	👤👤👤	IL	E M S W C G	A E G I L P O	C E G Hc H I M RI R Re S O	★★★★
Wold Architects & Engineers www.woldae.com	👤👤👤	MN	E M S W C G	A E G I L P O	C E G Hc H I M RI R Re S O	★★★
Wolfberg Alvarez & Partners www.wolfbergalvarez.com	👤	FL	E M S W C G	A E G I L P O	C E G Hc H I M RI R Re S O	★★★
Workshop Architects www.workshoparchitects.com	👤	WI	E M S W C G	A E G I L P O	C E G Hc H I M RI R Re S O	★★★
Worn Jerabek Architects www.wjaworks.com	👤	IL	E M S W C G	A E G I L P O	C E G Hc H I M RI R Re S O	★★★
WorthGroup Architects www.worthgroup.com	👤👤	CO	E M S W C G	A E G I L P O	C E G Hc H I M RI R Re S O	★★★
WTW Architects www.wtwarchitects.com	👤👤	PA	E M S W C G	A E G I L P O	C E G Hc H I M RI R Re S O	★★★
Yamasato, Fujiwara, Higa & Assoc. www.yamasato.com	👤	HI	E M S W C G	A E G I L P O	C E G Hc H I M RI R Re S O	★★★
Yost Grube Hall Architecture www.ygh.com	👤👤	OR	E M S W C G	A E G I L P O	C E G Hc H I M RI R Re S O	★★★
Zeidler Partnership Architects www.zeidlerpartnership.com	👤👤👤	CAN	E M S W C G	A E G I L P O	C E G Hc H I M RI R Re S O	★★★★
Ziegler Cooper Architects www.zieglercooper.com	👤👤	TX	E M S W C G	A E G I L P O	C E G Hc H I M RI R Re S O	★★★
Ziger/Snead Architects www.zigersnead.com	👤	MD	E M S W C G	A F G I L P O	C E G Hc H I M RI R Re S O	★★★
Zimmer Gunsul Frasca Archts. www.zgf.com	👤👤👤	OR	E M S W C G	A E G I L P O	C E G Hc H I M RI R Re S O	★★★★★
Zyscovich www.zyscovich.com	👤👤👤	FL	E M S W C G	A E G I L P O	C E G Hc H I M RI R Re S O	★★★

GEOGRAPHY: East (E), Midwest (M), South (S), West (W), Canada (C), Global (G)

TYPE: Architecture (A), Engineering (E), Graphic Design (G), Interior Design (I), Landscape Architecture (L), Planning/Urban Design (P), Other-including Industrial Design (O)

MARKETS: Corporate (C), Education (E), Government (G), Healthcare (Hc), Hospitality (H), Industrial (I) Museum/cultural (M), Religious (RI), Residential (R), Retail (Re), Sports (S), Other (O)

FIRMS | Statistics & Awards

People are the focus of chapters 3 through 5. This chapter, pertaining to people in firms, contains numerous vital statistics for professional reference and diversion. Awards to firms are also included.

(Note: Bolded text indicates additions to the existing list.)

Firm Anniversaries

The following currently practicing US architecture firms were founded in 1911, 1936, 1961, and 1986 respectively.

Firms Celebrating their 100th Anniversaries

IKM, Pittsburgh, PA

Firms Celebrating their 75th Anniversaries

Burt Hill, Butler, PA
CADM Architecture, El Dorado, AR
Gruzen Samton, New York, NY
JCJ Architecture, Hartford, CT
OBM Miami, Coral Gables, FL
Pinnacle Architects, Dayton, OH
Skidmore, Owings & Merrill, Chicago, IL

Firms Celebrating their 50th Anniversaries

Architects Delawie Wilkes Rodrigues Barker,
    San Diego, CA
Arrowstreet, Boston, MA
Bani Carville & Brown Architects,
    Baton Rouge, LA
Beery Rio Architects + Interiors,
    Springfield, VA
Bink Architectural Partnership, Camp Hill, PA
Blomquist and Associates Architects, Iron
    Mountain, MI
BLT Architects, Philadelphia, PA
BOA Architecture, San Pedro, CA
Bracke Hayes Miller Mahon Architects,
    Moline, IL
Carow Architects Plus, Chicago, IL
Cooke Douglass Farr Lemons, Jackson, MS
CSO Architects, Indianapolis, IN
Earl Swensson Associates, Nashville, TN
EwingCole, Philadelphia, PA
Fanning/Howey Associates, Celina, OH
Finegold Alexander + Associates, Boston, MA
HBRA Architects, Chicago, IL
Herbert Lewis Kruse Blunck Architecture, Des
    Moines, IA
Koch Hazard Architects, Sioux Falls, SD
Mantel Teter Architects, Kansas City, MO

M2 Architects, Huntsville, AL
Nearing Staats Prelogar & Jones,
    Kansas City, MO
Peacock + Lewis, North Palm Beach, FL
Rafferty Rafferty Tollefson Lindeke
    Architecture, Minneapolis, MN
Rancorn Wildman Architects,
    Newport News, VA
Regent Associates, Westborough, MA
Richard Fleischman Architects, Cleveland, OH
Werfel and Associates, Queens, NY
Zervas Group Architects, Bellingham, WA

Firms Celebrating their 25th Anniversaries

Aller Lingle Massey Architects,
    Fort Collins, CO
AOME Architects, Seattle, WA
Archicon, Phoenix, AZ
Architecture, Inc., Reston, VA
BCWH, Richmond, VA
BDA Architecture, Albuquerque, NM
Belmont Freeman Architects, New York, NY
Bjerke Architects, Helena, MT
BL Companies, Meriden, CT
Brawer & Hauptman, Architects,
    Philadelphia, PA
Brewer Ingram Fuller Architects, Knoxville, TN
Bryan Associates, Inc. Architects,
    Burr Ridge, IL
Childress & Cunningham, Cincinnati, OH
Chipman Adams, Park Ridge, IL
Cooper Johnson Smith, Tampa, FL
DNK Architects, Cincinnati, OH
Dominy + Associates Architects,
    San Diego, CA
Dull Olson Weekes Architects, Portland, OR
Ellis Browning Architects, Santa Fe, NM
ENB Architects, Jacksonville Beach, FL
Eskew+Dumez+Ripple, New Orleans, LA
ESP Associates, Charlotte, NC

Firm Anniversaries

Eubanks Harris Tyler Craig Architects,
Tyler, TX
Facility Design Group, Smyrna, GA
Field Paoli Architects, San Francisco, CA
FitzGerald Associates Architects, Chicago, IL
Fogle Stenzel Architects, Cleveland, OH
Forum Architecture & Interior Design,
Altamonte Springs, FL
Frazier Associates, Charlottesville, VA
Garavaglia Architecture, San Francisco, CA
Gerou & Associates, Evergreen, CO
GGLO, Seattle, WA
Golba & Associates Architecture,
Pittsburgh, PA
Group 3 Architecture, Interiors, Planning,
Hilton Head Island, SC
Holleran Duitsman Architects,
Chesterfield, MO
Howorth & Associates Architects, Oxford, MS
Jackson & Ryan Architects, Houston, TX
JAS Group Architects Planners, Miami, FL
Jones & Martinez Architects, Glendale, CA
JPC Architects, Bellevue, WA
Kang Associates, Sudbury, MA
Lee, Burkhart, Liu, Marina del Rey, CA
Lemay Erickson Willcox Architects, Reston, VA

LJM Architects, Sheboygan, WI
Lucchesi Galati Architects, Las Vegas, NV
Mamola Associates Architects, Novi, MI
Marshall Craft Associates, Baltimore, MD
McKinney Partnership Architects, Norman, OK
Moser Mayer Phoenix Associates,
Greensboro, NC
Notari Associates, Baltimore, MD
Novak Design Group, Cedar Rapids, IA
Pace Architects, Milwaukee, WI
Pitassi Architects, Rancho Cucamonga, CA
RMC Architects, Bellingham, WA
Roger Ferris + Partners, Westport, CT
Schmitt Walker Architects, Charleston, SC
Silva Studios Architecture, San Diego, CA
Sorg Architects, Washington, DC
Staikos Associates Architects, Wilmington, DE
Stirling Brown Architects, Winchester, MA
Sullivan Conard Architects, Seattle, WA
SWB Architects, Baltimore, MD
Tod Williams Billie Tsien Architects,
New York, NY
Tuthill and Wells Architects, Avon, CT
Vaught Frye Ripley Design, Fort Collins, CO
Wilson Architectural Group, Houston, TX
Zivic & Hurdle Architects, Fairfax, VA

Source: DesignIntelligence

Firm Statistics: Architecture

	Number of Establishments[1]	Annual Payroll ($1,000s)	Paid Employees[2]
Alabama	246	110,502	1,763
Alaska	54	43,293	576
Arizona	657	277,321	4,457
Arkansas	160	91,629	1,763
California	3,737	2,382,959	31,432
Colorado	908	344,062	5,140
Connecticut	342	181,324	2,477
Delaware	41	15,886	262
District of Columbia	162	243,814	3,048
Florida	1,927	761,350	12,426
Georgia	662	477,793	6,338
Hawaii	199	91,420	1,341
Idaho	170	53,695	932
Illinois	1,204	614,279	8,947
Indiana	293	161,445	2,676
Iowa	129	59,317	963
Kansas	172	103,147	1,560
Kentucky	159	66,824	1,126
Louisiana	295	106,778	1,852
Maine	121	44,712	771
Maryland	453	273,012	3,705
Massachusetts	814	562,064	7,738
Michigan	529	250,040	4,138
Minnesota	439	300,385	4,554
Mississippi	119	52,187	785
Missouri	443	323,589	4,776
Montana	157	46,807	965
Nebraska	98	78,510	1,323
Nevada	198	147,711	2,018
New Hampshire	80	29,846	448
New Jersey	781	330,811	5,176
New Mexico	176	58,529	1,152
New York	2,284	1,349,385	18,709

Firm Statistics: Architecture

	Number of Establishments[1]	Annual Payroll ($1,000s)	Paid Employees[2]
North Carolina	664	304,271	4,669
North Dakota	40	15,636	294
Ohio	644	377,183	6,139
Oklahoma	204	103,826	1,874
Oregon	391	214,041	3,507
Pennsylvania	771	552,736	8,295
Rhode Island	90	28,352	540
South Carolina	303	112,830	1,924
South Dakota	43	12,949	247
Tennessee	298	215,532	3,057
Texas	1,537	1,051,589	13,584
Utah	254	111,095	1,895
Vermont	94	21,610	418
Virginia	587	358,991	5,182
Washington	805	448,875	6,573
West Virginia	41	17,603	398
Wisconsin	306	159,825	2,686
Wyoming	50	14,465	257
US Total	**25,331**	**14,155,835**	**206,876**

[1] All numbers are 2008.
[2] Paid employees for the pay period including March 12.

Source: US Census Bureau

Firm Statistics: Number of Establishments

Architecture

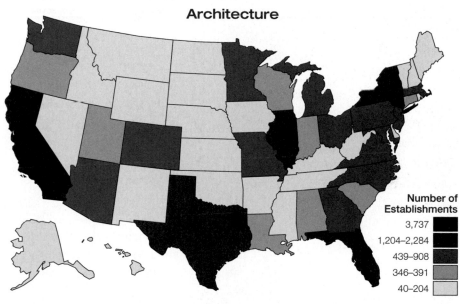

	Number of Establishments
3,737	
1,204–2,284	
439–908	
346–391	
40–204	

The District of Columbia contains 162 establishments. US Total Number of Establishments: 25,331.

Industrial Design

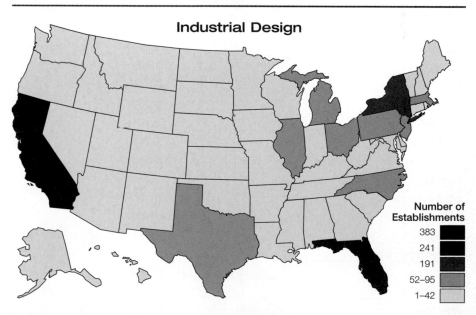

	Number of Establishments
383	
241	
191	
52–95	
1–42	

The District of Columbia contains 1 establishment. US Total Number of Establishments: 1,984.

Source: DesignIntelligence

Firm Statistics: Industrial Design

	Number of Establishments[1]	Annual Payroll ($1,000s)	Paid Employees[2]
Alabama	6	574	6
Alaska	1	Withheld	n/a
Arizona	32	6,130	n/a
Arkansas	6	983	n/a
California	383	172,722	2,424
Colorado	36	15,463	205
Connecticut	25	8,563	113
Delaware	2	Withheld	n/a
District of Columbia	1	Withheld	n/a
Florida	241	22,862	664
Georgia	37	7,510	134
Hawaii	3	Withheld	n/a
Idaho	8	Withheld	n/a
Illinois	87	23,825	387
Indiana	25	4,999	83
Iowa	7	557	17
Kansas	12	2,070	41
Kentucky	19	3,965	86
Louisiana	10	3,301	n/a
Maine	7	Withheld	n/a
Maryland	25	6,094	101
Massachusetts	54	48,270	552
Michigan	76	52,461	n/a
Minnesota	37	16,146	309
Mississippi	2	Withheld	n/a
Missouri	13	5,035	103
Montana	2	Withheld	n/a
Nebraska	3	Withheld	n/a
Nevada	26	3,611	n/a
New Hampshire	10	12,640	123
New Jersey	52	30,450	585
New Mexico	10	7,877	n/a
New York	191	91,818	1,376

	Number of Establishments[1]	Annual Payroll ($1,000s)	Paid Employees[2]
North Carolina	95	48,113	765
North Dakota	13	810	30
Ohio	78	36,335	595
Oklahoma	2	Withheld	n/a
Oregon	42	Withheld	n/a
Pennsylvania	65	41,726	796
Rhode Island	14	4,270	65
South Carolina	12	2,783	40
South Dakota	1	Withheld	n/a
Tennessee	11	Withheld	n/a
Texas	79	64,129	818
Utah	17	1,728	67
Vermont	12	2,245	48
Virginia	19	7,562	129
Washington	28	9,229	194
West Virginia	1	Withheld	n/a
Wisconsin	34	12,393	269
Wyoming	12	850	35
US Total	**1,984**	**780,099**	**11,160**

[1] All numbers are 2008.
[2] Paid employees for the pay period including March 12.

Source: US Census Bureau

Firm Statistics: Interior Design

	Number of Establishments[1]	Annual Payroll ($1,000s)	Paid Employees[2]
Alabama	109	8,470	289
Alaska	16	2,662	71
Arizona	321	41,600	1,073
Arkansas	70	5,846	241
California	1,923	448,642	8,436
Colorado	478	71,587	1,545
Connecticut	177	28,025	562
Delaware	42	6,476	163
District of Columbia	58	62,195	864
Florida	1,857	200,677	5,256
Georgia	557	87,891	1,832
Hawaii	43	7,792	148
Idaho	52	4,164	130
Illinois	699	105,265	2,273
Indiana	190	21,530	660
Iowa	69	4,502	190
Kansas	92	6,855	288
Kentucky	101	9,497	305
Louisiana	107	9,660	299
Maine	26	2,573	86
Maryland	289	45,875	1010
Massachusetts	309	53,039	973
Michigan	270	28,619	777
Minnesota	235	26,855	716
Mississippi	50	5,422	188
Missouri	160	25,903	597
Montana	41	3,246	104
Nebraska	67	7,312	268
Nevada	137	23,899	498
New Hampshire	36	3,885	73
New Jersey	434	60,153	1,502
New Mexico	49	3,834	144
New York	1,323	304,350	4,787

	Number of Establishments[1]	Annual Payroll ($1,000s)	Paid Employees[2]
North Carolina	402	39,565	1,325
North Dakota	15	1,246	48
Ohio	272	47,652	1,094
Oklahoma	113	9,455	290
Oregon	146	19,810	569
Pennsylvania	310	83,465	1,516
Rhode Island	41	8,596	170
South Carolina	193	16,666	595
South Dakota	15	795	41
Tennessee	171	22,668	551
Texas	818	154,708	3,446
Utah	104	9,360	327
Vermont	26	1,838	52
Virginia	379	54,023	1,306
Washington	267	32,155	858
West Virginia	25	1,604	n/a
Wisconsin	108	14,045	407
Wyoming	17	1,881	42
US Total	**13,809**	**2,247,833**	**48,985**

[1] All numbers are 2008.
[2] Paid employees for the pay period including March 12.

Source: US Census Bureau

Firm Statistics: Number of Establishments

Interior Design

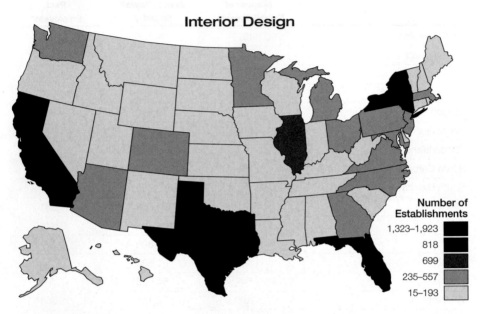

Number of Establishments

1,323–1,923	
818	
699	
235–557	
15–193	

The District of Columbia contains 58 establishments. US Total Number of Establishments: 13,809.

Landscape Architecture

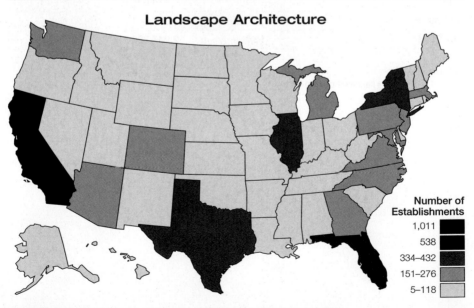

Number of Establishments

1,011	
538	
334–432	
151–276	
5–118	

The District of Columbia contains 23 establishments. US Total Number of Establishments: 6,630.

Source: DesignIntelligence

Firm Statistics: Landscape Architecture

	Number of Establishments[1]	Annual Payroll ($1,000s)	Paid Employees[2]
Alabama	40	7,481	184
Alaska	10	1,424	31
Arizona	175	80,130	1,790
Arkansas	28	4,477	174
California	1,011	470,530	9,507
Colorado	244	78,479	1,370
Connecticut	88	17,244	247
Delaware	27	6,182	141
District of Columbia	23	7,370	104
Florida	538	182,590	3,632
Georgia	177	48,821	1,077
Hawaii	38	14,920	227
Idaho	43	7,373	149
Illinois	396	104,774	1,904
Indiana	83	12,309	296
Iowa	30	5,204	122
Kansas	29	7,988	248
Kentucky	46	9,297	326
Louisiana	60	13,209	371
Maine	33	4,469	102
Maryland	158	43,658	931
Massachusetts	220	70,493	988
Michigan	167	33,498	656
Minnesota	90	18,774	401
Mississippi	25	4,970	174
Missouri	82	14,567	532
Montana	31	3,631	81
Nebraska	20	2,181	64
Nevada	40	23,272	546
New Hampshire	31	6,017	203
New Jersey	276	56,083	1,063
New Mexico	46	8,876	217
New York	432	114,559	1,857

Firm Statistics: Landscape Architecture

	Number of Establishments[1]	Annual Payroll ($1,000s)	Paid Employees[2]
North Carolina	255	68,800	1,526
North Dakota	5	317	n/a
Ohio	118	39,276	723
Oklahoma	51	10,648	349
Oregon	118	23,210	629
Pennsylvania	231	69,108	1,293
Rhode Island	30	5,483	119
South Carolina	96	22,093	672
South Dakota	13	1,957	48
Tennessee	110	28,881	740
Texas	334	114,561	2,498
Utah	84	13,560	377
Vermont	30	2,912	49
Virginia	151	49,254	1,011
Washington	170	46,162	964
West Virginia	8	749	39
Wisconsin	73	22,438	462
Wyoming	16	2,943	53
US Total	**6,630**	**2,007,202**	**41,267**

[1] All numbers are 2008.
[2] Paid employees for the pay period including March 12.

Source: US Census Bureau

Number of Registered Architects

Registered architects in each state are divided into two categories: resident and reciprocal, or non-resident, registrants. Based on current population levels, the chart below also calculates the per capita number of resident architects in each state. The following information is from the National Council of Architectural Registration Boards' 2008 survey.

State	Resident Architects	Reciprocal Registrations	Total	Population	Per capita # of Resident Arch. (per 100,000)
Alabama	856	1839	2,695	4,708,708	18
Alaska	242	330	572	698,473	35
Arizona	2,186	4,267	6,453	6,595,778	33
Arkansas	215	964	1,179	2,889,450	7
California	15,816	4,435	20,251	36,961,664	43
Colorado	3,243	4,197	7,440	5,024,748	65
Connecticut	1,556	2,992	4,548	3,518,288	44
Delaware	129	1,188	1,317	885,122	15
District of Columbia	556	2,457	3,013	599,657	93
Florida	4,754	4,221	8,975	18,537,969	26
Georgia	2,462	3,196	5,658	9,829,211	25
Hawaii	976	1233	2,209	1,295,178	75
Idaho	487	1,197	1,684	1,545,801	32
Illinois	5,301	3,624	8,925	12,910,409	41
Indiana	957	2,224	3,181	6,423,113	15
Iowa	522	1,285	1,807	3,007,856	17
Kansas	905	1,771	2,676	2,818,747	32
Kentucky	708	1,601	2,309	4,314,113	16
Louisiana	1,069	1,963	3,032	4,492,076	24
Maine	408	1124	1,532	1,318,301	31
Maryland	2,637	2,435	5,072	5,699,478	46
Massachusetts	3,460	2,911	6,371	6,593,587	52
Michigan	2,622	3,254	5,876	9,969,727	26
Minnesota	1,852	1,538	3,390	5,266,214	35
Mississippi	328	1599	1,927	2,951,996	11
Missouri	1,769	2,749	4,518	5,987,580	30
Montana	413	927	1,340	974,989	42

Number of Registered Architects

State	Resident Architects	Reciprocal Registrations	Total	Population	Per capita # of Resident Arch. (per 100,000)
Nebraska	519	1135	1,654	1,796,619	29
Nevada	611	2,770	3,381	2,643,085	23
New Hampshire	432	1931	2,363	1,324,575	33
New Jersey	3,013	4,815	7,828	8,707,739	35
New Mexico	711	1,506	2,217	2,009,671	35
New York	8,780	6,243	15,023	19,541,453	45
North Carolina	2,293	3,447	5,740	9,380,884	24
North Dakota	128	599	727	646,844	20
Ohio	3,276	3,499	6,775	11,542,645	28
Oklahoma	742	1,381	2,123	3,687,050	20
Oregon	1,521	1,166	2,687	3,825,657	40
Pennsylvania	3,483	3,645	7,128	12,604,767	28
Rhode Island	303	1,333	1,636	1,053,209	29
South Carolina	1023	2,639	3,662	4,561,242	22
South Dakota	98	673	771	812,383	12
Tennessee	1,288	1,836	3,124	6,296,254	20
Texas	6,910	3,423	10,333	24,782,302	28
Utah	735	1531	2,266	2,784,572	26
Vermont	295	751	1,046	621,760	47
Virginia	2,763	4,232	6,995	7,882,590	35
Washington	3,845	2,253	6,098	6,664,195	58
West Virginia	121	1190	1,311	1,819,777	7
Wisconsin	1,659	3,287	4,946	5,654,774	29
Wyoming	110	934	1,044	544,270	20
Totals	**101,088**	**117,740**	**218,828**	**307,006,550**	

Source: National Council of Architectural Registration Boards and DesignIntelligence

Oldest Architecture Firms

The following North American architecture firms were founded prior to 1912 (their specific founding dates indicated below) and are still operational today.

1827	Mason & Hanger, Lexington, KY	1885	Cromwell Architects Engineers, Little Rock, AR
1853	Luckett & Farley, Louisville, KY		
1853	SmithGroup, Detroit, MI	1885	HLW International. New York, NY
1868	Jensen and Halstead, Chicago, IL	1887	Bradley & Bradley, Rockford, IL.
1868	King & King Architects, Manlius, NY	1888	Parkinson Field Associates, Austin, TX
1870	Harriman, Auburn, ME	1889	CSHQA, Boise, ID
1871	Scholtz Gowey Gere Marolf Architects & Interior Designers, Davenport, IA	1889	MacLachlan, Cornelius & Filoni, Pittsburgh, PA
1873	Graham, Anderson, Probst, & White, Chicago, IL	1889	Wank Adams Slavin Associates, New York, NY
1874	Shepley Bulfinch Richardson and Abbott, Boston, MA	1890	Kendall, Taylor & Company, Billerica, MA
1876	Keffer/Overton Architects, Des Moines, IA	1890	Mathes Brierre Architects, New Orleans, LA
1878	The Austin Company, Kansas City, MO	1890	Plunkett Raysich Architects, Milwaukee, WI
1878	Ballinger, Philadelphia, PA	1891	SSP Architectural Group, Somerville, NJ
1880	Beatty, Harvey, Coco Architects, New York, NY	1892	FreemanWhite, Raleigh, NC
1880	Holabird & Root, Chicago, IL	1892	Architectural Design West, Logan, UT
1880	Zeidler Partnership Architects, Toronto, Canada	1893	Foor & Associates, Elmira, NY
1883	Hulsing and Associates Architects, Bismarck, ND	1894	Colgan Perry Lawler Aurell Architects, Nyack, NY
1883	Ritterbush-Elig-Hulsing, Bismarck, ND	1894	Freese and Nichols, Fort Worth, TX
1884	SMRT, Portland, ME	1895	Brooks Borg Skiles Architecture Engineering, Des Moines, IA
		1895	Albert Kahn Associates, Detroit, MI

Oldest Architecture Firms

1896	Hummel Architects, Boise, ID
1896	Kessels DiBoll Kessels, New Orleans, LA
1897	Baskervill, Richmond, VA
1898	Beardsley Design Associates, Auburn, NY
1898	Berners-Schober Associates, Green Bay, WI
1898	Burns & McDonnell, Kansas City, MO
1898	Eckles Architecture, New Castle, PA
1898	FEH Associates, Des Moines, IA
1898	Foss Architecture & Interiors, Fargo, ND & Moorhead, MN
1898	PageSoutherlandPage, Austin, TX
1899	Ittner Architects, St. Louis, MO
1900	DLR Group, Seattle, WA
1901	SHP Leading Design, Cincinnati, OH
1901	Wiley I Wilson, Lynchburg, VA
1902	WBRC, Bangor, ME
1906	AC Martin, Los Angeles, CA
1906	CJMW, Winston Salem, NC
1906	PMSM Architects, Santa Barbara, CA
1906	Ratcliff, Emeryville, CA
1906	Swanke Hayden Connell Architects, New York, NY
1906	Zimmerman Architectural Studios, Milwaukee, WI
1907	Ballou Justice Upton Architects, Richmond, VA
1907	Eppstein Uhen Architects, Milwaukee, WI
1907	Fletcher Thompson, Shelton, CT
1907	H2L2, Philadelphia, PA
1908	Ballard and Associates, Alexandria, VA
1908	Harley Ellis Devereaux, Southfield, MI
1908	Kahler Slater, Milwaukee, WI
1908	Somdal Associates, Shreveport, LA
1909	Altman & Altman, Architects, Uniontown, PA
1909	Ellerbe Becket, Minneapolis, MN
1909	Howell Rusk Dodson, Architects, Atlanta, GA
1909	Lionakis, Sacramento, CA
1909	Moeckel Carbonell Associates, Wilmington, DE
1909	TRO Jung	Brannen, Boston, MA
1910	Hart Freeland Roberts, Nashville, TN
1911	IKM, Pittsburgh, PA

Source: DesignIntelligence

Architecture Firm Award

The American Institute of Architects grants its Architecture Firm Award, **the highest honor the AIA can bestow on a firm, annually to an architecture firm for consistently producing distinguished architecture**. Eligible firms must claim collaboration within the practice as a hallmark of their methodology and must have been producing work as an entity for at least 10 years.

www.aia.org

1962	Skidmore, Owings & Merrill	1987	Benjamin Thompson & Associates
1963	*No award granted*	1988	Hartman-Cox Architects
1964	The Architects Collaborative	1989	Cesar Pelli & Associates
1965	Wurster, Bernardi & Emmons	1990	Kohn Pedersen Fox Associates
1966	*No award granted*	1991	Zimmer Gunsul Frasca Partnership
1967	Hugh Stubbins & Associates	1992	James Stewart Polshek & Partners
1968	I.M. Pei & Partners	1993	Cambridge Seven Associates
1969	Jones & Emmons	1994	Bohlin Cywinski Jackson
1970	Ernest J. Kump Associates	1995	Beyer Blinder Belle
1971	Albert Kahn Associates	1996	Skidmore, Owings & Merrill
1972	Caudill Rowlett Scott	1997	R.M. Kliment & Frances Halsband Architects
1973	Shepley Bulfinch Richardson and Abbott	1998	Centerbrook Architects and Planners
1974	Kevin Roche John Dinkeloo & Associates	1999	Perkins+Will
1975	Davis, Brody & Associates	2000	Gensler
1976	Mitchell/Giurgola Architects	2001	Herbert Lewis Kruse Blunck Architecture
1977	Sert Jackson and Associates	2002	Thompson, Ventulett, Stainback & Associates
1978	Harry Weese & Associates	2003	Miller|Hull Partnership
1979	Geddes Brecher Qualls Cunningham	2004	Lake/Flato Architects
1980	Edward Larrabee Barnes Associates	2005	Murphy/Jahn Architects
1981	Hardy Holzman Pfeiffer Associates	2006	Moore Ruble Yudell Architects & Planners
1982	Gwathmey Siegel & Associates, Architects	2007	Leers Weinzapfel Associates
1983	Holabird & Root	2008	KieranTimberlake Associates
1984	Kallmann, McKinnell & Wood Architects	2009	Olson Sundberg Kundig Allen Architects
1985	Venturi, Rauch and Scott Brown	**2010**	**Pugh + Scarpa**
1986	Esherick Homsey Dodge and Davis		

Source: American Institute of Architects

ASLA Firm Award

The American Society of Landscape Architects presents its annual ASLA Firm Award to a **landscape architecture firm that has produced a body of distinguished work for at least 10 years**. Nominees are reviewed for their influence on the profession, their collaborative environment, the consistent quality of their work, and their recognition among fellow practitioners, teachers, allied professionals, and the general public.

www.asla.org

2003	Jones & Jones Architects and Landscape Architects
2004	Wallace Roberts & Todd
2005	SWA Group
2006	OLIN
2007	Sasaki Associates, Inc.
2008	Design Workshop
2009	EDAW	AECOM
2010	**EDSA**

Source: American Society of Landscape Architects

Marketing Communications Awards

The annual Marketing Communications Awards are presented by the Society for Marketing Professional Services to recognize **excellence in marketing communications by firms in the design and building industry**. The diverse categories acknowledge the wide-ranging initiatives a marketing strategy can entail.

www.smps.org

2010 First-Place Winners

Advertising
Baker Concrete Construction

Annual Report
Gannett Fleming

Book/Monograph
Gresham, Smith and
   Partners

Brochure
GLY Construction
The Krill Co.*

Corporate Identity
BOND
ArchitectureIsFun*

Direct-Mail Campaign
RATIO Architects

Feature Writing
Cannon Design

Holiday Piece
USKH
Bloomfield Group*

**Internal
Communications**
EYP Architecture &
   Engineering

Magazine
HNTB

**Media Relations
Campaign**
HNTB

Newsletter, External
MulvannyG2 Architecture

Newsletter, Internal
Faithful+Gould

**Promotional
Campaign**
EYP Architecture &
   Engineering

**Recruitment
& Retention
Communications**
Degenkolb Engineers

**Social Media
Campaign**
Capelin Communications

Special Event
Hickok Cole Architects
MW Builders*

**Specific Project
Marketing**
HGA Architects and
   Engineers

Target Marketing
CBT

Web Site
RATIO Architects
Silverscape*

Best of Show Award
HGA Architects and
   Engineers
MW Builders*

**People's Choice
Award**
Degenkolb Engineers

*Small-firm winner

Source: Society for Marketing
Professional Services

Small Project Awards

The Small Project Awards sponsored by the American Institute of Architects **highlight the achievements of small-project practitioners for the high quality of their work and to promote excellence in small-project design**. The competition also strives to raise public awareness of the value and design excellence that architects bring to projects, no matter the limits of size and scope.

www.aia.org

2010 Winners

Architecture in the Public Interest
Art as Shelter
Raleigh, NC
Tonic Design

SplitFrame
Portland, CT
North Studio at Wesleyan University

Objects
Shadow Pavilion
Ann Arbor, MI
PLY Architecture

plug-in satellite office, Arizona State University
Phoenix, AZ
mark ryan studio

Prospect.1 Welcome Center
New Orleans, LA
Eskew+Dumez+Ripple

Puptent
New York, NY
Slade architecture

Structures
East Village Studio
New York, NY
jordan parnass digital architecture

Salve Staff Canteen
Milwaukee, WI
Johnsen Schmaling Architects

Kevin Mundy Memorial Bridge
Bozeman, MT
Intrinsik Architecture

[Wide] Band - Nomadic Café
Los Angeles, CA
Griffin Enright Architects

Source: American Institute of Architects

PEOPLE | Honors & Awards

Design leaders are featured in this chapter.
Induction as a fellow is an honor commonly
bestowed upon the industry's prominent
leaders. Many awards granted to individual
designers are also included.

(Note: Bolded text indicates additions to the existing list.)

Fellows of the American Academy of Arts and Sciences

Since its founding in 1780, the American Academy of Arts and Sciences has pursued as its goal **"to cultivate every art and science which may tend to advance the interest, honor, dignity, and happiness of a free, independent, and virtuous people."** Its diverse membership has included leaders from the arts, science, business, scholarship, and public affairs. Current members, also known as fellows, nominate and evaluate candidates for new membership.

Fellows: Design Professionals

Christopher Alexander
Edward Larrabee Barnes
Herbert Lawrence Block
Denise Scott Brown
Robert Campbell
Henry N. Cobb
Charles Correa* (India)
Elizabeth Diller
Carl Theodor Dreyer* (Denmark)
Peter Eisenman
Sir Norman Foster* (UK)
Kenneth Frampton
Frank Gehry
Lawrence Halprin
Steven Holl
Robert S.F. Hughes
Ada Louise Huxtable
Toyo Ito* (Japan)
Gerhard M. Kallmann
Rem Koolhaas* (Netherlands)
Phyllis Lambert* (Canada)
Ricardo Legorreta* (Mexico)
Michael Levitt
Maya Lin
Fumihiko Maki* (Japan)
Thom Mayne

N. Michael McKinnell
Richard Meier
Henry A. Millon
William Mitchell
Rafael Moneo* (Spain)
Oscar Niemeyer* (Brazil)
Guy Nordenson
I.M. Pei
Renzo Piano* (Italy)
James Stewart Polshek
William L. Rawn III
Kevin Roche
Elizabeth Barlow Rogers
Robert Rosenblum
Moshe Safdie
Ricardo Scofidio
Vincent J. Scully
Alvaro Siza* (Portugal)
Michael Sorkin
Robert A.M. Stern
Kenzo Tange* (Japan)
Billie Tsien
Robert Venturi
Tod Williams
Peter Zumthor* (Switzerland)

*Foreign honorary members

Source: American Academy of Arts and Sciences

Fellows of the American Institute of Architects

Fellowship in the American Institute of Architects recognizes members who have contributed notably to the **advancement of the architecture profession**. As an international counterpart, foreign architects may be granted honorary fellowship. For those who have demonstrated distinguished service to architecture and the allied arts and sciences and who are not otherwise eligible for membership in the AIA, the organization grants honorary membership.

2010 Fellows

Trevor Abramson
David Allison
Mark Anderson
Peter Arsenault
Michel Ashe
Richard Beard
Bruce Beinfield
G. Edwin Belk
Martha Bell
Hagy Belzberg
James Bershof
Bonnie Blake-Drucker
Christine Bodouva
Charles Boney Jr.
William Bonstra
Chris Brasier
Creed Brierre
Douglas Brinkley
Donna Carter
Richard Carter
Philip Castillo
William Chegwidden
Nelson Chen
Thomas Chessum
William Chilton
Sho-Ping Chin
Christopher Coe
Bruce Coldham
William Conway
Michael Corby
Juan Cotera
Lynn Craig

Ralph Cunningham
Michael Davis
Grover Dear
Sarah Ann Dennison
Edward Denton
Michael Doyle
Robert Dunay
Herman Dyal
Edmund Einy
Kevin Flynn
Anne Fougeron
Donald Fram
Kenn Gardner
Lia Gartner
Stephanie Gelb
Richard Gilyard
Sarah Graham
John Guenther
David Hacin
C. Richard Hall
Sam Halley
Thomas (Gunny) Harboe
Philip Harrison
Thomas Harvey
Hany Hassan
Diane Berry Hays
Richard Heinz
Kimberly Hickson
Albert Hightower
Charles Higueras
Mark Horton
James Housewright

Ted Hyman
Stephen Johnson
Susan Jones
Mary Louise Jurkowski
Philip Kennedy-Grant
Alice Kimm
Jerome King
James Kise
Alex Klatskin
Joan Krevlin
David Laffitte
Hugh Latimer
Michael Lauber
Michael LeBoeuf
William Ooi Lee Lim
James Loewenberg
Robert Luke
Sandro Marpillero
Bernard Marson
Joseph Mashburn
R. Kent Mather
Kenneth Mayer Jr.
Burton Miller
Leslie Gail Moldow
Robert Morris
Hubert Murray
James Nader
Dean Nota
Charles Oraftik
Paul O'Shea
Nicholas Peckham
Sue Pemberton-Haugh

Aubrey Pentecost III
Russell Perry
Bogdan Pestka
Peter Pfau
Jeffery Poss
Otto Poticha
Jeffery Potter
Gwynne Pugh
Elizabeth Ranieri
August Reno
James Robertson
Miguel Rodriguez
Bill Roschen

Jeffrey Rosenblum
James Russell
Dean Sakamoto
Lawrence Scarpa
Anthony Schirripa
Bradley Schulz
Walter Sedovic
Scott Shell
James Shields
Joan Soranno
Lars Stanley
Michael Strogoff
Yvonne Szeto

John Thodos
Benedetto Tiseo
Karen Van Lengen
Dean Vlahos
Joseph Waggonner III
John Waugh
Peter Weismantle
Richard Pardee Williams
Daniel Winey
Barry Yoakum
Francis Zwart III
Bernard Zyscovich

2010 Honorary Fellows

Rafael Aranda Quiles (Spain)
Mario Corea (Spain)
Jungsik Kim (Korea)
Richard Leplastrier (Australia)

Sheila O'Donnell (Ireland)
Carme Pigem Barcelo (Spain)
Brian Robert Rich
   (South Africa)

Ian Ritchie (UK)
John Tuomey (Ireland)
Lene Tranberg (Denmark)
Ramon Vilalta Pujol (Spain)

2010 Honorary Members

Patricia Daugherty
Parris Glendening

Jerrold Lea
Peter Miller

Gail Thomas
David Thurm

*Source: American Institute
of Architects*

Fellows of the American Institute of Certified Planners

Fellowship in the American Institute of Certified Planners is **one of the highest honors the AICP can bestow upon a member**. The AICP grants fellowships every two years to members who have achieved excellence in professional practice, teaching and mentoring, research, public and community service, and leadership.

2010–2011 Fellows

Norman Abbott
Ann Bagley
Robert Barber
Owen Beitsch
Richard Bickel
Charles Billand
Graham Billingsley
Richard Bolan
Roberta Burroughs
M. Perry Chapman
William Cohen
Pat Comarell
Charlie Compton

Gary Cooper
Jeanette Dinwiddie-Moore
Victor Fischer
C. Bickley Foster
Corinne Fox
Steve Gordon
William Gould
Cynthia Hoyle
Valerie Hubbard
Peter Lowitt
Weiming Lu
William McAllister
Robin McClelland

Robert Mulhere
Lee Nellis
Ben Orsbon
Rocky Piro
Joe Pobiner
Ralph Portmore
Orlando Riutort
John Shardlow
William Snowden
Ralph Willmer
Alfred Zelinka

Source: American Institute of Certified Planners

Fellows of the American Society of Interior Designers

The American Society of Interior Designers grants fellowship, the highest honor bestowed on its members, to those who have made **notable and substantial contributions to the interior design profession or ASID**. Those who have been professional ASID members for at least 10 continuous years are eligible for nomination.

2010 Fellows

Bruce Goff
Sari Graven
Calvin Hefner
Lisa Henry

Charles Larry Horne
D. Samantha McAskill
Rachelle Schoessler Lynn
Janice Young

Source: American Society of Interior Designers

Fellows of the American Society of Landscape Architects

The American Society of Landscape Architects grants fellowship to members of at least 10 years who have made **outstanding contributions to the profession in such areas as works of landscape architecture, administrative work, knowledge, and service**.

2010 Fellows

José M. Almiñana
William D. Almond
James P. Ballantyne
(Canada)
J. Robert Behling
Pamela M. Blough
Earl Broussard
Ignacio F. Bunster-Ossa
Jon Bryan Burley
Susan Cohen
Diane M. Dale
George F. Dark (Canada)
Harry S. Fuller
Joseph Geller

Jim Gordon Hagstrom
Michael S. Hamm
Douglas Hays
Frederick T. Hume
Heather Kinkade
Steven E. Koch
Tadd B. Kreun
Stephanie V. Landregan
Robby D. Layton
Marsha Lea
Todd Marshall McCurdy
Alistair T. McIntosh
Jana Dewey McKenzie
Hitesh Sukhlal Mehta

Dennis J. Mersky
James T. Penrod
April J. Philips
James P. Richards Jr.
Lucinda R. Sanders
Troy D. Sibelius
Greg Smallenberg (Canada)
Jerry A. Smith
Whitney A. Talcott
Elizabeth Thomas
Robert E. Truskowski
Donna Walcavage
Barbara E. Wilks
David J. Yocca

Source: American Society of Landscape Architects

Fellows of the Design Futures Council

Fellowship in the Design Futures Council is granted annually to an outstanding individual(s) who has provided noteworthy leadership to the advancement of design, design solutions, and/or the design professions. Senior fellows of the DFC are recognized for **significant contributions toward the understanding of changing trends, new research, and applied knowledge that improve the built environment and the human condition**. Any person worldwide may nominate candidates. The final selection of the senior fellows is made by the Senior Fellows Selection Committee.

Ava Abramowitz, George Washington
University Law School
Harold Adams, RTKL
David M. Adamson, UCL & UWE
David Adjaye, Adjaye Associates
Ray Anderson, Interface
Rodrigo Arboleda, One Laptop Per Child
Association
James F. Barker, Clemson University
Peter Beck, The Beck Group
Janine M. Benyus, Biomimicry & Sustainability
Expert
Robert J. Berkebile, BNIM Architects
Phil Bernstein, Autodesk & Yale University
Peter Bohlin, Bohlin Cywinski Jackson
Friedl Bohm, White Oaks Partners
Penny Bonda, *Interior Design* Magazine
John Seely Brown, Deloitte Center for Edge
Innovation
Barbara White Bryson, Rice University
Carrie Byles, Skidmore, Owings & Merrill
Santiago Calatrava, Santiago Calatrava
Architects
Robert Campbell, *The Boston Globe*
John Cary, *Next American City*
Wing Chao, Walt Disney Imagineering
David Childs, Skidmore, Owings & Merrill
Steve Chu, Secretary of Energy, U.S. Dept.
of Energy
Daniel P. Coffey, Daniel P. Coffey &
Associates
**Cindy Coleman, Frankel + Coleman &
School of the Art Institute of Chicago**
Carol Coletta, CEOs for Cities

James P. Cramer†, Design Futures Council
Co-Founder & Greenway Group
Michael Crichton*, Design Advocate, Author,
Film Director
Sylvester Damianos, Damianosgroup
Nigel Dancey, Foster + Partners
Clark Davis, HOK
Betsy del Monte, The Beck Group
Williston (Bill) Dye, TSA, Inc.
Phil Enquist, Skidmore, Owings & Merrill
Del Eulberg, Booz Allen Hamilton; USAF (ret.)
Richard Farson, Western Behavioral Sciences
Institute
**Rick Fedrizzi, United States Green Building
Council**
Edward A. Feiner, Perkins+Will
Martin Fischer, Center for Integrated Facility
Engineering, Stanford University
Tom Fisher, College of Design, University of
Minnesota
Stephen Fiskum, HGA Architects and
Engineers
Jim Follett, Gensler
Sir Norman Foster, Foster + Partners
Harrison Fraker, University of California,
Berkeley
Neil Frankel, Frankel + Coleman
Roger Frechette, PositivEnergy Practice
Ed Friedrichs, Friedrichs Group
R. Buckminster (Bucky) Fuller*, Engineer,
Inventor, Educator & Architectural Innovator
Thomas Galloway*, Georgia Institute of
Technology
Jan Gehl, Gehl Architects

Frank Gehry, Gehry Partners
M. Arthur Gensler, Gensler
Milton Glaser, Milton Glaser, Inc.
Roger Godwin, DAG Architects
Paul Goldberger, *The New Yorker*
Al Gore, Former Vice President of the United
States of America
David Gottfried, Regenerative Ventures
Michael Graves, Michael Graves & Associates
Robert Greenstreet, University of Wisconsin-
Milwaukee
Robert C. Grupe, USG Building Systems
Zaha Hadid, Zaha Hadid Architects
Gerry Hammond*, SHP Leading Design
Jeremy Harris, former Mayor of Honolulu
**Scott Harrison, President and Founder of
charity: water**
Craig W. Hartman, Skidmore, Owings & Merrill
Paul Hawken, Natural Capital Institute
H. Ralph Hawkins, HKS, Inc.
Barbara Heller, Design + Construction
Strategies
Jerry Hobbs, Boston Ventures
Carl Hodges, The Seawater Foundation
Robert Ivy, *Architectural Record*
Jane Jacobs*, Urban Theorist, Author,
Educator & Community Activist
Mary Margaret Jones, Hargreaves Associates
Louis I. Kahn*, Architect & Educator, University
of Pennsylvania
Blair Kamin, *The Chicago Tribune*
Don Kasian, Kasian Architecture Interior
Design and Planning
Tom Kelley, IDEO
Stephen Kieran, KieranTimberlake
A. Eugene Kohn, Kohn Pedersen Fox
Norman Koonce, Architect and Former CEO,
The American Institute of Architects
Theodore C. Landsmark, Boston Architectural
College
Gary Lawrence, AECOM
Laura Lee, Carnegie Mellon University
Maya Lin, Maya Lin Studio
Amory Lovins, Rocky Mountain Institute
Lucinda Ludwig*, LEO A DALY

Chris Luebkeman, Arup
John Maeda, Rhode Island School of Design
Janet Martin, Communication Arts (Stantec)
Bruce Mau, Bruce Mau Design
Thom Mayne, Morphosis
Ed Mazria, Architecture 2030
William McDonough, William McDonough
+ Partners
Alisdair McGregor, Arup
Richard Meier, Richard Meier & Partners
Architects
Sandra Mendler, Mithun
Raymond F. Messer, Walter P. Moore
Gordon Mills, Durrant
Glenn Murcutt, Professor and Architect
Douglas R. Parker, Greenway Group
Alexander (Sandy) Pentland, MIT Media Lab
Renzo Piano, Renzo Piano Building Workshop
B. Joseph Pine II, Strategic Horizons LLP
Dan Pink, Author & Economics Lecturer
William Bradley (Brad) Pitt, Actor &
Environmental Advocate
Jane Poynter, Paragon Space Development
Corp.
Witold Rybczynski, Wharton School of
Business, University of Pennsylvania
Moshe Safdie, Moshe Safdie and Associates
Jonas Salk*, Co-founder of the Design Futures
Council; Founder of The Salk Institute
Adele Santos, School of Architecture &
Planning, Massachusetts Institute of
Technology
Peter Schwartz, Global Business Network
Kate Schwennsen, School of Architecture,
Clemson University
Terrence J. Sejnowski, The Salk Institute
Stephen J. Senkowski, Xella Aircrete North
America
Scott Simpson, KlingStubbins
Adrian Smith, Adrian Smith + Gordon Gill
Architecture
Karen Stephenson, Rotterdam School of
Management, Erasmus University &
NetForm International

Fellows of the Design Futures Council

Cecil Steward, University of Nebraska-Lincoln & Joslyn Castle Institute for Sustainable Communities

RK Stewart, Perkins+Will

Sarah Susanka, Susanka Studios

David Suzuki, David Suzuki Foundation

Richard N. Swett, Swett Associates

Jack Tanis, Strategic Planning and Workplace Design Thought Leader

Marilyn Taylor, School of Design, University of Pennsylvania

April Thornton, Leading Voice for Integrated Design Services

James Timberlake, KieranTimberlake

Lene Tranberg, Lundgaard & Tranberg

Alan Traugott, CJL Engineering

Robert Tucker, The Innovation Resource

John Carl Warnecke*, Architect & Contextual Design Advocate

Alice Waters, Chez Panisse Foundation

Alan Webber, Author, *Rules of Thumb*; Founding Editor, *Fast Company*

Jon Westling, Boston University

Gary Wheeler, WHEELERKÄNIK

Allison Williams, Perkins + Will

Arol Wolford, SmartBIM

Richard Saul Wurman, Author, Information Architect and Founder, Access Guide and TED

Nicholas You, UN-HABITAT

* Deceased

† Resident fellow and foresight advisor

Source: Design Futures Council

Fellows of the Industrial Designers Society of America

Membership in the Industrial Designers Society of America's Academy of Fellows is conferred by a two-thirds majority vote of its board of directors. Fellows must be society members in good standing who have earned the **special respect and affection of the IDSA membership through distinguished service** to the organization and to the profession as a whole.

2010 Fellows

Michelle Berryman
Brian Vogel

Source: Industrial Designers Society of America

Fellows of the International Interior Design Association

Fellowship in the International Interior Design Association is a recognition of members who have demonstrated **outstanding service to IIDA**, the community, and the interior design profession.

2010 Fellows

Tama Duffy Day
David Hanson (Canada)
David Mourning

Source: International Interior Design Association

AIA Gold Medal

The Gold Medal is the **American Institute of Architects' highest award**. Eligibility is open to architects and non-architects, living or dead, whose contribution to the field of architecture has made a lasting impact. The AIA's board of directors grants at least one gold medal each year, occasionally granting none.

www.aia.org

1907	Sir Aston Webb (UK)	1967	Wallace K. Harrison
1909	Charles F. McKim	1968	Marcel Breuer
1911	George B. Post	1969	William Wurster
1914	Jean Louis Pascal (France)	1970	R. Buckminster Fuller
1922	Victor Laloux (France)	1971	Louis I. Kahn
1923	Henry Bacon	1972	Pietro Belluschi
1925	Sir Edwin Lutyens (UK)	1977	Richard Neutra* (Germany/US)
1925	Bertram Grosvenor Goodhue	1978	Philip Johnson
1927	Howard Van Doren Shaw	1979	I.M. Pei
1929	Milton B. Medary	1981	José Luis Sert (Spain)
1933	Ragnar Östberg (Sweden)	1982	Romaldo Giurgola
1938	Paul Philippe Cret (France/US)	1983	Nathaniel Owings
1944	Louis Sullivan	1985	William Wayne Caudill*
1947	Eliel Saarinen (Finland/US)	1986	Arthur C. Erickson (Canada)
1948	Charles D. Maginnis	1989	Joseph Esherick
1949	Frank Lloyd Wright	1990	E. Fay Jones
1950	Sir Patrick Abercrombie (UK)	1991	Charles Moore
1951	Bernard Maybeck	1992	Benjamin Thompson
1952	Auguste Perret (France)	1993	Thomas Jefferson*
1953	William Adams Delano	1993	Kevin Roche
1955	Willem Marinus Dudok (Netherlands)	1994	Sir Norman Foster (UK)
1956	Clarence S. Stein	1995	Cesar Pelli
1957	Ralph Thomas Walker	1997	Richard Meier
1957	Louis Skidmore	1999	Frank Gehry
1958	John Wellborn Root II	2000	Ricardo Legorreta (Mexico)
1959	Walter Gropius (Germany/US)	2001	Michael Graves
1960	Ludwig Mies van der Rohe (Germany/US)	2002	Tadao Ando (Japan)
1961	Le Corbusier (Charles Édouard Jeanneret) (Switzerland/France)	2004	Samuel Mockbee*
		2005	Santiago Calatrava (Spain)
1962	Eero Saarinen*	2006	Antoine Predock
1963	Alvar Aalto (Finland)	2007	Edward Larrabee Barnes*
1964	Pier Luigi Nervi (Italy)	2008	Renzo Piano (Italy)
1966	Kenzo Tange (Japan)	2009	Glenn Murcutt (Australia)
		2010	**Peter Bohlin**

* Honored posthumously

Source: American Institute of Architects

American Academy of Arts and Letters Awards

The American Academy of Arts and Letters grants its annual Academy Awards for Architecture to **American architects whose work is characterized by a strong personal direction**. It also presents a gold medal in the arts, rotating yearly among painting, music, sculpture, poetry, and architecture. An architect's entire career is weighed when being considered for this award.

www.artsandletters.org

Academy Awards for Architecture

1993	Franklin D. Israel	2005	Gisue Hariri and Mojgan Hariri
1994	Craig Hodgetts and Hsin-Ming Fung		Toshiko Mori
			Massimo and Lella Vignelli
1995	Mack Scogin and Merrill Elam	2006	Marwan Al-Sayed
1996	Maya Lin		Yung Ho Chang (China)
1997	Daniel Libeskind		Jeanne Gang
1998	Laurie D. Olin	2007	Wes Jones
1999	Eric Owen Moss		Tom Kundig
2000	Will Bruder		Lebbeus Woods
	Jesse Reiser and Nanako Umemoto	2008	Neil Denari
2001	Vincent James		Jim Jennings
	SHoP Architects		James Carpenter
2002	Rick Joy		Kenneth Frampton (UK)
	Office dA/Mónica Ponce de León with Nader Tehrani	2009	Stan Allen
			Wendell Burnette
2003	Greg Lynn		Jeffrey Kipnis
	Guy Nordenson	**2010**	**Stephen Cassell**
	Andrew Zago		**Michael Meredith**
2004	Preston Scott Cohen		**Hilary Sample**
	Marion Weiss and Michael Manfredi		**Michael Sorkin**
	James Corner		**Adam Yarinsky**

Gold Medal for Architecture

1912	William Rutherford Mead	1968	R. Buckminster Fuller
1921	Cass Gilbert	1973	Louis I. Kahn
1930	Charles Adams Platt	1979	I.M. Pei
1940	William Adams Delano	1984	Gordon Bunshaft
1949	Frederick Law Olmsted Jr.	1990	Kevin Roche
1953	Frank Lloyd Wright	1996	Philip Johnson
1958	Henry R. Shepley	2002	Frank Gehry
1963	Ludwig Mies van der Rohe	2008	Richard Meier

Source: American Academy of Arts and Letters

Arnold W. Brunner Memorial Prize

The American Academy of Arts and Letters annually awards the Arnold W. Brunner Memorial Prize to architects of any nationality who have contributed to architecture as an art. The award consists of a $5,000 prize. The prize is named in honor of the notable New York architect and city planner, Arnold William Brunner, who died in 1925.

www.artsandletters.org

1955	Gordon Bunshaft	1983	Frank Gehry
	Minoru Yamasaki*	1984	Peter Eisenman
1956	John Yeon	1985	William Pedersen and Arthur May
1957	John Carl Warnecke	1986	John Hejduk
1958	Paul Rudolph	1987	James Ingo Freed
1959	Edward Larrabee Barnes	1988	Arata Isozaki (Japan)
1960	Louis I. Kahn	1989	Richard Rogers (UK)
1961	I.M. Pei	1990	Steven Holl
1962	Ulrich Franzen	1991	Tadao Ando (Japan)
1963	Edward C. Bassett	1992	Sir Norman Foster (UK)
1964	Harry Weese	1993	Rafael Moneo (Spain)
1965	Kevin Roche	1994	Renzo Piano (Italy)
1966	Romaldo Giurgola	1995	Daniel Urban Kiley
1967	*No award granted*	1996	Tod Williams and Billie Tsien
1968	John M. Johansen	1997	Henri Ciriani (France)
1969	N. Michael McKinnell	1998	Alvaro Siza (Portugal)
1970	Charles Gwathmey and	1999	Fumihiko Maki (Japan)
	Richard Henderson	2000	Toyo Ito (Japan)
1971	John H. Andrews (Australia)	2001	Henry Smith-Miller and
1972	Richard Meier		Laurie Hawkinson
1973	Robert Venturi	2002	Kazuyo Sejima + Ryue Nishizawa
1974	Hugh Hardy with Norman Pfeiffer		(Japan)
	and Malcolm Holzman	2003	Elizabeth Diller and Ricardo Scofidio
1975	Lewis Davis and Samuel Brody	2004	Hans Hollein (Austria)
1976	James Stirling (UK)	2005	Shigeru Ban (Japan)
1977	Henry N. Cobb	2006	Jean Nouvel (France)
1978	Cesar Pelli	2007	Eric Owen Moss
1979	Charles Moore	2008	Peter Zumthor (Switzerland)
1980	Michael Graves	2009	Juhani Pallasmaa (Finland)
1981	Gunnar Birkerts	**2010**	**Michael Van Valkenburgh**
1982	Helmut Jahn		

* Honorable Mention

Source: American Academy of Arts and Letters

Arthur Ross Awards

Presented annually by the Institute of Classical Architecture & Classical America, the Arthur Ross Awards celebrate the **achievements and contributions of architects, painters, sculptors, artisans, landscape designers, educators, publishers, patrons, and others dedicated to preserving the classical tradition**. Award categories include architecture, community design, education, landscape design, and stewardship.

www.classicist.org

Architecture Recipients

1982	Philip Trammell Shutze	1993	William T. Baker
1983	Edward Vason Jones	1994	George M. White
	Samuel Wilson Jr.		Ernesto Buch
1984	Rurik F. Eckstrom	1995	Jaquelin Robertson
	David Anthony Easton	1996	Robert I. Cole
1985	A. Hays Town	1997	Milton Grenfell
	Douglas L. Greene	1998	Joseph Dixon III
	David Warren Hardwicke		Nell E. Davis
1986	Thomas C. Celli	1999	Curtis and Windham Architects
	Shahi Patel	2000	Harold H. Fisher
	Robert T. Meeker	2001	John Blatteau
1987	Norman Neuerberg	2002	Quinlan Terry (UK)
	David T. Mayernik	2003	Ferguson & Shamamian
	Thomas N. Rajkovich		Architects
1988	Frank Garretson	2004	Merrill and Pastor Architects
	David Anthony	2005	Demetri Porphyrios (UK)
1989	Floyd E. Johnson	2006	Hartman-Cox Architects
1990	Allan Greenberg	2007	Michael G. Imber Architects
1991	Boris Baranovich	2008	John Simpson (UK)
	Robert A.M. Stern	2009	John Milner Architects, Inc.
1992	Sherman Pardue	**2010**	**Historical Concepts**
	Thomas H. Beeby		

Source: Institute of Classical Architecture & Classical America

ASLA Medals

The American Society of Landscape Architects awards its highest honor, the ASLA Medal, to individuals who have made a **significant contribution to the field of landscape architecture** in such areas as landscape design, planning, writing, and public service. The ASLA Design Medal recognizes landscape architects who have produced a body of exceptional design work at a sustained level for at least 10 years.

www.asla.org

ASLA Medal

1971	Hideo Sasaki	1991	Meade Palmer
1972	Conrad L. Wirth	1992	Robert S. (Doc) Reich
1973	John C. Simonds	1993	Arthur E. Bye Jr.
1974	Campbell E. Miller	1994	Edward D. Stone Jr.
1975	Garrett Eckbo	1995	Ervin H. Zube
1976	Thomas Church	1996	John Lyle
1977	Hubert B. Owens	1997	Julius Fabos
1978	Lawrence Halprin	1998	Carol R. Johnson
1979	Norman T. Newton	1999	Stuart C. Dawson
1980	William G. Swain	2000	Carl D. Johnson
1981	Sir Geoffrey Jellicoe (UK)	2001	Robert E. Marvin
1982	Charles W. Eliot II	2002	Morgan (Bill) Evans
1983	Theodore Osmundson	2003	Richard Haag
1984	Ian McHarg	2004	Peter Walker
1985	Roberto Burle Marx (Brazil)	2005	Jane Silverstein Ries
1986	William J. Johnson	2006	Cameron R.J. Man
1987	Philip H. Lewis Jr.	2007	William B. Callaway
1988	Dame Sylvia Crowe (UK)	2008	Joseph A. Porter
1989	Robert N. Royston	2009	Joseph E. Brown
1990	Raymond L. Freeman	**2010**	**Edward L. Daugherty**

ASLA Design Medal

2003	Lawrence Halprin	2007	Richard Haag
2004	M. Paul Friedberg	2008	Kathryn Gustafson
2005	Laurie D. Olin	2009	Richard W. Shaw
2006	Steve Martino	**2010**	**James van Sweden**

Source: American Society of Landscape Architects

Auguste Perret Prize

The International Union of Architects (UIA) grants the triennial Auguste Perret Prize to an **internationally renowned architect or architects for work in applied technology in architecture**. The prize is named after notable French architect Auguste Perret, a leading pioneer of reinforced concrete design.

www.uia-architectes.org

Year		Year	
1961	Felix Candela (Mexico)	1978	Kiyonori Kitutake (Japan)
	Architect's office of the British		Piano & Rogers (Italy/UK)
	Ministry of Education (UK)*	1981	Günter Behnisch (GFR)
	Architects of the Office for the		Jacques Rougerie (France)*
	Study of Industrial and	1984	João Baptista Vilanova Artigas
	Agricultural Buildings of		(Brazil)
	Hungary (Hungary)*	1987	Santiago Calatrava (Spain)
1963	Kunio Mayekawa (Japan)		Clorindo Testa (Argentina)*
	Jean Prouvé (France)	1990	Adien Fainsilber (France)
1965	Hans Scharoun (GFR)	1993	KHR AS Arkitekten (Denmark)
	Heikki and Kaija Siren (Finland)*	1996	Thomas Herzog (Germany)
1967	Frei Otto and Rolf Gutbrod (GFR)	1999	Ken Yeang (Malaysia)
1969	Karel Hubacek (Czechoslovakia)	2002	Sir Norman Foster (UK)
1972	E. Pinez Pinero (Spain)	2005	Werner Sobek (Germany)
1975	Arthur C. Erickson and team	2008	Françoise-Hélène Jourda (France)
	(Canada)		
	J. Cardoso (Brazil)*		

*Honorary Mentions

Source: International Union of Architects

Designer of Distinction Award

With its Designer of Distinction Award, the American Society of Interior Designers rec-ognizes **individuals for their commitment to the profession as demonstrated by a significant, high-quality body of work that shows attention to social concerns and expresses creative, innovative concepts**. Eligibility is open to members in good stand-ing who have practiced interior design for at least 10 years.

www.asid.org

1979	William Pahlman	1998	Janet S. Schirn
1980	Everett Brown	1999	Gary Wheeler
1981	Barbara D'Arcy	2000	Paul Vincent Wiseman
1982	Edward J. Wormley	2001	William Hodgins
1983	Edward J. Perrault	2002	Hugh L. Latta
1984	Michael Taylor		Margaret McCurry
1985	Norman DeHaan	2003	Eleanor Brydone
1986	Rita St. Clair	2004	Deborah Lloyd Forrest
1987	James Merrick Smith	2005	Barbara Barry
1988	Louis Tregre	2006	Penny Bonda
1994	Charles D. Gandy	2007	Nila Leiserowitz
1995	Andre Staffelbach	2009*	Darrell Schmitt
1996	Joseph Minton	**2010**	**Kirsten Childs**
1997	Phyllis Martin-Vegue		

* No award was granted in 2008, when ASID adjusted the award schedule.

Source: American Society of Interior Designers

Designer of the Year

Contract magazine grants the annual Designer of the Year Award to a **mid-career designer or designers whose work demonstrates extraordinary creativity and innovative vision** and who is poised for great success in the future. The recipient is celebrated at the Annual Interiors Award Breakfast and in an issue of the magazine.

www.contractmagazine.com

1980	John F. Saladino	1996	Richard M. Brayton
1981	Michael Graves		Stanford Hughes
1982	Orlando Diaz-Azcuy	1997	Carolyn Iu
1983	Joseph Rosen		Neville Lewis
1984	Raul de Armas	1998	David Rockwell
1985	Francisco Kripacz	1999	William McDonough
1986	Charles Pfister	2000	Ralph Appelbaum
1987	Miguel Valcarel	2001	Shigeru Ban (Japan)
	Randy Gerner	2002	George Yabu (Canada)
	Judy Swanson		Glenn Pushelberg (Canada)
	Patricia Conway	2003	Peter Pfau
1988	Carol Groh	2004	Shashi Caan
1989	Scott Strasser	2005	Kendall Wilson
1990	Karen Daroff	2006	Mark Harbick
1991	Gregory W. Landahl	2007	Kelly Bauer
1992	Gary L. Lee		Jim Richärd
	Mel Hamilton	2008	Philip G. Freelon
1993	Juliette Lam	2009	John Peterson
1994	Lauren L. Rottet		John Cary
1995	Debra Lehman-Smith	**2010**	**Graft**

Source: Contract

Henry C. Turner Prize

The Henry C. Turner Prize for Innovation in Construction Technology is presented jointly by the National Building Museum and the Turner Construction Company to recognize **notable advances in construction**. It honors individuals, companies, and organizations for their inventions, innovative methodologies, and exceptional leadership in construction technology. The award is named for the founder of Turner Construction, which began operation in New York City in 1902.

www.nbm.org

2002	Leslie E. Robertson	2007	Gehry Partners
2003	I.M. Pei		Gehry Technologies
2004	Charles A. DeBenedittis	2008	Charles H. Thornton
2005	US Green Building Council	**2010**	**Engineers Without Borders-USA**
2006	Paul Teicholz		

Source: National Building Museum

IDSA Personal Recognition Award

The Industrial Designers Society of America presents its Personal Recognition Award to **designers and others whose involvement in and support of design has contributed to the profession's long-term welfare and importance**. Nominees are reviewed by a nominating committee, and IDSA's officers select the final winners.

www.idsa.org

1968	Dave Chapman	1999	Victor Papanek
1969	John Vassos	2000	Robert Schwartz
1978	Raymond Loewy	2001	Bill Stumpf
1980	William M. Goldsmith	2002	Viktor Schreckengost
1981	George Nelson	2003	Sam Farber
1982	Jay Doblin	2004	Henry Dreyfuss*
1985	Deane W. Richardson		Bruce Nussbaum
1986	Carroll M. Gantz	2005	*No award granted*
1991	Budd Steinhilber	2006	Robert Blaich
1992	Cooper C. Woodring		Charles (Chuck) Harrison
	Ellen Manderfield	2007	Walter Dorwin Teague*
1993	Raymond Spilman	2008	*No award granted*
	Brooks Stevens	2009	*No award granted*
1994	Belle Kogan	**2010**	**Peter Bressler**
1995	David B. Smith		**Gaylon White**
1996	Jane Thompson		
1997	Eva Zeisel	* Honored posthumously	
1998	Donald Dohner		

Source: Industrial Designers Society of America

Legend Award

Presented by *Contract* magazine, the Legend Award recognizes an outstanding **individual for lifetime achievement in design**. The recipient is celebrated at the Annual Interiors Award Breakfast and in an issue of the magazine.

www.contractmagazine.com

2002	Margo Grant Walsh	2007	William E. Valentine
2003	Hugh Hardy	2008	Moira Moser (Hong Kong)
2005	Neil Frankel	2009	Wing Chao
2006	Niels Diffrient	**2010**	**Arthur Gensler**

Source: Contract

Michelangelo Award

The Construction Specifications Institute's Michelangelo Award pays tribute to an **exceptional individual for a lifetime of distinguished, innovative service to the design and construction industry**. The recipient's career demonstrates a far-reaching effect in creating and sustaining the built environment. Only one winner may be selected each year. The honoree is celebrated at the annual CSI Show and presented with a bust of Michelangelo.

www.csinet.org

2005	Lawrence Halprin	2008	M. Arthur Gensler Jr.
2006	Charles H. Thornton	2009	*No award granted*
2007	*No award granted*	**2010**	***No award granted***

Source: Construction Specifications Institute

National Design Awards

The National Design Awards honor the best in American design. This annual program, sponsored by the Smithsonian's Cooper-Hewitt, National Design Museum, celebrates **design in various disciplines as a vital humanistic tool in shaping the world** and seeks to increase national awareness of design by educating the public and promoting excellence, innovation, and lasting achievement. The awards are granted for a body of work, not a specific project.

www.nationaldesignawards.org

2010 Recipients

Architectural Design
KieranTimberlake

Communication Design
Stephen Doyle

Corporate and Institutional Achievement
US Green Building Council

Design Mind
Ralph Caplan

Fashion Design
Rodarte

Interaction Design
Lisa Strausfeld

Interior Design
William Sofield

Landscape Design
James Corner Field Operations

Lifetime Achievement
Jane Thompson

Product Design
Smart Design

Source: Cooper-Hewitt, National Design Museum

Praemium Imperiale

The Praemium Imperiale is awarded by the Japan Art Association, Japan's premier cultural institution, for **lifetime achievement in the fields of painting, sculpture, music, architecture, and theater/film**. The following individuals received this honor for architecture, which includes a commemorative medal and a 15,000,000 yen ($130,000) honorarium.

www.praemiumimperiale.org

1989	I.M. Pei	2001	Jean Nouvel (France)
1990	James Stirling (UK)	2002	Sir Norman Foster (UK)
1991	Gae Aulenti (Italy)	2003	Rem Koolhaas (Netherlands)
1992	Frank Gehry	2004	Oscar Niemeyer (Brazil)
1993	Kenzo Tange (Japan)	2005	Taniguchi Yoshio (Japan)
1994	Charles Correa (India)	2006	Frei Otto (Germany)
1995	Renzo Piano (Italy)	2007	Jacques Herzog and Pierre de
1996	Tadao Ando (Japan)		Meuron (Switzerland)
1997	Richard Meier	2008	Peter Zumthor (Switzerland)
1998	Alvaro Siza (Portugal)	2009	Zaha Hadid (UK)
1999	Fumihiko Maki (Japan)	**2010**	**Toyo Ito (Japan)**
2000	Sir Richard Rogers (UK)		

Source: Japan Art Association

Pritzker Architecture Prize

In 1979, Jay and Cindy Pritzker established the Pritzker Architecture Prize to inspire **greater creativity in the profession** and to heighten public awareness about architecture. Today, it is revered as one of the field's highest honors. The prize, which includes a $100,000 grant, is awarded each year to a living architect whose body of work represents a long-standing, significant contribution to the built environment.

www.pritzkerprize.com

1979	Philip Johnson	1995	Tadao Ando (Japan)
1980	Luis Barragán (Mexico)	1996	Rafael Moneo (Spain)
1981	James Stirling (UK)	1997	Sverre Fehn (Norway)
1982	Kevin Roche	1998	Renzo Piano (Italy)
1983	I.M. Pei	1999	Sir Norman Foster (UK)
1984	Richard Meier	2000	Rem Koolhaas (Netherlands)
1985	Hans Hollein (Austria)	2001	Jacques Herzog and Pierre de
1986	Gottfried Boehm (Germany)		Meuron (Switzerland)
1987	Kenzo Tange (Japan)	2002	Glenn Murcutt (Australia)
1988	Gordon Bunshaft	2003	Jørn Utzon (Denmark)
	Oscar Niemeyer (Brazil)	2004	Zaha Hadid (UK)
1989	Frank Gehry	2005	Thom Mayne
1990	Aldo Rossi (Italy)	2006	Paulo Mendes da Rocha (Brazil)
1991	Robert Venturi	2007	Sir Richard Rogers (UK)
1992	Alvaro Siza (Portugal)	2008	Jean Nouvel (France)
1993	Fumihiko Maki (Japan)	2009	Peter Zumthor (Switzerland)
1994	Christian de Portzamparc (France)	**2010**	**Kazuyo Sejima (Japan)**
			Ryue Nishizawa (Japan)

Source: The Pritzker Architecture Prize

RAIC Gold Medal

The Royal Architectural Institute of Canada began its gold medal program in 1967 to recognize **architects or individuals in related fields who have made significant contributions to Canadian architecture**. As the RAIC Gold Medal is merit-based, awards are not necessarily granted annually.

www.raic.org

1967	Jean Drapeau	1992	Douglas Shadbolt
1968	Vincent Massey	1994	Barton Myers
1970	Eric R. Arthur	1995	Moshe Safdie (US)
	John A. Russell*	1997	Raymond Moriyama
1973	Serge Chermayeff (UK/US)	1998	Frank Gehry (US)
1976	Constantinos Doxiadis (Greece)	1999	Douglas Cardina
1979	John C. Parkin	2001	A.J. (Jack) Diamond
1981	Jane Jacobs	2006	Bruce Kuwabara
1982	Ralph Erskine (Sweden)	2007	Mario Saia
1984	Arthur C. Erickson	2008	Dan S. Hanganu
1985	John Bland	2009	John Patkau
1986	Eberhard Zeidler		Patricia Patkau
1989	Raymond T. Affleck	**2010**	**George Baird**
1991	Phyllis Lambert		

*Honored posthumously
Individuals are from Canada unless otherwise indicated.

Source: Royal Architectural Institute of Canada

RIBA Royal Gold Medal

The Royal Institute of British Architects' Royal Gold Medal was inaugurated by Queen Victoria in 1848. It is conferred annually on a **distinguished architect, person, or firm "whose work has promoted, either directly or indirectly, the advancement of architecture."**

www.riba.org

1848	Charles Robert Cockerell (UK)	1887	Ewan Christian (UK)
1849	Luigi Canina (Italy)	1888	Baron von Hansen (Austria)
1850	Sir Charles Barry (UK)	1889	Sir Charles T. Newton (UK)
1851	Thomas L. Donaldson (UK)	1890	John Gibson (UK)
1852	Leo von Klenze (Germany)	1891	Sir Arthur Blomfield (UK)
1853	Sir Robert Smirke (UK)	1892	Cesar Daly (France)
1854	Philip Hardwick (UK)	1893	Richard Morris Hunt
1855	Jacques Ignace Hittorff (France)	1894	Lord Frederic Leighton (UK)
1856	Sir William Tite (UK)	1895	James Brooks (UK)
1857	Owen Jones (UK)	1896	Sir Ernest George (UK)
1858	Friedrich August Stuler (Germany)	1897	Petrus Josephus Hubertus Cuypers (Netherlands)
1859	Sir George Gilbert Scott (UK)		
1860	Sydney Smirke (UK)	1898	George Aitchison (UK)
1861	Jean-Baptiste Cicéron Lesueur (France)	1899	George Frederick Bodley (UK)
		1900	Rodolfo Amadeo Lanciani (Italy)
1862	Robert Willis (UK)	1901	*No award granted due to the death of Queen Victoria*
1863	Anthony Salvin (UK)		
1864	Eugène Emmanuel Violett-le-Duc (France)	1902	Thomas Edward Collcutt (UK)
		1903	Charles F. McKim
1865	Sir James Pennethorne (UK)	1904	Auguste Choisy (France)
1866	Sir Matthew Digby Wyatt (UK)	1905	Sir Aston Webb (UK)
1867	Charles Texier (France)	1906	Sir Lawrence Alma-Tadema (UK)
1868	Sir Henry Layard (UK)	1907	John Belcher (UK)
1869	C.R. Lepsius (Germany)	1908	Honore Daumet (France)
1870	Benjamin Ferrey (UK)	1909	Sir Arthur John Evans (UK)
1871	James Fergusson (UK)	1910	Sir Thomas Graham Jackson (UK)
1872	Baron von Schmidt (Austria)	1911	Wilhelm Dorpfeld (Germany)
1873	Thomas Henry Wyatt (UK)	1912	Basil Champneys (UK)
1874	George Edmund Street (UK)	1913	Sir Reginald Blomfield (UK)
1875	Edmund Sharpe (UK)	1914	Jean Louis Pascal (France)
1876	Joseph Louis Duc (France)	1915	Frank Darling (Canada)
1877	Charles Barry Jr. (UK)	1916	Sir Robert Rowand Anderson (UK)
1878	Alfred Waterhouse (UK)	1917	Henri Paul Nenot (France)
1879	Marquis de Vogue (France)	1918	Ernest Newton (UK)
1880	John L. Pearson (UK)	1919	Leonard Stokes (UK)
1881	George Godwin (UK)	1920	Charles Louis Girault (France)
1882	Baron von Ferstel (Austria)	1921	Sir Edwin Lutyens (UK)
1883	Francis C. Penrose (UK)	1922	Thomas Hastings
1884	William Butterfield (UK)	1923	Sir John James Burnet (UK)
1885	H. Schliemann (Germany)	1924	*No award granted*
1886	Charles Garnier (France)	1925	Sir Giles Gilbert Scott (UK)

1926	Ragnar Östberg (Sweden)
1927	Sir Herbert Baker (UK)
1928	Sir Guy Dawber (UK)
1929	Victor Laloux (France)
1930	Sir Percy Scott Worthington (UK)
1931	Sir Edwin Cooper (UK)
1932	Hendrik Petrus Berlage (Netherlands)
1933	Sir Charles Reed Peers (UK)
1934	Henry Vaughan Lanchester (UK)
1935	Willem Marinus Dudok (Netherlands)
1936	Charles Henry Holden (UK)
1937	Sir Raymond Unwin (UK)
1938	Ivar Tengbom (Sweden)
1939	Sir Percy Thomas (UK)
1940	Charles Francis Annesley Voysey (UK)
1941	Frank Lloyd Wright
1942	William Curtis Green (UK)
1943	Sir Charles Herbert Reilly (UK)
1944	Sir Edward Maufe (UK)
1945	Victor Vesnin (USSR)
1946	Sir Patrick Abercrombie (UK)
1947	Sir Albert Edward Richardson (UK)
1948	Auguste Perret (France)
1949	Sir Howard Robertson (UK)
1950	Eleil Saarinen (Finland/US)
1951	Emanuel Vincent Harris (UK)
1952	George Grey Wornum (UK)
1953	Le Corbusier (Charles-Édouard Jeanneret) (Switzerland/France)
1954	Sir Arthur Stephenson (Australia)
1955	John Murray Easton (UK)
1956	Walter Gropius (Germany/US)
1957	Alvar Aalto (Finland)
1958	Robert Schofield Morris (Canada)
1959	Ludwig Mies van der Rohe (Germany/US)
1960	Pier Luigi Nervi (Italy)
1961	Lewis Mumford
1962	Sven Gottfrid Markelius (Sweden)
1963	Lord William Graham Holford (UK)
1964	E. Maxwell Fry (UK)
1965	Kenzo Tange (Japan)
1966	Ove Arup (UK)
1967	Sir Nikolaus Pevsner (UK)
1968	R. Buckminster Fuller

1969	Jack Antonio Coia (UK)
1970	Sir Robert Matthew (UK)
1971	Hubert de Cronin Hastings (UK)
1972	Louis I. Kahn
1973	Sir Leslie Martin (UK)
1974	Powell & Moya (UK)
1975	Michael Scott (Ireland)
1976	Sir John Summerson (UK)
1977	Sir Denys Lasdun (UK)
1978	Jørn Utzon (Denmark)
1979	The Office of Charles and Ray Eames
1980	James Stirling (UK)
1981	Sir Philip Dowson (UK)
1982	Berthold Lubetkin (Georgia)
1983	Sir Norman Foster (UK)
1984	Charles Correa (India)
1985	Sir Richard Rogers (UK)
1986	Arata Isozaki (Japan)
1987	Ralph Erskine (Sweden)
1988	Richard Meier
1989	Renzo Piano (Italy)
1990	Aldo van Eyck (Netherlands)
1991	Sir Colin Stansfield Smith (UK)
1992	Peter Rice (UK)
1993	Giancarlo de Carlo (Italy)
1994	Sir Michael and Lady Patricia Hopkins (UK)
1995	Colin Rowe (UK/US)
1996	Harry Seidler (Australia)
1997	Tadao Ando (Japan)
1998	Oscar Niemeyer (Brazil)
1999	Barcelona, Spain
2000	Frank Gehry
2001	Jean Nouvel (France)
2002	Archigram (UK)
2003	Rafael Moneo (Spain)
2004	Rem Koolhaas (Netherlands)
2005	Frei Otto (Germany)
2006	Toyo Ito (Japan)
2007	Jacques Herzog and Pierre de Meuron (Switzerland)
2008	Edward Cullinan (UK)
2009	Álvaro Siza (Portugal)
2010	**I.M. Pei**

Source: Royal Institute of British Architects

Richard H. Driehaus Prize for Classical Architecture

The Richard H. Driehaus Prize annually honors an **outstanding contributor to the field of traditional architecture**. The award was established and endowed by the founder of Chicago's Driehaus Capital Management Company. Winners receive $200,000 and a model of the Choregic Monument of Lysikrates in Athens, Greece, known as the first use of the Corinthian order.

www.driehausprize.org

2003	Léon Krier (UK)	2008	Andrés Duany and
2004	Demetri Porphyrios (Greece)		Elizabeth Plater-Zyberk
2005	Quinlan Terry (UK)	2009	Abdel-Wahed El-Wakil (Egypt)
2006	Allan Greenberg	**2010**	**Rafael Manzano Martos (Spain)**
2007	Jaquelin Robertson		

Source: University of Notre Dame School of Architecture

Russel Wright Award

The Russel Wright Award honors **individuals who are working in the tradition of design pioneer Russel Wright** (1904–1976), a well-known home furnishings and housewares designer whose works date mainly from 1930 to 1950. The award is sponsored by the Russel Wright Design Center, located at Manitoga, the 75-acre wooded landscape Wright sculpted in Garrison, NY.

www.russelwrightcenter.org

2000	Michael Graves	2005	Knoll, Inc.
2001	Lella and Massimo Vignelli		Palisades Interstate Park Commission
	William T. Golden	2006	Frances D. Fergusson
	Cooper-Hewitt National Design		Viktor Schreckengost
	Museum, Smithsonian Institution	2007	Herman Miller
2002	Murray Moss		Mitchell Wolfson Jr.
	Frances S. Reese	2008	Lara Deam Anne
	Eva Zeisel		Constantine Sidamon-Eristoff
2003	Jack Lenor Larsen	2009	Donald Albrecht
	Harvey Keyes Flad		Carol Levy Franklin
	Rob Forbes		
2004	Jens Risom	*Source: Russel Wright Design Center*	
	Michael and Stephen Maharam		
	The Institute of Ecosystems Studies		

Star Award

The International Interior Design Association's Star Award celebrates **individuals and organizations that have made extraordinary contributions to the interior design profession**. As the Star Award is merit-based, it is not necessarily granted each year. Although non-members are eligible, the IIDA board of directors (the selection body) only accepts nominations from IIDA fellows, chapter presidents, and directors.

www.iida.org

1985	Lester Dundes	1998	Charles and Ray Eames
1986	William Sullivan	1999	Michael Brill
1987	Orlando Diaz-Azcuy	2000	Eva L. Maddox
1988	Paul Brayton	2001	Andrée Putman (France)
1989	Florence Knoll Bassett	2002	Karim Rashid
1990	Beverly Russell	2003	Ray Anderson
1991	Stanley Abercrombie	2004	Kevin Kampschroer
1992	M. Arthur Gensler Jr.	2005	Target Corporation
1993	Sivon C. Reznikoff	2006	*Fast Company*
1994	Michael Kroelinger	2007	Karen Stephenson
1995	Douglas R. Parker	2008	Gordon Segal
1997	Michael Wirtz	2009	Hilda Longinotti
		2010	**Majora Carter**

Source: International Interior Designers Association

Curtis Fentress

Thomas Jefferson Award for Public Architecture

The American Institute of Architects grants the Thomas Jefferson Award for Public Architecture to recognize **design excellence in government and infrastructure projects**. Awards are presented in three categories: private sector architects who have amassed a portfolio of distinguished public facilities, public sector architects who produce quality projects within their agencies, and public officials or others who have been strong advocates for design excellence.

www.aia.org

1992	James Ingo Freed	2000	Charles E. Peterson
	George M. White		Jay Chatterjee
	Daniel Patrick Moynihan	2001*	Terrel M. Emmons
1993	Jack Brooks		J. Stroud Watson
1994	Richard Dattner	2003	Edmund W. Ong
	M.J. (Jay) Brodie		Susan Williams
	Joseph P. Riley Jr.	2005	Carol Ross Barney
1995	Herbert S. Newman		Diane Georgopulos
	Edward A. Feiner		Charles H. Atherton
	Henry G. Cisneros	2007	David D. Dixon
1996	Thomas R. Aidala		Michael A. Fitts
	Douglas P. Woodlock	2009	Roger Boothe
1997	John Tarantino		Philip G. Freelon
	Richard A. Kahan		Donald J. Stastny
	Hunter Morrison	**2010**	**Curtis Fentress**
1998	Arthur Rosenblatt		**Les Shepherd**
1999	Lewis Davis		**Ken Greenberg**
	Robert Kroin		

* Between 2001 and 2009, the award was granted biennially.

Source: American Institute of Architects

UIA Gold Medal

Every three years at its World Congress, the International Union of Architects awards its Gold Medal to a **living architect who has made outstanding achievements in the field of architecture**. This honor recognizes the recipient's lifetime of distinguished practice, contribution to the enrichment of mankind, and the promotion of the art of architecture.

www.uia-architectes.org

1984	Hassan Fathy (Egypt)	1999	Ricardo Legorreta (Mexico)
1987	Reima Pietila (Finland)	2002	Renzo Piano (Italy)
1990	Charles Correa (India)	2005	Tadao Ando (Japan)
1993	Fumihiko Maki (Japan)	2008	Teodoro González de León
1996	Rafael Moneo (Spain)		(Mexico)

Source: International Union of Architects

5

OBITUARIES |

This chapter is a celebration of the lives and contributions of the design and preservation leaders, patrons, and advocates who died between August 1, 2009, and July 31, 2010.

Shusaku Arakawa, 73

Shusaku Arakawa, the artist and designer who preferred to use only his surname, died May 18, 2010, of unknown causes. With his wife, artist Madeline Gins, he endeavored to write, draw, paint, and design a reality that challenged the notion that one must age and imminently die. They called their philosophy "Reversible Destiny," and it manifested itself architecturally in buildings that challenged occupants and kept them from forming a comfortable, complacent attitude toward their surroundings.

In the couple's 2008 Bioscleave House (Lifespan Extending Villa) built on Long Island, floors sloped and undulated like dunes, windows were placed slightly higher or lower than expected, switches were oddly placed, more than 36 paint colors were utilized, and no doors separated interior spaces. The intent was to keep those who entered on their toes—to stimulate and to provoke. Arakawa and Gins believed comfort created anxiety because it shortens life rather than prolonging it.

Born and educated in Japan, Arakawa arrived in New York in 1961 with $14 and Marcel Duchamp's phone number in his pocket. He attended art school in the Brooklyn Museum (for the visa, not the education, he said) in 1962 and met Gins there. In their more than 40 years together, the couple collaborated on large-scale paintings and books, among many projects, operating from a SoHo loft. They later suffered large financial losses by investing with Bernard Madoff. A series of 83 large paintings called "The Mechanism of Meaning" was displayed worldwide and supported the couple's projects.

Arakawa and Gins won a competition to design housing for a 75-acre landfill in Tokyo and, though unrealized, a few of the couple's Reversible Destiny lofts were constructed there. Undeniably asserting form over function, rooms in the units are spheres, cubes, and cylinders. The project was dedicated to Helen Keller for demonstrating that reversing one's destiny is possible.

In addition to visual art, Arakawa and Gins wrote several books, including *The Mechanism of Meaning* (1971), *Reversible Destiny: We Have Decided Not to Die* (1997), and *Making Dying Illegal* (2006).

Jeanne-Claude Denat de Guillebon, 74

Jeanne-Claude Denat de Guillebon, known simply as Jeanne-Claude, wife of conceptual artist Christo, died November 18, 2009, from complications from a brain aneurysm suffered after a fall. The pair is responsible for some of the largest, most dramatic public art installations in the world, including covering Germany's Reichstag building in fabric, "mummifying" Paris' Pont Neuf, surrounding a string of islands off the coast of Florida in pink nylon, and erecting 7,500 fabric gates in New York's Central Park. Their projects were executed on a grand scale, first credited only to Christo but later to both. Jeanne-Claude acted as project manager for the couple's theatrical endeavors, while Christo prepared sketches, drawings, and plans that would later be sold to fund the projects. Their temporary installations often relied on millions of yards of fabric and a permitting process that could take years, if it happened at all. Together they completed 19 projects; 37 had to be abandoned because permission was refused.

Born on the same day in the same year, Jeanne-Claude most often spoke for both of them. She was a large personality, with her bright red hair, progressive fashion sense and her focused, intense energy. Introduced to each other in 1958 by Jeanne-Claude's mother, an admirer of his portraiture, she encouraged the young artist, born Christo Javacheff in Bulgaria, to expand the scope of his projects beyond painting and small sculptural installations. Soon he was wrapping cars, trees, and landscape features in textiles. The larger the project, the more publicity it generated.

With their young son, Cyril Christo, they immigrated to New York from Paris in 1964. Six of their projects were the subject of documentary films by Albert Maysles, including "Christo's Valley Curtain" in 1974, which was nominated for an Oscar. It was the first of Maysles' films about the pair's projects, documenting the planning, construction, and display of a giant orange fabric dam in Colorado. At the time of Jeanne-Claude's death, the pair was working on a plan to cover six miles of the Arkansas River with fabric.

Paul Devrouax, 67

Leading DC-area architect Paul Devrouax died March 22, 2010, of a heart attack. His firm, Devrouax & Purnell Architects, with business partner Marshall Purnell, was one of the largest black-owned firms in Washington. Their projects included the Walter E. Washington Convention Center, the Pepco Building, the Frank D. Reeves Municipal Center, and, Nationals Park with HOK Sport + Venue + Event. He had also been a past president of the National Organization of Minority Architects.

Though the firm was founded in 1978, it was 1995 before it contributed a "significant building" to the area landscape. This project, a 190,000-square-foot addition to the Freddie Mac campus in McLean, VA, marked the first time a black-led architecture firm designed a headquarters for a Fortune 500 company. Though not one to invoke the issue of race, Devrouax did tell the *Washington Post*, "We went to all the meetings and got to know all the movers and shakers. But our phone didn't ring."

Through the years, the firm gained traction and did design many prominent spaces in Washington, including the underground garage and luxury boxes at Verizon Center, an information center at Howard University, the Studio Theater, and the African American Civil War Memorial, as well as historical renovations and some international projects. In 1998 it was awarded the design of a new building for Pepco, a large area electric services provider. Erected between Mies van der Rohe's Martin Luther King Jr. Library and the 19th-century Patent Office Building, now home of the National Portrait Gallery, the modern glass, limestone, granite and stainless steel Pepco Building was hailed for bringing freshness to Ninth Street. *Washington Post* architecture critic Benjamin Forgey wrote it was "as sure-handed a piece of architectural urbanism as Washington has seen in many a moon."

A native of New Orleans, Devrouax was living with his uncle in Los Angeles when prominent black residential architect Paul R. Williams gave a talk at his high school. He returned to Louisiana and studied architecture at Southern University at Baton Rouge. Following graduation, he worked for a subsidiary of Westinghouse, practiced briefly in Miami, and set up shop permanently in DC in 1973. He was active in many civic and professional organizations and was named a fellow of the American Institute of Architects. Devrouax took great pride in mentoring young architects; former Devrouax & Purnell employees have started over 14 firms.

The firm's other founder, Marshall Purnell, served as 2008 AIA National President, the first African-American to do so in the organization's history.

Joan Goody, 73

Joan Goody, a founding partner of Boston's Goody, Clancy & Associates, died of cancer September 8, 2009. A graduate of the Harvard Graduate School of Design, she became not only one of the first leading women in the field, but a prolific and sensitive designer and civic leader whose many projects dot the Boston cityscape.

The former Joan Edelman married architect and MIT professor Marvin Goody and joined his firm in 1960, becoming a partner in 1968. He died in 1980, and under her leadership the firm grew to over 100 employees with a long and varied project list. In an interview with the *Boston Globe*, Goody chose a few of her favorites, including Boston's Harbor Point, where she led the transformation of a troubled housing project into a successful mixed-income neighborhood. She also cited the restoration of H.H. Richardson's Trinity Church at Copley Square in Boston; a federal courthouse in Wheeling, WV; the Salomon Center for Teaching at Brown University; and Heaton Court, an affordable housing project in Stockbridge, MA. Recently the firm was selected as lead designer for the transformation of St. Elizabeth's Hospital in Washington, DC, into new headquarters for the Department of Homeland Security.

Goody eschewed showy design and practiced architecture that worked for the greatest social benefit, focusing early on public and urban housing. In the 1970s, she taught at Harvard, and she was active many years in Boston civic organizations. She chaired the Boston Civic Design Commission for many years, reviewing every major building design proposal presented to the city. She also served as president of Boston's Saturday Club, a group that met to enjoy lunch and lively discussions on a number of topics.

Realizing she had a responsibility to help mentor younger women trying to enter the design profession, Goody helped found an advocacy group called Women Architects, Landscape Architects and Planners (WALAP) in 1970. In a room of over 100 women at that time, Goody was one of only two principals.

Goody married poet and writer Peter Davidson in 1984. He was editor of *Atlantic Monthly* for many years and published numerous books of his own poetry. Though he died in 2004, Goody remained close to his children and grandchildren. She died in the converted Beacon Hill carriage house where she lived many years.

Bruce Graham, 84

Bruce Graham, designer of Chicago's iconic John Hancock Center and Sears Tower (now Willis Tower), died March 6, 2010, of complications from Alzheimer's disease. He led the Chicago office of Skidmore, Owings & Merrill from the 1960s through the 1980s and has been called the most important Chicago architect of his generation. With a staff that included Gordon Bunshaft, Walter Netsch, and famed structural engineer Fazlur Khan, SOM was a design powerhouse during this period, responsible for prominent contributions to the built environment all over the world.

Graham is himself responsible not only for the Sears Tower, the world's tallest building for many years and still the tallest in the US, and the Hancock Center ("Big John" to locals) but for projects in London, Barcelona, Egypt, Korea, Guatemala, Houston, Los Angeles, Boston, Atlanta, Kansas City, Milwaukee, Wichita, Nashville, Tulsa, Madison, and many other locales. Famed for his gruff, steely countenance, Graham is of course best known for his tall buildings in Chicago. Their revolutionary design, engineered by Khan, placed the structural supporting elements on the outside, greatly reducing construction costs and providing vast open interiors. The Hancock Center especially, with its hefty exterior X bracing, defined the "muscular" style for which Chicago became known. And in its wake, a distinguished area of tall buildings and commerce now graces a formerly bleak section of the city.

Born in Colombia to a Canadian banker father and a Peruvian mother and raised in Puerto Rico, Graham's first language was Spanish. He arrived in the US to study engineering, but a stint in the Navy during World War II interrupted his studies. When he returned to school he changed his field of study to architecture and graduated from the University of Pennsylvania in 1948. His first wife was from Chicago, so Graham headed there and he sought counsel from Mies van der Rohe, who advised him to apprentice with Holabird, Root and Burgee. Graham did so from 1949 to 1951 and then departed for the growing firm of Skidmore, Owings & Merrill. By 1960 he was a design partner and would remain in leadership at SOM through his retirement in 1989.

His 1957 Inland Steel building—the first significant office building constructed in downtown Chicago since the Great Depression—featured the use of structural columns on the building's perimeter and a separate adjoining tower for elevators and other services to open up the interiors. It was named an official landmark by the City of Chicago in 1998, its trademark stainless steel exterior an icon of mid-century design on West Monroe Street. Similarly, the Hancock Center won the AIA's 25-Year Award, presented to a significant, successful building over 25 years old, in 1999.

With William Hartmann, another partner at SOM, Graham developed the Chicago 21 Plan of 1973 for the Chicago Central Area Committee, a group of business leaders that Graham himself led in 1980. It called for alterations and additions to Chicago's lakefront as the city entered the 21st century, including rebuilding the dilapidated Navy Pier into a tourist destination and the creation of the museum campus—projects that had a transformative effect on the city. In the mid-1980s, however, a plan he helped develop with other architects for a 1992 Chicago World's Fair failed to come to fruition as local governmental support and objections by community activists to the 500 planned acres of infill along the lake doomed the project.

Following retirement, Graham and his second wife Jane, a former interior architect at SOM, established the practice of Graham and Graham. She died in 2004.

Lawrence Halprin, 93

Landscape architect and environmental planner Lawrence Halprin died October 25, 2009, of complications from a fall. Based in the San Francisco Bay area, Halprin designed some of the country's most famous public spaces, including Ghirardelli Square in San Francisco and the Franklin Delano Roosevelt Memorial in Washington, DC.

He was married to a dancer, the former Anna Schuman, and described his blend of modernism, environmentalism, and movement as a choreography. It was a blending of materials, including concrete, and attention to how places should influence the interaction of people, predominantly in urban settings, that distinguished his work. Before committing to a design, he often held a workshop with different constituencies—artists, community activists, clients, developers—to gauge emotional responses to different places.

His many projects included the plazas and grand fountains of Portland, OR; Seattle Freeway Park; Nicollet Mall in Minneapolis; and the Approach to Yosemite Falls in Yosemite National Park, dedicated in 2005. One of his most prominent projects was not an urban area but a residential development on the California coast that required great environmental sensitivity, Sea Ranch. For this Sonoma County development of 1,500 homes on 5,000 acres, Halprin preserved and enhanced the natural features of the site, planting more than a half-million trees. It was the subject of his 1995 book *The Sea*

Ranch...Diary of an Idea. Halprin wrote nearly a dozen books during the course of his career on projects and the process of design.

Born in Brooklyn, Halprin's mother took him to Palestine in 1933 to work on a kibbutz near Haifa. He returned to study plant sciences at Cornell University, and then he did his master's degree work in horticulture at the University of Wisconsin, where he met his wife. A trip to Taliesin in Spring Green, WI, at her suggestion, inspired Halprin's interest in design, and he then pursued a second bachelor's degree from Harvard's Graduate School of Design. During World War II he served on the destroyer USS *Morris* in the Pacific, and was injured when a kamikaze attack destroyed the ship. He was sent to San Francisco for leave, and set up his practice there.

Halprin's many awards included the Thomas Jefferson Foundation Medal in Architecture, the AIA Gold Medal for Distinguished Achievement, the National Medal of Arts, and the Design Medal from the American Society of American Architects.

Robert Lautman, 85

Architectural photographer Robert Lautman died of pancreatic cancer on October 20, 2009. Based in Washington, DC, Lautman's meticulous photographs of commercial buildings, institutions, and residences earned him a Gold Medal for Architectural Photography from the American Institute of Architects in 1973. He is perhaps best known for his images of the Washington National Cathedral, which he documented for over 40 years.

Born in Butte, MT, Lautman, a twice-decorated photographer during World War II, worked in New York for several years and then settled in Washington in 1948. He opened his studio just as modernism was creeping into American design, and he had many loyal modernist clients. Developer James Rouse sent him across the country in 1960, and he worked regularly with architects Hugh Newell Jacobsen, Charles M. Goodman, and Arthur H. Keyes. Lautman's work began appearing regularly in magazines like *House and Garden*, *House Beautiful*, *Architectural Digest*, *Elle*, *Smithsonian*, and *Architectural Record*. He carried pole-climbing equipment with him and sometimes shot from a construction crane. He left no detail unattended, from the choice of camera or lens to waiting until the light moved into a perfect position.

Lautman shot a series of 19th-century-style photos of Monticello for documentary filmmaker Ken Burns' PBS series on Thomas Jefferson, and those photos became the subject of a book. When the old Pension Building in Washington, DC, faced destruction, his series of pro-bono photographs of the structure is credited with helping save it. The building now houses the National Building Museum, to which Lautman donated over 30,000 of his prints and negatives in 2006.

William Mitchell, 65

Former MIT School of Architecture and Planning dean William (Bill) Mitchell died June 11, 2010, after a long battle with cancer. An architect and urban theorist, he founded and led the Smart Cities research group at the MIT Media Lab and oversaw a $1 billion building campaign on the campus.

Mitchell's work with the Smart Cities group explored the relationship between cities, people, and digital technology. Theorizing that cities are becoming smarter—more aware of the activities of their inhabitants—he looked for ways to improve the urban experience for residents and the environment. He was particularly interested in transportation, and he helped develop the CityCar, a folding stacking electric vehicle with all essential mechanical systems housed in its wheels. His lab also produced designs for a folding electric RoboScooter and GreenWheel, a design to turn an ordinary bike into an electric-assisted one.

As dean of architecture and planning, he served as advisor to then MIT President Charles M. Vest on an ambitious building plan, adding nearly 1 million square feet of space to the university's campus. The project included five buildings by some of the world's leading designers: Frank Gehry's Stata Center, Kevin Roche's Zesiger Sports and Fitness Center, Steven Holl's Simmons Hall, Charles Correa's Brain and Cognitive Sciences Complex, and Fumihiko Maki's Media Lab Complex. Mitchell wrote about the process of realizing the five buildings—from conception to completion—in his 2007 book *Imagining MIT*.

A native of Australia, Mitchell joined the MIT faculty in 1992 after serving as director of the Master in Design Studies Program at the Harvard Graduate School of Design. He had also been head of the architecture/urban design program at UCLA's Graduate School of Architecture and Urban Planning, and had taught previously at Yale, Carnegie-Mellon and Cambridge universities.

His many books included *Reinventing the Automobile* (2010) with Christopher Borroni-Bird and Lawrence Burns; *World's Greatest Architect: Making, Meaning and Network Culture* (2008), and 1977's seminal work *Computer-Aided Architectural Design*. Mitchell had been a leading early voice in favor of computer-aided design; by integrating it into the university curricula where he taught, he is credited with playing a large part in its adoption.

Following undergraduate study in Australia, Mitchell received a Master of Environmental Design from Yale and a Master of Arts from Cambridge University. The recipient of six honorary doctorates, he was a fellow of both the Royal Australian Institute of Architects and the American Academy of Arts and Sciences.

John Carl Warnecke, 91

To those of a certain age, John Carl (Jack) Warnecke is remembered as "Kennedy's archi-tect," the designer who helped shape the District of Columbia and plan John F. Kennedy's grave at Arlington Cemetery. To a younger generation, he is the man revealed to have been romantically involved with Jacqueline Kennedy following her husband's assassination, as reported in outlets from *People* magazine to TV newsmagazine *60 Minutes*. Warnecke, whose San Francisco firm was once the largest in the US, died in April 17, 2010, of com-plications from pancreatic cancer at his ranch in Healdsburg, CA.

The son of architect Carl I. Warnecke, Jack rose to prominence as a leading con-textualist. As a Stanford University undergraduate, Warnecke played left tackle on their undefeated "Wow Boys" team of 1941. He then enrolled in the Harvard Graduate School of Design where he studied under Walter Gropius, completing the three-year course of study in one year. After a short stint with his father's firm, Warnecke established his own practice in the early 1950s and began designing acclaimed schools and university proj-ects. Later, his 1950s design for a new United States Embassy in Bangkok, though never realized, was widely praised for its unique blending of Western and indigenous styles. He similarly fused modernism with 19th century Hawaiian design in his plan for a civic center and capitol building for what was then a new state.

Warnecke's work with the Kennedys began in the early 1960s when he was asked by President Kennedy to redesign Lafayette Square, a historic area across from the White House. A plan previously submitted by another firm that called for the razing of historic buildings there to construct modern office buildings spurred Mrs. Kennedy to persuade her husband that a new plan should be developed. Over the course of the next decade, Warnecke's design took shape, preserving the historic row houses and integrating two office buildings—the National Courts Building and the New Executive Office Building—in courtyards behind them.

These buildings reflect the context-sensitive approach that was a common thread in his work. Warnecke was a pioneer of the concept of urban contextualism in which he believed that a building could relate to its neighbors and the general locale through its architectural details, historical overtones, and climatic considerations. By integrating these principles into his designs, Warnecke strove to create visual harmony by evoking a sense of place rather than producing buildings that dominate and exclude their surroundings.

President Kennedy appointed Warnecke to the Commission of Fine Arts in 1963, a body that approved all federal building projects in Washington. He had developed a new master plan for the Naval Academy at Annapolis and was working with the president on early designs for his presidential library when Kennedy was killed. He was then called upon to design the Kennedy gravesite at Arlington. Warnecke's design for the memorial was unveiled in 1964 at the National Gallery of Art, and the final project was completed in 1967. Critically acclaimed, his plan called for a four-part landscape design, leading down to a grave platform with the Eternal Flame at its center.

By the mid 1970s, Warnecke's firm, John Carl Warnecke & Associates, was the nation's largest with offices in San Francisco, Los Angeles, New York, Boston, DC, and Honolulu and was responsible for many diverse, large-scale projects of the era. These included the AT&T Long Lines Building in Manhattan; the Soviet Embassy and Hart Senate Office Building, both in DC; and the South Terminal at Logan Airport in Boston. He began to scale back his practice in the late 1970s, eventually retiring to his picturesque ranch in Alexander Valley in Sonoma County where he grew a variety of grapes that were used to produce many award-winning wines.

Frank Williams, 73

Frank Williams, an architect of many New York tall buildings, died February 25, 2010, from osophagcal canccr. Though not a marquee name, Williams quietly designed or collaborated on over 20 high-rise buildings in Manhattan, including Trump Place and 515 Park Avenue. He had a reputation for good quality and good contemporary design (i.e., not too Modern) that made for good relationships with clients, mostly developers.

Born in Georgia, Williams attended the University of California, Berkeley, and then received his master's degree from the Harvard Graduate School of Design before locating permanently in New York. He taught at Columbia University four years before opening his own firm, Frank Williams and Partners Architects. During this period, Williams was a consultant to the Regional Plan Association in New York City and, with Rai Okamoto, authored 1969's *Urban Design Manhattan*, an influential study on managing growth in Midtown Manhattan.

During the lean years of the 1970s in New York, Williams worked abroad in Iran before receiving a commission in 1983 (with Theodore Liebman) from developer William Zeckendorf Sr. for the design of the Columbia, an apartment house at 96th and Broadway. Williams continued to design high-rise luxury apartment towers for Zeckendorf, as well as work for Donald Trump, Madison Equities, and the Monian Group. At the time of his death, Williams' Mercury City tower in Moscow was nearing completion, and towers in Dubai and Seoul were on the drawing board. In New York, Williams was also responsible for designing the W Hotel at Times Square, the residential portion of World Wide Plaza on Ninth Avenue, and the Four Seasons Hotel on East 57th Street in collaboration with I.M. Pei. He is the subject of a 1995 monograph by Michael J. Crosbie, *The Architecture of Frank Williams*.

Raimund Abraham, 77

Austrian architect and educator Raimund Abraham died March 3, 2010, in a car accident following a lecture at the Southern California Institute of Architecture, where he was a visiting faculty member. He also taught and lectured at Pratt Institute and Cooper Union. Renown for his drawing, Abraham was responsible for several significant buildings, including the 2002 avant-modern Austrian Cultural Forum on East 52nd Street in New York.

Günter Behnisch, 88

Günter Behnisch, a prominent German architect credited with helping reshape the face of post-war Germany, died July 12, 2010. His airy modern buildings included the Munich Olympic Stadium (with engineer Frei Otto) for the 1972 games; the 1992 Plenary Complex of the German Parliament in Bonn, Germany; 2003's Genzyme Center in Cambridge, MA; and 2005's Centre for Cellular and Bimolecular Research in Toronto, Canada. He opened his office in Stuttgart in 1952, and it evolved into Behnisch & Partner, which dissolved in 2008.

Aaron Benjamin, 78

Urban planner and housing specialist Aaron Benjamin died June 13, 2010, of complications from pneumonia. He worked 22 years for the US State Department's Agency for International Development (USAID) as the Housing and Urban Development Officer. He was involved worldwide, often following a disaster, in reconstruction, export development, and disaster preparedness response programming. He received degrees in urbanism and city planning and then worked in the architectural offices of Victor Gruen and Skidmore, Owings & Merrill. He served on the New York City Housing and Development Board and was the director of planning and development for the City of Elizabeth, NJ.

George Bissell, 82

California architect George Bissell died on January 2, 2010, of complications from lymphoma. His many California projects included the San Francisco Solano Catholic Church in Rancho Santa Margarita, Our Lady of the Rosary Cathedral in San Bernardino, and a redesign of the Bowers Museum in Santa Ana. He was also active in the American Institute of Architects, where he was also a fellow, serving as president of the Orange County chapter, president of the AIA California Council, and director of the AIA National Board. He received a lifetime achievement award from the AIA California Council in 2002.

Frances L. Brody, 93

California philanthropist and art collector Frances Brody died November 12, 2009. The daughter of advertising magnate Arthur Lasker, Brody was a founding benefactor of the Los Angeles County Museum of Art and a guiding patron of The Huntington in San Marino, CA. Encouraged to collect art by her family, Brody helped found and later became president of the UCLA Art Council in the early 1950s, and helped bring a ground-breaking Matisse retrospective to UCLA as well as an important Pablo Picasso exhibit in honor of his 80th birthday.

Leslie Buck, 87

Leslie Buck, a paper cup company executive who designed the iconic "Anthora" Greek-motif cardboard coffee cup, died April 26, 2010, of complications from Parkinson's disease. The cup, with its Greek key trim and "We Are Happy To Serve You" message, is a cultural icon as synonymous with New York as the Statue of Liberty or Grand Central Station. It sold hundreds of millions annually and is still available, though no longer a standard catalog item.

Pierre Cabrol, 84

Pierre Cabrol, an architect with Los Angeles firm Welton Becket and Associates died October 8, 2009. The firm's iconic projects included the Capitol Records Building, the Pan Pacific Auditorium, and the Cinerama Dome, a project that Cabrol led. While with Welton Becket, he worked as a designer on many projects, including the General Electric Pavilion at the 1964 New York World's Fair and the Grand Ole Opry House in Nashville, TN. A native of France and graduate of the École des Beaux-Arts in Paris, Cabrol attended the Massachusetts Institute of Technology on a scholarship, studying under Buckminster Fuller.

Jack Ladd Carr, 84

Jack Carr, the first planning director of Annapolis, MD, died January 10, 2010, of complications following a heart attack. He joined the city in 1961 and later was a planner for the Roman Catholic Diocese of Maryland. In the mid-1960s, he was a senior manager of statewide historical, cultural, and art programs for the state; in the mid-1980s he was named deputy director of all programs concerning the historical heritage of the State of Maryland. A native of Philadelphia, Carr was a World War II veteran and a graduate of St. John's College and Temple University.

Eduardo Catalano, 92

Argentinean architect and professor Eduardo Catalano died January 28, 2010. Born and educated in Buenos Aires, he was awarded scholarships to study at the University of Pennsylvania and later the Harvard Graduate School of Design under Walter Gropius. He taught at North Carolina State University School and then the Massachusetts Institute of Technology for almost 20 years. Among his many projects he is best known for the modernist home he designed for himself in Raleigh, NC, in 1954 that was razed in 2001. The home, with its innovative 4,000-square-foot undulating parabolic roof over a glass-walled structure, was named "House of the Decade" in the 1950s by *House and Home* magazine.

W.I.B. Crealock, 89

Yacht designer, sailor, and author William Ion Belton Crealock died September 29, 2009, after breaking his hip. In his studio in Newport Beach, CA, Crealock meticulously crafted by hand mostly fiberglass boats of every size—from dinghies to yachts—for boating enthusiasts, including many members of Hollywood's elite. His Pacific Seacraft 37 design was inducted into the American Sailboat Hall of Fame in 2002. Born in Great Britain, Crealock studied nautical architecture at Glasgow University and worked in the Glasgow shipyard during World War II. Following numerous sailing adventures in such exotic places as the South Pacific, he settled in California.

Joe Deal, 62

Photographer Joe Deal died June 18, 2010, from bladder cancer. He had been a founder of the New Topographies photography movement as well as a university professor. Concerned with the changing American landscape, his artistic portraits of scenic vistas marred by new tract homes, smog, and other indications of man's relentless sprawl were a highlight of his early career. He taught at numerous schools, including the University of California, Riverside; Washington University in St. Louis, where he was dean of the art school; and the Rhode Island School of Design, where he served as provost. He is also known for documenting the construction of the Getty Center; his decade's worth of photos hung inside the facility when it opened in 1997.

Vernon Phillip Deines, 80

Vernon Deines, a cofounder and early chair of the American Planning Association's Small Town and Rural Planning Division, died March 30, 2010. A professor at Kansas State University for 40 years, he taught architecture, mechanical engineering, and regional planning. He was also a founding member of the APA and the American Institute of Certified

Planners, and was involved in the process that eventually resulted in the APA/ACSP accreditation program for planning schools.

David Dillon, 68

Longtime *Dallas Morning News* architecture critic David Dillon died June 3, 2010, of a heart attack. He had been with the paper for 25 years. A native New Englander, he also taught architecture at Amherst College and the University of Massachusetts at Amherst. Dillon was the author of over 200 articles in such publications as *Architectural Record*, *Domus,* and *Harvard Design Review*. He also wrote more than a dozen books, including *Dallas Architecture: 1936–1986, The Architecture of O'Neil Ford*, and *Extending the Legacy: Planning the Nation's Capital for the 21st Century*.

Alfred Eckersberg, 89

Alfred Eckersberg, a leading Chicago-area planner who helped lead the city's 1950s urban renewal, died January 10, 2010. A native of the city, Eckersberg received a master's degree in economic planning from the University of Chicago and served as senior planner and assistant executive director of the Chicago Plan Commission as well as director of planning for the Chicago Conservation Board. An expert in real estate analysis and projections, Eckersberg later became senior vice president of the Real Estate Research Corporation and a principal in CASL, consulting on many real estate developments worldwide.

Barry Elbasani, 69

Barry Elbasani, a founder of ELS Architecture and Urban Design, died June 29, 2010, from brain cancer. Through the years, ELS gained a reputation as leading planners and designers of projects that helped revitalize urban spaces. Working with the Rouse Company through the 1980s and 1990s, ELS designed the Grand Avenue in Milwaukee; the mixed-use Pioneer Place in downtown Portland, OR; the Shops at Arizona Center in Phoenix, AZ; and the Village of Merrick Park in Coral Gables, FL. The firm also created the master plan for Summerlin, NV, and designed the Denver Pavilions in Colorado. Elbasani was also a lecturer at the University of California, Berkeley's College of Environmental Design.

David Van Fraser, 79

Atlanta, Georgia, architect David Van Fraser died May 3, 2010, of prostate cancer. After studying at Virginia Tech and Auburn University, he settled in Atlanta and spent many years in private practice there, contributing to many of the city's most prominent buildings and many area schools. He became director of architectural services for Norfolk

Southern Railway in 1978, supervising a staff of 11 that designed hundreds of projects for the company across 21 states.

Lane Greene, 74

Leading Georgia preservationist and architect Lane Greene died December 20, 2009. Over the course of his 30-year career, he was responsible for the preservation of numerous homes, churches, businesses, and community buildings throughout Georgia, particularly in the historic city of Madison and in surrounding Morgan County. He was a graduate of the Georgia Institute of Technology and worked for many Atlanta-area architecture firms before establishing his own practice in 1978. He is credited with the preservation and/or restoration of numerous structures in Georgia, including the First A.M.E. Church and Morton Theater in Athens; the Crawford W. Long House and Madison County Courthouse in Danielsville; and the Wren's Nest, home of *Uncle Remus* author Joel Chandler Harris, in Atlanta.

Henry T. Hopkins, 81

Henry Hopkins, a former director of the San Francisco Museum of Modern Art and later an arts leader in Southern California, died September 28, 2009, from complications caused by a brain tumor. A graduate of the School of the Art Institute of Chicago, Hopkins began his arts career in 1961 as assistant curator and an educator at the Los Angeles County Museum of History, Science and Art (now the Los Angeles County Museum of Art). He relocated to Texas in the late 1960s, serving as the head of the Modern Art Museum of Fort Work for six years, and then became director of the San Francisco Museum of Modern Art for eight years. He later went on to chair the UCLA art department and then become director of the Hammer Museum.

Stephen Kanner, 54

Stephen Kanner, a Los Angeles architect and cofounder of the Los Angeles Architecture and Design Museum died July 2, 2010, of cancer. Among his award-winning designs are the Harvard Apartments in Koreatown and the In-N-Out Burger on Gayley Avenue in Westwood that is a tribute to 1950s jet-age architecture. Inspired by a museum he had seen in Finland, in 2001 he cofounded the Architecture and Design museum in Los Angeles to promote architecture and design.

Claude Lévi-Strauss, 100

The French anthropologist, considered by many to be the father of modern anthropology, Claude Lévi-Strauss, died of natural causes on October 30, 2009. His theory of structuralism—which argues that common features exist within human societies—provided a level playing field for Western civilizations and so-called primitive societies, which he cautioned were not societies without advanced thought processes but rather were "societies without writing." The implications of his theories to architecture are essential to understanding the universal importance of honest contextual buildings built with indigenous materials expressive of a particular culture. "One of the giants of the 20th century" (dubbed by UNESCO Director-General Koichiro Matsuura), Lévi-Strauss studied law and philosophy at the Sorbonne and went on to teach at the newly created University of São Paulo while visiting the Amazon interior and living among various tribes for four years while formulating his groundbreaking theories about universal human principles of existence and habitation.

Barbara Lukermann, 79

Planner Barbara Lukermann, an educator at the Humphrey Institute at the University of Minnesota, died April 23, 2009, from cancer. A former chair of the American Institute of Certified Planners, she served on the AICP committee that developed the profession's first certification exam. Her expertise was tapped numerous times at the local, national, and international levels, including work on the National Academy of Sciences steering committee for the Cooperative Agreement with the Navajo Nation, as a delegate for the Municipal Planning Board of China, and as a trainer for USAID environmental programs in Romania. She received the American Planning Association's Award for Distinguished Leadership by a Professional Planner in 2004.

Donal McLaughlin, 102

Donal McLaughlin, an architect and graphic designer whose design for the United Nations logo has become one of the most recognized symbols in the world, died September 27, 2009, of esophageal cancer. Working as the head of graphics for the Office of Strategic Services (the precursor to the CIA), McLaughlin led a team charged with putting together the printed elements for the 1945 United Nations Conference on International Organization in San Francisco, including the emblem that eventually became the UN's logo. Trained as an architect, he collaborated with Walter Dorwin Teague and Raymond Loewy on exhibits for the 1939 World's Fair and designed a bottle for Pepsi-Cola and the interiors of Tiffany & Company's Fifth Avenue store before joining the OSS to develop visual material for the military.

Jack Meltzer, 88

Urban planner Jack Meltzer died May 5, 2010, from complications from emphysema. He helped plan and design the controversial 1950s urban renewal of Hyde Park, the South Side Chicago neighborhood that surrounds the University of Chicago. As director of planning for the South East Chicago Commission, he was charged with reshaping the majority of Hyde Park in what was widely recognized as an effort to keep minorities out of the area, including demolishing older structures and planning new development in their wake. A graduate of Wayne State University, Meltzer later started his own urban planning firm. He had also been chair of the public affairs program at the University of Chicago's School of Social Service Administration.

Bitte Bertilson Miller, 75

Bitte Bertilson Miller, Swedish artist and long-time companion, caregiver, and confidant to architect John Carl Warnecke, died July 2, 2010, in Sonoma County, CA. While still mourning Warnecke's death only 10 weeks after his passing, she suffered a ruptured aortic aneurysm. As an accomplished artist she excelled in many mediums—painting, ceramics, fibers, sculpting. An award-winning vintner and gourmet cook, she always selflessly gave of her time and talents to Warnecke's fellow architect/friends during their relationship spanning two decades.

Allyn Morris, 87

Allyn Morris, a Southern California modernist architect, died August 1, 2009. Though not widely known, his many residential projects are products of a unique vision. His first residential design was 1956's concrete, glass and steel Brubeck House in Eagle Rock, CA, whose multileveled interlocking spaces created a dynamic effect not found in most modernist architecture of the period. He also designed numerous houses and apartments throughout Los Angeles, including the Murakami house and his own studio-home. His work was photographed by Julius Shulman and Marvin Rand and included in the *Guide to Architecture in Los Angeles & Southern California*.

Barbara Morris, 90

Barbara Morris, a curator at Britain's Victoria and Albert Museum, died July 15, 2009. An artist, she joined the V&A circulation department in 1947 and under Peter Floud helped organize the 1952 exhibit "Victorian and Edwardian Decorative Arts." The program helped establish the museum as a leader in the field of Victorian design, and she later became an expert in the Arts and Crafts movement and led the museum's department of ceramics, retiring in 1978. She then worked six years for Sotheby's as part of its educational department, and finally joined the team of experts on the BBC's *Antiques Roadshow*.

Kemper Nomland Jr., 90

Southern California architect Kemper Nomland died December 25, 2009, of natural causes. He designed Case Study House No. 10 with his father; they formed their firm Nomland & Nomland after World War II. Their Case Study home, part of a program sponsored by *Arts & Architecture* magazine that promoted the design of modernist postwar housing, was constructed in 1947 in Pasadena. Nomland later designed a home for actress Jane Russell as well as over a dozen others in the Los Angeles area.

Bob Noorda, 82

Bob Noorda, a leading mid-century graphic designer who brought the clean look of modernism to corporate communications as well as the New York City subway system died January 11, 2010, from complications from a fall. With Massimo Vignelli, among others, he was a founding partner of the international graphics firm Unimark International. A native of the Netherlands who spent his career in Milan, Noorda and his firm were hired to redesign the look of the signage and wayfinding system for the New York City subway in 1966. Their clean designs, use of sans serif type, and color-coded markings remain largely intact today. Noorda also briefly led design for the Italian tire maker Pirelli and later worked on signage for the Milan and Naples subway systems in Italy and in São Paulo, Brazil.

Perry Norton

Perry Norton, a leading planner, teacher, and author, died December 23, 2009. He was the first full-time executive director of the American Institute of Planners, a predecessor of the American Planning Association. He had also been a member of the commission of the American Institute of Certified Planners; he was inducted into the AICP's first class of fellows in 1999. Norton was a frequent contributor to the urban planning website Cyburbia.org, where many of his writings on planning are posted.

Monica Pidgeon, 95

Monica Pidgeon, former editor of the British architecture magazine *Architectural Design* and a strong voice for modernism in the UK, died September 17, 2009. With Theo Crosby, later a cofounder of the design firm Pentagram, Pidgeon is credited with transforming the magazine into a thought leader in the design and art worlds. The pair also collaborated on the book *An Anthology of Houses* (1960), featuring cutting-edge modernist designs of the 1950s. In 1979 she began interviewing well-known architects and designers, and in recent years she made that material available online at the Pidgeon Digital Archive.

Robert S. Reich, 97

Robert Reich, the longtime Louisiana State University professor who is regarded as the "father of landscape architecture in Louisiana," died July 31, 2010. Known to friends and colleagues as "Doc," Reich joined the LSU faculty in 1941; intending to stay for a year, he retired from full-time teaching in 1983 when he reached the university's mandatory retirement age of 70. He founded the school's world-class landscape architecture program in 1946; it was renamed the Dr. Robert S. Reich School of Landscape Architecture in 2007. He was awarded LSU's highest teaching award, Alumni Professor, and won the American Society of Landscape Architect's ALSA Medal in 1992. He was the recipient of the ALSA's Jot D. Carpenter Teaching Medal for sustained and significant contributions to landscape architecture education in 2005.

Alan H. Rider, 79

Architect Alan Rider died May 25, 2010, of congestive heart failure. He had been an associate with John Carl Warnecke & Associates in the 1960s, and worked on many significant projects for the firm, including the memorial for President John F. Kennedy at Arlington National Cemetery. A resident of the Georgetown area of Washington, DC, Rider also helped develop a master plan for the US Naval Academy in Annapolis and the hangar for Air Force One at Andrews Air Force Base. He later joined the firm of Daniel, Mann, Johnson & Mendenhall where he contributed to renovations at the Pentagon as well as buildings at the Naval Academy and Howard University.

John B. Rogers, 85

John Rogers, a cofounder of Denver-based architecture firm RNL, died July 12, 2010, in his sleep. His wife Bette preceded him in death by 14 hours. Rogers and Jerry Nagel founded a firm in 1961, and five years later merged with another firm to form Rogers Nagel Langhart Architects and Engineers. Today RNL has over 200 employees working from offices in Denver, Los Angeles, Phoenix, and Dubai. Rogers' many designs included the Colorado History Museum, the *Rocky Mountain News* building, and Colorado's Ocean Journey aquarium. He was elected to the AIA College of Fellows in 1979 and was named Architect of the Year by AIA Colorado in 1991.

James Rossant, 81

Architect and planner James Rossant died December 15, 2009, at his home in Normandy, France, of complications of leukemia. His many projects include the planning of Reston, VA, and the 1966 master plan of lower Manhattan that led to the building of Battery Park City. He also taught architecture at the Pratt Institute for 35 years and urban design at

New York University. His first significant project was the co-design of 1962's Butterfield House, a modern apartment building in a Greenwich Village neighborhood of historic townhomes. It was named one of the 10 best post-war apartment buildings in New York by architecture critic Paul Goldberger. His partner for that project was William J. Conklin, with whom he practiced until 1995. Their design for Reston, a city of 75,000 outside DC for developer Robert E. Simon, included planning commercial and residential districts, landscaping, recreation, and culture. He was a graduate of the University of Florida and the Harvard Graduate School of Design where he studied under Walter Gropius.

Daniel Rowen, 56

Daniel Rowen, a New York architect with a client list that included hotelier Ian Schrager, art dealer Larry Gagosian, and Martha Stewart Living Omnimedia, died November 17, 2009, of neuroendocrine cancer. A protégé of modernist Charles Gwathmey, he formed a firm with Frank Lupo, another former Gwathmey employee, called New York Architects. He later formed his own firm, Daniel Rowan Architect. Whether designing an all-white Park Avenue apartment; the expansive headquarters for Martha Stewart's company with its combination of small, well-appointed workspaces and large loft-like areas; or the office and apartment of Schrager, Rowen's work was always in demand.

David Sarkisyan, 62

David Sarkisyan, director of the Shchusev State Museum of Architecture in Moscow, Russia, and a champion of that city's architectural treasures, died January 7, 2010, of lymphoma. A former physiologist, pharmacologist, and film director, Sarkisyan embarked on his "fourth life," heading the museum, in early 2000. With nearly all of its state funding cut and its infrastructure crumbling, Sarkisyan became a champion, not only of his own institution but of Moscow's many historical buildings, many of which met the wrecking ball despite his efforts. He planned many successful shows at the museum and brought the work of some of the world's best contemporary architects to Russia. Nicolai Ouroussoff writing in the *New York Times* said of Sarkisyan: "He was an extraordinary if anachronistic example of what a single person at the helm of a crumbling institution with few financial resources could accomplish—even in a world that seemed bent on silencing him."

Mario L. Schack, 81

Longtime Baltimore architect, educator, and design critic Mario Schack died June 17, 2010. He had been an architecture professor and department chair at Cornell University and a partner in several Baltimore-based firms, including RTKL Associates; Marks, Cooke, Schack and Thomas (now Marks, Thomas Architects), and MLS Associates. He had served on several panels charged with reviewing building proposals for the city of Baltimore, including the Design Advisory Panel, the Architectural Review Board, and the Urban Design and Architecture Review Panel. As a designer, Schack's projects included the Charles Center South office tower in Charles Center in Baltimore, the Albin O. Kuhn Library on the University of Maryland campus, and the Geological Sciences building at Cornell. He was named an AIA Fellow in 1980.

Der Scutt, 75

Der Scutt, the designer of Manhattan's Trump Tower, died March 14, 2010, of liver failure. He was a developer's architect, and his many New York projects included One Astor Plaza overlooking Times Square; 100 United Nations Plaza Tower; and the Corinthian at First Avenue and 37th Street, designed with Michael Schimenti. In recent years Scutt redesigned facades for older buildings, often replacing masonry with glass curtain walls. It was his early 1980s addition to Fifth Avenue for Donald Trump—a bronzed glass modern tower that brought new energy to its stodgy block—for which Scutt is best known. Before founding his own firm in 1981, Scutt worked for Kahn & Jacobs and then for Swanke Hayden Connell Architects. Following graduation from Yale's graduate architecture program, he ran the office of Paul Rudolph, then dean of the program, for several years.

Karle Seydel, 59

Denver architect and urban activist Karle Seydel died May 12, 2010. He is credited with having an instrumental role in the siting of Coors Field and for his efforts to revitalize the neighborhoods around the stadium. He advocated for better lighting and street beautification for the lower downtown area of the city and worked to preserve some of the older and sometimes neglected buildings there. Seydel operated his own design firm, Urban Options.

Dennis Sharp, 76

British architect, writer, and educator Dennis Sharp died May 6, 2010. He was a practicing designer with a keen interest in British modernism, environmental design, and professional activism. A graduate of the Architectural Association in London, Sharp remained involved with the school for the rest of his life as a vice president and a teacher. His firm, Dennis Sharp Architects, was responsible for many historic renovation projects, including Norman Foster's Renault Distribution Centre in Swindon, Wiltshire. Sharp also designed Strawdance studio, the least-expensive national lottery-funded project to date in the UK, using straw bales, timber, and clear plastic. He was also the author of many books and articles on British architects and 20th-century buildings.

James Stageberg, 85

James Stageberg, a leading Minnesota architect and longtime University of Minnesota professor, died July 7, 2010, of complications from Parkinson's disease. A graduate of the Harvard Graduate School of Design, Stageberg practiced many years in Minnesota. His many projects include the Walter Library, Elmer L. Andersen Library, and Aquatic Center at the University of Minnesota in Minneapolis; the Mary Mother of the Church in Burnsville; and many houses. He was awarded the Gold Medal by AIA Minnesota and was voted by its members as one of the state's 12 all-time best architects. The first hire for Ralph Rapson, Stageberg was awarded the U of M Ralph Rapson award for Distinguished Teaching in 1991. With his wife, Susan Allen, he wrote 1991's *A House of One's Own: An Architect's Guide to Designing the House of Your Dreams.*

Stewart L. Udall, 90

Conservationist and former US secretary of the interior Stewart Udall died March 20, 2010. His long career in public service was highlighted by his work on land and environmental conservation, especially in his native West. Born in Arizona and a graduate of the University of Arizona law school, he was elected to the congress from Arizona in 1954, and served as secretary of the interior under presidents Kennedy and Johnson. He spearheaded the addition of 3.85 million acres of new holdings to the National Park system, including the Appalachian National Scenic Trail and Redwood National Park in California. Udall also had a hand in the enactment of many environmental laws, including the Endangered Species Act. He also worked to preserve historic sites, including Carnegie Hall in New York. He was the author or co-author of many books, including his bestselling 1963 book foretelling a conservation crisis, *The Quiet Crisis*.

Edgar Wayburn, 103

Former longtime Sierra Club president Edgar Wayburn died March 5, 2010. He is credited with protecting more parks and wilderness areas than any other American. For his years of service, Wayburn was awarded the Presidential Medal of Freedom well as the Albert Schweitzer Prize for Humanitarianism. A native of Georgia, Wayburn graduated from Harvard Medical School in 1930 and moved to California to practice medicine. He joined the Sierra Club in 1939 so he could participate in the group's burro trips into the Sierras. During his work with the group he is credited with helping establish Redwood National Park, the Golden Gate National Recreation Area, Point Reyes National Seashore, and many others.

Malcolm Wells, 83

Architect Malcolm Wells, a pioneer of the green roof movement, died November 27, 2009, of congestive heart failure. A practicing architect many years, Wells refocused his priorities after realizing the pavilion he designed for RCA at the 1964 World's Fair would soon be torn down and consigned to a landfill. He then looked for ways to build in harmony with the land and to leave as light a footprint on it as possible. He designed numerous homes and offices with green roofs, most with passive heat. Wells wrote numerous books and articles on the subject and lectured at architectural schools and universities across the country throughout the 1970s and '80s.

Norval White, 83

Norval White, co-author of the *AIA Guide to New York City*, died December 26, 2009, of a heart attack. Authoritative and opinionated, the guide is credited with playing a pivotal role in increasing America's awareness of its architectural past. A native New Yorker, White taught architecture at the Cooper Union and then became founding chairman of the City College School of Architecture and Environmental Studies (now the Bernard and Anne Spitzer School of Architecture). The original guide, with its notes on neighborhoods, landmarks, and other less-known buildings, introduced readers to a host of little-known designers and increased appreciation for their work.

Tobias Wong, 35

Conceptual artist Tobias (Tobi) Wong died May 30, 2010; the cause of death was suicide. He rose to prominence through his provocative reimagining of designers' products and his own subversive work. He created a "pad" of $100 bills, a gold-plated McDonald's coffee stir, and a duvet made of bulletproof Kevlar. He turned a Phillippe Starck Bubble Club chair into a lamp, and fashioned a copy of Karim Rashid's book *I Want to Change the World* into the shape of a gun. Fashion icon Issey Miyake issued a cease-and-desist order when Wong made computer-screen covers from his Pleats Please dress. Wong's work was included in the MOMA's 2005 exhibition "SAFE: Design Takes on Risk."

BUILDINGS | Awards

Buildings are highlighted in chapters 6 and 7.
Awards to buildings are presented here: the
skyscraper building type is followed by general awards, then specific award types, such
as schools and libraries, and industrial design.

(Note: Bolded text indicates additions to the existing list.)

Best Tall Building Awards

The Best Tall Building Awards recognize projects that have made **extraordinary contributions to the advancement of tall buildings and the urban environment, including sustainability**. The projects must also exhibit processes or innovations that have enhanced the design profession and enriched the cities and lives of their inhabitants. The program is sponsored by the Council on Tall Buildings and Urban Habitats.

www.ctbuh.org

2010 Winners

Americas
Bank of America Tower
New York, NY
Cook + Fox Architects

Europe
Broadcasting Place
Leeds, UK
Feilden Clegg Bradley Studios (UK)

Asia & Australasia
Pinnacle @ Duxton
Singapore
ARC Studio Architecture + Urbanism
(Singapore)

Middle East & Africa
Burj Khalifa
Dubai, UAE
Skidmore, Owings & Merrill

Source: Council on Tall Buildings and Urban Habitats

Emporis Skyscraper Award

Emporis, an international provider of architectural and building information, bestows its annual Skyscraper Award to an **outstanding building over 100 meters (328 feet)** completed in the previous year. The selection process favors solutions that provide for people's physical, social, and economic needs as well as respond to cultural and spiritual expectations. Particular attention is given to buildings that use local resources and appropriate technology in an innovative way.

www.emporis.com

2009 Winners

Skyscraper of the Year
Aqua
Chicago, IL
Studio Gang Architects

Silver Award
O-14
Dubai, UAE
Reiser + Umemoto RUR Architecture

Bronze Award
The Met
Bangkok, Thailand
WOHA Architects (Singapore)

Runners Up (listed in order)
Torres de Hércules
Los Barrios, Spain
Rafael de La-Hoz Arquitectos (Spain)

Trump International Hotel & Tower
Chicago, IL
Skidmore, Owings & Merrill

The Red Apple
Rotterdam, Netherlands
KCAP Architects & Planners (Netherlands)

Bank of America Tower
New York, NY
Cook + Fox Architects with Adamson
    Associates Architects

Almas Tower
Dubai, UAE
Atkins Middle East (UAE)

Millennium Tower
San Francisco, CA
Handel Architects

William Beaver House
New York, NY
Tsao & McKown Architects with SLCE
    Architects

Source: Emporis

Lynn S. Beedle Achievement Award

The Lynn S. Beedle Lifetime Achievement Award recognizes individuals who have made **extraordinary contributions to tall buildings and the urban environment**. Candidates may be from any area of specialization, including architecture, structures, building systems, construction, academia, planning, development, or management. The award is named for the founder and former director (1969–2000) of the Council on Tall Buildings and Urban Habitats.

www.ctbuh.org

2002	Lynn S. Beedle
2003	Charles A. DeBenedittis
2004	Gerald D. Hines
2005	Alan G. Davenport
2006	Ken Yeang (Malaysia)
2007	Lord Norman Foster (UK)
2008	Cesar Pelli
2009	John Portman
2010	**William Pedersen**

Source: Council on Tall Buildings and Urban Habitats

Tallest Buildings in the World

The following list ranks the world's 100 tallest buildings as determined by the Council on Tall Buildings and Urban Habitat. Buildings that have reached their full height but are still under construction are deemed eligible and are indicated with a UC in the year category along with the anticipated completion date, if known.

	Building	Yr.	Location	Height (ft./m.)	(# stories)	Architect
1	Burj Khalifa	2010	Dubai, UAE	2,717/828	163	Skidmore, Owings & Merrill
2	Makkah Royal Clock Tower Hotel	UC11	Makkah, Saudi Arabia	1,972/601	95	Dar al-Handasah Shair & Partners (Lebanon)
3	Taipei 101	2004	Taipei, Taiwan	1,667/508	101	C.Y. Lee & Partners (Taiwan)
4	Shanghai World Financial Center	2008	Shanghai, China	1,614/492	101	Kohn Pedersen Fox; East China Architectural Design & Research Institute Co. Ltd. (China)
5	International Commerce Centre	2010	Hong Kong, China	1,588/484	108	Wong & Ouyang Ltd. (Hong Kong); Kohn Pedersen Fox Associates
6	Petronas Tower 1	1998	Kuala Lumpur, Malaysia	1,483/452	88	Cesar Pelli & Associates
7	Petronas Tower 2	1998	Kuala Lumpur, Malaysia	1,483/452	88	Cesar Pelli & Associates
8	Nanjing Greenland Financial Center	2010	Nanjing, China	1,476/450	66	Skidmore, Owings & Merrill
9	Willis Tower	1974	Chicago, IL	1,451/442	108	Skidmore, Owings & Merrill
10	Kingkey Finance Tower	UC12	Shenzhen, China	1,449/442	98	Terry Farrell and Partners (UK)
11	Guangzhou International Finance Center	2010	Guangzhou, China	1,446/441	103	Wilkerson Eyre Architects (UK)
12	Trump International Hotel & Tower	2009	Chicago, IL	1,398/423	98	Skidmore, Owings & Merrill
13	Jin Mao Building	1999	Shanghai, China	1,380/421	88	Skidmore, Owings & Merrill
14	Princess Tower	UC11	Dubai, UAE	1,358/414	101	Eng. Adnan Saffarini (UAE)
15	Al Hamra Tower	UC11	Kuwait City, Kuwait	1,354/413	77	Skidmore, Owings & Merrill; Al Jazera Consultants (Kuwait); Callison
16	Marina 101	UC12	Dubai, UAE	1,352/412	101	National Engineering Bureau (UAE)
17	Two International Finance Centre	2003	Hong Kong, China	1,352/412	88	Cesar Pelli & Associates
18	CITIC Plaza	1996	Guangzhou, China	1,280/390	80	Dennis Lau & Ng Chun Man Architects & Engineers (China)

	Building	Yr.	Location	Height (ft./m.)	(# stories)	Architect
19	23 Marina	UC11	Dubai, UAE	1,276/389	90	KEO International Consultants (UAE)
20	Shun Hing Square	1996	Shenzhen, China	1,260/384	69	K.Y. Cheung Design Associates (China)
21	The Domian	UC12	Abu Dhabi, UAE	1,251/382	88	Foster + Partners (UK)
22	Empire State Building	1031	New York, NY	1,250/381	102	Shreve, Lamb & Harmon
23	Emirates Park Towers Hotel & Spa 1	UC11	Dubai, UAE	1,234/376	77	Archgroup Consultants (UAE)
24	Emirates Park Towers Hotel & Spa 2	UC11	Dubai, UAE	1,234/376	77	Archgroup Consultants (UAE)
25	Central Plaza	1992	Hong Kong, China	1,227/374	78	Ng Chun Man & Associates (China)
26	Bank of China	1989	Hong Kong, China	1,205/367	70	Pei Cobb Freed & Partners
27	Bank of America Tower	2009	New York, NY	1,200/366	55	Cook + Fox Architects; Adamson Associates Architects
28	Almas Tower	2008	Dubai, UAE	1,191/363	68	WS Atkins & Partners (UK)
29	Emirates Tower One	2000	Dubai, UAE	1,163/355	54	Norr Group Consultants (Canada)
30	Tuntex Sky Tower	1997	Kaohsiung, Taiwan	1,140/348	85	C.Y. Lee & Partners (Taiwan); Hellmuth, Obata & Kassabaum
31	Aon Centre	1973	Chicago, IL	1,136/346	83	Edward Durrell Stone & Associates
32	The Center	1998	Hong Kong, China	1,135/346	73	Dennis Lau & Ng Chun Man Architects & Engineers (China)
33	The Torch	UC11	Dubai, UAE	1,132/345	80	Khatib & Alami (UAE)
34	John Hancock Center	1969	Chicago, IL	1,128/344	100	Skidmore, Owings & Merrill
35	Tianjin World Financial Center	UC11	Tianjin, China	1,106/337	76	Skidmore, Owings & Merrill
36	Shimao International Plaza	2006	Shanghai, China	1,094/333	60	Ingenhoven Architekten (Germany); East China Architectural Design & Research Institute Co. Ltd. (China)
37	Rose Rayhaan by Rotana	2007	Dubai, UAE	1,093/333	72	Khatib & Alami (Lebanon)
38	Minsheng Bank Building	2008	Wuhan, China	1,087/331	68	Wuhan Architectural Design Institute (China)
39	Ryugyong Hotel	UC*	Pyongyang, North Korea	1,083/330	105	Baikdoosan Architects & Engineers (North Korea)

* Topped out in 1995 but never completed

Tallest Buildings in the World

Building	Yr.	Location	Height (ft./m.)	(# stories)	Architect
40	United International Mansion	UC11	Chongqing, China	1,083/330	72	Unknown
41	China World Trade Center Tower III	2009	Beijing, China	1,083/330	74	Skidmore, Owings & Merrill
42	The Index	2010	Dubai, UAE	1,076/328	80	Foster + Partners (UK); Woods Bagot (UAE); Khatib & Alami (UAE)
43	Hanging Village of Huaxi	UC11	Jiangyin, China	1,076/328	74	A+E Design Co. (China)
44	Al Yaqoub Tower	UC11	Dubai, UAE	1,076/328	69	Eng. Adnan Saffarini (UAE)
45	The Landmark	UC11	Abu Dhabi, UAE	1,063/324	72	Pelli Clarke Pelli Architects
46	Q1	2005	Gold Coast, Australia	1,058/323	78	The Buchan Group (Australia)
47	Wenzhou Trade Center	2010	Wenzhou, China	1,056,322	68	RTKL Associates Inc.; Shanghai Institute of Architectural Design & Research Co.Ltd (China)
48	Burj al Arab Hotel	1999	Dubai, UAE	1,053/321	56	WS Atkins & Partners (UK)
49	Nina Tower I	2007	Hong Kong, China	1,046/319	80	Arthur CS Kwok Architects & Associates Ltd. (China); Casa Design International Ltd. (China); Dennis Lau & Ng Chun Man Architects & Engineers (China)
50	Chrysler Building	1930	New York, NY	1,046/319	77	William Van Alen
51	New York Times Tower	2007	New York, NY	1,046/319	52	Renzo Piano Building Workshop (Italy); FXFOWLE Architects
52	HHHR Tower	2010	Dubai, UAE	1,042/318	72	Al Hashemi (UAE)
53	Bank of America Plaza	1993	Atlanta, GA	1,039/317	55	Kevin Roche John Dinkeloo & Associates
54	Sky Tower	2010	Dubai, UAE	1,024/312	74	Arquitectonica
55	U.S. Bank Tower	1990	Los Angeles, CA	1,018/310	73	Pei Cobb Freed & Partners
56	Ocean Heights	UC10	Dubai, UAE	1,017/310	82	Aedas (UAE) with ECG Engineering Consultants Group (Egypt)
57	Menara Telekom Headquarters	2000	Kuala Lumpur, Malaysia	1,017/310	55	Hijjas Kasturi Associates (Malaysia)
58	Pearl River Tower	UC11	Guangzhou, China	1,016/310	71	Skidmore, Owings & Merrill
59	Emirates Tower Two	2000	Dubai, UAE	1,014/309	56	Norr Group Consultants (Canada)
60	AT&T Corporate Center	1989	Chicago, IL	1,007/307	60	Skidmore, Owings & Merrill

	Building	Yr.	Location	Height (ft./m.)	(# stories)	Architect
61	Infinity Tower	UC11	Dubai, UAE	1,005/306	76	Skidmore, Owings & Merrill
62	The Address Downtown Burj Dubai	2008	Dubai, UAE	1,004/306	63	WS Atkins & Partners (UK)
63	Etihad Tower 2	UC11	Abu Dhabi, UAE	1,002/305	79	DBI Design (Pty Ltd). (Australia)
64	JP Morgan Chase Tower	1982	Houston, TX	1,002/305	75	I.M. Pei & Partners
65	NE Asia Trade Tower	2010	Incheon, South Korea	1,001/305	68	Kohn Pedersen Fox
66	Baiyoke Tower II	1997	Bangkok, Thailand	997/304	85	Plan Architects Co. (Thailand)
67	Two Prudential Plaza	1990	Chicago, IL	995/303	64	Loebl Schlossman Dart & Hackl
68	Leatop Plaza	UC11	Guangzhou, China	994/303	64	Murphy/Jahn
69	Wells Fargo Plaza	1983	Houston, TX	992/302	71	Skidmore, Owings & Merrill
70	Kingdom Centre	2002	Riyadh, Saudi Arabia	991/302	41	Ellerbe Becket; Omrania & Associates (Saudi Arabia)
71	Capital City Moscow Tower	2010	Moscow, Russia	989/302	76	NBBJ
72	Arraya Tower	2009	Kuwait City, Kuwait	984/300	60	Fentress Architects
73	Aspire Tower	2007	Doha, Qatar	984/300	36	AREP Group (France) with Hadi Simaan Partners (Qatar)
74	One Island East	2008	Hong Kong, China	979/298	69	Wong & Ouyang Ltd. (Hong Kong)
75	First Bank Tower	1975	Toronto, ON, Canada	978/298	72	Bregman + Hamann Architects (Canada)
76	Shanghai Wheelock Square	2010	Shanghai, China	978/298	59	Kohn Pedersen Fox Associates
77	Eureka Tower	2006	Melbourne, Australia	975/297	91	Fender Katsalidis Architects (Australia)
78	Comcast Center	2008	Philadelphia, PA	974/297	57	Robert A.M. Stern Architects with Kendall/Heaton Associates
79	Trump Ocean Club	UC11	Panama City, Panama	961/293	68	Arias Serna Saravia (Columbia)
80	Landmark Tower	1993	Yokohama, Japan	972/296	73	The Stubbins Associates
81	Emirates Crown	2008	Dubai, UAE	971/296	63	DAR Consult (Sudan)
82	Khalid Al Attar Tower 2	UC10	Dubai, UAE	965/294	65	Eng. Adnan Saffarini (UAE)

Tallest Buildings in the World

	Building	Yr.	Location	Height (ft./m.)	(# stories)	Architect
83	Islamic Bank Office Tower	UC11	Dubai, UAE	964/294	49	Hopkins Architects (UK)
84	311 South Wacker Drive	1990	Chicago, IL	961/293	65	Kohn Pedersen Fox
85	SEG Plaza	2000	Shenzhen, China	957/292	71	Hua Yi Designing Consultants Ltd (China)
86	American International Building	1932	New York, NY	952/290	67	Clinton & Russell
87	Key Tower	1991	Cleveland, OH	947/289	57	Cesar Pelli & Associates
88	Plaza 66	2001	Shanghai, China	945/288	66	Kohn Pedersen Fox Associates with East China Architectural Design & Research Institute Co. Ltd. (China) and Frank C.Y. Feng Architects & Associates (China)
89	One Liberty Place	1987	Philadelphia, PA	945/288	61	Murphy/Jahn
90	Excellence Century Plaza Tower 1	UC10	Shenzhen, China	945/288	60	LEO A DALY
91	SPG Global Tower 1	UC11	Suzhou, China	938/286	54	East China Architectural Design & Research Institute Co., Ltd. (China)
92	SPG Global Tower 2	UC11	Suzhou, China	938/286	54	East China Architectural Design & Research Institute Co., Ltd. (China)
93	Sulafa Tower	UC10	Dubai, UAE	935/285	75	National Engineering Bureau (UAE)
94	Millennium Tower	2006	Dubai, UAE	935/285	59	WS Atkins & Partners (UK)
95	Tomorrow Square	2003	Shanghai, China	934/285	58	John Portman & Associates
96	Columbia Center	1984	Seattle, WA	933/284	76	Chester Lindsey Architects
97	Chongqing World Trade Center	2005	Chongqing, China	929/283	60	Haines Lundberg Waehler
98	Cheung Kong Centre	1999	Hong Kong, China	928/283	63	Cesar Pelli & Associates; Leo A Daly
99	The Trump Building	1930	New York, NY	927/283	71	H. Craig Severance
100	Bank of America Plaza	1985	Dallas, TX	921/281	72	JPJ Architects

Source: ©Council on Tall Buildings and Urban Habitat

World's Best Skylines

This list ranks the impressiveness of the world's skylines by calculating the density and height of each city's skyscrapers. All buildings taller than 295 feet (90 meters)—excluding spires—contribute points to its home city's score equal to the number of feet it exceeds this benchmark height.

http://homepages.ipact.nl/~egram/skylines.html

	City	Points	# Bldgs. over 295 ft/90 m
1	Hong Kong, China	86,076	3037
2	New York, NY (incl. Jersey City, Fort Lee, Guttenburg)	36,784	882
3	Tokyo, Japan (incl. Kawaguchi, Kawasaki, Ichikawa)	20,476	656
4	Dubai, UAE	19,170	308
5	Shanghai, China	18,957	548
6	Chicago, IL	16,578	344
7	Bangkok, Thailand	14,500	448
8	Guangzhou, China	11,374	348
9	Chongqing, China	9,296	363
10	Singapore	9,019	354
11	Seoul, South Korea	8,902	289
12	Shenzhen, China	8,895	251
13	Kuala Lumpur, Malaysia (incl. Petaling Jaya, Subang Jaya)	7,959	233
14	Manila, Philippines (incl. metro areas)	7,151	190
15	Jakarta, Indonesia	6,860	189
16	Toronto, ON, Canada (incl. Mississauga)	6,641	239
17	Osaka, Japan (incl. Sakai, Amagasaka)	5,698	155
18	Beijing, China	5,543	260
19	Nanjing, China	5,201	102
20	Miami, FL (incl. Miami Beach)	4,992	111
21	Houston, TX (incl. Pasadena)	4,983	117
22	Moscow, Russia	4,954	165
23	Sydney, Australia (incl. N. Sydney)	4,739	138
24	Panama City, Panama	4,303	113
25	São Paulo, Brazil	4,073	293

Note: To serve as a tribute to the old towers and the victims, the World Trade Center will be included in the calculations for New York's points until the Freedom Tower/One World Trade Center is topped out.

Source: Egbert Gramsbergen and Paul Kazmierczak

Top Ranked Buildings

The following rankings provide a glimpse into the minds of architects, architecture critics, and the general public as they reflected at various points in history on the question of what are the best buildings.

1885 Poll by American Architect and Building News

1. Trinity Church
   Boston, MA, 1877
   H.H. Richardson

2. US Capitol
   Washington, DC, 1793–1865
   William Thornton, Benjamin Henry
     Latrobe, Charles Bulfinch, Thomas
     Ustick Walter

3. Vanderbilt House
   New York, NY, 1883
   Richard Morris Hunt

4. Trinity Church
   New York, NY, 1846
   Richard Upjohn

5. Jefferson Market Courthouse
   New York, NY, 1877
   Frederick Withers & Calvert Vaux

6. Connecticut State Capitol
   Hartford, CT, 1879
   Richard Upjohn

7. Albany City Hall
   Albany, NY, 1883
   H.H. Richardson

8. Sever Hall, Harvard University
   Cambridge, MA, 1880
   H.H. Richardson

9. New York State Capitol
   Albany, NY, 1886
   H.H. Richardson

10. Town Hall
    North Easton, MA, 1881
    H.H. Richardson

Source: American Architect *and* Building News

100 Years of Signature Buildings, 1857–1956

In 1956 *Architectural Record* asked a panel of 50 architects and scholars to name "about 20 buildings in existence today whose overall significance, in your opinion, has been most important in the stage-by-stage development of our architecture."

1. Wainwright Building
   St. Louis, MO, 1891
   Louis Sullivan

   Carson Pirie Scott
   Chicago, IL, 1904
   Louis Sullivan

2. Rockefeller Center
   New York, NY, 1940
   Reinhard & Hofmeister; Corbett,
     Harrison & MacMurray; Hood &
     Fouilhoux

3. Lever House
   New York, NY, 1952
   Skidmore, Owings & Merrill

4. Trinity Church
   Boston, MA, 1877
   H.H. Richardson

5. PSFS Building
   Philadelphia, PA, 1931
   Howe & Lescaze

6. General Motors Technical Center
Warren, MI, 1957
Saarinen, Saarinen & Associates

7. Lake Shore Apartments
Chicago, IL, 1951
Ludwig Mies van der Rohe

8. S.C. Johnson & Son Administration
Building
Racine, WI, 1936
Frank Lloyd Wright

9. Daily News Building
New York, NY, 1930
Howells & Hood

Monadnock Block
Chicago, IL, 1891
Burnham & Root

TVA Norris Dam & Powerhouse
Clinch River, Anderson County, TN, 1936
Roland Wank

10. Boston Public Library
Boston, MA, 1889
McKim, Mead and White

State Fair Livestock Pavilion
(now Dorton Arena)
Raleigh, NC, 1952
Matthew Nowicki and William Dietrick

11. First Church of Christ, Scientist
Berkeley, CA, 1910
Bernard Maybeck

12. Crow Island School
Winnetka, IL, 1940
Saarinen & Saarinen with Perkins,
Wheeler & Will

Manufacturers Trust Building
New York, NY, 1954
Skidmore, Owings & Merrill

Woolworth Building
New York, NY, 1913
Cass Gilbert

13. Nebraska State Capitol
Lincoln, NE, 1926
Bertram Grosvenor Goodhue

Unity Temple
Oak Park, IL, 1908
Frank Lloyd Wright

14. United Nations Secretariat
New York, NY, 1950
W.K. Harrison & Consultants

S.C. Johnson & Son Laboratory Building
Racine, WI, 1949
Frank Lloyd Wright

15. Kresge Auditorium, Massachusetts
Institute of Technology
Cambridge, MA, 1955
Eero Saarinen and Associates

Lincoln Memorial
Washington, DC, 1917
Henry Bacon

16. Equitable Savings and Loan Association
Building
Portland, OR, 1948
Pietro Belluschi

17. Allegheny County Buildings
Pittsburgh, PA, 1887
H.H. Richardson

Cranbrook School
Bloomfield Hills, MI, 1930
Eliel Saarinen

Minerals & Metals Research Building,
Illinois Institute of Technology
Chicago, IL, 1943
Ludwig Mies van der Rohe (Germany/US)

University Club
New York, NY, 1900
McKim, Mead and White

18. Alcoa Building
Pittsburgh, PA, 1952
Harrison & Abramovitz

Top Ranked Buildings

19. Museum of Modern Art
    New York, NY, 1939
    Philip L. Goodwin and Edward Durrell
      Stone

20. 100 Memorial Drive Apartments
    Cambridge, MA, 1950
    Kennedy, Koch, DeMars, Rapson & Brown

    Dodge Truck Plant
    Detroit, MI, 1938
    Albert Kahn Associates

Central Lutheran Church
Portland, OR, 1951
Pietro Belluschi

Experimental School
Los Angeles, CA, 1935
Richard Neutra (Germany/US)

Pennsylvania Station
New York, NY, 1906
McKim, Mead and White

Source: Architectural Record, *June 1956–July 1957*

100 Years of Signature Houses, 1857–1956

As part of the 1956 "100 Years of Signature Buildings" series, *Architectural Record* ranked houses separate from other buildings.

1. Fallingwater
   Mill Run, PA, 1936
   Frank Lloyd Wright

   Robie House
   Chicago, IL, 1909
   Frank Lloyd Wright

2. Taliesin West
   Scottsdale, AZ, 1937
   Frank Lloyd Wright

4. Henry Villard Houses
   New York, NY, 1885
   McKim, Mead and White

5. Avery Coonley House
   Riverside, IL, 1908
   Frank Lloyd Wright

   William Watts Sherman House
   Newport, RI, 1876
   H.H. Richardson

6. Gamble House
   Pasadena, CA, 1908
   Greene and Greene

7. Glass House
   New Caanan, CT, 1950
   Philip Johnson

   Ward Willitts House
   Highland Park, IL, 1902
   Frank Lloyd Wright

8. Walker Guest House
   Sanibel Island, FL, 1953
   Paul Rudolph

9. Ellen Scripps House
   La Jolla, CA, 1917
   Irving Gill

   Lovell House
   Los Angeles, CA, 1929
   Richard Neutra (Germany/US)

   Weston Havens House
   Berkeley, CA, 1940
   Harwell Hamilton Harris

10. Farnsworth House
    Plano, IL, 1951
    Ludwig Mies van der Rohe
      (Germany/US)

Source: Architectural Record, *June 1956–May 1957*

Top Works of Architecture, 1891–1991

The following ranking resulted from a readers' poll conducted by *Architectural Record* in 1991 regarding the best buildings worldwide of the past century.

1. Fallingwater
   Mill Run, PA, 1936
   Frank Lloyd Wright

2. Villa Savoye
   Poissy, France, 1931
   Le Corbusier (Switzerland/France)

3. Barcelona Pavilion
   Barcelona, Spain, 1929
   Ludwig Mies van der Rohe
     (Germany/US)

4. Notre Dame du Haut
   Ronchamp, France, 1955
   Le Corbusier (Switzerland/France)

5. Kimbell Art Museum
   Fort Worth, TX, 1972
   Louis I. Kahn

6. Robie House
   Chicago, IL, 1909
   Frank Lloyd Wright

7. Seagram Building
   New York, NY, 1954–58
   Ludwig Mies van der Rohe
     (Germany/US)

8. Chrysler Building
   New York, NY, 1930
   William Van Alen

9. Rockefeller Center
   New York, NY, 1940
   Reinhard & Hofmeister; Corbett,
     Harrison & MacMurray; Hood &
     Fouilhoux

10. Lever House
    New York, NY, 1952
    Skidmore, Owings & Merrill

11. Wainwright Building
    St. Louis, MO, 1891
    Louis Sullivan

12. Pompidou Center
    Paris, France, 1977
    Piano & Rogers (Italy/UK)

13. S.C. Johnson & Son Administration
      Building
    Racine, WI, 1939
    Frank Lloyd Wright

14. Unity Temple
    Oak Park, IL, 1908
    Frank Lloyd Wright

15. Bauhaus
    Dessau, Germany, 1926
    Walter Gropius (Germany/US)

16. Carson Pirie Scott
    Chicago, IL, 1904
    Louis Sullivan

17. Dulles International Airport, Terminal
      Building
    Chantilly, VA, 1962
    Eero Saarinen & Associates

18. Sydney Opera House
    Sydney, Australia, 1973
    Jørn Utzon (Denmark)

19. Salk Institute
    La Jolla, CA, 1966
    Louis I. Kahn

    Glasgow School of Art
    Glasgow, Scotland, UK, 1909
    Charles Rennie Mackintosh (UK)

Source: Architectural Record, *July 1991*

Top Ranked Buildings

2000, Top 10 Buildings of the 20th Century

At the 2000 AIA convention, attendees were asked to vote for their top 10 favorite structures of the century.

1. Fallingwater
   Mill Run, PA, 1936
   Frank Lloyd Wright

2. Chrysler Building
   New York, NY, 1930
   William Van Alen

3. Seagram Building
   New York, NY, 1958
   Ludwig Mies van der Rohe (Germany/US)

4. Thorncrown Chapel
   Eureka Springs, AR, 1980
   E. Fay Jones

5. Terminal Building, Dulles International
   Airport
   Chantilly, VA, 1962
   Eero Saarinen & Associates

6. Salk Institute
   La Jolla, CA, 1966
   Louis I. Kahn

7. Vietnam Veterans Memorial
   Washington, DC, 1982
   Maya Lin

8. Robie House
   Chicago, IL, 1909
   Frank Lloyd Wright

9. East Wing, National Gallery
   Washington, DC, 1978
   I.M. Pei & Partners

10. S.C. Johnson & Son Administration
    Building
    Racine, WI, 1939
    Frank Lloyd Wright

Source: American Institute of Architects

2001, Architecture Critics' Top Rated Buildings

US architecture critics rated the top US buildings in a 2001 study conducted by Columbia University's National Arts Journalism Program.

1. Brooklyn Bridge
   New York, NY, 1883
   John Augustus Roebling

2. Grand Central Terminal
   New York, NY, 1913
   Warren & Wetmore; Reed & Stem

3. Chrysler Building
   New York, NY, 1930
   William Van Alen

4. Monticello
   Charlottesville, VA, 1769–84, 1796–1809
   Thomas Jefferson

5. University of Virginia
   Charlottesville, VA, 1826
   Thomas Jefferson

6. Robie House
   Chicago, IL, 1909
   Frank Lloyd Wright

7. Carson Pirie Scott Building
   Chicago, IL, 1904
   Louis Sullivan

8. Empire State Building
   New York, NY, 1931
   Shreve, Lamb & Harmon

9. S.C. Johnson & Son Administration
    Building
    Racine, WI, 1939
    Frank Lloyd Wright

10. Unity Temple
    Oak Park, IL, 1908
    Frank Lloyd Wright

Source: The Architecture Critic, *National Arts Journalism Program, Columbia University*

2002, Great Architectural Works of the 21st Century

In 2002, *USA Weekend* magazine asked a panel of jurors to determine the great architectural works of the 21st century (listed alphabetically).

3Com Midwest Headquarters
Rolling Meadows, IL, 1999
Valerio Dewalt Train Associates

Quadracci Pavilion, Milwaukee Art Museum
Milwaukee, WI, 2001
Santiago Calatrava (Spain) with Kahler
    Slater

Rose Center for Earth and Space, American
    Museum of Natural History
New York, NY, 2000
Polshek Partnership Architects

Sandra Day O'Connor US Courthouse
Phoenix, AZ, 2001
Richard Meier & Partners Architects

Westside Light Rail Transit System
Portland, OR, 1998
Zimmer Gunsul Frasca Architects

Source: USA Weekend, Sept. 1, 2002

2006, Most Important Houses in America

A panel of architects, builders, and home enthusiasts convened by *Fine Homebuilding* in 2006 selected the following 25 buildings as the most important houses in America (listed chronologically).

Ashley House
Deerfield, MA, 1730
John Wells

Monticello
Charlottesville, VA, 1769–84, 1796–1809
Thomas Jefferson

Isaac Small House
Truro, MA, c. 1780
Royal Barry Willis

Roseland Cottage
Woodstock, CT, 1848
Joseph Collin Wells

William Watts Sherman House
Newport, RI, 1875
H.H. Richardson

W.G. Low House
Bristol, RI, 1887
McKim, Mead and White

Biltmore
Ashville, NC, 1889
Richard Morris Hunt

Gamble House
Pasadena, CA, 1908
Greene and Greene

Top Ranked Buildings

Sears Kit House
Nationwide, 1908–1937
Sears, Roebuck and Company

Schindler House
West Hollywood, CA, 1921
Rudolph Schindler (Austria/US)

Wharton Esherick House and Studio
Paoli, PA, 1926–1966
Wharton Esherick

Gregory Farmhouse
Scotts Valley, CA, 1928
William Wurster

Cyrus McCormick Jr. House
Santa Fe, NM, 1931
John Gaw Meem

Jacobs I House
Madison, WI, 1936
Frank Lloyd Wright

Wallen II House
Kensington, CA, 1937
Bernard Maybeck

Fallingwater
Mill Run, PA, 1938
Frank Lloyd Wright

Levittown Ranch
Levittown, NY, 1949
Levitt and Sons

Farnsworth House
Plano, IL, 1951
Ludwig Mies van der Rohe (Germany/US)

Hedgerow Houses
Sea Ranch, CA, 1966
Joseph Esherick

Integral Urban House
Berkeley, CA, 1973
Sim van der Ryn

Unit One/Balcomb House
Santa Fe, NM, 1976
Walter Lumpkin

Seaside
Seaside, FL, 1986
Duany Plater-Zyberk & Company

Wright Guest House
The Highlands, WA, 1987
James Cutler Architects

Harris (Butterfly) House
Hale County, AL, 1997
Rural Studio

McMansions
Nationwide, 1980s–present
Various architects, builders, and developers

Source: Fine Homebuilding, *Spring/Summer 2006*

2007 America's Favorite Architecture

The American Institute of Architects, in conjunction with its 150th anniversary in 2007, conducted a public poll of the 150 best works of architecture. The full list is available at *www.aia150.org*.

1. Empire State Building
   New York, NY, 1931
   Shreve, Lamb & Harmon

2. White House
   Washington, DC, 1800
   James Hoban

3. Washington National Cathedral
   Washington, DC, 1907–1990
   George Frederick Bodley (UK),
   Henry Vaughan and Philip Frohman

4. Thomas Jefferson Memorial
   Washington DC, 1943
   John Russell Pope

5. Golden Gate Bridge
   San Francisco, CA, 1937
   Irving F. Morrow and Gertrude C.
     Morrow

6. US Capitol
   Washington, DC, 1793–1865
   William Thornton, Benjamin Henry
     Latrobe, Charles Bulfinch, Thomas
     Ustick Walter

7. Lincoln Memorial
   Washington, DC, 1917
   Henry Bacon

8. Biltmore
   Asheville, NC, 1889
   Richard Morris Hunt

9. Chrysler Building
   New York, NY, 1930
   William Van Alen

10. Vietnam Veterans Memorial
    Washington, DC, 1982
    Maya Lin

Source: American Institute of Architects

2010, Architecture's Modern Marvels

Vanity Fair magazine asked the world's leading architects, critics, and deans of architecture schools to answer the question, what are the five most important buildings, bridges, or monuments constructed since 1980? Below are the top 21, in order of popularity.

1. Guggenheim Museum
   Bilbao, Spain, 1997
   Frank O. Gehry and Associates, Inc.

2. Menil Collection
   Houston, TX, 1987
   Renzo Piano Building Workshop (Italy)

3. Thermal Baths
   Vals, Switzerland, 1996
   Peter Zumthor (Switzerland)

4. HSBC Building
   Hong Kong, 1985
   Foster + Associates (UK)

5. Seattle Central Library
   Seattle, WA, 2004
   Office for Metropolitan Architecture
     (Netherlands)

   Mediatheque Building
   Sendai, Japan, 2001
   Toyo Ito & Associates, Architects (Japan)

Top Ranked Buildings

Neue Staatsgalerie
Stuttgart, Germany, 1984
James Stirling Michael Wilford and
  Associates (UK)

Church of the Light
Osaka, Japan, 1989
Tadao Ando Architect and Associates
  (Japan)

9. Vietnam Veterans Memorial
    Washington, DC, 1982
    Maya Lin

10. Millau Viaduct
    Millau, France, 2004
    Foster + Partners (UK)

Jewish Museum
Berlin, Germany, 1998
Studio Daniel Libeskind

Lloyd's Building
London, UK, 1984
Richard Rogers Partnership (UK)

13. Bird's Nest Stadium
    Beijing, China, 2008
    Jacques Herzog and Pierre de Meuron
      (Switzerland)

CCTV Building
Beijing, China, under construction
Office for Metropolitan Architecture
  (Netherlands)

Casa da Musica
Porto, Portugal, 2005
Office for Metropolitan Architecture
  (Netherlands)

Cartier Foundation
Paris, France, 1994
Jean Nouvel Ateliers (France)

BWM Welt
Munich, Germany, 2007
Coop Himmelb(l)au (Austria)

Nelson-Atkins Museum, addition
Kansas City, MO, 2007
Steven Holl Architects

Cooper Union building
New York, NY, 2009
Morphosis

Parc de la Villette
Paris, France, 1987
Bernard Tschumi Architects (France)

Yokohama Port Terminal
Yokohama, Japan, 2002
Foreign Office Architects (UK)

Source: www.vanityfair.com, June 30, 2010

Aga Khan Award for Architecture

The Aga Khan Trust for Culture grants the triennial Aga Khan Award for Architecture to **outstanding projects**—including individual buildings, restoration and reuse schemes, large-scale community developments, and environmental initiatives—**in the Muslim world**. Submissions are reviewed for their ability to meet people's physical, social, and economic needs as well as their cultural and spiritual expectations. An award of $500,000 is apportioned among the winners.

www.akdn.org

2010 Winners

Bridge School
Xiashi, Fujian Province, China
Li Xiaodong Atelier (China)

Ipekyol Textile Factory
Edirne, Turkey
Emre Arolat Architects (Turkey)

Madinat al Zahra Museum
Cordoba, Spain
Nieto Sobejano Architects (Spain)

Revitalization of the Recent Heritage of Tunis
Tunis, Tunisia
Association de Sauvegarde de la Medina de
 Tunis (Tunisia)

Wadi Hanifa Wetlands
Riyadh, Saudi Arabia
Moriyama & Teshima Planners Limited
 (Canada) / Buro Happold (UK)—
 joint venture

Source: Aga Khan Trust for Culture

Paul Rivera/ArchPhoto

TKTS Booth and the Redevelopment of Father Duffy Square, New York, NY | Perkins Eastman

AIA Honor Awards

The American Institute of Architects' Honor Awards celebrate **outstanding design in three areas: architecture, interior architecture, and regional and urban design**. Juries for each category, comprised of designers and executives for the respective disciplines, select the winners.

www.aia.org

2010 Architecture Winners

Alice Tully Hall
New York, NY
Diller Scofidio + Renfro; FXFOWLE Architects

Austin E. Knowlton School of Architecture,
    Ohio State University
Columbus, OH
Mack Scogin Merrill Elam Architects

Beauvoir
Biloxi, MS
Albert & Associates Architects

Brochstein Pavilion and Central Quad, Rice
    University
Houston, TX
Thomas Phifer and Partners

Camino Nuevo High School
Los Angeles, CA
Daly Genik Architects

Campus Restaurant and Event Space
Stuttgart, Germany
Barkow Leibinger Architects (Germany)

Macallen Building
Boston, MA
Office dA; Burt Hill

Outpost
Central Idaho
Olson Kundig Architects

Serta International Center
Hoffman Estates, IL
Epstein | Metter Studios

Skirkanich Hall
Philadelphia, PA
Tod Williams Billie Tsien Architects

Step Up on 5th
Santa Monica, CA
Pugh + Scarpa

TKTS Booth and the Revitalization of Father
    Duffy Square
New York, NY
Perkins Eastman; Choi Ropiha; PKSB
    Architects

Urban Outfitters Corporate Campus
Philadelphia, PA
Meyer, Scherer & Rockcastle

Kahn Building Renovation, Yale University Art
    Gallery
New Haven, CT
Polshek Partnership Architects

Cesar Rubio

Cathedral of Christ the Light, Oakland, CA I **Skidmore, Owings & Merrill; Kendall/Heaton Associates**

AIA Honor Awards

2010 Interior Architecture Winners

Cathedral of Christ the Light
Oakland, CA
Skidmore, Owings & Merrill; Kendall/Heaton
    Associates

CHANEL Robertson Blvd.
Los Angeles, CA
Peter Marino Architect

Craftsteak
New York, NY
Bentel & Bentel Architects/Planners

Data
Omaha, NE
Randy Brown Architects

Exeter Schools Multipurpose Space
Exeter, MO
Dake Wells Architecture

Historic Central Park West Residence
New York, NY
Shelton, Mindel & Associates

Vera Wang Boutique SoHo
New York, NY
Gabellini Sheppard Associates

2010 Regional Urban Design Winners

A Civic Vision for the Central Delaware River
Philadelphia, PA
Wallace Roberts & Todd

Connections: MacArthur Park District Master
    Plan
Little Rock, AR
Conway+Schulte Architects

Greenwich South Strategic Framework
New York, NY
Architecture Research Office

U.S. House Office Buildings Facilities Plan and
    Preliminary South Capitol Area Plan
Washington, DC
Wallace Roberts & Todd

Monumental Core Framework Plan
Washington, DC
US Government

Ryerson University Master Plan
Toronto, ON, Canada
Kuwabara Payne McKenna Blumberg
    Architects (Canada)

Savannah East Riverfront Extension
Savannah, GA
Sottile & Sottile

Source: American Institute of Architects

Bruce Damonte Photography

University of California Davis Graduate School of Management, Davis, CA I Sasaki Associates, Inc.

BIM Awards

The annual Building Information Model (BIM) Awards honor **projects that have strategically used integrated processes and interoperable models**. The program is sponsored by the American Institute of Architects' Technology in Architectural Practice knowledge community. Winning projects showcase proven strategies and the latest trends in design and technology in the building industry.

www.aia.org

2010 Citation Winners

BIM Excellence Awards
Aurora Medical Center
Summit, WI
Albert Kahn Associates

Palomar Medical Center West
Escondido, CA
CO Architects

Design/Delivery Process Innovation
Sutter Medical Center Castro Valley
Castro Valley, CA
Devenney Group Architects

Academic Program or Curriculum Development
Intergrating BIM in Academia
Pennsylvania State University

2010 Honorable Mentions

BIM Excellence Awards
Veterans Affairs Medical Center
Central Florida
RLF

Outstanding Sustainable Design
University of California Davis Graduate School
of Management
Davis, CA
Sasaki Associates, Inc.

Academic Program or Curriculum Development
B III M
University of Southern California, School of
Architecture

Source: American Institute of Architects

Engineering Excellence Awards

The American Council of Engineering Companies' annual Engineering Excellence Awards grant one Grand Conceptor Award and up to 23 grand and honor awards. A panel of engineers and infrastructure experts reviews submissions for **uniqueness and originality, technical value to the engineering profession**, social and economic considerations, complexity, and ability to meet the needs of the client.

www.acec.org

2010 Winners

Grand Conceptor Award
Gills Onions Advanced Energy Recovery
    System
Oxnard, CA
HDR Engineering, Inc.

Grand Awards
Cowboys Stadium
Arlington, TX
Walter P. Moore Engineers + Consultants

Sea-to-Sky Highway Improvement Project
Horseshoe Bay to Whistler, BC, Canada
Hatch Mott MacDonald

TMI Steam Generator Transport Project
Middletown, PA
Michael Baker Jr., Inc.

Littleton/Englewood Wastewater Treatment
    Plant
Englewood, CO
Brown and Caldwell

Bob Kerrey Pedestrian Bridge
Omaha, NE
HNTB Corporation

Dee and Charles Wyly Theatre
Dallas, TX
Magnusson Klemencic Associates

Sound Transit's Light Rail Beacon Hill Station
    and Tunnels
Seattle, WA
Hatch Mott MacDonald/Jacobs (Joint Venture)

Honor Awards
Housatonic River Museum
Pittsfield, MA
Dagher Engineering

David Kreitzer Lake Hodges Bicycle
    Pedestrian Bridge
San Diego, CA
T.Y. Lin International

King & King Office Building
Syracuse, NY
IBC Engineering

Harmon Shop Replacement
Croton-on-Hudson, NY
Jacobs/Parsons Brinckerhoff (Joint Venture)

Marquette Interchange Reconstruction
Milwaukee, WI
Milwaukee Transportation Partners

Portal 31 Exhibition Mine
Lynch, KY
Engineering Consulting Services, Inc.

Nebraska City 2 Power Plant
Nebraska City, NE
HDR Engineering, Inc.

Relocated I-195 and New Providence River
    Bridge
Providence, RI
Maguire Group

North Avenue Bridge Reconstruction
Chicago, IL
HNTB Corporation

TKTS Booth, Times Square
New York, NY
Dewhurst Macfarlane and Partners

O-14
Dubai, UAE
Ysrael A. Seinuk

Levee Certification Using Geospatial
   Technologies
Wichita, KS
Merrick & Company

Lake Delton and STH A Restoration
Lake Delton, WI
Mead & Hunt, Inc./MSA Professional Services,
   Inc. (Joint Venture)

Union Station Bicycle Transit Center
Washington, DC
Parsons Brinckerhoff

Port of Long Beach Cold Ironing Project
Long Beach, CA
AECOM

Wetland Treatment of Glycol Impaired Runoff
Cheektowaga, NY
Urban Engineers of New York; Jacques
   Whitford Stantec LTD

Source: American Council of Engineering Companies

GSA Design Awards

The US General Services Administration presents its biennial design awards as part of its Design Excellence Program, which seeks **the best in design, construction, and restoration for all federal building projects**. The awards were developed to encourage and recognize innovative design in federal buildings and to honor noteworthy achievements in the preservation and renovation of historic structures.

www.gsa.gov

2008 Honor Awards

Architecture
Wayne Lyman Morse United States
   Courthouse
Eugene, OR
Morphosis

San Francisco Federal Building
San Francisco, CA
Morphosis

Preservation
United States Post Office and Courthouse
Brooklyn, NY
Kliment Halsband Architects

Sustainability
San Francisco Federal Building
San Francisco, CA
Morphosis

Construction Excellence Honor
Wayne Lyman Morse United States
   Courthouse
Eugene, OR
Morphosis

Art in Architecture Honor
Wayne Lyman Morse United States Courthouse
Eugene, OR
Morphosis

2008 Citations

Architecture
United States Courthouse
Springfield, MA
Moshe Safdie and Associates

United States Land Port of Entry
Raymond, MT
Hammond Beeby Rupert Ainge

Architecture/On the Boards
United States Courthouse
Austin, TX
Mack Scogin Merrill Elam Architects

United States Land Port of Entry
Donna, TX
Hodgetts + Fung Design and Architecture

United States Land Port of Entry
Warroad, MN
Julie Snow Architects

United States Land Port of Entry
Massena, NY
Smith-Miller + Hawkinson Architects

Modernization

Byron G. Rogers United States Courthouse
Denver, CO
Bennett Wagner & Grody Architects

Richard Bolling Federal Building
Kansas City, MO
Helix Architecture + Design

Lease Construction

United States Courthouse
Alpine, TX
PageSoutherlandPage

Graphic Design/Signage

Wayne Lyman Morse United States
    Courthouse
Eugene, OR
Morphosis

Art in Architecture Book
Cox and Associates, Inc.

Landscape Architecture

Anthony J. Celebreeze Federal Building
Cleveland, OH
OLIN

Source: US General Services Administration

National Design-Build Awards

The annual National Design-Build Awards honor **projects that exemplify the principles that characterize the design-build delivery method**: interdisciplinary teamwork, innovation, and problem solving. Created by the Design-Build Institute of America, the competition is open to design-build projects completed within the previous three years. In addition to the National Design-Build Award, the jury may also grant Design-Build Excellence Awards and merit awards.

www.dbia.org

2009 National Design-Build Award Winners

Best Overall
I-35W (St. Anthony Falls) Bridge
Minneapolis, MN
Flatiron-Manson (a joint venture)

Public Sector Building Over $25 Million
Walter Cronkite School of Journalism and
    Mass Communication, Arizona State
    University
Phoenix, AZ
Sundt Construction

Private Sector Building Over $25 Million
Pacific Beacon
San Diego, CA
Clark Builders Group

Private Sector Building Under $25 Million
Washington Christian Academy
Olney, MD
Forrester Construction Company

Transportation Over $50 Million
I-35W (St. Anthony Falls) Bridge
Minneapolis, MN
Flatiron-Manson (a joint venture)

Rehabilitation/Renovation/ Restoration
St. Bernard Parish Pump Station
    Rehabilitation
New Orleans, LA
CDM

Overhead Coverage System Program:
    Enhanced Force Protection for US Military
    and Government Personnel
Iraq (various locations)
Perini Corporation

Source: Design-Build Institute of America

Twenty-five Year Award

The American Institute of Architects' Twenty-five Year Award celebrates **buildings that excel under the test of time.** Eligible projects must have been completed within the past 25 to 35 years by a licensed US architect, though the buildings may be located worldwide. Winning designs are still operating under the tenets of the original program, demonstrating continued viability in function and form, and contributing meaningfully to American life and architecture.

www.aia.org

1969   Rockefeller Center
        New York, NY, 1931–40
        Reinhard & Hofmeister with
            Corbett, Harrison & MacMurray
            and Hood & Fouilhoux

1971   Crow Island School
        Winnetka, IL, 1939
        Perkins, Wheeler & Will and Eliel
            and Eero Saarinen

1972   Baldwin Hills Village
        Los Angeles, CA, 1941
        Reginald D. Johnson with Wilson,
            Merrill & Alexander and
            Clarence S. Stein

1973   Taliesin West
        Paradise Valley, AZ, 1938
        Frank Lloyd Wright

1974   S.C. Johnson & Son Administration
            Building
        Racine, WI, 1939
        Frank Lloyd Wright

1975   Philip Johnson Residence
            (The Glass House)
        New Canaan, CT, 1949
        Philip Johnson

1976   860-880 North Lakeshore Drive
            Apartments
        Chicago, IL, 1948–51
        Ludwig Mies van der Rohe

1977   Christ Lutheran Church
        Minneapolis, MN, 1948–51
        Saarinen, Saarinen & Associates
            with Hills, Gilbertson & Hays

1978   Eames House
        Pacific Palisades, CA, 1949
        Charles and Ray Eames

1979   Yale University Art Gallery
        New Haven, CT, 1954
        Louis I. Kahn with Douglas W. Orr

1980   Lever House
        New York, NY, 1952
        Skidmore, Owings & Merrill

1981   Farnsworth House
        Plano, IL, 1950
        Ludwig Mies van der Rohe

1982   Equitable Savings and Loan
            Association Building
        Portland, OR, 1948
        Pietro Belluschi

1983   Price Tower
        Bartlesville, OK, 1956
        Frank Lloyd Wright

1984   Seagram Building
        New York, NY, 1957
        Ludwig Mies van der Rohe

1985   General Motors Technical Center
        Warren, MI, 1951
        Saarinen, Saarinen & Associates
            with Smith, Hinchman and
            Grylls Associates

1986   Solomon R. Guggenheim
            Museum
        New York, NY, 1959
        Frank Lloyd Wright

Twenty-five Year Award

1987   Bavinger House
        Norman, OK, 1953
        Bruce Goff

1988   Dulles International Airport
            Terminal Building
        Chantilly, VA, 1962
        Eero Saarinen & Associates

1989   Vanna Venturi House
        Chestnut Hill, PA, 1964
        Robert Venturi

1990   Gateway Arch
        St. Louis, MO, 1965
        Eero Saarinen & Associates

1991   Sea Ranch Condominium I
        The Sea Ranch, CA, 1965
        Moore Lyndon Turnbull Whitaker

1992   Salk Institute for Biological Studies
        La Jolla, CA, 1966
        Louis I. Kahn

1993   Deere & Company Administrative
            Center
        Moline, IL, 1963
        Eero Saarinen & Associates

1994   Haystack Mountain School of Crafts
        Deer Isle, ME, 1962
        Edward Larrabee Barnes
            Associates

1995   Ford Foundation Headquarters
        New York, NY, 1968
        Kevin Roche John Dinkeloo &
            Associates

1996   Air Force Academy Cadet Chapel
        Colorado Springs, CO, 1962
        Skidmore, Owings & Merrill

1997   Phillips Exeter Academy Library
        Exeter, NH, 1972
        Louis I. Kahn

1998   Kimbell Art Museum
        Fort Worth, TX, 1972
        Louis I. Kahn

1999   John Hancock Center
        Chicago, IL, 1969
        Skidmore, Owings & Merrill

2000   Smith House
        Darien, CT, 1967
        Richard Meier & Partners Architects

2001   Weyerhaeuser Headquarters
        Tacoma, WA, 1971
        Skidmore, Owings & Merrill

2002   Fundació Joan Miró
        Barcelona, Spain, 1975
        Sert Jackson and Associates

2003   Design Research Headquarters
            Building
        Cambridge, MA, 1969
        BTA Architects Inc.

2004   East Building, National Gallery of Art
        Washington, DC, 1978
        I.M. Pei & Partners

2005   Yale Center for British Art
        New Haven, CT, 1977
        Louis I. Kahn

2006   Thorncrown Chapel
        Eureka Springs, AR, 1980
        E. Fay Jones

2007   Vietnam Veterans Memorial
        Washington, DC, 1982
        Maya Lin

2008   Atheneum
        New Harmony, IN, 1979
        Richard Meier & Partners Architects

2009   Faneuil Hall Marketplace
        Boston, MA various renovations
        Benjamin Thompson & Associates

**2010   Hajj Terminal, King Abdul Aziz
            International Airport
        Jeddah, Saudi Arabia, 1981
        Skidmore, Owings & Merrill**

Source: American Institute of Architects

Best of 50+ Housing Awards

The National Association of Home Builders' 50+ Housing Council annually presents the Best of 50+ Housing Awards. Winning projects are chosen for their **ability to meet the needs of the ever-changing seniors' housing market**, including marketability, budget, density, and program. Gold, silver, and innovation awards are presented in a range of categories based on project type and size.

www.nahb.org/50plusawards

2009 Gold Winners

Repositioned 50+ Housing Project
Westminster Village
Scottsdale, AZ
Perkins Eastman

Renovated 50+ Housing
Sherwood Village Senior Apartments
Salinas, CA
The Paul Davis Partnership

WoodCrest Retirement Residence
Moon, PA
design by us

Small CCRC, Up to 200 Units
Varenna
Santa Rosa, CA
Oakmont Senior Living

Large CCRC, Over 200 Units
Sun City Palace Tsukaguchi
Osaka, Japan
BAR Architects

CCRC Common Area
Lenbrook
Atlanta, GA
Interior Design Associates

Congregate/Independent Living Community
The Bellettini
Bellevue, WA
Wattenbarger Architects

Touchmark at Mt. Bachelor Village - Cliff
Lodge
Bend, OR
LRS Architects

Assisted Living Community
Sunrise Senior Living - Monterey
Monterey, CA
Arbor Building Group, Inc.

Multifamily Rental 50+ Community
Market Rate
Towne Club at Peachtree City
Peachtree City, GA
Niles Bolton Associates

Affordable
Victoria Park at Walkersville
Walkersville, MD
Grimm + Parker Architects

Active Adult Community
Up to 500 Homes
Parkview Court
Torrance, CA
Withee Malcolm Architects

Over 500 Homes
Sun City Festival
Buckeye, AZ
SHJ Studio

Best of 50+ Housing Awards

Clubhouse at an Active Adult Community
Up to 8,000 Square Feet
Traditions Community Center
Paso Robles, CA
gbh Partners

Over 8,000 Square Feet
Heritage Todd Creek
Brighton, CO
KEPHART

Detached Home at an Active Adult Community
Up to 2,000 Square Feet
Eskaton National Demonstration Home
Roseville, CA
BSB Design

Over 2,000 Square Feet
Residences at Bulle Rock
Havre de Grace, MD
Clark Turner Signature Homes

Attached Home at an Active Adult Community
Up to 2,000 Square Feet
Plan 2, Valencia Terrace
Corona, CA
Irwin Pancake Dawson Architects

Over 2,000 Square Feet
Chester River Landing
Chestertown, MD
Morgan Design Group

Model Home Merchandising at an Active Adult Community
Over 2,000 Square Feet
Plan 2556, The Boulevard at Lakeway
Austin, TX
Mary DeWalt Design Group

The Case Model, Highland Meadows
Weston, MA
Design East Interiors

Repositioned 50+ Housing Project On the Boards
San Joaquin Gardens
Fresno, CA
Irwin Pancake Dawson Architects

Small CCRC, Up to 200 Units, On the Boards
Walnut Village
Anaheim, CA
Ankrom Moisan Associated Architects

Large CCRC, Over 200 Units, On the Boards
Sun City Palace Showa Kinen Koen
Tokyo, Japan
BAR Architects

Congregate/Independent Living Community, On the Boards
The Palace at Weston II - Senior Living
Weston, FL
Anne Jackaway Architecture

Assisted Living Community, On the Boards
Warrington Senior Commons
Warrington, PA
JKR Partners

Special Needs Community, On the Boards
SEASONS at Compton
Compton, CA
Nardi Associates

Multifamily Rental 50+ Community Market Rate, On the Boards
NoHo Senior Artists Colony
North Hollywood, CA
John Cotton Architects

Affordable, On the Boards
Echo Park
Echo Park, CA
KTGY Group

Active Adult Community, On the Boards, Up to 500 Homes
Maison du Lac
St. Tammany Parish, LA
Basham & Lucas Design Group

Clubhouse at an Active Adult Community, On the Boards
Fieldstone Club, Chatfield Farms
Beacon Falls, CT
Wyndham Homes, Inc.

Detached Home at an Active Adult Community, On the Boards
Emerson II, Denver Traditions Series at
  Stapleton
Denver, CO
Olson Architecture, Inc.

Attached Home at an Active Adult Community, On the Boards
The Chatham, Gibson's Grant
Chester, MD
Morgan Design Group

Source: National Association of Home Builders

Pioneer Middle School, DuPont, WA | DLR Group

Exhibition of School Architecture Awards

The Exhibition of School Architecture Awards, sponsored by the American Association of School Administrators, American Institute of Architects, and Council of Educational Facility Planners International, **showcase how well-designed schools facilitate student achievement**. The Shirley Cooper Award recognizes the project that best meets the educational needs of students. The Walter Taylor Award honors the project that best addresses a difficult design challenge.

www.aasa.org

2010 Winners

Shirley Cooper Award
Barbara Ingram School for the Arts
Hagerstown, MD
Cho Benn Holback + Associates

Frisco CTE Career & Technical Education
    Design Model
Frisco, TX
SHW Group

Walter Taylor Award
Thurston Elementary School
Springfield, OR
Mahlum

Honorable Mentions
Pioneer Middle School
DuPont, WA
DLR Group

C.W. Morey Elementary School
Lowell, MA
Flansburgh Architects

Gray Middle School
Tacoma, WA
Mahlum Architects

Poquoson Elementary School
Poquoson, VA
VMDO Architects

Source: American Association of School Administrators

Jeff Goldberg/ESTO

AEC Headquarters, Autodesk, Waltham, MA | KlingStubbins

Good Design Is Good Business Awards

The BusinessWeek/Architectural Record Awards are granted annually to organizations that prove good design is good business. Sponsored by *Architectural Record* and *BusinessWeek* magazines, the award's special focus is on **collaboration and the achievement of business goals through architecture**. Eligible projects must have been completed within the past four years and may be submitted by any architect registered in the United States or abroad.

www.archrecord.com

2009 Winners

Award of Excellence
Architecture of Discovery Green
Houston, TX
PageSouthernlandPage; Hargreaves
   Associates

AEC Headquarters, Autodesk
Waltham, MA
KlingStubbins

Barbie Shanghai Store
Shanghai, China
Slade Architecture

Eversheds Law Offices
London, UK
Woods Bagot (UK)

Hawks Boots Sustainable Manufacturing
   Facility
Duluth, MN
Salmela Architects

Peterborough Regional Health Centre
Peterborough, ON, Canada
Stantec Architecture (Canada)

The Lab Gastropub
Los Angeles, CA
AC Martin

Urban Outfitters Corporate Campus
Philadelphia, PA
Meyer, Scherer & Rockcastle

Citations for Excellence
East Harlem School
New York, NY
Peter L. Gluck and Partners

Gregg's Cycles
Bellevue, WA
Weinstein Architects + Urban Designers

International Fund for Animal Welfare
   Headquarters
Yarmouth Port, MA
designLAB

Southbrook Vineyards
Niagara-On-The-Lake, ON, Canada
Diamond and Schmitt

Source: BusinessWeek/Architectural Record

Housing Awards

The AIA's Housing Awards recognize the **importance of good housing as a necessity of life, a sanctuary for the human spirit, and a valuable national resource**. Licensed AIA-member architects are eligible to enter US-built projects.

www.aia.org

2010 Winners

One/Two Family Custom Housing
Diamond Project
San Francisco, CA
Terry & Terry Architecture

Ferrous House
Milwaukee, WI
Johnsen Schmaling Architects

Port Townsend Residence
Port Townsend, WA
Bohlin Cywinski Jackson

Dry Creek Outbuildings
Woodside, CA
Bohlin Cywinski Jackson

Sky Ranch
Seattle, WA
Miller Hull Partnership

Spiral House
Old Greenwich, CT
Joeb Moore + Partners Architects

Sheldon Gatehouse
Cle Elum, WA
Bohlin Cywinski Jackson

T42 House
Minneapolis, MN
VJAA

One/Two Family Production Housing
Cellophane House
New York, NY
KieranTimberlake

14 Townhouses
Brooklyn, NY
Rogers Marvel Architects

Multifamily Living
Gish Apartments
San Jose, CA
Office of Jerome King, FAIA

OneEleven Mixed-Use Development
Baton Rouge, LA
Remson | Haley | Herpin Architects

Formosa 1140
West Hollywood, CA
Lorcan O'Herlihy Architects

Safari Drive
Scottsdale, AZ
Miller Hull Partnership

The Waterworks at Chestnut Hill
Chestnut Hill, MA
GUND Partnership

Special Housing
Step Up on 5th
Santa Monica, CA
Pugh + Scarpa

The Housing Tower
Stockbridge, MA
The Rose + Guggenheimer Studio

Residence Halls, Swarthmore College
Swarthmore, PA
William Rawn Associates, Architects, Inc.

Source: American Institute of Architects

Hugh Ferriss Memorial Prize

The American Society of Architectural Illustrators annually bestows the Hugh Ferriss Memorial Prize, the highest honor conferred by the organization, for the **best graphic representation of architecture**. The prize is part of Architecture in Perspective, an annual international competition, traveling exhibition, and catalog comprised of the Hugh Ferriss winner as well as 60 other pieces intended to promote the field of architectural illustration.

www.asai.org

1986	*Worth Square Building*
	Lee Dunnette
	The State Capitol Dome, Texas
	James Record
1987	*One Montvale Avenue*
	Richard Lovelace
1988	*Proposed Arts and Cultural Center*
	Thomas Wells Schaller
1989	*Edgar Allen Poe Memorial (detail)*
	Daniel Willis
1990	*The Interior of the Basilica Ulpia*
	Gilbert Gorski
1991	*Affordable Housing Now!*
	Luis Blanc
1992	*BMC Real Properties Buildings*
	Douglas E. Jamieson
1993	*Additions and Renovations to Tuckerton Marine Research Field Station*
	David Sylvester
1994	*3rd Government Center Competition*
	Rael D. Slutsky
1995	*The Pyramid at Le Grand Louvre*
	Lee Dunnette
1996	*Hines France Office Tower*
	Paul Stevenson Oles

1997	*World War II Memorial*
	Advanced Media Design
1998	*Baker Library Addition, Dartmouth College*
	Wei Li
1999	*Five Star Deluxe Beach Hotel*
	Serge Zaleski
2000	*1000 Wilshire Blvd.*
	Thomas Wells Schaller
2001	*The Royal Ascot, Finishing Post*
	Michael McCann
2002	*Chicago 2020*
	Gilbert Gorski
2003	*Edge City*
	Ronald Love
2004	*Project Japan*
	Michael Reardon
2005	*Resort, Evening*
	Chris Grubbs
2006	*Arthur V. McCarthy Memorial*
	Dennis Allain
2007	*Harry's Island – The Coral Helix*
	Ana Carolina Monnaco
2008	*Quartet on Stage*
	Frank M. Costantino
2009	*RDL Eindhoven*
	Maarten van Dooren
2010	***Algae Harvester***
	Jon Kletzien

Source: American Society of Architectural Illustrators

Library Buildings Awards

The American Institute of Architects and American Library Association present the biennial Library Buildings Awards to encourage **excellence in the design and planning of libraries**. Architects licensed in the United States are eligible to enter any public or private library project from around the world, whether a renovation, addition, conversion, interior project, or new construction. The jury consists of three architects and three librarians with extensive library building experience.

www.ala.org

2009 Winners

Arabian Library
Scottsdale, AZ
richärd+bauer

C.V. Starr East Asian Library, University
    of California Berkeley
Berkeley, CA
Tod Williams Billie Tsien Architects

Chongqing Library
Chongqing, China
Perkins Eastman

Biblioteca Central Estatal Wigberto Jiménez
    Moreno
León, Guanajuato, Mexico
Pei Partnership Architects

Francis Martin Library
Bronx, NY
1100 Architect

Gentry Public Library
Gentry, AR
Marlon Blackwell Architect

Minneapolis Central Library
Minneapolis, MN
Pelli Clarke Pelli Architects

Palo Verde Library/Maryvale Community
    Center
Phoenix, AZ
Gould Evans; Wendell Burnette Architects

Source: American Library Association

Mies van der Rohe Award

The biennial Mies van der Rohe Award highlights **notable contemporary European architecture** that demonstrates an innovative character and excellence in design and execution. The award consists of a cash prize of 50,000 euros and a sculpture by Xavier Corberó, inspired by the Mies van der Rohe Pavilion in Barcelona, Spain. Recipients of the Emerging Architect Special Mention, which celebrates young architects, receive 10,000 euros and a sculpture.

www.miesbcn.com

1988   Borges e Irmão Bank
        Vila do Conde, Portugal
        Alvaro Siza (Portugal)

1990   New Terminal Development,
            Stansted Airport
        London, UK
        Foster + Partners (UK)

1992   Municipal Sports Stadium
        Badalona, Barcelona, Spain
        Esteve Bonell and Francesc Rius
            (Spain)

1994   Waterloo International Station
        London, UK
        Nicholas Grimshaw & Partners (UK)

1996   Bibliotèque Nationale de France
        Paris, France
        Dominique Perrault (France)

1999   Art Museum in Bregenz
        Bregenz, Austria
        Peter Zumthor (Switzerland)

2001   Kursaal Congress Centre
        San Sebastian, Spain
        Rafael Moneo (Spain)

        Kaufmann Holz Distribution Centre*
        Bobingen, Germany
        Florian Nagler, Florian Nagler
            Architekt (Germany)

2003   Car Park & Terminal Hoenheim
            North
        Strasbourg, France
        Zaha Hadid (UK)

        Scharnhauser Park Town Hall*
        Ostfildern, Germany
        H.J. Mayer (Germany)

2005   Netherlands Embassy Berlin
        Berlin, Germany
        Office for Metropolitan
            Architecture (Netherlands)

        Basket Bar*
        Utrecht, Netherlands
        NL Architects (Netherlands)

2007   MUSAC – Contemporary Art
            Museum of Castilla y León
        León, Spain
        Mansilla + Tuñón (Spain)

        Faculty of Mathematics*
        Ljubljana, Slovenia
        Bevk Perovic arhitekti (Slovania)

2009   **Norwegian National Opera &
            Ballet**
        Oslo, Norway
        Snøhetta (Norway)

        Gymnasium 46°09'N/16°50E*
        Koprivnica, Croatia
        STUDIO UP (Croatia)

*Emerging Architect Special Mention

Source: Mies van der Rohe Foundation

Patient Care Tower, Advocate Lutheran General Hospital and Advocate Lutheran General Children's Hospital, Park Ridge, IL | Cannon Design

National Healthcare Design Awards

The National Healthcare Design Awards showcase the **best of healthcare building design and health design-oriented research**. The program is sponsored by the American Institute of Architects and the Academy of Architecture for Health. Winning projects exhibit conceptual strength and solve aesthetic, civic, urban, and social concerns in addition to the requisite functional and sustainability concerns of a healthcare facility.

www.aia.org/aah

2010 Winners

Less than $25 Million
Duke Integrative Medicine, Duke University
Durham, NC
Duda/Paine Architects

Advocate Lutheran General Hospital Center
 for Advanced Care
Park Ridge, IL
OWP/P | Cannon Design

More Than $25 Million
Children's Medical Center Legacy
Dallas, TX
Zimmer Gunsul Frasca Architects

Unbuilt
Seoul National University Hospital Medical Mall
Seoul, South Korea
Gresham, Smith and Partners

Source: American Institute of Architects

Building 23, US Centers for Disease Control and Prevention, Atlanta, GA | HDR Architecture, Inc.

HDR Architecture, Inc.; © 2010 Phillip Spears

John W. Fisher Heart Center, Ball Memorial Hospital, Muncie, IN I HDR Architecture, Inc.

Jeff Totaro

St. Paul's Episcopal Church, Indianapolis, IN | Atkin Olshin Schade Architects

Palladio Awards

The Palladio Awards honor **outstanding achievement in traditional design** reflecting the creative interpretation or adaptation of the principles of the Renaissance architect Andrea Palladio. Entries are judged for their refinement and appropriateness, adherence to the program, use of materials, quality of construction and craftsmanship, and overall design excellence. Winners receive bronze trophies and are featured in *Traditional Building* magazine.

www.palladioawards.com

2010 Commercial, Institutional, and Public Winners

New Design & Construction
Flinn Hall and Edelman Hall, Hotchkiss School
Lakeville, CT
Robert A.M. Stern Architects

Alan B. Miller Hall, Mason School of Business,
    College of William & Mary
Williamsburg, VA
Robert A.M. Stern Architects

Restoration/Renovation
Basilica of the Assumption
Baltimore, MD
John G. Waite Associates Architects

Parks, Plazas, Gardens & Streetscapes
Lake Marilyn, Somerset Bridge and
    Seagarden
Alys Beach, FL
Khoury & Vogt Architects

Sympathetic Addition
St. Paul's Episcopal Church
Indianapolis, IN
Atkin Olshin Schade Architects

2010 Residential Winners

Gardens & Landscapes
English Country Home
Atlanta, GA
Richard Anderson Landscape Architect

Multifamily
211 Elizabeth Street
New York, NY
Roman and Williams Buildings and Interiors

New Design & Construction
New Residence
Seaside, FL
Braulio Casas Architects

New Residence
Westport, CT
Ferguson & Shamamian Architects

Restoration & Renovation
Maycroft
North Haven, NY
James Merrell Architects

Sympathetic Addition
Medina River Ranch
Medina, TX
Michael G. Imber Architects

Special Award
Pool Pavilion
Undisclosed location, Western Massachusetts
David Scott Parker Architects

Source: Traditional Building

Michael Moran

B'nai Israel Synagogue, Rochester, MN | HGA Architects and Engineers

Religious Art & Architecture Design Awards

The annual Religious Art & Architecture Design Awards, co-sponsored by *Faith & Form* magazine and the Interfaith Forum on Religion, Art and Architecture (a professional interest area of the American Institute of Architects), reward the **highest achievements in architecture, liturgical design, and art for religious spaces.** Architects, liturgical consultants, interior designers, artists, and craftpersons worldwide are eligible to enter. Winning projects are featured in *Faith & Form*.

www.faithandform.com

2009 Honor Awards

New Facilities
Church Sun-pu
Shizuoka prefecture, Japan
Taira Nishizawa Architects (Japan)

Liturgical/Interior Design
Petters Pavillion and Blessed Sacrament
    Chapel, Saint John's Abbey
Collegeville, MN
VJAA

Sacred Heart Cathedral, Renovations and
    Additions
Rochester, NY
Williamson Pounders Architects; LaBella
    Associates

Sacred Landscape
WesSukkah, Wesleyan Center for Jewish Life
Middletown, CT
North Studio, Wesleyan University

Visual Arts
 "Designation," Bartholomew Chapel
Paderborn, Germany
Kunst aaO GmbH (Germany)

2009 Merit Awards

New Facilities
Chapel Addition, Shepherd of the Valley
    United Methodist Church
Hope, RI
3six0 Architecture

B'nai Israel Synagogue
Rochester, MN
HGA Architects and Engineers

All Saints Chapel, Texas Military Institute
San Antonio, TX
Ford Powell & Carson

Cathedral of Christ the Light
Oakland, CA
Skidmore, Owings & Merrill

Renovation
Christ Church Tower Restoration
Poughkeepsie, NY
Barry Donaldson, Architect at Lichten Craig
    Architects

Religious Art & Architecture Design Awards

Liturgical/Interior Design

Light Gallery and Interaction Gallery, Ogen
 Center
Tokyo, Japan
UA OFFICE Co. (Japan)

Cathedral of Christ the Light
Oakland, CA
Skidmore, Owings & Merrill

Visual Arts

Stations of the Cross, South Sydney Uniting
 Church
Waterloo, NSW, Australia
Miriam Cabello (Australia)

"I Will Bless You" Triptych, Union for Reform
 Judaism
New York, NY
Sarah Hall Studio (Canada)

Source: Faith & Form

residential architect Design Awards

The residential architect Design Awards honor the **best in American housing**. Projects may be submitted in one of 14 categories, though judges may eliminate, add, or combine categories—bestowing as many awards (or none) as they see fit. The jury, comprised of top residential architects, also selects the residential project of the year from among the winning entries. Winning projects are published in *residential architect* magazine.

www.residentialarchitect.com

2010 Project of the Year

Tea Houses
Silicon Valley, CA
Swatt | Miers Architects

2010 Grand Prize Winners

Custom, More Than 3,000 Square Feet
Yingst Retreat
Empire, MI
Salmela Architects

Custom, 3,000 Square Feet or Less
L-Stack House
Fayetteville, AR
Marlon Blackwell Architect

Mod Cott
Burnet, TX
Mell Lawrence Architects

Restoration/Preservation
Spreter Studio
Gladwyne, PA
Martin Jay Rosenblum, AIA & Associates

Multifamily
Formosa 1140
West Hollywood, CA
Lorcan O'Herlihy Architects

OneEleven Mixed-Use Development
Baton Rouge, LA
Remson | Haley | Herpin Architects

Christopher Barrett/Hendrich Blessing

Claremont House, Chicago, IL | Brininstool, Kerwin & Lynch

residential architect Design Awards

2010 Merit Winners

Custom, More Than 3,000 Square Feet
Black White Residence
Bethesda, MD
David Jameson Architect

Claremont House
Chicago, IL
Brininstool, Kerwin & Lynch

Montecito Residence
Santa Barbara, CA
Olson Kundig Architects

LC Ranch
Three Forks, MT
Lake/Flato Architects

Custom, 3,000 Square Feet or Less
Coffou Cottage
Michigan City, IN
Brininstool, Kerwin & Lynch

Renovation
Hollywood Hills Residence
Los Angeles, CA
Griffin Enright Architects

Residence e2
Washington, DC
Robert M. Gurney, FAIA

Addition to a Historic Cape on a Coastal Farm
Little Compton, RI
Bohlin Cywinski Jackson

Pilates Studio and Carport
Dallas, TX
Susan Appleton Architecture

Restoration/Preservation
Bubeshko Apartments
Los Angeles, CA
DSH

Multifamily
Hancock Mixed-Use
West Hollywood, CA
Koning Eizenberg Architecture

Single-Family Production, Detached
Elm
Hidden Creek, NE
Randy Brown

Affordable
Step Up on Fifth
Santa Monica, CA
Pugh + Scarpa

Lolomas
Clovis, NM
Rockhill and Associates

Architectural Design Detail
Claremont House
Chicago, IL
Brininstool, Kerwin & Lynch

Salt Spring Island Cabin
Salt Spring, BC, Canada
Olson Kundig Architects

On the Boards
House 99
Houston, TX
Borden Partnership; Atelier Andrews

Community | City: Between Building and
 Landscape: Affordable, Sustainable Infill
 for Smoketown
Louisville, KY
Marilys R. Nepomechie Architect

Porchscapes
Fayetteville, AR
University of Arkansas Community Design
 Center

Source: residential architecture

SADI Awards

Retail Traffic magazine annually presents the SADI (Superior Achievement in Design and Imaging) Awards to recognize **outstanding retail design achievements**. The jury, comprised of leading US retail architects and designers, reviews projects for criteria such as problem solving, general aesthetics, image building, and implementation. Any architecture or design firm, retailer, or developer of a new or renovated retail store, shopping center, or restaurant is eligible to enter.

www.retailtrafficmag.com

2010 Grand Winner

Dolce Vita Tejo
Lisbon, Portugal
RTKL Associates Inc.

2010 Winners

New Enclosed Center
Dolce Vita Tejo
Lisbon, Portugal
RTKL Associates Inc.

Renovated or Expanded Enclosed Center
Chadstone Shopping Centre
Melbourne, Australia
RTKL Associates Inc.

New Fast/Casual Dining
Carrefour Laval Food Court
Laval, QC, Canada
GHA design studios (Canada)

2010 Honorable Mentions

New Store — Less Than 5,000 Square Feet
The Shops at Fountainebleau
Miami, FL
Mancini - Duffy

New Store — More Than 5,000 Square Feet
Stark & Whyte
Brossard, QC, Canada
Ruscio Studio Inc. (Canada)

Renovated or Expanded Enclosed Center
Cherry Hill Mall
Cherry Hill, NJ
JPRA Associates

New Community/Power Center
Countryside Marketplace
Menifee, CA
Perkowitz + Ruth Architects

2010 Editor's Choice

Renovated Store — More Than 5,000 Square Feet
Saks Fifth Avenue (Third Floor)
New York, NY
Mancini - Duffy

New Mixed-Use or Multi-Use Development
Annapolis Towne Center at Parole
Annapolis, MD
The Martin Architectural Group; ka; Mulvanny
      G2 Architecture

Source: Retail Traffic

Ryan Gobuty/Gensler

Los Angeles Police Department Memorial, Los Angeles, CA | Gensler

SEGD Design Awards

The Society for Environmental Graphic Design's Design Awards recognize the **best in environmental design**: the planning, design, and specifying of graphic elements in the built and natural environments. Eligible projects include signage, wayfinding systems, mapping, exhibit design, themed environments, retail spaces, sports facilities, and campus design. A jury of professionals reviews the entries to determine which projects best identify, direct, inform, interpret, and visually enhance our surroundings.

www.segd.org

2010 Honor Awards

Boeing Future Factory
Everett, WA
NBBJ

California Academy of Sciences Exhibits
San Francisco, CA
Volume Inc.; Cinnabar Inc.

Green Community
Washington, DC
Matter Architecture Practice; MGMT. design

Los Angeles Police Department Memorial
Los Angeles, CA
Gensler

Legible London
London, UK
Applied Information Group (UK); Lacock
    Gullam (UK)

Official NYC Information Center
New York, NY
Local Projects; WXY Architecture

Rugerero Survivors Village Sunflower Oil
    Cooperative
Gisenyi, Rwanda
ex;it Foundation

Rugerero Sunflower Oil Project
Gisenyi, Rwanda
Antoinette Westphal College of Media
    Arts and Design, Drexel University; ex;it
    Foundation

Theatre and Auditorium Poitiers
Poitiers, France
P-06 Atelier (Portugal)

*The Wayfinding Handbook: Information Design
    for Public Places*
David Gibson with Two Twelve

Source: Society for Environmental Graphic Design

Tucker Design Awards

The Tucker Design Awards honor projects that demonstrate **design excellence in the use of natural stone**. This biennial competition, sponsored by the Building Stone Institute, is open to architects, landscape architects, interior designers, and others whose work integrates and showcases natural stone. First presented in 1977, the award is named in honor of the late Beverly R. Tucker Jr., a past president of the institute.

www.buildingstoneinstitute.org

2010 Winners

Chapel of Our Lady of the Most Holy Trinity,
    Thomas Aquinas College
Santa Paula, CA
Duncan G. Stroik Architect

Kogod Courtyard at the Reynolds Center for
    American Art and Portraiture, Smithsonian
    Institution
Washington, DC
Foster + Partners (UK)

Abby Aldrich Rockefeller Sculpture Garden,
    Museum of Modern Art
New York, NY
Zion Breen Richardson Associates

Sun Valley Pavilion
Sun Vally, ID
Ruscitto/Latham/Blanton Architectura; FTL
    Design Engineering Studio

Ambassador John L. Loeb Jr. Visitors Center
Newport, RI
Newport Collaborative

Kroon Hall, School of Forestry and
    Environmental Studies, Yale University
New Haven, CT
Hopkins Architects (UK)

Douglas B. Gardner '83 Integrated Athletic
    Center, Haverford College
Haverford, PA
Bohlin Cywinski Jackson

Federal Reserve Bank of Kansas City
Kansas City, MO
Pei Cobb Freed & Partners

OC Tanner Store Renovation
Salt Lake City, UT
MJSA Architects

Lily Lake Residence
Dalton, PA
Bohlin Cywinski Jackson

New Canaan Pool and Pool House
New Canaan, CT
Amanda Martocchio Architecture + Design
    with Devore Associates

Ravine Residence
Toronto, ON, Canada
Hariri Pontarini Architects (Canda)

Source: Building Stone Institute

USITT Architecture Awards

Sponsored by the United States Institute for Theatre Technology, the USITT Architecture Awards honor **excellence in theater design**. Created in 1994, the program recognizes superior design work and provides resource material about contemporary theater architecture. Submissions are evaluated for their creative image, contextual resonance, community contribution, explorations in new technologies, and functional operations.

www.usitt.org

2010 Winners

Honor Awards
TELUS Centre for Performance and Learning,
    Royal Conservatory of Music
Toronto, ON, Canada
Kuwabara Payne McKenna Blumberg
    Architects (Canada)

Merit Awards
Vukovich Center for Communication Arts
Meadville, PA
Polshek Partnership Architects

Henry Miller's Theatre
New York, NY
Cook + Fox Architects

Winspear Opera House
Dallas, TX
Foster + Partners

Theatre De Quat'sous
Montreal, QC, Canada
Les Architectes FABG (Canada)

Renée and Henry Segerstrom Concert Hall
    and Samueli Theater
Costa Mesa, CA
Pelli Clarke Pelli Architects

Iwaki Performing Arts Center
Fukushima, Japan
Naomi Sato Architects (Japan); Shimizu
    Corporation (Japan)

Source: United States Institute for Theatre Technology

Hubert Kang

Richmond Olympic Oval, Richmond, BC, Canada | Cannon Design

Wood Design Awards

The Wood Design Awards annually recognize **excellence in wood architecture throughout North America**. Winning projects push the boundaries of conventional wood building practices and highlight the special qualities, versatility, and sheer beauty of wood as a building material, though buildings need not be constructed entirely of wood. A special award issue of *Wood Design & Building* magazine features the winning projects.

www.wooddesignandbuilding.com

2009 Winners

Honor Awards
Chapel of the Sky
Granite, CO
Anderson Mason Dale Architects

Creekside House
Woodside, CA
Bohlin Cywinski Jackson

Prefab Cottage for Two Families
Muskoka, ON, Canada
Kohn Shnier Architects

Richmond Olympic Oval
Richmond, BC, Canada
Cannon Design

Merit Awards
Koerner Hall, Royal Conservatory of Music
Toronto, ON, Canada
Kuwabara Payne McKenna Blumberg
    Architects (Canada)

Louver House
Long Island, NY
Leroy Street Studio

Spiral House
Old Greenwich, CT
Joeb Moore + Partners Architects

Tillamook Forest Interpretive Complex
Tillamook, OR
Miller Hull Partnership

Citation Awards
Camouflage House
Green Lake, WI
Johnsen Schmaling Architects

Source: Wood Design & Building

Best of NeoCon

The Best of NeoCon competition honors the **best new products introduced to the US contract market** during the past year. A jury of industry professionals selects gold, silver, editor's choice, and innovation winners. From these, one product is chosen as the best of competition. Winners are announced at NeoCon, the interior design industry's annual showcase for the latest products and trends.

www.contractmagazine.com

2010 Best of Competition

ON
Wilkhahn

2010 Gold Winners

Architectural Products
Kids Glass
Skyline Design

Carpet Fiber
TruBlend Fiber Technology
Antron INVISTA

Carpet
Broadloom
Palisades Collection
Milliken Constantine

Modular
Memphis Collection
InterfaceFLOR

Casegoods
Proximus
Halcon

Conference Room Furniture
SITE Collection
Davis

Education Solutions
Dewey 6-Top by Fixtures Furniture
Izzy+

Flooring Resilient
Urban Nature Powerbond Hybrid Resilient
Tandus Flooring

Furniture Systems
Collective and Innovative Teaming
　　Enhancements
Groupe Lacasse

Furniture Systems
Enhancements
Stride Benching
Allsteel

Healthcare
Allay Sleep Sofa
Wieland

Healthcare
Furniture
Compass System
Herman Miller Healthcare

Fabrics
Entwined
Pallas Textiles

Textiles
Silica
Momentum Textiles

Lighting
Decorative
Heat
Joel Berman Glass Studio

Task/Desktop, Furniture-Integrated
Conflux LED Lighting
Teknion

Office Accessories
Humanair Personal Zone Air Purifier
Humanscale

Seating
Benches
dna Collaborative Lounge Seating & Tables
Teknion

Conference
Very Task Conference
Haworth

Ergonomic Desk/Task
ON
Wilkhahn

Guest
Corvo
Bernhardt Design

Sofas & Lounge
Cahoots
Keilhauer

Stacking
Seek
Allsteel

Software Technologies
Next-Generation Spec Tool
Polycor Inc.

Surfacing Materials
Silver Gray Phylite
Stone Source

Tables
Occasional
CurioTables
Bernhardt Design

Training
Fleet
Nucraft

Technology Support
Mobile Monitor Stand
Nucraft

Textiles
Upholstery
Rodarto for Knoll Luxe
Knoll Luxe

Wall Treatments
Dimension Walls Eco
MDC Wallcoverings

Walls
Movable
Enclose Frameless Glass
Haworth

Window Treatments
UrbanShade
MechoShade Systems

Workplace Technologies
Room Wizard
Steelcase

Worksurfaces
Height-Adjustable
Wing-It
SurfaceWorks

Source: Contract

I.D. Annual Design Review

Since 1954, the I.D. Annual Design Review has recognized the best in product, furniture, graphic, and environment design and chronicled the evolution of design. A jury of leading practitioners reviews the submissions and grants awards on three levels: best of category, design distinction, and honorable mention. Winning entries are showcased on the award's website.

http://annualdesignreview.id-mag.com/

2010 Best of Category

Concepts
Palette concept for the Future Present Exhibit
IDEO; Hakuhodo (Japan)

Consumer Products
Meyerhoffer Surfboard
Thomas Meyerhoffer

Environments
One Shelley Street
Sydney, Australia
Clive Wilkinson Architects with Woods Bagot
   (Australia)

Equipment
Motorola MC9500 Mobile Computer
Motorola; Kaleidoscope

Furniture
Click, an immaterial lamp
Patrick Martinez

Graphics
X Exhibition Space
SenseTeam

Interactive
www.wechoosethemoon.org
The Martin Agency; Domani Studios

Packaging
Amazon Kindle DX Packaging
Lab 126

Student Work
Es Tiempo Cervical Cancer Prevention
   Campaign
Art Center College of Design

Transportation
Swiss International Air Lines Ltd First Class
   Suite
Priestmangoode (UK)

Source: F+W Media

International Design Excellence Awards

The annual International Design Excellence Awards (IDEA), produced by the Industrial Designers Society of America (IDSA) and sponsored by *Fast Company*, **honor outstanding industrial design projects worldwide**. A jury of business and design executives select winners from categories ranging from commercial and industrial products to interactive product experiences and service design. Gold, silver, and bronze awards are granted.

www.idsa.org

2010 Gold Winners

Commercial & Industrial
ESR 5000 Series Reach Truck
Crown Equipment Corporation; Formation
  Design Group

Geocell RDFW™
Geocell Systems; Eastman Chemical
  Company

Electrosurgery Unit Tester (ESU Tester)
  for developing countries
Hiemstra Product Development

Communication Tools
Jawbone ICON Headset
fuseproject

LaCie lamaKey, CooKey and WhisKey
  USB flash drives
5.5 designers (France)

Computer Equipment
External HDD G Series
Samsung Electronics (South Korea)

Design Strategy
Lifetuner.org
AARP; Essential; Peer Insight

Li-Ning Design Strategy
Ziba and Li-Ning (China)

Lançamento da Lata Guaraná Jesus (The
  launching of Guaraná Jesus new can)
Dia Comunicação (Brazil)

Ecodesign
PACT Underwear
fuseproject

Entertainment
Slingbox 700U
NewDealDesign; SlingMedia Inc.

Beats by Dr. Dre Solo
Ammunition; Dr. Dre

Environments
Media Bus Shelter
Seoul, South Korea
Seoul National University (South Korea); CA
  plan Co., Ltd. (South Korea); Hyundaicard
  Co., Ltd. (South Korea)

Museu do Futebol (The Soccer Museum)
São Paulo, Brazil
Souza Design (Brazil)

Urban Graphic Design for Bixiga
  Neighborhood (Trabalho Gráfica Urbana
  para o Bairro do Bixiga)
São Paulo, Brazil
Padovano Arquitetura em Rede Ltda. (Brazil)

International Design Excellence Awards

Home Living
Hwaro
Woongjin Coway Co. Ltd. (South Korea)

LED Light Bulb
Panasonic Corporation (Japan)

Easy Latrine
IDE; Rainwater Cambodia (Cambodia); LienAid
(Singapore); Ministry of Rural Development
(Cambodia)

Fuego Element
Ammunition; Fuego North America

Herman Miller Ardea Light
fuseproject

Virus Doctor
Samsung Electronics (South Korea)

Woven Bin (Cesto Trama)
Bertussi Designdustrial (Brazil)

Interactive Product Experiences
CompleteSpeech Palatometer
Rocketship, Inc., CompleteSpeech

Virtual Wallet for PNC Financial Services
Group
IDEO; PNC Financial Services Group

Zune HD
Zune Design Team; ASTRO Studios

Leisure & Recreation
Meyerhoffer™ Surfboard
Meyerhoffer Inc.

Medical & Scientific Products
SILS Port
Covidien

Fitbit Tracker
NewDealDesign

Ventus PROVENT® Professional Sleep Apnea
Therapy
LUNAR; Ventus Medical

Office & Productivity
LIM (Light in Motion)
Pablo Designs; Haworth

Very seating family
Haworth; Simon Desanta Industrial Design
(Germany)

Packaging & Graphics
Method Laundry Detergent with Smartclean
Technology™
Method Products, Inc.

litl webbook packaging
litl; Pentagram

Research
Lilly Patient Posters
IDEO; Eli Lilly and Company

Service Design
Collaborative Service for Best Western
IDEO

Student Designs
CAS AIr System
Malin Grummas, Umeå Institute of Design
(Sweden)

980 TATOU - sport shoe for Le Parkour
Annika Lüber, University of Applied Science
Schwäbisch Gmünd (Germany)

ONEDOWN
Aakash Dewan, DSK ISD International School
of Design (India)

Source: Industrial Designers Society of America

BUILDING TYPES |

Listings of architecturally significant airports, aquariums, art museums, convention centers, and sports stadiums, with their requisite architectural statistics, are available in this chapter.

Airports: 1990–2010

Airports have evolved over the past century from small, utilitarian structures to sprawling multi-purpose complexes. Engineering challenges, the popularity of regional airlines, the need to accommodate larger jets, and expansion in Asia have resulted in the construction of countless new airport terminals since 1990. Many of those noteworthy for their architecture or engineering are listed in the following chart.

Airport	Location	Architect	Opened
Astana International Airport (KZT), Passenger Terminal	Astana, Kazakhstan	Kisho Kurokawa Architect & Associates (Japan)	2005
Barcelona International Airport (BCN), T1	Barcelona, Spain	Taller de Arquitectura (Spain)	2009
Barcelona International Airport (BCN), South Terminal	Barcelona, Spain	Taller de Arquitectura (Spain)	2005
Beihai Fucheng Airport (BHY), Domestic Terminal	Beihai, Guangxi, China	Llewelyn-Davies Ltd. (UK)	2000
Beijing Capital International Airport (PEK), Terminal 3	Beijing, China	Foster + Partners (UK) with Beijing Institute of Architectural Design (China)	2008
Ben Gurion Airport (TLV), Airside Complex, Terminal 3	Tel Aviv, Israel	Moshe Safdie and Associates and TRA Architects—a joint venture	2004
Ben Gurion Airport (TLV), Landside Complex, Terminal 3	Tel Aviv, Israel	Skidmore, Owings & Merrill; Moshe Safdie and Associates; Karmi Associates (Israel); Lissar Eldar Architects (Israel)—a joint venture	2002
Bilbao Airport (BIO), Terminal Building	Bilbao, Spain	Santiago Calatrava (Spain)	2000
Buffalo Niagara International Airport (BUF), Passenger Terminal	Cheektowaga, NY	Cannon Design; William Nicholas Bodouva + Associates; Kohn Pedersen Fox— a joint venture	1997
Carrasco International Airport (MVD), New Terminal	Montevideo, Uruguay	Rafael Viñoly Architects with Carla Bechelli Arquitectos (Argentina)	2009
Central Japan International Airport (NGO)	Tokoname City, Aichi Prefecture, Japan	Nikken Sekkei (Japan); Azusa Sekkei (Japan); Hellmuth, Obata & Kassabaum/ Arup (UK)—a joint venture	2005
Changi Airport (SIN), Terminal 3	Singapore	CPG Corporation (Singapore); Skidmore, Owings & Merrill	2008
Charles de Gaulle Airport (CDG), Terminal 2E	Paris, France	Aéroports de Paris (France)	2003

Airports: 1990–2010

Airport	Location	Architect	Opened
Charles de Gaulle Airport (CDG), Terminal 2F	Paris, France	Aéroports de Paris (France)	1998
Chicago-O'Hare International Airport (ORD), Terminal 5	Chicago, IL	Perkins+Will with Heard & Associates	1994
Chongqing Jiangbei International Airport (CKG)	Chongqing, China	Llewelyn-Davies Ltd. (UK) with Arup (UK)	2004
Cologne/Bonn Airport (CGN), Terminal 2	Cologne, Germany	Murphy/Jahn	2000
Copenhagen International Airport (CPH), Terminal 3	Copenhagen, Denmark	Vilhelm Lauritzen AS (Denmark)	1998
Dallas-Fort Worth International Airport (DFW), Terminal D	Dallas/Fort Worth, TX	HNTB Architecture; HKS, Inc.; Corgan	2005
Denver International Airport (DEN)	Denver, CO	Fentress Bradburn Architects	1995
Detroit Metropolitan Wayne County Airport (DTW), North Terminal	Romulus, MI	Gensler; GHAFARI; Hamilton Anderson Associates	2008
Detroit Metropolitan Wayne County Airport (DTW), McNamara Terminal	Romulus, MI	SmithGroup	2002
Dubai International Airport (DXB), Terminal 3	Dubai, UAE	Paul Andreu Architecte (France)	2007
Dusseldorf International Airport (DUS)	Dusseldorf, Germany	JSK Architekten (Germany); Perkins+Will	2001–2003
Enfidha – Zine el Abidine Ben Ali Airport (NBE)	Enfidha, Tunisia	ADPi Designers & Planners (France)	2009
EuroAirport Basel-Mulhouse-Freiburg (BSL), South Terminal	Saint Louis Cédex, France	Aegerter and Bosshardt (Switzerland)	2005
Frankfurt Airport (FRA), Terminal 2	Frankfurt, Germany	Perkins+Will; JSK Architekten (Germany)	1994
Fukuoka International Airport (FUK), International Terminal	Hakata-ku, Fukuoka City, Japan	Hellmuth, Obata & Kassabaum; Azusa Sekkei (Japan); Mishima Architects (Japan); MHS Planners, Architects & Engineers Co. (Japan)	1999
Gardermoen Airport (GEN)	Oslo, Norway	AVIAPLAN (Norway); Niels Torp Architects (Norway)	1998
Graz International Airport (GRZ), Passenger Terminal	Graz, Austria	Pittino & Ortner Architekturbüro (Austria)	2005
Graz International Airport (GRZ), Passenger Terminal expansion	Graz, Austria	Riegler Riewe Architekten (Austria)	1994
Guangzhou Baiyun International Airport (CAN)	Guangdong, China	Parsons Brinckerhoff with URS Corporation	2004

Airport	Location	Architect	Opened
Hamburg Airport (HAM), New Terminal 1	Hamburg, Germany	gmp Architekten (Germany) with von Gerkan, Marg & Partner Architekten (Germany)	2005
Hamburg Airport (HAM), Terminal 4 (now Terminal 2)	Hamburg, Germany	von Gerkan, Marg & Partner Architekten (Germany)	1991
Haneda Airport (HND), New International Terminal	Tokyo, Japan	Unknown	2010
Haneda Airport (HND), Terminal 2	Tokyo, Japan	Cesar Pelli & Associates; Jun Mitsui & Associates Inc. Architects (Japan)	2004
Heathrow Airport (LHR), Terminal 5	London, UK	Richard Rogers Partnership (UK)	2008
Heathrow Airport (LHR), Pier 4A	London, UK	Nicholas Grimshaw & Partners (UK)	1993
Heathrow Airport (LHR), Europier	London, UK	Richard Rogers Partnership (UK)	1992
Hong Kong International Airport (HKG)	Hong Kong, China	Foster + Partners (UK)	1998
Incheon International Airport (ICN), Integrated Transportation Center	Seoul, South Korea	Terry Farrell and Partners (UK)	2002
Incheon International Airport (ICN)	Seoul, South Korea	Fentress Bradburn Architects with BHJW and Korean Architects Collaborative International (South Korea)	2001
Indianapolis Airport (IND), Passenger Terminal	Indianapolis, IN	Hellmuth, Obata & Kassabaum	2008
Indira Ghandi International Airport (DEL), Terminal 3	New Delhi, India	Hellmuth, Obata & Kassabaum with Mott MacDonald Group (UK)	2010
Jinan International Airport (TNA)	Jinan, China	Integrated Design Associates	2005
John F. Kennedy International Airport (JFK), Terminal 5	Jamaica, NY	Gensler	2008
John F. Kennedy International Airport (JFK), American Airlines Terminal, Phase 1	Jamaica, NY	DMJM Harris	AECOM	2005–2007
John F. Kennedy International Airport (JFK), Terminal 4	Jamaica, NY	Skidmore, Owings & Merrill	2001
John F. Kennedy International Airport (JFK), Terminal 1	Jamaica, NY	William Nicholas Bodouva + Associates	1998
Jorge Chávez International Airport (LIM), New Terminal	Lima, Peru	Arquitectonica	2005
Kansai International Airport (KIA)	Osaka Bay, Japan	Renzo Piano Building Workshop (Italy) with Nikken Sekkei (Japan), Aéroports de Paris (France), Japan Airport Consultants Inc. (Japan)	1994

Airports: 1990–2010

Airport	Location	Architect	Opened
King Fahd International Airport (DMM)	Dammam, Saudi Arabia	Minoru Yamasaki Associates (Japan)	1999
King Shaka International Airport (DUR)	Durban, South Africa	Osmond Lange Architects and Planners (South Africa)	2010
Kuala Lumpur International Airport (KUL)	Kuala Lumpur, Malaysia	Kisho Kurokawa Architect & Associates (Japan) with Akitek Jururancang (Malaysia)	1998
Learmonth International Airport (LEA)	Exeter, Australia	JCY Architects and Urban Designers (Australia)	1999
Lester B. Pearson International Airport (YYZ), Pier F at Terminal 1	Toronto, ON, Canada	Architects Canada; Moshe Safdie and Associates; Skidmore, Owings & Merrill; Adamson Associates Architects (Canada)	2007
Lester B. Pearson International Airport (YYZ), New Terminal 1	Toronto, ON, Canada	Skidmore, Owings & Merrill; Moshe Safdie and Associates; Adamson Associates Architects (Canada)	2004
Logan International Airport (BOS), Terminal A	Boston, MA	Hellmuth, Obata & Kassabaum with C&R/ Rizvi, Inc.	2005
Madrid Barajas International Airport (MAD), Terminal 3	Madrid, Spain	Richard Rogers Partnership (UK) with Estudio Lamela (Spain)	2005
Málaga Airport (AGP), Terminal 3	Malaga, Spain	Bruce S. Fairbanks (Spain)	2010
Malaga Airport (AGP), Pablo Ruiz Picasso Terminal	Malaga, Spain	Taller de Arquitectura (Spain)	1991
McCarran International Airport (LAS), Satellite D	Las Vegas, NV	LEO A DALY; Tate & Snyder	1998
Mineta San José International Airport (SJC), Terminal B Concourse	San José, CA	Gensler with Steinberg Architects	2010
Ministro Pistarini International Airport (EZE), Terminal A	Buenos Aires, Argentina	Estudio M/SG/S/S/S (Spain) with Urgell/Fazio/Penedo/Urgell (Spain)	2000
Munich International Airport (MUC), Terminal 2	Munich, Germany	K+P Architekten und Stadtplaner (Germany)	2003
Munich International Airport (MUC), Airport Center	Munich, Germany	Murphy/Jahn	1999
Munich International Airport (MUC)	Munich, Germany	Von Busse & Partners (Germany)	1992
Orlando International Airport (MCO), Airside 2	Orlando, FL	Hellmuth, Obata & Kassabaum	2000
Ottawa International Airport (YOW), Passenger Terminal	Ottawa, ON, Canada	Brisbin Brook Beynon Architects (Canada); Stantec	2003
Philadelphia International Airport (PHL), International Terminal A-West	Philadelphia, PA	Kohn Pedersen Fox	2003

Airport	Location	Architect	Opened
Pointe à Pitre Le Raizet International Airport (PTP)	Pointe à Pitre, Guadeloupe	Aéroports de Paris (France)	1996
Raleigh-Durham International Airport (RDU), Terminal 2 Phase 1	Raleigh, NC	Fentress Architects	2008
Ronald Reagan Washington National Airport (DCA), North Terminal	Washington, DC	Cesar Pelli & Associates; LEO A DALY	1997
San Francisco International Airport (SFO), International Terminal	San Francisco, CA	Skidmore, Owings & Merrill with Del Campo & Maru and Michael Willis Architects	2000
San Pablo Airport (SVQ)	Seville, Spain	Rafael Moneo (Spain)	1992
Seattle-Tacoma International Airport (SEA), Central Terminal	Seattle, WA	Fentress Bradburn Architects	2005
Seattle-Tacoma International Airport (SEA), Concourse A	Seattle, WA	NBBJ	2004
Sendai International Airport (SDJ)	Natori, Japan	Hellmuth, Obata & Kassabaum; Nikken Sekkei (Japan)	1998
Shanghai Pudong International Airport (PVG), Terminal 2	Shanghai, China	Shanghai Xian Dai Architectural Design Group (China)	2007
Shanghai Pudong International Airport (PVG)	Shanghai, China	Aéroports de Paris (France)	1999
Shenzhen Baoan International Airport (SZX), Domestic Terminal	Shenzhen, China	Llewelyn-Davies Ltd. (UK)	2001
Sheremetyevo International Airport (SVO), Terminal 3	Moscow, Russia	ADPi Designers & Planners (France)	2009
Southampton Airport (SOU)	Southampton, UK	Manser Associates (UK)	1994
Stansted Airport (STN)	London, UK	Foster + Partners (UK)	1991
Suvarnabhumi Airport (BK)	Samut Prakarn (Bangkok), Thailand	MJTA (Murphy/Jahn; TAMS Consultants Inc.; ACT Engineering)	2006
Tianjin Binhai International Airport (TSN), Terminal	Dongli, China	Kohn Pedersen Fox with Netherlands Airport Consultants (Netherlands)	2008
Toulouse-Blagnac International Airport (TLS), Hall D	Toulouse, France	Cardete Huet Architectes (France)	2010
Zurich Airport (ZRH), Airside Centre	Zurich, Switzerland	Nicholas Grimshaw & Partners (UK) with Itten+Brechbühl (Switzerland)	2004

Source: DesignIntelligence

Aquariums

The opening of Boston's New England Aquarium in 1969 ushered in a new age for aquariums, combining the traditional ideas found in the classic aquariums of the early 20th century with new technology and revised educational and research commitments. Aquariums have since proliferated. The following pages highlight the major free-standing aquariums in the United States.

Aquarium	Location	Opened	Cost
Alaska SeaLife Center	Seward, AK	1998	$56 M
Aquarium of the Bay	San Francisco, CA	1996	$38 M
Aquarium of the Pacific	Long Beach, CA	1998	$117 M
Audubon Aquarium of Americas	New Orleans, LA	1990	$42 M
Belle Isle Aquarium	Royal Oak, MI	1904	$175,000
Birch Aquarium at Scripps Institution of Oceanography, UCSD	La Jolla, CA	1992	$14 M
Colorado's Ocean Journey	Denver, CO	1999	$94 M
Flint RiverQuarium	Albany, GA	2004	$30 M
Florida Aquarium	Tampa, FL	1994	$84 M
Georgia Aquarium	Atlanta, GA	2005	$280 M
Great Lakes Aquarium	Duluth, MN	2000	$34 M
John G. Shedd Aquarium	Chicago, IL	1930	$ 3.25 M ($45 M addition)
Maritime Aquarium at Norwalk	Norwalk, CT	1988	$11.5 M ($9 M addition)
Monterey Bay Aquarium	Monterey, CA	1984	$55 M ($57 M addition)
Mystic Aquarium	Mystic, CT	1973	$1.74 M ($52 M expansion)
National Aquarium	Washington, DC	1931	n/a
National Aquarium in Baltimore	Baltimore, MD	1981	$21.3 M ($35 M 1990 addition $66 M 2005 addition)

Total Square Ft. (original/current)	Tank Capacity (orig./current, in gal.)	Architect
115,000	400,000	Cambridge Seven Associates with Livingston Slone
48,000	707,000	Esherick Homsey Dodge and Davis
156,735	900,000	A joint venture of Hellmuth, Obata & Kassabaum and Esherick Homsey Dodge and Davis
110,000	1.19 M	The Bienville Group: a joint venture of The Mathes Group, Eskew + Architects, Billes/Manning Architects, Hewitt Washington & Associates, Concordia
10,000	32,000	Albert Kahn Associates, Inc.
34,000	150,000	Wheeler Wimer Blackman & Associates
107,000	1 M	Odyssea: a joint venture of RNL and Anderson Mason Dale Architects
30,000	175,000	Antoine Predock Architect with Robbins Bell Kreher Inc.
152,000	1 M	Hellmuth, Obata & Kassabaum and Esherick Homsey Dodge and Davis
500,000	8 M	Thompson, Ventulett, Stainback & Associates
62,382	170,000	Hammel, Green and Abrahamson
225,000/395,000	1.5 M/3 M	Graham, Anderson, Probst, & White (Lohan Associates, 1991 addition)
102,000/135,000	150,000	Graham Gund Architects Inc. (original building and 2001 addition)
216,000/307,000	900,000/1.9 M	Esherick Homsey Dodge and Davis (original building and 1996 addition)
76,000/137,000	1.6 M/2.3 M	Flynn, Dalton and van Dijk (Cesar Pelli & Associates, 1999 expansion)
13,500	32,000	York & Sawyer Architects
209,000/324,000/ 389,400	1 M/1.5 M/ 1.578 M	Cambridge Seven Associates (Grieves & Associates, 1990 addition; Chermayeff, Sollogub and Poole, 2005 addition)

Aquariums

Aquarium	Location	Opened	Cost
New England Aquarium	Boston, MA	1969	$8 M ($20.9 M 1998 addition $19.3 M 2001 expansion)
New Jersey State Aquarium	Camden, NJ	1992	$52 M
New York Aquarium at Coney Island	Brooklyn, NY	1957	n/a
Newport Aquarium	Newport, KY	1999	$40 M ($4.5 M expansion)
North Carolina Aquarium at Fort Fisher	Kure Beach, NC	1976	$1.5 M ($17.5 M expansion)
North Carolina Aquarium at Pine Knoll Shores	Pine Knoll Shores, NC	1976	$4 M ($25 M expansion)
North Carolina Aquarium on Roanoke Island	Manteo, NC	1976	$1.6 M ($16 M expansion)
Oklahoma Aquarium	Tulsa, OK	2003	$15 M
Oregon Coast Aquarium	Newport, OR	1992	$25.5 M
Ripley's Aquarium	Myrtle Beach, SC	1997	$40 M
Ripley's Aquarium of the Smokies	Gatlinburg, TN	2000	$49 M
Seattle Aquarium	Seattle, WA	1977	n/a ($20 M expansion)
South Carolina Aquarium	Charleston, SC	2000	$69 M
Steinhart Aquarium at the California Academy of Science	San Francisco, CA	2008	$438 M*
Tennessee Aquarium	Chattanooga, TN	1992	$45 M ($30 M addition)
Texas State Aquarium	Corpus Christi, TX	1990	$31 M ($14 M addition)
Virginia Aquarium & Science Center	Virginia Beach, VA	1986	$7.5 M ($35 M expansion)
Waikiki Aquarium	Honolulu, HI	1955	$400,000
Wonders of Wildlife at the American National Fish and Wildlife Museum	Springfield, MO	2001	$34 M

* Combines figures for the Steinhart Aquarium, Morrison Planetarium, and Kimball Natural History Museum.

Source: DesignIntelligence

Total Square Ft. (original/current)	Tank Capacity (orig./current, in gal.)	Architect
75,000/1 M	1 M	Cambridge Seven Associates (Schwartz/Silver Architects, 1998 addition; E. Verner Johnson and Associates, 2001 expansion)
120,000	1 M	The Hillier Group
150,000	1.8 M	n/a
100,000/121,200	1 M/1.01 M	GBBN Architects (original and 2005 expansion)
30,000/84,000	77,000/455,000	Cambridge Seven Associates (BMS Architects, 2002 expansion)
29,000/93,000	25,000/433,000	Hayes, Howell & Associates (BMS Architects, 2006 expansion)
34,000/68,000	5,000/400,000	Lyles, Bissett, Carlisle and Wolff Associates of North Carolina Inc. with Cambridge Seven Associates (BMS Architects, 2000 expansion)
71,600	500,000	SPARKS
51,000	1.4 M	SRG Partnership
87,000	1.3 M	Enartec
115,000	1.3 M	Helman Hurley Charvat Peacock/Architects
68,000/86,000	753,000/873,000	Fred Bassetti & Co. (Miller Hull Partnership and Mithun, 2007 expansion)
93,000	1 M	Eskew + Architects with Clark and Menefee Architects
410,000*	500,000	Renzo Piano Building Workshop (Italy) with Stantec Architecture
130,000/190,000	400,000/1.1 M	Cambridge Seven Associates (Chermayeff, Sollogub & Poole, 2005 addition)
43,000/73,800	325,000/725,000	Phelps, Bomberger, and Garza (Corpus Christi Design Associates, 2003 addition)
41,500/120,000	100,000/800,000	E. Verner Johnson and Associates (original building and 1996 expansion)
19,000	152,000	Hart Wood and Edwin A. Weed with Ossipoff, Snyder, and Rowland
92,000	500,000	Cambridge Seven Associates

Art Museums

By some calculations there are more than 16,000 museums in the United States. While the collections they hold are often priceless, the facilities that contain them are frequently significant, especially amidst the recent museum-building boom led by world-class architects. The following chart, while not comprehensive, lists architecturally significant US art museums.

Museum	Location	Architect (original)
Akron Art Museum	Akron, OH	Dalton, van Dijk, Johnson & Partners (conversion of the original 1899 post office)
Albright-Knox Art Gallery	Buffalo, NY	Edward B. Green
Allen Memorial Art Museum	Oberlin, OH	Cass Gilbert
American Folk Art Museum	New York, NY	Tod Williams Billie Tsien Architects
Amon Carter Museum	Fort Worth, TX	Philip Johnson
Anchorage Museum of History and Art	Anchorage, AK	Kirk, Wallace, and McKinley with Schultz/Maynard
Art Institute of Chicago	Chicago, IL	Shepley, Rutan, and Coolidge
Art Museum of South Texas	Corpus Christi, TX	Philip Johnson
Arthur M. Sackler Museum	Cambridge, MA	James Stirling Michael Wilford and Associates (UK)
Asian Art Museum	San Francisco, CA	Gae Aulenti (Italy) with Hellmuth, Obata & Kassabaum, LDa Architects, and Robert Wong Architects (adapted the 1917 main library by George Kelham)
Baltimore Museum of Art	Baltimore, MD	John Russell Pope
Barnes Foundation	Merion, PA	Paul Philippe Cret
Bass Museum of Art	Miami, FL	B. Robert Swartburg (adapted the 1930 Miami Beach Library by Russell Pancoast)
Bellevue Art Museum	Bellevue, WA	Steven Holl Architects
Berkeley Art Museum + Pacific Film Archive	Berkeley, CA	Mario J. Ciampi & Associates
Birmingham Museum of Art	Birmingham, AL	Warren, Knight and Davis
Bowdoin College Museum of Art	Brunswick, ME	McKim, Mead and White

Opened	Architect (expansion)
1981	Coop Himmelb(l)au (Austria) with Westlake Reed Leskosky, 2007 John S. and James L. Knight Building
1905	Skidmore, Owings & Merrill, 1961 addition
1917	Venturi, Scott Brown and Associates, 1977 addition
2001	—
1961	Johnson/Burgee Architects, 1977 expansion; Philip Johnson/Alan Ritchie Architects, 2001 expansion
1968	Kenneth Maynard Associates, 1974 addition; Mitchell	Giurgola Architects with Maynard and Partch, 1986 addition; David Chipperfield Architects with Kumin Associates Inc., 2009 expansion
1893	Skidmore, Owings & Merrill, 1977 Arthur Rubloff Building; Hammond, Beebe and Babka, 1988 Daniel F. and Ada L. Rice Building; Renzo Piano Building Workshop, with Interactive Design Inc., 2009 Modern Wing
1972	Legorreta + Legorreta (Mexico) with Dykema Architects, 2006 William B. and Maureen Miller Building
1985	—
2003	—
1929	John Russell Pope, 1937 Jacobs Wing; Wrenn, Lewis & Jancks, 1950 May Wing, 1956 Woodward Wing and 1957 Cone Wing; Bower Lewis & Thrower Architects, 1994 West Wing for Contemporary Art
1925	—
1964	Arata Isozaki & Associates (Japan) with Spillis Candela DMJM	AECOM, 2002 expansion
2001	—
1970	—
1959	Warren, Knight and Davis, 1965 west wing, 1967 east wing, 1974 expansion, 1979 addition, and 1980 expansion; Edward Larrabee Barnes Associates, 1993 expansion
1894	Machado and Silvetti Associates, 2007 entry pavilion

Art Museums

Museum	Location	Architect (original)
Brooklyn Museum	Brooklyn, NY	McKim, Mead, and White
Butler Institute of American Art	Youngstown, OH	McKim, Mead and White
Cincinnati Art Museum	Cincinnati, OH	James McLaughlin
Cleveland Museum of Art	Cleveland, OH	Benjamin Hubbell and W. Dominick Benes
Colorado Springs Fine Arts Center	Colorado Springs, CO	John Gaw Meem
Columbus Museum of Art	Columbus, OH	Richards, McCarty and Bulford
Contemporary Art Museum St. Louis	St. Louis, MO	Allied Works Architecture
Contemporary Arts Museum, Houston	Houston, TX	Gunnar Birkerts and Associates
Corcoran Gallery of Art	Washington, DC	Ernest Flagg
Cranbrook Art Museum	Cranbrook, MI	Eliel Saarinen
Crocker Art Museum	Sacramento, CA	Seth Babson (architect of the original 1872 Crocker family mansion and art gallery)
Dallas Museum of Art	Dallas, TX	Edward Larrabee Barnes Associates
Dayton Art Institute	Dayton, OH	Edward B. Green
de Young Museum	San Francisco, CA	Herzog & de Meuron (Switzerland) with Fong & Chan Architects
Denver Art Museum	Denver, CO	Gio Ponti (Italy) with James Sudler Associates
Denver Museum of Contemporary Art	Denver, CO	Adjaye Associates (UK)
Des Moines Art Center	Des Moines, IA	Eliel Saarinen
Detroit Institute of Arts	Detroit, MI	James Balfour
Elvehjem Museum of Art	Madison, WI	Harry Weese
Everson Museum of Art	Syracuse, NY	I.M. Pei & Associates
Figge Art Museum	Davenport, IA	David Chipperfield Architects (UK) with Herbert Lewis Kruse Blunck Architecture
Fogg Art Museum	Cambridge, MA	Coolidge, Shepley, Bulfinch, and Abbott
Frances Lehman Loeb Art Center	Poughkeepsie, NY	Cesar Pelli & Associates
Fred Jones Jr. Museum of Art	Norman, OK	Howard and Smais

Opened	Architect (expansion)
1897–1927	Prentice & Chan, Ohlhausen, 1978 addition; Arata Isozaki & Associates (Japan) and James Stewart Polshek & Partners, 1991 Iris and B. Gerald Cantor Auditorium; Polshek Partnership Architects, 2004 front entrance and public plaza addition
1919	Paul Boucherie, 1931 north and south wings; C. Robert Buchanan & Associates, 1967 addition; Buchanan, Ricciuti & Associates, 1986 west wing addition
1886	Daniel H. Burnham, 1907 Schmidlapp Wing; Garber and Woodward, 1910 Ropes Wing and 1930 Emery, Hanna & French Wings; Rendigs, Panzer and Martin, 1937 Alms Wing; Potter, Tyler, Martin and Roth, 1965 Adams-Emery Wing
1916	J. Byers Hays and Paul C. Ruth, 1958 addition; Marcel Breuer and Hamilton P. Smith, 1971 addition; Dalton, van Dijk, Johnson & Partners, 1984 addition; Rafael Viñoly Architects, 2009 East Wing
1936	—
1931	Van Buren and Firestone, Architects, Inc., 1974 addition
2003	—
1972	—
1897	Charles Adams Platt, 1927 expansion
1941	Rafael Moneo (Spain), 2002 addition
1978	Gwathmey Siegel & Associates Architects with HMR Architects, Inc., 2010 expansion
1984	Edward Larrabee Barnes Associates, 1985 decorative arts wing and 1991 Nancy and Jake L. Hamon Building
1930	Levin Porter Associates, 1997 expansion
2005	—
1971	Studio Daniel Libeskind with Davis Partnership Architects, 2006 Frederic C. Hamilton Building
2006	—
1948	I.M. Pei & Associates, 1968 addition; Richard Meier & Partners Architects, 1985 addition
1888	Cret, Zantzinger, Borie and Medary, 1927 addition; Harley, Ellington, Cowin and Stirton, with Gunnar Birkerts and Associates, 1966 south wings; Harley, Ellington, Cowin and Stirton, 1966 north wing; Michael Graves & Associates with SmithGroup, 2007 expansion
1970	—
1968	—
2005	—
1927	—
1993	—
1971	Hugh Newell Jacobsen, 2005 Mary and Howard Lester Wing

Art Museums

Museum	Location	Architect (original)
Frederick R. Weisman Art Museum	Minneapolis, MN	Frank O. Gehry and Associates, Inc.
Freer Gallery Art	Washington, DC	Charles Adams Platt
Frist Center for the Visual Arts	Nashville, TN	Tuck Hinton Architects (adapted the 1934 US Post Office by Marr and Holman Architects)
Frost Art Museum, Florida International University	Miami, FL	Hellmuth, Obata & Kassabaum
Frye Art Museum	Seattle, WA	Paul Albert Thiry
Grand Rapids Art Museum	Grand Rapids, MI	wHY Architecture with Design Plus
Herbert F. Johnson Museum of Art	Ithaca, NY	I.M. Pei & Partners
High Museum of Art	Atlanta, GA	Richard Meier & Partners Architects
Hirshhorn Museum and Sculpture Garden	Washington, DC	Skidmore, Owings & Merrill
Hood Museum of Art	Hanover, NH	Charles Moore and Centerbrook Architects and Planners
Hunter Museum of American Art	Chattanooga, TN	Mead and Garfield (architects of the 1905 mansion adapted to a museum in 1952)
Indiana University Art Museum	Bloomington, IN	I.M. Pei & Partners
Indianapolis Museum of Art	Indianapolis, IN	Richardson, Severns, Scheeler and Associates
Institute for Contemporary Art	Boston, MA	Diller Scofidio + Renfro
Iris & B. Gerald Cantor Center for Visual Arts	Stanford, CA	Percy & Hamilton Architects with Ernest J. Ransome
J. Paul Getty Museum	Los Angeles, CA	Richard Meier & Partners Architects
Joslyn Art Museum	Omaha, NE	John and Alan McDonald
Kemper Museum of Contemporary Art and Design	Kansas City, MO	Gunnar Birkerts and Associates
Kimbell Art Museum	Fort Worth, TX	Louis I. Kahn
Kreeger Museum	Washington, DC	Philip Johnson with Richard Foster
Lois & Richard Rosenthal Center for Contemporary Art	Cincinnati, OH	Zaha Hadid Architects (UK) with KZF Design
Los Angeles County Museum of Art	Los Angeles, CA	William L. Pereira & Associates
Mead Art Museum	Amherst, MA	McKim, Mead and White
Memphis Brooks Museum of Art	Memphis, TN	James Gamble Rogers with Carl Gutherz

Opened	Architect (expansion)
1993	—
1923	—
2001	—
2008	
1952	Olson Sundberg Kundig Allen Architects, 1997 expansion
2007	—
1973	—
1983	Renzo Piano Building Workshop (Italy) with Lord, Aeck and Sargent, 2005 addition
1974	—
1985	—
1952	Derthick, Henley and Wilkerson Architects, 1975 addition; Randall Stout Architects with Derthick, Henley and Wilkerson Architects and Hefferlin + Kronenberg Architects, 2005 addition
1982	—
1970	Edward Larrabee Barnes Associates and John M.Y. Lee, 1990 Mary Fendrich Hulman Pavilion; Browning Day Mullins Dierdorf Architects, 2005 expansion
2006	—
1894	Polshek Partnership Architects, 1999 addition
1997	—
1931	Foster + Partners (UK), 1994 Walter and Suzanne Scott Pavilion
1994	—
1972	—
1967	—
2003	—
1965	Hardy Holzman Pfeiffer Associates, 1986 Art of the Americas Building; Bruce Goff, 1988 Pavilion for Japanese Art; Albert C. Martin and Associates, 1998 LACAMA West building (originally the 1946 May Co. building); Renzo Piano Building Workshop (Italy), 2008 Broad Contemporary Art Museum
1949	—
1916	Walk Jones and Francis Mah, 1973 addition; Skidmore, Owings & Merrill with Askew, Nixon, Ferguson & Wolf, 1989 expansion

Art Museums

Museum	Location	Architect (original)
Menil Collection	Houston, TX	Renzo Piano Building Workshop (Italy) with Richard Fitzgerald & Partners
Metropolitan Museum of Art	New York, NY	Calvert Vaux and J. Wrey Mould
Milwaukee Art Museum	Milwaukee, WI	Eero Saarinen with Maynard Meyer
Minneapolis Institute of Arts	Minneapolis, MN	McKim, Mead and White
Modern Art Museum of Fort Worth	Fort Worth, TX	Tadao Ando (Japan)
Munson-Williams-Proctor Arts Institute	Utica, NY	Philip Johnson
Museum of Arts and Design	New York, NY	Allied Works Architecture (renovated the 1965 building by Edward Durrell Stone & Associates)
Museum of Contemporary Art, Chicago	Chicago, IL	Josef Paul Kleihues (Germany)
Museum of Contemporary Art/Denver	Denver, CO	Adjaye Associates (UK)
Museum of Contemporary Art, Los Angeles (at California Plaza)	Los Angeles, CA	Arata Isozaki & Associates (Japan)
Museum of Contemporary Art, San Diego	La Jolla, CA	Irving Gill (originally designed as a residence in 1916)
Museum of Fine Arts, Boston	Boston, MA	Guy Lowell
Museum of Fine Arts, Houston	Houston, TX	William Ward Watkin
Museum of Fine Arts, St. Petersburg	St. Petersburg, FL	John L. Volk
Museum of Modern Art	New York, NY	Philip L. Goodwin and Edward Durrell Stone & Associates
Nasher Museum of Art	Durham, NC	Rafael Viñoly Architects
Nasher Sculpture Center	Dallas, TX	Renzo Piano Building Workshop (Italy) with Peter Walker and Partners
National Gallery of Art, East Building	Washington, DC	I.M. Pei & Partners
National Gallery of Art, West Building	Washington, DC	John Russell Pope

Opened	Architect (expansion)
1987	—
1880	Theodore Weston, 1888 SW wing; Richard Morris Hunt and Richard Howland Hunt, 1902 Central Fifth Avenue facade; McKim, Mead and White, 1906 side wings along Fifth Avenue; Brown, Lawford & Forbes, 1965 Thomas J. Watson Library; Kevin Roche John Dinkeloo & Associates, 1975 Lehman Wing, 1979 Sackler Wing, 1980 American Wing, 1981 Michael C. Rockefeller Wing for Primitive Art, 1988 European Sculpture and Decorative Art Wing
1957	Kahler, Fitzhugh and Scott, 1975 addition; Santiago Calatrava (Spain) with Kahler Slater, 2001 Quadracci Pavilion
1915	Kenzo Tange Associates (Japan), 1974 addition; Michael Graves & Associates with RSP Architects, 2006 Target Wing
2002	—
1960	Lund McGee Sharpe Architecture, 1995 Education Wing
2008	—
1996	—
2007	—
1986	—
1941	Mosher & Drew, 1950 transition to museum; Mosher & Drew, 1959 Sherwood Auditorium; Venturi, Scott Brown and Associates, 1996 expansion and renovation
1909	Guy Lowell, 1915 Robert Dawson Evans Wing; John Singer Sargent, 1921 Rotunda and 1925 Colonnade; Guy Lowell, 1928 Decorative Arts Wing; Hugh Stubbins & Associates, 1968 Forsyth Wickes Galleries and 1970 George Robert White Wing; I.M. Pei & Partners, 1981 West Wing; Foster + Partners (UK) with Childs Bertman Tseckares, 2010 Art of the Americas Wing and Ruth and Carl J. Shapiro Family Courtyard
1924–26	Kenneth Franzheim, 1953 Robert Lee Blaffer Memorial Wing; Mies van der Rohe, 1958 Cullinan Hall and 1974 Brown Pavilion; Isamu Noguchi (Japan), 1986 Lillie and Hugh Roy Cullen Sculpture Garden; Rafael Moneo (Spain), 2000 Audrey Jones Beck Building
1965	Hellmuth, Obata & Kassabaum, 2008 Hazel Hough Wing
1939	Philip Johnson, 1964 east wing; Cesar Pelli & Associates, 1984 tower; Taniguchi Associates (Japan) with Kohn Pedersen Fox and Cooper, Robertson & Partners, 2004 expansion and 2006 Lewis B. and Dorothy Cullman Education Building
2005	—
2003	—
1978	—
1941	—

Art Museums

Museum	Location	Architect (original)
National Portrait Gallery and American Art Museum	Washington, DC	Faulkner, Stenhouse, Fryer (adapted the 1836–67 Old Patent Office Building by Robert Mills and Thomas Ustick Walter)
Nelson Fine Arts Center	Tempe, AZ	Antoine Predock Architect
Nelson-Atkins Museum of Art	Kansas City, MO	Wight and Wight
Nevada Museum of Art	Reno, NV	will bruder + PARTNERS
New Museum of Contemporary Art	New York, NY	SANAA with Gensler
New Orleans Museum of Art	New Orleans, LA	Samuel Marx
North Carolina Museum of Art	Raleigh, NC	Edward Durell Stone
Oakland Museum of California	Oakland, CA	Kevin Roche John Dinkeloo & Associates
Ohr-O'Keefe Museum of Art	Biloxi, MS	Gehry Partners; Eley Guild Hardy Architects
Parrish Art Museum	Southampton, NY	Grosvenor Atterbury
Pennsylvania Academy of the Fine Arts	Philadelphia, PA	Frank Furness and George W. Hewitt
Philadelphia Museum of Art	Philadelphia, PA	Horace Trumbauer with Zantzinger, Borie, and Medar
Phoenix Art Museum	Phoenix, AZ	Alden B. Dow
Portland Art Museum	Portland, OR	Pietro Belluschi
Portland Museum of Art	Portland, ME	John Calvin Stevens
Princeton University Art Museum	Princeton, NJ	Ralph Adams Cram
Pulitzer Foundation for the Arts	St. Louis, MO	Tadao Ando (Japan)
Renwick Gallery	Washington, DC	James Renwick Jr.
Rodin Museum	Philadelphia, PA	Paul Philippe Cret and Jacques Gréber
Saint Louis Art Museum	St. Louis, MO	Cass Gilbert
San Diego Museum of Art	San Diego, CA	William Templeton Johnson with Robert W. Snyder
San Francisco Museum of Modern Art	San Francisco, CA	Mario Botta (Italy)
Santa Barbara Museum of Art	Santa Barbara, CA	David Adler (adapted the 1914 Old Post Office designed by Francis Wilson)
Seattle Art Museum	Seattle, WA	Venturi, Scott Brown and Associates
Shaw Center for the Arts	Baton Rouge, LA	Schwartz/Silver Architects with Eskew+Dumez+ Ripple and Jerry M. Campbell Associates
Sheldon Memorial Art Gallery	Lincoln, NE	Philip Johnson

Opened	Architect (expansion)
1968	Foster + Partners (UK) with SmithGroup, 2007 Robert and Arlene Kogod Courtyard
1989	—
1933	Steven Holl Architects with BNIM Architects, 2007 Bloch Building
2003	—
2007	—
1911	August Perez with Arthur Feitel, 1971 Wisner Education Wing, City Wing, and Stern Auditorium; Eskew Filson Architects with Billes/Manning Architects, 1993 expansion
1984	Thomas Phifer and Partners with Pierce Brinkley Cease + Lee, 2010 expansion
1969	—
2010	—
1897	Grosvenor Atterbury, 1902 and 1913 wings
1876	—
1928	Gluckman Mayner Architects, 2008 renovation of the Perelman Building (originally designed by Zantzinger, Borie, and Medary in 1927)
1959	Alden B. Dow, 1965 east wing; Tod Williams Billie Tsien Architects, 1996 and 2006 expansions
1932	Pietro Belluschi, 1939 Hirsch Wing; Pietro Belluschi, with Wolff, Zimmer, Gunsul, Frasca, and Ritter, 1970 Hoffman Wing; Ann Beha Architects, 2000 expansion; Ann Beha Architects with SERA Architects, 2005 expansion
1911	I.M. Pei & Partners, 1983 Charles Shipman Payson Building
1922	Steinman and Cain, 1966 expansion; Mitchell	Giurgola Architects, 1989 Mitchell Wolfson Jr. Wing
2001	
1859	John Carl Warnecke & Associates and Hugh Newell Jacobsen, 1971 restoration
1929	
1903	
1926	Robert Mosher & Roy Drew, Architects, 1966 west wing; Mosher, Drew, Watson & Associates with William Ferguson, 1974 east wing
1995	
1941	Chester Carjola, 1942 Katherine Dexter McCormick Wing; Arendt/Mosher/Grants Architects, 1961 Preston Morton Wing and 1962 Sterling Morton Wing; Paul Gray, 1985 Alice Keck Park Wing; Edwards & Pitman, 1998 Peck Wing
1991	Allied Works Architecture with NBBJ, 2007 expansion
2005	—
1963	—

* The museum opened in 1994, but all of its former buildings were destroyed in Hurricane Katrina.

Art Museums

Museum	Location	Architect (original)
Solomon R. Guggenheim Museum	New York, NY	Frank Lloyd Wright
Speed Art Museum	Louisville, KY	Arthur Loomis
Sterling and Francine Clark Art Institute	Wiliamstown, MA	Daniel Perry
Tacoma Art Museum	Tacoma, WA	Antoine Predock Architect with Olson Sundberg Kundig Allen Architects
Tampa Museum of Art	Tampa, FL	Natoma Architects
Taubman Museum of Art	Roanoke, VA	Randall Stout Architects with Rodriguez Ripley Maddux Motley Architects
Terra Museum of American Art	Chicago, IL	Booth Hansen Associates
Toledo Museum of Art	Toledo, OH	Green & Wicks with Harry W. Wachter
UCLA Hammer Museum of Art	Los Angeles, CA	Edward Larrabee Barnes Associates
University of Michigan Museum of Art	Ann Arbor, MI	Donaldson and Meier Architects
Virginia Museum of Fine Arts	Richmond, VA	Peebles and Ferguson Architects
Wadsworth Atheneum Museum of Art	Hartford, CT	Ithiel Town and Alexander Jackson Davis
Walker Art Center	Minneapolis, MN	Edward Larrabee Barnes Associates
Wexner Center for the Arts	Columbus, OH	Eisenman Architects with Richard Trott & Partners
Whitney Museum of American Art	New York, NY	Marcel Breuer and Associates
Yale Center for British Art	New Haven, CT	Louis I. Kahn
Yale University Art Gallery	New Haven, CT	Louis I. Kahn

Source: DesignIntelligence

Opened	Architect (expansion)
1959	Gwathmey Siegel & Associates Architects, 1992 addition
1927	Nevin and Morgan, 1954 Preston Pope Satterwhite Wing; Brenner, Danforth, and Rockwell, 1973 north wing; Robert Geddes, 1983 south wing
1955	Pietro Belluschi and The Architects Collaborative, 1973 addition; Tadao Ando Architect & Associates (Japan) and Gensler, 2008 Stone Hill Center
2003	—
2010	—
2008	—
1987	—
1912	Edward B. Green and Sons, 1926 wing and 1933 expansion; Frank O. Gehry and Associates, Inc., 1992 Center for the Visual Arts addition; SANAA (Japan), 2006 Glass Pavilion
1990	—
1910	Allied Works Architecture with IDS, 2009 Maxine and Stuart Frankel and Frankel Family Wing
1936	Merrill C. Lee, Architects, 1954 addition; Baskervill & Son Architects, 1970 South Wing; Hardwicke Associates, Inc., 1976 North Wing; Hardy Holzman Pfeiffer Associates, 1985 West Wing; Rick Mather Architect (UK) with SMBW, 2010 addition
1844	Benjamin Wistar Morris, 1910 Colt Memorial and 1915 Morgan Memorial; Morris & O'Connor, 1934 Avery Memorial; Huntington, Darbee & Dollard, Architects, 1969 Goodwin Wing
1971	Herzog & de Meuron (Switzerland) with Hammel, Green and Abrahamson, 2005 expansion
1989	—
1966	Gluckman Mayner Architects, 1998 expansion
1977	—
1953	—

Convention Centers

In the past decade public spending on convention centers has doubled to $2.4 billion annually, and since 1990 convention space in the US has increased by more than 50 percent. The following is *DesignIntelligence*'s list of the largest US convention centers with their requisite architectural statistics.

Convention Center	Location	Opened	Exhibit Halls (sq. ft.)
America's Center	St. Louis, MO	1977	502,000
AmericasMart Atlanta	Atlanta, GA	1961	800,000
Anaheim Convention Center	Anaheim, CA	1967	815,000
Atlantic City Convention Center	Atlantic City, NJ	1997	518,300
Austin Convention Center	Austin, TX	1992	246,097
Baltimore Convention Center	Baltimore, MD	1979	300,000
Boston Convention and Exhibition Center	Boston, MA	2004	516,000
Charlotte Convention Center	Charlotte, NC	1995	280,000
Cobo Conference/Exhibition Center	Detroit, MI	1960	700,000
Colorado Convention Center	Denver, CO	1990	584,000
Dallas Convention Center	Dallas, TX	1973	726,726
David L. Lawrence Convention Center	Pittsburgh, PA	2003	313,400
Donald E. Stephens Convention Center	Rosemont, IL	1974	840,000
Ernest N. Morial Convention Center	New Orleans, LA	1985	1.1 M
Fort Worth Convention Center	Fort Worth, TX	1968	253,226

Architect (original)	Architect (expansion)
Hellmuth, Obata & Kassabaum	Hellmuth, Obata & Kassabaum, 1993 and 1995 expansions
Edwards and Portman, Architects (Merchandise Mart)	Edwards and Portman, Architects, 1968 Merchandise Mart addition; John Portman & Associates, Architects, 1979 Apparel Mart, 1986 Merchandise Mart addition, 1989 Apparel Mart addition, 1992 Gift Mart; John Portman & Associates, 2009 Building 2 WestWing
Adrian Wilson & Associates	HNTB Architecture, 1974, 1982, 1990, and 1993 expansions; HOK Sport + Venue + Event, 1999–2001 expansion
Wallace Roberts & Todd	—
PageSoutherlandPage	Austin Collaborative Venture (PageSoutherlandPage; Cotera Kolar Negrete & Reed Architects; Limbacher & Godfrey Architects), 2002 expansion
NBBJ with Cochran, Stephenson & Donkervoet expansion	LMN Architects with Cochran, Stephenson & Donkervoet, 1996
HNTB Architecture/Rafael Viñoly Architects, joint venture	—
Thompson, Ventulett, Stainback & Associates with The FWA Group	—
Giffels & Rossetti	Sims-Varner & Associates, 1989 expansion
Fentress Bradburn Architects	Fentress Bradburn Architects, 2004 expansion
Harrell + Hamilton Architects (adapted and expanded the 1957 Dallas Memorial Auditorium by George L. Dahl Architects and Engineers Inc.)	Omniplan, 1984 expansion; JPJ Architects, 1994 expansion; Skidmore, Owings & Merrill and HKS, Inc., 2002 expansion
Rafael Viñoly Architects	—
Anthony M. Rossi Limited	Anthony M. Rossi Limited, subsequent expansions
Perez & Associates and Perkins & James	Perez & Associates and Billes/Manning Architects, 1991 expansion; Convention Center III Architects (Cimini, Meric, Duplantier Architects/Planners, Billes/Manning Architects, and Hewitt Washington & Associates), 1999 expansion
Parker Croston	Carter & Burgess, Inc. and HOK Sport + Venue + Event, 2003 addition

Convention Centers

Convention Center	Location	Opened	Exhibit Halls (sq. ft.)
George R. Brown Convention Center	Houston, TX	1987	893,590
Georgia World Congress Center	Atlanta, GA	1976	1.4 M
Greater Columbus Convention Center	Columbus, OH	1993	426,000
Hawaii Convention Center	Honolulu, HI	1996	204,249
Henry B. Gonzalez Convention Center	San Antonio, TX	1968	440,000
Indianapolis Convention Center & RCA Dome	Indianapolis, IN	1972	308,700
Jacob K. Javits Convention Center	New York, NY	1986	814,000
Kansas City Convention Center	Kansas City, MO	1976	388,800
Las Vegas Convention Center	Las Vegas, NV	1959	2 M
Long Beach Convention & Entertainment Center	Long Beach, CA	1978	224,000
Los Angeles Convention Center	Los Angeles, CA	1972	720,000
Mandalay Bay Convention Center	Las Vegas, NV	2003	934,731
McCormick Place	Chicago, IL	1971	2.6 M
Miami Beach Convention Center	Miami Beach, FL	1958	503,000

Architect (original)	Architect (expansion)
Goleman & Rolfe Associates, Inc.; John S. Chase; Molina & Associates; Haywood Jordan McCowan, Inc.; Moseley Architects with Bernard Johnson and 3D/International	Golemon & Bolullo Architects, 2003 expansion
Thompson, Ventulett, Stainback & Associates	Thompson, Ventulett, Stainback & Associates, 1985 and 1992 expansions; Thompson, Ventulett, Stainback & Associates with Heery International, 2003 expansion
Eisenman Architects with Richard Trott & Partners	Eisenman Architects, Karlsberger, and Thompson, Ventulett, Stainback & Associates, 2001 expansion
LMN Architects with Wimberly Allison Tong & Goo	—
Noonan and Krocker; Phelps and Simmons and Associates	Cerna Raba & Partners, 1986 expansion; Thompson, Ventulett, Stainback & Associates with Kell Muñoz Architects and Haywood Jordon McCowan, Inc., 2001 expansion
Lennox, James and Loebl (Lennox, Matthews, Simmons and Ford; James Associates; Loebl Schlossman Bennett & Dart)	Blackburn Architects and Browning Day Mullins Dierdorf Architects with Hellmuth, Obata & Kassabaum, 1993 and 2001 expansions
I.M. Pei & Partners	—
C.F. Murphy Associates with Seligson Associates, Hormer and Blessing, and Howard Needles Tammen & Bergendoff	Convention Center Associates, Architects; BNIM Architects; HNTB Architecture, 1994 expansion
Adrian Wilson & Associates with Harry Whitney Consulting Architect	Jack Miller & Associates, 1967 South Hall; Adrian Wilson & Associates, 1971 C3 expansion; Jack Miller & Associates, 1975 C4 expansion; JMA, 1980 C5 expansion and 1990 expansion; Domingo Cambeiro Corp. Architects, 1998 North Hall and 2002 South Hall
Killingsworth, Brady, Smith and Associates	Thompson, Ventulett, Stainback & Associates, 1994 expansion
Charles Luckman & Associates	Pei Cobb Freed & Partners with Gruen Associates, 1993 expansion; Gruen Associates, 1997 Kentia Hall addition
Klai Juba Architects	—
C.F. Murphy Associates	Skidmore, Ownings & Merrill, 1986 North Hall; Thompson, Ventulett, Stainback & Associates with Architects Enterprise, 1996 South Hall; Thompson, Ventulett, Stainback & Associates and Mc4West, 2007 West Hall
B. Robert Swartburg	Gilbert M. Fein, 1968 Hall D; Edward Durrell Stone & Associates, Gilbert M. Fein, and Watson, Deutschmann, Kruse & Lyon, 1974 addition; Thompson, Ventulett, Stainback & Associates with Borrelli, Frankel, Biltstein, 1989 and 1991 expansions

Convention Centers

Convention Center	Location	Opened	Exhibit Halls (sq. ft.)
Minneapolis Convention Center	Minneapolis, MN	1989–91	475,000
Moscone Center	San Francisco, CA	1981	741,308
Orange County Convention Center	Orlando, FL	1983	2.1 M
Oregon Convention Center	Portland, OR	1990	315,000
Pennsylvania Convention Center	Philadelphia, PA	1993	440,000
Phoenix Convention Center	Phoenix, AZ	1985	502,500
Reliant Center	Houston, TX	2004	706,213
Reno-Sparks Convention Center	Reno, NV	1965	381,000
Salt Palace Convention Center	Salt Lake City, UT	1996	515,000
San Diego Convention Center	San Diego, CA	1989	615,701
Tampa Convention Center	Tampa, FL	1990	200,000
Washington Convention Center	Washington, DC	2003	703,000
Washington State Convention and Trade Center	Seattle, WA	1988	205,700

Source: DesignIntelligence

Architect (original)	Architect (expansion)
Leonard Parker Associates; Setter Leach & Lindstrom; LMN Architects	Convention Center Design Group (Leonard Parker Associates; Setter Leach & Lindstrom; LMN Architects), 2001 expansion
Hellmuth, Obata & Kassabaum	Gensler/DMJM Associate Architects, joint venture, 1992 North Hall; Gensler/Michael Willis Architects/Kwan Henmi, joint venture, 2003 West Hall
Helman Hurley Charvat Peacock/Architects, Inc.	Hellmuth, Obata & Kassabaum and Vickey/Ovresat Assumb Associates, Inc., 1989-90 expansion; Hunton Brady Pryor Maso Architects and Thompson, Ventulett, Stainback & Associates, 1996 expansion; Helman Hurley Charvat Peacock/Architects, Thompson, Ventulett, Stainback & Associates, Inc. and Hunton Brady Pryor Maso Architects, 2003 expansion
Zimmer Gunsul Frasca Partnership	Zimmer Gunsul Frasca Architects, 2003 expansion
Thompson, Ventulett & Stainback Associates with VITETTA and Kelly/Maiello Architects and Planners (including the adaption of the 1893 Reading Terminal Headhouse by Wilson Brothers and F.H. Kimball)	—
GSAS Architects and Planners, Inc. with Howard Needles Tammen & Bergendoff	LEO A DALY/HOK Sport + Venue + Event with van Dijk Westlake Reed Leskosky, 2006 expansion; HOK Sport + Venue + Event and SmithGroup, 2008 North Building
Hermes Reed Architects	—
Richard Neutra with Lockard, Casazza & Parsons	Parsons Design Group, 1981 North Hall; Sheehan, Van Woert Architects, 1991 East Hall; LMN Architects, 2002 expansion
Thompson, Ventulett, Stainback & Associates with GSBS Architects	Leonard Parker Associates with MHTB Architects, 2000 expansion; Edwards & Daniels Architects, Inc., 2006 expansion
Arthur Erickson Architect with Deems Lewis McKinley	HNTB Architecture with Tucker Sadler Architects, 2002 expansion
Hellmuth, Obata & Kassabaum	—
TVS–D&P–Mariani PLLC (Thompson, Ventulett, Stainback & Associates; Devrouax & Purnell Architects; and Mariani Architects Engineers)	—
TRA Architects	LMN Architects, 2001 expansion

Minor League Ballparks

Half of today's AAA ballparks were built within the last 10 years, and baseball's other minor leagues have also seen quite a bit of building activity, their increasingly sophisticated ballpark designs following the trend of the major leagues. The following charts list all the AAA ballparks and their requisite architectural statistics, as well as other minor-league ballparks that have opened since 2000.

AAA Ballparks

Team	League/Affiliation	Stadium	Location
Albuquerque Isotopes	Pacific Coast/Los Angeles Dodgers	Isotopes Park	Albuquerque, NM
Buffalo Bisons	International/New York Mets	Coca-Cola Field	Buffalo, NY
Charlotte Knights	International/Chicago White Sox	Knights Stadium	Fort Mill, SC
Colorado Springs Sky Sox	Pacific Coast/Colorado Rockies	Security Services Field	Colorado Springs, CO
Columbus Clippers	International/Cleveland Indians	Huntington Park	Columbus, OH
Durham Bulls	International/Tampa Bay Rays	Durham Bulls Athletic Park	Durham, NC
Fresno Grizzlies	Pacific Coast/San Francisco Giants	Chukchansi Park	Fresno, CA
Gwinnett Braves	International/Atlanta Braves	Gwinnett Stadium	Lawrenceville, GA
Indianapolis Indians	International/Pittsburgh Pirates	Victory Field	Indianapolis, IN
Iowa Cubs	Pacific Coast/Chicago Cubs	Principal Park	Des Moines, IA
Lehigh Valley IronPigs	International/Philadelphia Phillies	Coca-Cola Park	Allentown, PA
Las Vegas 51s	Pacific Coast/Toronto Blue Jays	Cashman Field	Las Vegas, NV
Louisville Bats	International/Cincinnati Reds	Louisville Slugger Field	Louisville, KY
Memphis Redbirds	Pacific Coast/St. Louis Cardinals	AutoZone Park	Memphis, TN
Nashville Sounds	Pacific Coast/Milwaukee Brewers	Herschel Greer Stadium	Nashville, TN
New Orleans Zephyrs	Pacific Coast/Florida Marlins	Zephyr Field	New Orleans, LA
Norfolk Tides	International/Baltimore Orioles	Harbor Park	Norfolk, VA
Oklahoma City RedHawks	Pacific Coast/Texas Rangers	AT&T Bricktown Ballpark	Oklahoma City, OK
Omaha Royals	Pacific Coast/Kansas City Royals	Rosenblatt Stadium	Omaha, NE
Pawtucket Red Sox	International/Boston Red Sox	McCoy Stadium	Pawtucket, RI
Portland Beavers	Pacific Coast/San Diego Padres	PGE Park	Portland, OR

Architect	Opened	Cost (original)	Capacity (current)	Naming Rights (amt. & expiration)
HOK Sport + Venue + Event	2003	$25 M	11,075	—
HOK Sports Facilities Group	1988	$40 M	21,050	Undisclosed
Odell	1990	$12 M	10,002	—
HNTB Architecture	1988	$3.7 M	8,500	$1.5 M (12 yrs.)
360 Architecture	2009	$56 M	10,000	$12 M (23 yrs.)
HOK Sports Facilities Group	1995	$16 M	10,000	—
HOK Sport + Venue + Event	2002	$46 M	12,500	$16 M (15 yrs.)
HKS, Inc.	2009	$64 M	10,099	—
HOK Sports Facilities Group	1996	$18 M	15,696	—
HOK Sports Facilities Group	1992	$11.5 M	11,000	$2.5 M (Indefinite)
HOK Sport + Venue + Event	2008	$48.4 M	10,000	Undisclosed
Tate & Snyder	1983	$26 M	9,334	—
HNTB Architecture and K. Norman Berry & Associates	2000	$26 M	13,131	—
Looney Ricks Kiss with HOK Sports Facilities Group	2000	$46 M	14,320	$4.5 M (15 yrs.)
Stoll-Reed Architects Inc.	1977	$1 M	10,130	—
HOK Sports Facilities Group	1997	$25 M	10,000	—
HOK Sports Facilities Group	1993	$16 M	12,067	—
Architectural Design Group	1998	$32.4 M	13,066	Undisclosed
LEO A DALY	1948	$750,000	21,871	—
Mark Linenthal and Thomas E. Harding (Heery International, 1999 renovation)	1942	$1.2 M ($16 M, 1999 renovation)	10,031	—
A.E. Doyle (Ellerbe Becket with Fletcher Farr Ayotte, 2001 renovation)	1926	$502,000 ($38.5 M, 2001 renovation)	18,000	$7.1 M (10 yrs.)

Minor League Ballparks

AAA Ballparks

Team	League/Affiliation	Stadium	Location
Reno Aces	Pacific Coast/Arizona Diamondbacks	Aces Ballpark	Reno, NV
Rochester Red Wings	International/Minnesota Twins	Frontier Field	Rochester, NY
Round Rock Express	Pacific Coast/Houston Astros	Dell Diamond	Round Rock, TX
Sacramento River Cats	Pacific Coast/Oakland A's	Raley Field	Sacramento, CA
Salt Lake Bees	Pacific Coast/Los Angeles Angels of Anaheim	Spring Mobile Ballpark	Salt Lake City, UT
Scranton-Wilkes Barre Yankees	International/New York Yankees	PNC Field	Moosic, PA
Syracuse Chiefs	International/Washington Nationals	Alliance Bank Stadium	Syracuse, NY
Tacoma Rainiers	Pacific Coast/Seattle Mariners	Cheney Stadium	Tacoma, WA
Toledo Mud Hens	International/Detriot Tigers	Fifth Third Field	Toledo, OH

Other New Minor League Ballparks: 2000–2010

Team	League/Affiliation	Stadium	Location
Aberdeen IronBirds	Class A New York-Penn League/ Baltimore Orioles	Ripken Stadium	Little Aberdeen, MD
Arkansas Travelers	Class AA Texas League/Los Angeles Angeles of Anaheim	Dickey-Stephens Park	North Little Rock, AR
Bowling Green Hot Rods	Class A Midwest League/ Tampa Bay Rays	Bowling Green Ballpark	Bowling Green, KY
Brooklyn Cyclones	Class A New York-Penn League/ New York Mets	MCU Park	Brooklyn, NY
Camden Riversharks	Independent Atlantic League	Campbell's Field	Camden, NJ
Casper Ghosts	Rookie Pioneer Leaguo/ Colorado Rockies	Mike Lansing Field	Casper, WY
Cedar Rapids Kernels	Class A Midwest League/ Los Angeles Angels of Anaheim	Veterans Memorial Stadium	Cedar Rapids, IA
Chattanooga Lookouts	Class AA Southern League/ Los Angeles Dodgers	AT&T Field	Chattanooga, TN
Clearwater Threshers	Class A Florida State League/ Philadelphia Phillies	Bright House Field	Clearwater, FL
Corpus Christi Hooks	Class AA Texas League/ Houston Astros	Whataburger Field	Corpus Christi, TX

Architect	Opened	Cost (original)	Capacity (current)	Naming Rights (amt. & expiration)
HNTB Architecture	2009	$50 M	9,100	—
Ellerbe Beckett	1997	$35.3 M	10,868	$3.5 M (20 yrs.)
HKS, Inc.	2002	$25 M	9,816	$2.5 M (15 yrs.)
HNTB Architecture	2000	$40 M	11,092	$15 M (20 yrs.)
HOK Sports Facilities Group	1994	$22 M	15,500	Undisclosed
GSGS&B	1989	$25 M	11,432	$1.1 M (3 yrs.)
HOK Sports Facilities Group	1997	$16 M	11,602	$2.8 M (20 yrs.)
E.L Mills & Associates	1960	$940,000	9,600	—
HNTB Architecture	2002	$39.2 M	10,000	$5 M (15 yrs.)

Architect	Opened	Cost (original)	Capacity (current)	Naming Rights (amt. & expiration)
Tetra Tech, Inc.	2002	$35 M	6,000	—
HKS, Inc.	2007	$40.4 M	5,288	—
DLR Group	2009	$28 M	4,559	—
Jack L. Gordon Architects	2001	$35 M	8,000	Undisclosed
Clarke, Caton and Hintz	2001	$20.5 M	6,425	$3 M (10 yrs.)
GSG Architecture	2001	$4 M	2,500	—
Heinlein Schrock Stearns	2002	$14 M	6,100	—
DLR Group with TWH Architects	2000	$10 M	6,157	$1 M (10 yrs.)
HOK Sport + Venue + Event with EwingCole	2004	$32 M	7,000	$1.7 M (10 yrs.)
HKS, Inc.	2005	$27.7 M	8,255	Undisclosed

Minor League Ballparks

Other New Minor League Ballparks: 2000–2010

Team	League/Affiliation	Stadium	Location
Dayton Dragons	Class A Midwest League/ Cincinnati Reds	Fifth Third Field	Dayton, OH
Eugene Emeralds San Diego Padres	Class A Northwest League/	PK Park	Eugene, OR
Fort Wayne TinCaps	Class A Midwest League/ San Diego Padres	Parkview Field	Fort Wayne, IN
Frisco RoughRiders	Class AA Texas League/ Texas Rangers	Dr Pepper Ballpark	Frisco, TX
Gary SouthShore RailCats	Independent Northern League	U.S. Steel Yard	Gary, IN
Great Lakes Loons	Class A Midwest League/ Los Angeles Dodgers	Dow Diamond	Midland, MI
Greensboro Grasshoppers	Class A South Atlantic League/ Florida Marlins	NewBridge Bank Park	Greensboro, SC
Greenville Drive	Class A South Atlantic League/ Boston Red Sox	Fluor Field at the West End	Greenville, SC
Idaho Falls Chukars	Rookie Pioneer League/ Kansas City Royals	Melaleuca Field	Idaho Falls, ID
Jacksonville Suns	Class AA Southern League/ Florida Marlins	Baseball Grounds of Jacksonville	Jacksonville, FL
Joliet Jackhammers	Independent Northern League	Silver Cross Field	Joliet, IL
Kansas City T-Bones	Independent Northern League	CommunityAmerica Ballpark	Kansas City, KS
Lake County Captains	Class A Midwest League/ Cleveland Indians	Classic Park	Eastlake, OH
Lake Erie Crushers	Independent Frontier League	All-Pro Freight Stadium	Avon, OH
Lakewood BlueClaws	Class A South Atlantic/ Philadelphia Phillies	FirstEnergy Park	Lakewood, NJ
Lancaster Barnstormers	Independent Atlantic League	Clipper Magazine Stadium	Lancaster, PA
Lexington Legends	Class A South Atlantic League/ Houston Astros	Applebee's Park	Lexington, KY
Lincoln Saltdogs	Independent American Association	Haymarket Park	Lincoln, NE
Long Island Ducks	Independent Atlantic League	Citibank Park	Central Islip, NY
Midland RockHounds	Class AA Texas League/Oakland A's	Citibank Ballpark	Midland, TX

Architect	Opened	Cost (original)	Capacity (current)	Naming Rights (amt. & expiration)
HNTB Architecture	2000	$22.7 M	7,250	Undisclosed
DLR Group	2009	$19.2 M	4,000	—
Populous	2009	$30.6 M	8,100	$3 M (10 yrs.)
David M. Schwarz Architects, with HKS, Inc.	2003	$28 M	10,600	Undisclosed
HNTB Architecture	2003	$45 M	6,000	Undisclosed
HOK Sport + Venue + Event	2007	$28 M	5,500	—
Moser Mayer Phoenix Associates	2005	$20 M	5,021	$3 M (10 yrs.)
DLR Group	2006	$14.5 M	5,700	Undisclosed
Elliott Workgroup Architects	2007	$5.6 M	3,400	600,000
HOK Sport + Venue + Event	2003	$34 M	10,000	—
Sink Combs Dethlefs	2002	$27 M	6,915	$1.5 M (10 yrs.)
Heinlein Schrock Stearns	2003	$15 M	5,500	Undisclosed
DLR Group	2003	$19.5 M	7,273	$4.26 M (15 yrs.)
OSports	2009	$12.1 M	5,000	Undisclosed
HNTB Architecture	2001	$20 M	6,588	$4.5 M (20 yrs.)
Tetra Tech, Inc.	2005	$23.4 M	6,500	$2.5 M (10 yrs.)
Brisbin Brook Beynon Architects (Canada)	2001	$13.5 M	6,994	$3 M (10 yrs.)
DLR Group	2001	$32 M	4,500	—
HNTB Architecture with Beatty Harvey Associates, Architects	2000	$14 M	6,200	Undisclosed
HOK Sport + Venue + Event	2002	$25 M	5,000	$2.1 M (25 yrs.)

Minor League Ballparks

Other New Minor League Ballparks: 2000–2010

Team	League/Affiliation	Stadium	Location
Mississippi Braves	Class AA Southern League/ Atlanta Braves	Trustmark Park	Pearl, MS
Missoula Osprey	Rookie Pioneer League/ Arizona Diamondbacks	Ogren Park at Allegiance Field	Missoula, MT
Montgomery Biscuits	Class AA Southern League/ Tampa Bay Rays	Montgomery Riverwalk Stadium	Montgomery, AL
New Hampshire Fisher Cats	Class AA Eastern League/ Toronto Blue Jays	Merchantsauto.com Stadium	Manchester, NH
Northwest Arkansas Naturals	Class AA Texas League/ Kansas City Royals	Arvest Ballpark	Springdale, AR
Peoria Chiefs	Class A Midwest League/ Chicago Cubs	O'Brien Field	Peoria, IL
Rockford RiverHawks	Independent Northern League	Road Ranger Stadium	Loves Park, IL
Rome Braves	Class A South Atlantic/ Atlanta Braves	State Mutual Stadium	Rome, GA
Southern Illinois Miners	Independent Frontier League	Rent One Park	Marion, IL
Springfield Cardinals	Class AA Texas League/ St. Louis Cardinals	Hammons Field	Springfield, MO
State College Spikes	Class A New York-Penn League/ Pittsburgh Pirates	Medlar Field at Lubrano Park	University Park, PA
Staten Island Yankees	Class A New York-Penn League/ New York Yankees	Richmond County Bank Ballpark at St. George	Staten Island, NY
Stockton Ports	Class A California League/ Oakland A's	Banner Island Ballpark	Stockton, CA
Tennessee Smokies	Class AA Southern League/ Chicago Cubs	Smokies Park	Kodak, TN
Traverse City Beach Bums	Independent Frontier League	Wuerfel Park	Traverse City, MI
Tri-City ValleyCats	Class A New York-Penn League/ Houston Astros	Joseph L. Bruno Stadium	Troy, NY
Tulsa Drillers	Class AA Texas League/ Colorado Rockies	ONEOK Field	Tulsa, OK
West Viginia Power	Class A South Atlantic League/ Pittsburgh Pirates	Appalachian Power Park	Charleston, WV
Winston-Salem Dash	Class A Carolina League/ Chicago White Sox	BB&T Ballpark	Winston-Salem, NC
York Revolution	Independent Atlantic League	Sovereign Bank Stadium	York, PA

Architect	Opened	Cost (original)	Capacity (current)	Naming Rights (amt. & expiration)
HOK Sport + Venue + Event with Dale and Associates Architects	2005	$25 M	7,062	$25 M (10 yrs.)
Heery International with CTA Architects	2004	$10.2 M	3,500	$1 M
HOK Sport + Venue + Event	2004	$26 M	7,000	—
HNTB Architecture	2005	$20 M	7,000	Undisclosed
HOK Sport + Venue + Event	2008	$32 M	6,500	Undisclosed
HNTB Architecture	2000	$24 M	7,500	—
CSHQA	2005	$7 M	4,000	Undisclosed
Brisbin Brook Beynon Architects (Canada)	2003	$14.8 M	6,100	Undisclosed
360 Architecture	2007	$18 M	4,380	Undisclosed
Pellham Phillips Hagerman	2004	$32 M	8,056	—
L. Robert Kimball & Associates; DLR Group	2006	$24 M	6,000	—
HOK Sport + Venue + Event	2001	$34 M	6,886	Undisclosed
HKS, Inc.	2005	$14.5 M	5,000	—
HNTB Architecture	2000	$20 M	6,412	—
Fuller Nichols Architects	2006	$8 M	3,518	—
DLR Group	2002	$14 M	4,500	—
Populous	2010	$39.2 M	7,833	$5 M (20 yrs.)
HNTB Architecture	2005	$23 M	4,500	$1.25 M (10 yrs.)
360 Architecture	2010	$48.7 M	5,500	Undisclosed
Tetra Tech, Inc.; Murphy and Dittenhafer	2007	$32.5 M	5,200	$2.7 (10 yrs.)

Sports Stadiums

From classic ballparks to cutting-edge arenas and stadiums, the following charts provide statistical and architectural highlights for all major-league baseball, basketball, football, and hockey venues in the United States. All cost and architectural information refers to the stadiums as they were originally built and does not include additions, renovations, or expansions.

Baseball

Team	League	Stadium	Location	Opened
Arizona Diamondbacks	National	Chase Field	Phoenix, AZ	1998
Atlanta Braves	National	Turner Field	Atlanta, GA	1997
Baltimore Orioles	American	Oriole Park at Camden Yards	Baltimore, MD	1992
Boston Red Sox	American	Fenway Park	Boston, MA	1912
Chicago Cubs	National	Wrigley Field	Chicago, IL	1914
Chicago White Sox	American	U.S. Cellular Field	Chicago, IL	1991
Cincinnati Reds	National	Great American Ball Park	Cincinnati, OH	2003
Cleveland Indians	American	Progressive Field	Cleveland, OH	1994
Colorado Rockies	National	Coors Field	Denver, CO	1995
Detroit Tigers	American	Comerica Park	Detroit, MI	2000
Florida Marlins	National	Sun Life Stadium	Miami, FL	1987
Houston Astros	National	Minute Maid Park	Houston, TX	2000
Kansas City Royals	American	Kauffman Stadium	Kansas City, MO	1973
Los Angeles Angels of Anaheim	American	Angel Stadium of Anaheim	Anaheim, CA	1966
Los Angeles Dodgers	National	Dodger Stadium	Los Angeles, CA	1962
Milwaukee Brewers	National	Miller Park	Milwaukee, WI	2001
Minnesota Twins	American	Target Field	Minneapolis, MN	2010
New York Mets	National	Citi Field	Flushing, NY	2009
New York Yankees	American	Yankee Stadium	Bronx, NY	2009
Oakland A's	American	McAfee Coliseum	Oakland, CA	1966
Philadelphia Phillies	National	Citizens Bank Park	Philadelphia, PA	2004
Pittsburgh Pirates	National	PNC Park	Pittsburgh, PA	2001

Architect	Cost (original)	Capacity (current)	Roof Type	Naming Rights (amt. & expiration)
Ellerbe Becket with Bill Johnson	$355 M	49,033	Convertible	$33.1 M (30 yrs.)
Heery International; Williams-Russell & Johnson, Inc.; Ellerbe Becket	$250 M	49,831	Open-Air	Undisclosed
HOK Sports Facilities Group with RTKL Associates Inc.	$210 M	48,876	Open-Air	—
Osborn Engineering Company	$365,000	33,871	Open-Air	—
Zachary Taylor Davis	$250,000	38,765	Open-Air	—
HOK Sports Facilities Group	$150 M	44,321	Open-Air	$68 M (20 yrs.)
HOK Sport + Venue + Event with GBBN Architects	$290 M	42,053	Open-Air	$75 M (30 yrs.)
HOK Sports Facilities Group	$173 M	43,345	Open-Air	$54 M (15 yrs.)
HOK Sports Facilities Group	$215 M	50,445	Open-Air	$15 M (indefinite)
HOK Sports Facilities Group; SHG Inc.	$300 M	40,637	Open-Air	$66 M (30 yrs.)
HOK Sports Facilities Group	$125 M	47,662	Open-Air	$20 M (5 yrs.)
HOK Sports Facilities Group	$248.1 M	40,950	Retractable	$170 M (28 yrs.)
HNTB Architecture	$50.45 M	40,625	Open-Air	—
Robert A.M. Stern Architects	$25 M	45,050	Open-Air	—
Emil Praeger	$24.47 M	56,000	Open-Air	—
HKS, Inc. with NBBJ and Eppstein Uhen Architects	$399.4 M	42,500	Retractable	$41 M (20 yrs.)
Populous	$545 M	39,504	Open-Air	Undisclosed
Populous	$660 M	41,800	Open-Air	$400 M (20 yrs.)
Populous	$1.5 B	52,325	Open-Air	—
Skidmore, Owings & Merrill	$25.5 M	48,219	Open-Air	$6 M (5 yrs.)
EwingCole with HOK Sport + Venue + Event	$346 M	43,000	Open-Air	$57.5 M (25 yrs.)
HOK Sport + Venue + Event; L.D. Astorino Companies	$262 M	38,000	Open-Air	$30 M (20 yrs.)

Sports Stadiums

Baseball

Team	League	Stadium	Location	Opened
San Diego Padres	National	Petco Park	San Diego, CA	2004
San Francisco Giants	National	AT&T Park	San Francisco, CA	2000
Seattle Mariners	American	Safeco Field	Seattle, WA	1999
St. Louis Cardinals	National	Busch Stadium	St. Louis, MO	2006
Tampa Bay Rays	American	Tropicana Field	St. Petersburg, FL	1990
Texas Rangers	American	Rangers Ballpark in Arlington	Arlington, TX	1994
Toronto Blue Jays	American	Rogers Centre	Toronto, ON, Canada	1989
Washington Nationals	National	Nationals Park	Washington, DC	2008

Basketball

Team	Conference	Stadium	Location	Opened
Atlanta Hawks	Eastern	Philips Arena	Atlanta, GA	1999
Boston Celtics	Eastern	TD Garden	Boston, MA	1995
Charlotte Bobcats	Eastern	Time Warner Cable Arena	Charlotte, NC	2005
Chicago Bulls	Eastern	United Center	Chicago, IL	1994
Cleveland Cavaliers	Eastern	Quicken Loans Arena	Cleveland, OH	1994
Dallas Mavericks	Western	American Airlines Center	Dallas, TX	2001
Denver Nuggets	Western	Pepsi Center	Denver, CO	1999
Detroit Pistons	Eastern	Palace of Auburn Hills	Auburn Hills, MI	1988
Golden State Warriors	Western	Oracle Arena	Oakland, CA	1966
Houston Rockets	Western	Toyota Center	Houston, TX	2003
Indiana Pacers	Eastern	Conseco Fieldhouse	Indianapolis, IN	1999
Los Angeles Clippers	Western	Staples Center	Los Angeles, CA	1999
Los Angeles Lakers	Western	Staples Center	Los Angeles, CA	1999
Memphis Grizzlies	Western	FedEx Forum	Memphis, TN	2004

Architect	Cost (original)	Capacity (current)	Roof Type	Naming Rights (amt. & expiration)
Antoine Predock Architect with HOK Sport + Venue + Event	$453 M	46,000	Open-Air	$60 M (22 yrs.)
HOK Sports Facilities Group	$345 M	40,800	Open-Air	$50 M (24 yrs.)
NBBJ	$517.6 M	46,621	Retractable	$40 M (20 yrs.)
HOK Sport + Venue + Event	$344 M	46,816	Open-Air	Undisclosed
HOK Sports Facilities Group; Lescher & Mahoney Sports; Criswell, Blizzard & Blouin Architects	$138 M	45,360	Dome	$30 M (30 yrs.)
David M. Schwarz Architects; HKS, Inc.	$190 M	49,115	Open-Air	—
Rod Robbie and Michael Allen	C$500 M	50,516	Retractable	C$20 M (10 yrs.)
HOK Sport + Venue + Event with Devrouax & Purnell	$611 M	41,888	Open-Air	—

Architect	Cost (original)	Capacity (current)	Naming Rights (amt. & expiration)
HOK Sports Facilities Group; Arquitectonica	$213.5 M	20,300	$180 M (20 yrs.)
Ellerbe Becket	$160 M	18,624	Undisclosed
Ellerbe Becket with Odell and The Freelon Group	$265 M	18,500	Undisclosed
HOK Sports Facilities Group; Marmon Mok; W.E. Simpson Company	$175 M	21,711	$25 M (20 yrs.)
Ellerbe Becket	$152 M	20,562	Undisclosed
David Schwarz/Architectural Services, Inc. with HKS, Inc.	$420 M	19,200	$40 M (20 yrs.)
HOK Sports Facilities Group	$160 M	19,309	$68 M (20 yrs.)
Rossetti	$70 M	21,454	—
HNTB Architecture	n/a	19,200	$30 M (10 yrs.)
HOK Sports + Venue + Event	$175 M	18,300	Undisclosed
Ellerbe Becket	$183 M	18,345	$40 M (20 yrs.)
NBBJ	$330 M	20,000	$100 M (20 yrs.)
NBBJ	$330 M	20,000	$100 M (20 yrs.)
Ellerbe Becket with Looney Ricks Kiss	$250 M	18,165	$90 M (20 yrs.)

Sports Stadiums

Basketball

Team	Conference	Stadium	Location	Opened
Miami Heat	Eastern	American Airlines Arena	Miami, FL	1998
Milwaukee Bucks	Eastern	Bradley Center	Milwaukee, WI	1988
Minnesota Timberwolves	Western	Target Center	Minneapolis, MN	1990
New Jersey Nets	Eastern	Prudential Center	Newark, NJ	2007
New Orleans Hornets	Western	New Orleans Arena	New Orleans, LA	1999
New York Knicks	Eastern	Madison Square Garden	New York, NY	1968
Oklahoma City Thunder	Western	Ford Center	Oklahoma City, OK	2002
Orlando Magic	Eastern	Amway Center	Orlando, FL	2010
Philadelphia 76ers	Eastern	Wells Fargo Center	Philadelphia, PA	1996
Phoenix Suns	Western	US Airways Center	Phoenix, AZ	1992
Portland Trail Blazers	Western	Rose Garden	Portland, OR	1995
Sacramento Kings	Western	ARCO Arena	Sacramento, CA	1988
San Antonio Spurs	Western	AT&T Center	San Antonio, TX	2002
Toronto Raptors	Eastern	Air Canada Centre	Toronto, ON, Canada	1999
Utah Jazz	Western	EnergySolutions Arena	Salt Lake City, UT	1991
Washington Wizards	Eastern	Verizon Center	Washington, DC	1997

Football

Team	League	Stadium	Location	Opened
Arizona Cardinals	NFC	University of Phoenix Stadium	Glendale, AZ	2006
Atlanta Falcons	NFC	Georgia Dome	Atlanta, GA	1992
Baltimore Ravens	AFC	M&T Bank Stadium	Baltimore, MD	1998
Buffalo Bills	AFC	Ralph Wilson Stadium	Orchard Park, NY	1973
Carolina Panthers	NFC	Bank of America Stadium	Charlotte, NC	1996
Chicago Bears	NFC	Soldier Field	Chicago, IL	2003
Cincinnati Bengals	AFC	Paul Brown Stadium	Cincinnati, OH	2000
Cleveland Browns	AFC	Cleveland Browns Stadium	Cleveland, OH	1999
Dallas Cowboys	NFC	Cowboys Stadium	Arlington, TX	2009

Architect	Cost (original)	Capacity (current)	Naming Rights (amt. & expiration)
Arquitectonica	$175 M	19,600	$42 M (20 yrs.)
HOK Sports Facilities Group	$90 M	18,717	—
KMR Architects	$104 M	19,006	$18.75 M (15 yrs.)
HOK Sport + Venue + Event with Morris Adjmi Architects	$375 M	17,615	$105.3 M (20 yrs.)
Arthur Q. Davis, FAIA & Partners	$112 M	18,500	—
Charles Luckman	$116 M	19,763	—
The Benham Companies	$89 M	19,599	$8.1 M (15 yrs.)
Populous	$480 M	18,500	$195 M (30 yrs.)
Ellerbe Becket	$206 M	20,444	$40 M (29 yrs.)
Ellerbe Becket	$90 M	19,023	$26 M (30 yrs.)
Ellerbe Becket	$262 M	21,538	—
Rann Haight Architect	$40 M	17,317	$7 M (10 yrs.)
Ellerbe Becket with Lake/Flato Architects and Kell Muñoz Architects	$186 M	18,500	$85 M (20 yrs.)
HOK Sports Facilities Group; Brisbin Brook Beynon Architects (Canada)	C$265 M	19,800	C$40 M (20 yrs.)
FFKR Architects	$94 M	19,911	$20 M (10 yrs.)
Ellerbe Becket	$260 M	20,674	$44 M (15 years)

Architect	Cost (original)	Capacity (current)	Roof Type	Naming Rights (amt. & expiration)
Peter Eisenman with HOK Sport + Venue + Event	$370.6 M	65,000	Retractable	$154.5 M (20 yrs.)
Heery International	$214 M	71,149	Dome	—
HOK Sports Facilities Group	$220 M	69,084	Open-Air	$75 M (15 yrs.)
HNTB Architecture	$22 M	73,800	Open-Air	—
HOK Sports Facilities Group	$248 M	73,258	Open-Air	Undisclosed
Wood + Zapata, Inc. with Lohan Caprile Goettsch	$365 M	62,000	Open-Air	—
NBBJ	$400 M	65,535	Open-Air	—
HOK Sports Facilities Group	$283 M	73,200	Open-Air	—
HKS, Inc.	$1.1 B	80,000	Retractable	—

Sports Stadiums

Football

Team	Conference	Stadium	Location	Opened
Denver Broncos	AFC	Invesco Field at Mile High Stadium	Denver, CO	2001
Detroit Lions	NFC	Ford Field	Allen Park, MI	2002
Green Bay Packers	NFC	Lambeau Field	Green Bay, WI	1957
Houston Texans	AFC	Reliant Stadium	Houston, TX	2002
Indianapolis Colts	AFC	Lucas Oil Stadium	Indianapolis, IN	2008
Jacksonville Jaguars	AFC	Jacksonville Municipal Stadium	Jacksonville, FL	1995
Kansas City Chiefs	AFC	Arrowhead Stadium	Kansas City, MO	1972
Miami Dolphins	AFC	Sun Life Stadium	Miami, FL	1987
Minnesota Vikings	NFC	Hubert H. Humphrey Metrodome	Minneapolis, MN	1982
New England Patriots	AFC	Gillette Stadium	Foxboro, MA	2002
New Orleans Saints	NFC	Louisiana Superdome	New Orleans, LA	1975
New York Giants	NFC	New Meadowlands Stadium	E. Rutherford, NJ	2010
New York Jets	AFC	New Meadowlands Stadium	E. Rutherford, NJ	2010
Oakland Raiders	AFC	Oakland-Alameda County Coliseum	Oakland, CA	1966
Philadelphia Eagles	NFC	Lincoln Financial Field	Philadelphia, PA	2003
Pittsburgh Steelers	AFC	Heinz Field	Pittsburgh, PA	2001
San Diego Chargers	AFC	Qualcomm Stadium	San Diego, CA	1967
San Francisco 49ers	NFC	Candlestick Park	San Francisco, CA	1960
Seattle Seahawks	NFC	Qwest Field	Seattle, WA	2002
St. Louis Rams	NFC	Edward Jones Dome	St. Louis, MO	1995
Tampa Bay Buccaneers	NFC	Raymond James Stadium	Tampa, FL	1998
Tennessee Titans	AFC	LP Field	Nashville, TN	1999
Washington Redskins	NFC	FedEx Field	Landover, MD	1996

Architect	Cost (original)	Capacity (current)	Roof Type	Naming Rights (amt. & expiration)
HNTB Architecture with Fentress Bradburn Architects and Bertram A. Burton and Associates	$400.8 M	76,125	Open-Air	$120 M (20 yrs.)
SmithGroup	$500 M	64,355	Dome	$40 M (40 yrs.)
John Somerville	$960,000	60,890	Open-Air	—
HOK Sport + Venue + Event	$325 M	69,500	Retractable	$300 M (30 yrs.)
HKS, Inc.	$625 M	63,000	Retractable	$122 (20 yrs.)
HOK Sports Facilities Group	$138 M	73,000	Open-Air	—
Kivett and Meyers	$43 M	79,409	Open-Air	—
HOK Sports Facilities Group	$125 M	74,916	Open-Air	$20 M (5 yrs.)
Skidmore, Owings & Merrill	$55 M	64,121	Dome	—
HOK Sport + Venue + Event	$325 M	68,000	Open-Air	Undisclosed
Curtis & Davis Architects	$134 M	69,065	Dome	—
EwingCole; Skanska; 360 Architecture	$1.6 B	82,566	Open-Air	—
EwingCole; Skanska; 360 Architecture	$1.6 B	82,566	Open-Air	—
Skidmore, Owings & Merrill	$25.5 M	62,026	Suspension (fixed)	—
NBBJ	$320 M	66,000	Open-Air	$139.6 M (20 yrs.)
HOK Sport + Venue + Event with WTW Architects	$281 M	64,440	Open-Air	$58 M (20 yrs.)
Frank L. Hope and Associates	$27 M	71,294	Open-Air	$18 M (20 yrs.)
John & Bolles	$24.6 M	69,843	Open-Air	—
Ellerbe Becket with LMN Architects	$360 M	67,000	Partial Roof	$75.27 M (15 yrs.)
HOK Sports Facilities Group	$280 M	66,000	Dome	$31.8 M (12 yrs.)
HOK Sports Facilities Group	$168.5 M	66,000	Open-Air	$32.5 M (13 yrs.)
HOK Sports Facilities Group	$290 M	67,000	Open-Air	$30 M (10 yrs.)
HOK Sports Facilities Group	$250.5 M	80,116	Open-Air	$205 M (27 yrs.)

Sports Stadiums

Hockey

Team	Conference	Stadium	Location	Opened
Anaheim Ducks	Western	Honda Center	Anaheim, CA	1993
Atlanta Thrashers	Eastern	Philips Arena	Atlanta, GA	1999
Boston Bruins	Eastern	TD Garden	Boston, MA	1995
Buffalo Sabres	Eastern	HSBC Arena	Buffalo, NY	1996
Calgary Flames	Western	Pengrowth Saddledome	Calgary, AB, Canada	1983
Carolina Hurricanes	Eastern	RBC Center	Raleigh, NC	1999
Chicago Blackhawks	Western	United Center	Chicago, IL	1994
Colorado Avalanche	Western	Pepsi Center	Denver, CO	1999
Columbus Blue Jackets	Western	Nationwide Arena	Columbus, OH	2000
Dallas Stars	Western	American Airlines Center	Dallas, TX	2001
Detroit Red Wings	Western	Joe Louis Arena	Detroit, MI	1979
Edmonton Oilers	Western	Rexall Place	Edmonton, AB, Canada	1974
Florida Panthers	Eastern	BankAtlantic Center	Sunrise, FL	1998
Los Angeles Kings	Western	Staples Center	Los Angeles, CA	1999
Minnesota Wild	Western	Xcel Energy Center	St. Paul, MN	2000
Montreal Canadiens	Eastern	Bell Centre	Montreal, QC, Canada	1996
Nashville Predators	Western	Bridgestone Arena	Nashville, TN	1997
New Jersey Devils	Eastern	Prudential Center	Newark, NJ	2007
New York Islanders	Eastern	Nassau Veterans Memorial Coliseum	Uniondale, NY	1972
New York Rangers	Eastern	Madison Square Garden	New York, NY	1968
Ottawa Senators	Eastern	Scotiabank Place	Kanata, ON, Canada	1996
Philadelphia Flyers	Eastern	Wells Fargo Center	Philadelphia, PA	1996
Phoenix Coyotes	Western	Jobing.com Arena	Glendale, AZ	2003
Pittsburgh Penguins	Eastern	Consol Energy Center	Pittsburgh, PA	2010
San Jose Sharks	Western	HP Pavillion	San Jose, CA	1993
St. Louis Blues	Western	Scottrade Center	St. Louis, MO	1994
Tampa Bay Lightning	Eastern	St. Pete Times Forum	Tampa, FL	1996
Toronto Maple Leafs	Eastern	Air Canada Centre	Toronto, ON, Canada	1999
Vancouver Canucks	Western	General Motors Place	Vancouver, BC, Canada	1995
Washington Capitals	Eastern	Verizon Center	Washington, DC	1997

Source: DesignIntelligence

Architect	Cost (original)	Capacity (current)	Naming Rights (amt. & expiration)
HOK Sports Facilities Group	$120 M	17,174	$60 M (15 yrs.)
HOK Sports Facilities Group; Arquitectonica	$213.5 M	18,750	$180 M (20 yrs.)
Ellerbe Becket	$160 M	17,565	Undisclosed
Ellerbe Becket	$127.5 M	18,595	$24 M (30 yrs.)
Graham Edmunds Architecture (Canada); Graham McCourt Architects (Canada)	C$176 M	20,140	C$20 M (20 yrs.)
Odell	$158 M	18,176	$80 M (20 yrs.)
HOK Sports Facilities Group; Marmon Mok; W.E. Simpson Co.	$175 M	20,500	$25 M (20 yrs.)
HOK Sports Facilities Group	$160 M	18,129	$68 M (20 yrs.)
Heinlein Schrock Stearns; NBBJ	$150 M	18,500	$135 M (indefinite)
David M. Schwarz Architects with HKS, Inc.	$420 M	18,000	$40 M (20 yrs.)
Smith, Hinchmen and Grylls Associates	$57 M	18,785	—
Phillips, Barrett, Hillier, Jones & Partners with Wynn, Forbes, Lord, Feldberg & Schmidt	C$22.5 M	16,900	Undisclosed
Ellerbe Becket	$212 M	19,452	$27 M (10 yrs.)
NBBJ	$330 M	18,500	Undisclosed
HOK Sports Facilities Group	$130 M	18,064	$75 M (25 yrs.)
Consortium of Quebec Architects (Canada)	C$280 M	21,273	$100 M (20 yrs.)
HOK Sports Facilities Group	$144 M	17,500	Undisclosed
HOK Sport + Venue + Event with Morris Adjmi Architects	$375 M	17,615	$105.3 M (20 yrs.)
Welton Becket	$31 M	16,297	—
Charles Luckman	$116 M	18,200	—
Rossetti	C$200 M	18,500	C$20 M (15 yrs.)
Ellerbe Becket	$206 M	18,168	$40 M (29 yrs.)
HOK Sport + Venue + Event	$220 M	17,653	$25 M (10 yrs.)
Populous	$321 M	18,087	Undisclosed
Sink Combs Dethlefs	$162.5 M	17,483	$55.8 M (18 yrs.)
Ellerbe Becket	$170 M	19,260	Undisclosed
Ellerbe Becket	$139 M	19,500	$25 M (12 yrs.)
HOK Sports Facilities Group; Brisbin Brook Beynon Architects (Canada)	C$265 M	18,800	C$40 M (20 yrs.)
Brisbin Brook Beynon Architects (Canada)	C$160 M	18,422	C$18.5 M (20 yrs.)
Ellerbe Becket	$260 M	19,700	$44 M (13 yrs.)

1724 California Street NW, Washington, DC | RTKL Associates Inc.

OUTSIDE & INSIDE SPACES | Awards

Awards granted to outside spaces and inside spaces are featured in this chapter. Outdoor awards include landscape architecture, urban planning, and spaces such as waterfronts. Interior spaces are comprised of general awards to interiors followed by specific awards to restaurants, libraries, healthcare, and lighting.

(Note: Bolded text indicates additions to the existing list.)

Communal Water
Source and area light

Additional Landscape
To Provide Shade and
Soften Architecture

Potential Roof
Mounted Solar
Collectors

Banana Trees
As Food and
Landscaping

Vegetable Garden
As Landscape

Local Cobblestone Paving
With Underground Water
And Sewer Utilities,
Pedestrian, Bicycle, and
Motorbike Access

Rainwate
Harvestir
From Roc

Russ Butler

Kigali Conceptual Master Plan, Kigali, Rwanda | AECOM

ASLA Professional Awards

With the annual Professional Awards program, the American Society of Landscape Architects honors the **best in landscape architecture from around the globe**. Recipients receive coverage in *Landscape Architecture* magazine; winners in the residential category are also featured in *Garden Design* magazine. The Landmark Award recognizes a distinguished landscape architecture project completed 15 to 50 years ago that retains its original design integrity and contributes significantly to the public realm.

www.asla.org

2010 Award of Excellence Winners

General Design
Shanghai Houtan Park: Landscape as a
    Living System
Shanghai, China
Turenscape (China); Peking University
    Graduate School of Landscape
    Architecture (China)

Residential Design
Lakeside Retreat
New England
Richardson & Associates, Landscape
    Architects

Analysis and Planning Category
Kigali Conceptual Master Plan
Kigali, Rwanda
AECOM Design + Planning

Communications Category
Pioneers Oral History Series
The Cultural Landscape Foundation

Landmark Award
Bryant Park
New York, NY
OLIN

2010 Honor Award Winners

General Design
Qinhuangdao Beach Restoration: An
    Ecological Surgery
Qinhuangdao City, Hebei Province, China
Turenscape (China); Peking University
    Graduate School of Landscape Architecture
    (China)

Tianjin Qiaoyuan Park: The Adaptation Palettes
Tianjin City, China
Turenscape (China); Peking University
    Graduate School of Landscape Architecture
    (China)

Nueva School
Hillsborough, CA
Andrea Cochran Landscape Architecture

Square Four
Beirut, Lebanon
Vladimir Djurovic Landscape Architecture
    (Lebanon)

Connecticut Water Treatment Facility
New Haven, CT
Michael Van Valkenburgh Associates

High Line, Section 1
New York, NY
James Corner Field Operations; Diller Scofidio
    + Renfro

Underwood Family Sonoran Landscape
    Laboratory
Tucson, AZ
Ten Eyck Landscape Architects

D. A. Horchner/Design Workshop

Catalina Foothills, Tucson, AZ | Design Workshop

ASLA Professional Awards

Brochstein Pavilion, Rice University
Houston, TX
The Office of James Burnett

Crosswaters Ecolodge , Nankun Mountain
   Reserve
Guangdong Province, China
EDSA

Rooftop Haven for Urban Agriculture
Chicago, IL
Hoerr Schaudt Landscape Architects

Theater Group Retreat
Western Maine
Landworks Studio

Residential Design
Urban Play Garden
San Francisco, CA
Blasen Landscape Architecture

Padaro Lane
Carpinteria, CA
Keith LeBlanc Landscape Architecture

Pamet Valley
Truro, MA
Keith LeBlanc Landscape Architecture

Catalina Foothills
Tucson, AZ
Design Workshop

Pacific Cannery Lofts
Oakland, CA
Miller Company Landscape Architects

Transformative Water
Pitkin County, CO
Design Workshop, Inc.

Parkside Garden
San Francisco, CA
Scott Lewis Landscape Architecture

Bridle Road Residence
Cape Town, South Africa
Rees Roberts & Partners

Lily Lake Residence
Dalton, PA
Michael Vergason Landscape Architects, Ltd.

North Sea Residence
Southampton, NY
Rumsey Farber

San Francisco Residence
San Francisco, CA
Lutsko Associates

Power House
Dallas, TX
Hocker Design Group

Pool House
Dallas, TX
Hocker Design Group

Analysis and Planning Category
Remodeling Paradise —Landscape
   Renovation Round West Lake Region in
   Hangzhou
Hangzhou, China
Hangzhou Landscape Architecture Design
   Institute (China); Beijing Forestry University
   (China); Atelier DYJG (China)

Gowanus Canal Sponge Park
Brooklyn, NY
dlandstudio

Sungei Buloh Wetland Reserve Master Plan
Lim Chu Kang, Northern Singapore
National Parks Board (Singapore)

Adam Elliott / Elliott Photographic

Isla Palenque Project, Golfo de Chiriqui, Panama | Design Workshop

ASLA Professional Awards

Isla Palenque
Golfo de Chiriqui, Panama
Design Workshop

Orongo Station Conservation Master Plan
Poverty Bay, North Island, New Zealand
Nelson Byrd Woltz Landscape Architects

California Institute of Technology Landscape
     Master Plan
Pasadena, CA
Nelson Byrd Woltz Landscape Architects

Resuscitating the Fez River
Fez, Morocco
Bureau E.A.S.T. (Morocco)

Seattle Green Factor
Seattle, WA
City of Seattle Department of Planning and
     Development

Transit Revitalization Investment District
     Master Plan
Philadelphia, PA
Interface

Park 20/20: A Cradle to Cradle Inspired
     Master Plan
Haarlemmermeer, Netherlands
William McDonough + Partners

PGHSNAP: Neighborhood Data and Map
     Resource
Pittsburgh, PA
City of Pittsburgh, PA Department of City
     Planning

Communications Category

Ken Smith Landscape Architect Monograph
Ken Smith Landscape Architect

SAFARI 7
Columbia University GSAPP/Urban Landscape
     Lab+; MTWTF

Grid/Street/Place: Essential Elements of
     Sustainable Urban Districts
RTKL Associates Inc.

Water Lites
Del Mar, CA
Schmidt Design Group

City Plates
Rios Clementi Hale Studios

Landscape Infrastructures Emerging Practices,
     Paradigms & Technologies Reshaping the
     Contemporary Urban Landscape
John H. Daniels Faculty of Architecture,
     Landscape, and Design, University of
     Toronto (Canada)

Research Category

The Forensics of Ancient Landscape
     Architecture: Methods and Approaches to
     Excavating Relict Gardens and Designed
     Landscapes
Kathryn Gleason, Cornell University

Getting to Minus 80: Defining the Contribution
     of Urban Form to Achieving Greenhouse
     Gas Emission Reduction Targets
The Design Centre for Sustainability at the
     University of British Columbia (Canada)

Access to Nature for Older Adults: Promoting
     Health Through Landscape Design
Center for Health Systems & Design, Texas
     A&M University

Source: American Society of Landscape Architects

Design Guidelines for Emory University's Clifton Community Partnership, Atlanta, GA | Goody Clancy & Associates

Charter Awards

Presented by the Congress for the New Urbanism, the Charter Awards honor projects that **best fulfill and advance the principles of the Charter of the New Urbanism**, which defines the essential qualities of outstanding buildings and urban places. The awards recognize architecture, landscape architecture, and urban design projects that improve the human experience and are built in harmony with their physical and social contexts.

www.cnu.org

2010 Winners

Metropolis, City, Town
Southeast Lee County Plan for Conservation
    and Development
Lee County, FL
Dover, Kohl, & Partners

Southlands: Agricultural Urbanism
Tsawwassen, BC, Canada
Duany Plater-Zyberk & Company

Lifelong Communities
Atlanta, GA
Duany Plater-Zyberk & Company

Neighborhood, District, Corridor
State Center
Baltimore, MD
Design Collective

Salon Des Refuses
Katy, TX
Droiling Terrones Architecture; Crabtree
    Rohrbaugh & Associates

Design Guidelines for Emory University's
    Clifton Community Partnership
Atlanta, GA
Goody Clancy & Associates

Block, Street, Building
A Plaça in the Pyrenees
Sant Julia de Loria, Andorra
Fairfax and Sammons Architects

Academic
Barrio Capital de Analco
Santa Fe, NM
School of Architecture, Andrews University

Source: Congress for the New Urbanism

Cityscape Architectural Review Awards

Cityscape, an international development conference, and the British magazine *Architectural Review*, jointly grant the Cityscape Architectural Review Awards to promote **design excellence in the Middle East, Africa, Central and Eastern Asia, Australasia (excluding Japan, Australia, and New Zealand), and South America**. Entries are judged on innovation, environmental awareness, and appropriateness to the site and culture.

www.cityscape.ae

2009 Winners

Commercial/Mixed Use, Built
Qatar Science & Technology Park
Doha, Qatar
Woods Bagot (Australia)

Commercial/Mixed Use, Future
Masdar HQ
Abu Dhabi, UAE
Agi Architects (Kuwait)

Community, Built
Malawi Schools Project
Malawi (various locations)
John McAslan + Partners (UK)

Community, Future
Astana National Library
Astana, Kasakhstan
BIG Architects (Denmark)

Leisure, Future
Oberoi Resort
Al Khiran, Oman
Bernard Khoury (Lebanon)

Residential, Built
S.A. Residence, House #37, Road #100,
    Gulshan #2
Dhaka, Bangladesh
Shatotto Architecture for Green Living
    (Bangladesh)

Residential, Future
Z House
Muscat, Oman
Nabil Gholam Architects (Lebanon)

Tourism, Travel and Transport, Built
Libertas Rixos Hotel
Dubrovnik, Croatia
Melkan Gursel and Murat Tabanlioglu (Turkey)

Tourism, Travel and Transport, Future
Dubai Metro
Dubai, UAE
RTA (UAE)

Special Award: Environmental
Masdar Plaza, Masdar Masterplan
Abu Dhabi, UAE
LAVA (Laboratory for Visionary Architecture)
    (Australia)

Special Award: Islamic Architecture
Al-Asmariya Universlty
Zilten, Libya
RMJM

Special Award: Master Planning
Bund Waterfront
Shanghai, China
Chan Krieger Sieniewicz, Inc.

Source: Cityscape Architectural Review Awards

European Prize for Urban Public Space

The European Prize for Urban Public Space is a biennial competition to celebrate and encourage the **recovery and creation of cohesive spaces in Europe's cities**. First awarded in 2000, the prize is presented both to the designers of the project and the sponsor institutions in order to encourage the rejuvenation of public spaces to improve the quality of urban life. A commemorative plaque is installed at each winning site.

www.publicspace.org

2010 Winners

Winners
Open-Air-Library
Magdeburg, Germany
KARO Architekten (Germany) with
    Architektur+Netzwerk (Germany)

Norwegian National Opera and Ballet
Oslo, Norway
Snøhetta (Norway)

Special Mentions
Urban Activators: Theater Podium and Brug
    Grotekerkplein
Rotterdam, Netherlands
Atelier Kempe Thill (Netherlands)

Paseo Marítimo de la Playa Poniente
Benidorm, Spain
Office of Architecture in Barcelona (Spain)

Passage 56 / Espace Culturel Écologique
Paris, France
atelier d'architecture autogérée (France)

Casetas de Pescadores en el Puerto
Cangas do Morrazo, Spain
Irisarri + Piñera (Spain)

Source: Public Space

Dixi Carrillo

Waterfront Gateway Project and Fanfare, Port of Los Angeles, San Pedro, CA | AECOM

Excellence on the Waterfront Awards

Lauding projects that **convert abandoned or outmoded waterfronts into constructive spaces**, the Excellence on the Waterfront Awards are presented annually by the nonprofit Waterfront Center. Judging criteria include the design's sensitivity to the water, quality and harmony, civic contribution, environmental impact, and educational components. The group also presents a Clearwater Citizens Award to recognize outstanding grassroots initiatives.

www.waterfrontcenter.org

2009 Top Honor Award

The Confluence Project
Vancouver and Iwaco, WA, and Troutdale, OR
Jones & Jones Architects and Landscape
    Architects

2009 Honor Awards

Environmental Protection and Enhancement
Qinhuangdao Beach Restoration
Qinhuangdao City, China
Turenscape (China); Qinhuangdao City
    Landscape Bureau (China)

Historic or Maritime Preservation/ Adaptive Reuse
Erie Canal Harbor Project
Buffalo, NY
Flynn Battaglia Architects; New York State
    Empire State Development Corp.

Commercial/Mixed Use
Ferry Terminal at the World Financial Center
New York, NY
Port Authority of New York and New Jersey

Park/Walkway/Recreational
Southeast False Creek Waterfront, Phase 1
Vancouver, BC, Canada
PWL Partnership Landscape Architects
    Inc. (Canada); City of Vancouver Parks,
    Planning and Engineering (Canada)

San Pedro Waterfront Gateway Project and
    Fanfare at San Pedro
San Pedro, CA
Port of Los Angeles; EDAW/AECOM; WET

West Harlem Piers Park
New York City, NY
W Architecture & Landscape Architecture;
    New York Economic Development Corp.

Residential or Resort
South Pier District Redevelopment
Sheboygan, WI
City of Sheboygan; Eduard J. Freer; WET

Public Works
Castleford Bridge
Castleford, West Yorkshire, UK
McDowell+Benedetti (UK); Wakefield
    Metropolitan District Council (UK)

Plan
Trinity River Corridor Design Guidelines
Dallas, TX
Wallace Roberts & Todd; City of Dallas

Excellence on the Waterfront Awards

Waterfront Zoning Text Amendment
New York, NY
City of New York

Brooklyn Bridge Park
Brooklyn, NY
Michael Van Valkenburgh Associates; Brooklyn
Bridge Park Development Corporation

Student Awards
Aquatecture: Water-based Architecture in the
Netherlands
Rebecca Pasternack, University of Southern
California

Revival of a Canal City, Chuo Ward Waterfront
Tokyo, Japan
Dustin Stevens and Robert Cheng, Harvard
Graduate School of Design

2009 Clearwater Award

Vision Map & Report
Seattle, WA
Duwamish River Cleanup Coalition

Oakland-Alameda Waterfront Maps Project
Oakland, CA
Oakland Waterfront Coalition

Friends for Our Riverfront
Memphis, TN

Source: Waterfront Center

J.C. Nichols Prize

The Urban Land Institute's J.C. Nichols Prize for Visionary Urban Development rewards individuals and institutions whose work demonstrates a **high commitment to responsible development**. The award's namesake, Jesse Clyde Nichols, was a visionary developer whose work embodied ULI's mission to foster responsible land use. Winners, who receive a $100,000 honorarium, may include architects, researchers, developers, journalists, public officials, planners, and academics.

www.nicholsprize.org

2000	Joseph P. Riley Jr.	2006	Peter Calthorpe
2001	Daniel Patrick Moynihan	2007	Sir Stuart Lipton
2002	Gerald D. Hines	2008	Bart Harvey and Enterprise
2003	Vincent J. Scully		Community Partners
2004	Richard D. Baron	2009	Amanda M. Burden
2005	Forest City Enterprises, Inc. and Albert B. Ratner	2010	Richard M. Daley

Source: Urban Land Institute

National Planning Excellence Awards

Through its National Planning Awards program, the American Planning Association recognizes the role cutting-edge planning achievements and outstanding individual contributions play in creating **communities of lasting value**. Excellence Awards are granted to outstanding initiatives by planning agencies, planning teams or firms, community groups, and local authorities.

www.planning.org

2010 Winners

Best Practices
Indianapolis Regional Center Design
  Guidelines
Indianapolis, IN

Implementation
University District Revitalization
Columbus, OH

Public Outreach
Wicker Park Bucktown Master Plan
Chicago, IL

Innovation in Best Practices for Sustainability
Hilltop Hanover, A Westchester County Farm
  and Environmental Center
Westchester County, NY

Hard-Won Victory
New Orleans City Park
New Orleans, LA

Source: American Planning Association

Rudy Bruner Award for Urban Excellence

The biennial Rudy Bruner Award for Urban Excellence celebrates projects that approach **urban problems through the creative inclusion of often competing political, community, environmental, and formal considerations**. Established in 1987, the program grants one gold medal, along with a $50,000 cash prize, and four silver medals, each with a $10,000 prize. A multidisciplinary jury performs an on-site evaluation of the final five projects before selecting the gold-medal recipient.

www.brunerfoundation.org

2009 Winners

Gold
Inner-City Arts
Los Angeles, CA

Silver
Hunts Point Riverside Park
Bronx, NY

Millennium Park
Chicago, IL

St. Joseph Rebuild Center
New Orleans, LA

The Community Chalkboard and Podium: An
Interactive Monument to Free Expression
Charlottesville, VA

Source: Bruner Foundation

SCUP/AIA-CAE Excellence in Planning, Landscape Architecture, and Architecture Awards

The Society for College and University Planning and the American Institute of Architects' Committee on Architecture for Education jointly present the annual Excellence in Planning, Landscape Architecture, and Architecture Awards to **outstanding projects developed for higher education institutions**. The jury considerations include the quality of the physical environment as well as the comprehensiveness of the planning process. The award is presented to all members of the project team.

www.scup.org

2010 Honor Awards

Planning for an Established Campus
Campus Master Plan, Haverford College
Haverford, PA
Venturi, Scott Brown and Associates

Architecture for a New Building
Student Center, Bennington College
Bennington, VT
Taylor & Burns Architects

Architecture Addition
Julliard School Expansion and Renovation
New York, NY
Diller Scofidio + Renfro with FXFOWLE
   Architects

Museum of Art, University of Michigan
Ann Arbor, MI
Allied Works Architecture

2010 Merit Awards

Planning for New Campus
Habib University City Campus
Karachi, Pakistan
Ahed Associates (Pakistan)

Planning for a District or Campus Component
AKU Faculty of Arts and Sciences University
   Village Land Use Plan, Aga Khan University
Karachi, Pakistan
Goody Clancy

Science & Engineering Quad, Stanford
   University
Palo Alto, CA
BOORA Architects

Planning for an Established Campus
VCU 2020: 2004 Master Plan Site, Virginia
   Commonwealth University
Richmond, VA
BCWH

Campus Master Plan, University of Utah
Salt Lake City, UT
Skidmore, Owings & Merrill

Landscape Architecture
West Campus Plaza, Duke University
Durham, NC
Hargreaves Associates

Anton Grassl/Esto

North Campus Residence Hall, Roger Williams University, Bristol, RI | Perkins + Will

SCUP/AIA-CAE Excellence in Planning, Landscape Architecture, and Architecture Awards

Architecture for a New Building

School of Art & Art History, University of Iowa
Iowa City, IA
Steven Holl Architects

Arts and Social Sciences Complex, Simon
    Fraser University
Burnaby, BC, Canada
Busby Perkins+Will (Canada)

North Campus Residence Hall, Roger Williams
    University
Bristol, RI
Perkins+Will

Architecture Addition

Peirce Hall, Kenyon College
Gambier, OH
GUND Partnership

Architecture Renovation/Adaptive Reuse

Owen Graduate Center Refurbishment,
    Michigan State University
East Lansing, MI
SmithGroup

San Francisco Conservatory of Music
San Francisco, CA
Perkins+Will

2010 Special Citations

Academic Commons at Goddard Library,
    Clark University
Worcester, MA
Perry Dean Rogers | Partners Architects

William Oxley Thompson Memorial Library,
    Ohio State University
Columbus, OH
GUND Partnership

Source: Society for College and University Planning

SCUP/AIA-CAE Excellence in Planning, Landscape Architecture, and Architecture Awards

Tim Griffith

San Francisco Conservatory of Music, San Francisco, CA | Perkins+Will

Tim Griffith

ULI Awards for Excellence

The Urban Land Institute's Awards for Excellence consider the full development process. Winning entries demonstrate superior design, improve the **quality of the built environment**, exhibit a sensitivity to the community, display financial viability, and are relevant to contemporary issues. Since it was established in 1979, the program has evolved into separate juried competitions for the Americas, Europe, and Asia Pacific. The developer responsible for each winning project is listed below.

www.uli.org

2010 Americas Winners

Andares
Guadalajara, Mexico
Desarrolladora Mexicana de Inmuebles S.A.
 (Mexico)

Bethel Commercial Center
Chicago, IL
Bethel New Life

Columbia Heights
Washington, DC
Government of the District of Columbia

Foundry Square
San Francisco, CA
Wilson Meany Sullivan

L.A. Live
Los Angeles, CA
AEG

Madison at 14th Apartments
Oakland, CA
Affordable Housing Associates

Sundance Square
Fort Worth, TX
Sundance Square Management

Thin Flats
Philadelphia, PA
Onion Flats

Vancouver Convention Centre West
Vancouver, BC, Canada
BC Pavilion Corporation (Canada)

The Visionaire
New York, NY
Albanese Organization; Starwood Capital

2010 Europe, Middle East, and Africa Winners

Citilab
Barcelona, Spain
Fundació per la promoció de la societat del
 coneixement (Spain)

MUMUTH Music Theatre
Graz, Austria
BIG Bundesimmobiliengesellschaft m.b.H
 (Austria)

New District "Miasteczko Wilanów"
Warsaw, Poland
Prokom Investments (Poland) with IN-VI
 Investment Environments (Poland)

Palazzo Tornabuoni
Florence, Italy
Kitebrook Partners; R.D.M. Real Estate
 Development (Italy)

2010 Asia Pacific Winners

Dragon Lake Bridge Park
Bengbu, China
Xincheng Comprehensive Development Zone
   Bengbu (China)

Greenbelt 5
Makati City, Philippines
Ayala Land, Inc. (Philippines)

Newton Suites
Singapore
UOL Group Ltd. (Singapore)

Rouse Hill Town Centre
Rouse Hill, NSW, Australia
The GPT Group (Australia)

The Southern Ridges
Singapore
Urban Redevelopment Authority of Singapore
   (Singapore)

Source: Urban Land Institute

Power House Restoration, St. Louis, MO | Cannon Design

Annual Interiors Awards

The Annual Interiors Awards recognize **interior design excellence in multiple commercial categories**. A jury of design professionals selects winning projects based on aesthetics, design creativity, function, and achievement of client objectives. Winners are honored at an awards breakfast in New York, and their projects are published in *Contract* magazine.

www.contractmagazine.com

2010 Winners

Adaptive Reuse
Andel's Hotel Lodz
Lodz, Poland
Jestico + Whiles (UK)

Education
Fashion Institute of Design and Merchandising
San Diego, CA
Clive Wilkinson Architects

Environmental
The Power House
St. Louis, MO
Cannon Design

Exhibit
Prospect.1 Welcome Center
New Orleans, LA
Eskew+Dumez+Ripple

Healthcare
Peterborough Regional Health Centre
Peterborough, ON, Canada
Stantec Architecture (Canada)

Historic Restoration
Woodward Building
Washington, DC
Hartman Design Group

Hotel
Andaz
West Hollywood, CA
Janson Goldstein

Large Office
Fornari Headquarters
Milan, Italy
Giorgio Borruso Design

Public Space
Agave Library
Phoenix, AZ
will bruder+PARTNERS

Restaurant
ULTRA
Toronto, ON, Canada
Munge Leung Design Associates (Canada)

Retail
Barbie Shanghai
Shanghai, China
Slade Architecture

Showroom
Osram Light Studio Showroom
Treviso, Italy
Cerquiglini & Rossi Architecture (Italy)

Annual Interiors Awards

Small Office
A confidential financial client
San Francisco, CA
Gensler

Spa/Fitness
Center for Wellness, College of New Rochelle
New Rochelle, NY
ikon.5 architects; Galina Design Group

Sports/Entertainment Winner
Exeter Schools Multipurpose Space
Exeter, MO
Dake Wells Architecture

Source: Contract *magazine*

Gold Key Awards

For over 20 years, the Gold Key Awards for Excellence in Hospitality Design have honored **outstanding hospitality projects**. Judging criteria include aesthetic appeal, practicality and functionality, and innovative design concepts. The awards are presented by the International Hotel/Motel & Restaurant Show and sponsored by *Interior Design* and *HOTELS* magazines. Winners in each category are profiled in both sponsoring publications.

www.ihmrs.com

2009 Winners

Best Hotel Design/Resort
Four Seasons Bora Bora
Bora Bora, French Polynesia
BAMO

Best Hotel Design/Urban
Las Alcobas
Polanco, Mexico
Yabu Pushelberg (Canada)

Guest Room
Miraval Guestrooms
Catalina, AZ
Clodagh

Lobby/Reception
Shangri-La's Far Eastern Plaza Hotel
Tainan, Taiwan
AB Concept (Hong Kong)

Lounge/Bar
Mondrian Miami
Miami Beach, FL
Marcel Wanders Studio (Netherlands)

Restaurants/Casual Dining
Jen Cafe at Hotel Jen
Hong Kong
AB Concept (Hong Kong)

Restaurants/Fine Dining
Corton
New York, NY
Stephanie Goto

Spa
Lapis at Fontainebleau Miami Beach
Miami Beach, FL
Richardson Sadeki

The Spa at Four Seasons Bora Bora
Bora Bora, French Polynesia
BAMO

Suite
Four Seasons Bora Bora
Bora Bora, French Polynesia
BAMO

Source: International Hotel/Motel & Restaurant Show

HDR Architecture, Inc./© 2010 Farshid Assassi

Bellevue Medical Center, Bellevue, NE | HDR Architecture, Inc.

Healthcare Environment Awards

Since 1989, the annual Healthcare Environment Awards have recognized **innovative, life-enhancing designs**. The program is sponsored by the Center for Health Design, *Contract* magazine, Medquest Communications, and the American Institute of Architecture Students and is open to architects, interior designers, healthcare executives, and students. The winners are honored at the annual Healthcare Design Conference and featured in an issue of *Contract* magazine.

www.healthdesign.org

2010 Winners

Acute Care
Bellevue Medical Center
Bellevue, NE
HDR Architecture, Inc.

Conceptual Design
Patient Room 2020
Clemson University Architecture + Health

Health and Fitness
Central Harlem STD Clinic
New York, NY
Stephen Yablon Architect

Long-Term Care
NewBridge on the Charles
Dedham, MA
Perkins Eastman

2010 Honorary Mentions

Acute Care
MultiCare Medical Center Emergency
    Department
Tacoma, WA
GBJ Architecture

Student
Ollie and Me
Caylee Raber, Emily Carr University

Source: The Center for Health Design

Chris Cooper

NewBridge on the Charles, Hebrew SeniorLife, Dedham, MA | Perkins Eastman

Building 23, US Centers for Disease Control and Prevention, Atlanta, GA | HDR Architecture, Inc.

Benny Chan, Fotoworks

Guess? Inc. Headquarters, Los Angeles, CA | STUDIOS Architecture

Interior Design Competition

The Interior Design Competition is presented jointly each year by the International Interior Design Association and *Interior Design* magazine. The program was established in 1973 to recognize **outstanding interior design projects and to foster new ideas and techniques**. Winning projects appear in the magazine, and the best-of-competition winner receives a $5,000 cash prize.

www.iida.org

2010 Winners

Best of Competition
LYNNsteven
Vancouver, BC, Canada
mgb ARCHITECTURE + DESIGN (Canada)

Winners
FIDM
San Diego, CA
Clive Wilkinson Architects

Rennie Art Gallery and Offices
North Vancouver, BC, Canada
mgb ARCHITECTURE + DESIGN (Canada)

Dubai Mall Medical Center
Dubai, UAE
NBBJ

Guess? Inc. Headquarters
Los Angeles, CA
STUDIOS Architecture

MUMUTH Music Theatre
Graz, Austria
UNStudio (Netherlands)

Source: International Interior Design Association

HDR Architecture, Inc.; © 2010 www.balloggphoto.com

Faith Regional Health Services, Bed Tower, Norfolk, NE | HDR Architecture, Inc.

Unilever, US Headquarters, Englewood Cliffs, NJ | HDR Architecture, Inc.

HDR Architecture, Inc.; © Ari Burling

James Beard Restaurant Design Award

The James Beard Foundation annually presents the James Beard Restaurant Design Award to the project that best demonstrates **excellence in restaurant design or renovation**. Architects and interior designers are eligible to enter restaurant projects completed within the preceding three years. The award is presented at the annual Beard Birthday Fortnight celebration.

www.jamesbeard.org

1995	Fifty Seven Fifty Seven New York, NY Chhada Siembieda and Partners
1996	Bar 89 New York, NY Ogawa/Depardon Architects
1997	Paci Restaurant Westport, CT Ferris Architects
1998	Monsoon Toronto, ON, Canada Yabu Pushelberg
1999	MC Squared San Francisco, CA Mark Cavagnero Associates
2000	Brasserie New York, NY Diller & Scofidio
2001	Russian Tea Room New York, NY Leroy Adventures
2002	Blackbird Restaurant Chicago, IL Thomas Schlesser & Demian Repucci
2003	L'Impero Restaurant New York, NY Vicente Wolf Associates

2004	PUBLIC New York, NY AvroKO
2005	Solea Restaurant, W Hotel Mexico City, Mexico Studio Gaia
	Avec Chicago, IL Thomas Schlesser Design
2006	The Modern New York, NY Bentel & Bentel Architecture/Planners
2007	Xing Restaurant New York, NY Lewis.Tsurumaki.Lewis
2008	Morimoto New York, NY Tadao Ando Architect and Associates (Japan)
2009	The Publican Chicago, IL Design Bureaux, Inc.
2010	The Wright New York, NY Andre Kikoski Architect

Source: James Beard Foundation

Library Interior Design Awards

The Library Interior Design Awards program is a biennial competition that honors **excellence in the design of library interiors and promotes innovative concepts and design excellence**. Projects are judged on aesthetics, design creativity, function, and satisfaction of the client's objectives. The program is administered by the American Library Association in partnership with the International Interior Design Association.

www.ala.org

2008 Winners

Academic Libraries

Under 30,000 Square Feet
Susan P. and Richard A. Friedman Study
    Center, Brown University
Providence, RI
Architecture Research Office

Over 30,000 Square Feet
Hastings College of Law Library, University
    of California
San Francisco, CA
SmithGroup

Public Libraries

Under 30,000 Square Feet
Arabian Public Library
Scottsdale, AZ
richärd+bauer

Honorable Mention
Durham County Regional Library, North
    Branch
Durham, NC
The Freelon Group

Over 30,000 Square Feet
Ramsey County Library
Maplewood, MN
HGA Architects and Engineers

Single Space
Evanston Public Library Teen Room, The Loft
Evanston, IL
Nagle Hartray Danker Kagan McKay Penney;
    ArchitectureIsFun

Innovation in Sustainable Design
Hazel McCallion Academic Learning Center,
    University of Toronto Mississauga
Toronto, ON, Canada
Shore Tilbe Irwin & Partners (Canada)

Outstanding Historic Renovation
Restoration
Lionel Pincus and Princess Firyal Map
    Division, New York Public Library
New York, NY
Davis Brody Bond Aedas

Adaptive Reuse
Fleet Library, Rhode Island School of Design
Providence, RI
Office dA

On the Boards
Prescott Valley Public Library
Prescott Valley, AZ
richärd+bauer

Honorable Mention
Phoenix Public Library, Harmon Branch
Phoenix, AZ
richärd+bauer

**Note, this award was suspended for the 2010 cycle.
It will resume in 2012.*

Source: American Library Association

Lighting Design Awards

Presented for lighting installations that couple aesthetic achievement with technical expertise, the Lighting Design Awards are bestowed annually by the International Association
of Lighting Designers. The program emphasizes **design innovation with attention to
energy usage, economics, and sustainable design**. One project receives the Radiance
Award, the finest example of lighting design excellence among all submissions.

www.iald.org

2010 Winners

Radiance Award for Excellence in Lighting Design

Sheikh Zayed Bin Sultan Al Nahyan Mosque,
Exterior Lighting
Abu Dhabi, UAE
Speirs & Major Associates (UK)

Awards of Excellence

Chipotle Mexican Grill, New Concept
Prototype
New York, NY
Arc Light Design

First National Bank Metro Crossing, Glass
Feature Wall
Council Bluffs, IA
RDG Planning & Design

Infinity Bridge
Stockton on Tees, UK
Speirs & Major Associates

Nyborg Bridges
Two Highway Bridges F45/46 on Highway
E20, Denmark
ÅF - Hansen & Henneberg (Denmark)

Utah State Capitol Restoration
Salt Lake City, UT
Randy Burkett Lighting Design

Vastra Eriksberg Crane and Dock
Gothemburg, Sweden
Ljusarkitektur (Sweden)

Award of Excellence & Sustainability

New Acropolis Museum
Athens, Greece
Arup Lighting (UK)

Awards of Merit

Auto Storage Facility
Westchester, NY
Schwinghammer Lighting

Canada Line Rapid Transit System
Vancouver, BC, Canada
Total Lighting Solutions (Canada)

Chanel Encore
Las Vegas, NV
Fisher Marantz Stone

Macquarie Park & University Stations, Epping-
Chatswood Railway
North Ryde, Sydney, NSW, Australia
PointOfView (Australia)

Joyeria D (D Jewelry Shop)
Pamplona, Spain
architectural lighting solutions (UK)

Maki Office Building, Novartis Campus
Basel, Switzerland
Licht Kunst Licht AG (Germany)

Private San Francisco Residence
San Francisco, CA
Fisher Marantz Stone

Sands Bethworks Retained Edifices
Bethlehem, PA
Speirs & Major Associates (UK)

Stephen M. Ross School of Business,
   University of Michigan
Ann Arbor, MI
Lam Partners Inc.

National Portrait Gallery
Canberra, Australia
Steensen Varming Australia (Australia)

Puli Hotel
Shanghai, China
The Flaming Beacon (Australia)

USGBC Headquarters
Washington, DC
Clanton & Associates

Special Citations
Showroom ROCA
Barcelona, Spain
artec3 (Spain)

Modern Wing, Art Institute of Chicago
Chicago, IL
Arup Lighting (UK)

Source: International Association of Lighting Designers

© Maxwell MacKenzie

Courtesy of Architect of the Capitol

US Capitol Visitor Center, Washington, DC | RTKL Associates Inc.

SUSTAINABILITY | Green Design & Historic Preservation

Sustainability for the stewardship of our
planet's resources is the subject of this chapter
in its dual aspects of green design and historic
preservation. Recent winners of sustainable
design awards (buildings, products, and
leaders), in addition to historic preservation
awards and timely alerts, are presented.

(Note: Bolded text indicates additions to the existing list.)

Beyond Green Awards

The Sustainable Buildings Industry Council grants its annual Beyond Green Awards to recognize **initiatives that shape and catalyze the high-performance building market**. Entries are judged on their successful application of the whole building approach and their ability to balance the design objectives (accessible, aesthetic, cost effective, functional, historic, productive, safe/secure, and sustainable) of a high-performance building with energy and environmental considerations.

www.sbicouncil.org

2009 High-Performance Buildings Winners

First Place
Empire State Building, Integrated Energy
    Efficiency Retrofit
New York, NY
Rocky Mountain Institute; Jones Lang LaSalle;
    Clinton Climate Initiative; Johnson Controls

Citations
Emerson Energy-Efficient Global Data Center
St. Louis, MO
Emerson Electric Company

Charlotte Vermont House
Charlotte, VT
Pill-Maharam Architects

Kroon Hall, School of Forestry &
    Environmental Studies, Yale University
New Haven, CT
Centerbrook Architects and Planners

2009 High-Performance Initiative Winners

Citation
Water Independence in Oregon's Buildings
Portland, OR
SERA Architects; Interface Engineering

Source: Sustainable Buildings Industry Council

Bloom Awards

The Bloom Awards, sponsored by the American Society of Interior Designers and *Interiors & Sources* magazine, celebrate sustainable commercial interior design products that are also innovative and unique. **Entries are judged for their environmental innovation, aesthetics, promotion of sustainability, material selection, resource efficiency, and recycling and waste management within the manufacturing process.** The winners are featured in an issue of *Interiors & Sources*.

www.bloomawards.com

2010 Winners

Flooring
Powerbond ethos Cushion
Tandus

Systems Furniture
Silea Desk System
Gunlocke

Occasional Furniture
XCube
Southern Aluminum

Innovative Materials
Refined Line
IceStone

Textiles
Tabrasa
Ideapaint

Source: American Society of Interior Designers

BSA Sustainable Design Awards

The Boston Society of Architects bi-annually presents the Sustainable Design Awards to **projects worldwide that have a minimal impact on the environment**. The judging criteria include energy-efficiency and minimal ecological impact of materials integrated with traditional design requirements.

www.architects.org

2009 Winners

Honor Award for Design Excellence
Children's Museum
Boston, MA
Cambridge Seven Associates

International Fund for Animal Welfare
    Headquarters
Yarmouth Port, MA
designLAB

Awards for Design
New England Biolabs
Ipswich, MA
TRO Jung | Brannen

Garthwaite Center for Science and Art,
    Cambridge School of Weston
Weston, MA
Architerra

Gary C. Comer Geochemistry Building,
    Lamont-Doherty Earth Observatory
Palisades, NY
Payette

Starr Library, Middlebury College
Middlebury VT
CBT

Citation, Low-Waste Flexibility in a Modern Office Space
Post Office Square
Boston, MA
Audrey O'Hagan Architects

Citation, Off-Grid Housing
West Basin House
Santa Fe, NM
Signer Harris Architects

Citation, Innovative Use of Solar Technology
GreenPix
Beijing, China
Simone Giostra & Partners | Architects (China)

Citation, Social Sustainability
Jamaica Plain Cohousing
Jamaica Plain, MA
Kraus-Fitch Architects; Domenech Hicks &
    Krockmalnic Architects

Citation, Reusability of Materials and Components
Cellophane House Exhibit, Museum of
    Modern Art
New York, NY
KieranTimberlake

Citation, Student Housing
Davis Student Village, College of the Atlantic
Bar Harbor, ME
Coldham & Hartman Architects

Citation, Urban Chicago Development
Southworks Lakeside Chicago Development
Chicago, IL
Sasaki Associates, Inc.; Skidmore, Owings &
    Merrill

Source: Boston Society of Architects

Earth-Minded Award

The Earth-Minded Award program recognizes the achievement and advancement of **green design in the hospitality industry**. Sponsored by the American Society of Interior Designers and *Hospitality Design* magazine, the competition annually honors one hospitality project and one hospitality product that are environmentally innovative and aesthetically pleasing, promote sustainability, incorporate recycling and waste management, and use materials that were carefully selected.

www.asid.org

2010 Winners

Hospitality Products
Glass Series Guest Interface Device Suite
INNCOM

Hospitality Projects
ARIA Resort and Casino
Las Vegas, NV

Alila Villas Uluwatu
Bali, Indonesia

Student Hospitality Project
AIS Senior Studio
Michelle Kiese

Source: American Society of Interior Designers

ED+C Excellence in Design Awards

Environmental Design + Construction's Excellence in Design Awards celebrate **buildings that demonstrate a commitment to green building and sustainable design**. Any architect, interior designer, contractor, building owner, or engineer is eligible to submit projects completed within the previous two years. A jury of professionals reviews entries for such green features as energy efficiency, indoor air quality, water conservation, sustainable or recycled materials, and site selection.

www.edcmag.com

2010 Winners

Commercial
Blue Cross Blue Shield of Rhode Island,
 Corporate Headquarters
Providence, RI
SMMA

Government
Roosevelt Community Center
San Jose, CA
Group 4 Architecture, Research + Planning

Educational
Kroon Hall, Yale School of Forestry and
 Environmental Studies
New Haven, CT
Centerbrook Architects and Planners

Institutional
Center for Global Conservation, Bronx Zoo
Bronx, NY
FXFOWLE Architects

Residential
Los Vecinos
Chula Vista, CA
Wakeland Housing and Development
 Corporation

Source: Environmental Design + Construction *magazine*

Green Roof Awards of Excellence

Green Roofs for Healthy Cities established the Green Roof Awards of Excellence to recognize **green roof projects that exhibit leadership in integrated design and implementation and increase public awareness of the benefits of green roofs**. Entries are evaluated for their aesthetic, economic, functional, and ecological components. In addition, the jury grants the Civic Award of Excellence and other special awards as warranted.

www.greenroofs.org

2009 Winners

Industrial/Commercial, Extensive
Building 607, O'Hare Modernization Program
Chicago, IL
McDonough Associatess

Industrial/Commercial, Intensive
Broadway Tech Centre
Victoria, BC, Canada
Bunting Coady Architects (Canada)

Institutional, Extensive
Burnside Gorge Community Centre
Victoria, BC, Canada
Garyali Architect Inc. (Canada)

Institutional, Intensive
Gary Comer Youth Center
Chicago, IL
Hoerr Schaudt Landscape Architects

Residential, Extensive
Big Sur
Big Sur, CA
Carver + Schicketanz

Residential, Intensive
Macallen Building Condominiums
Boston, MA
Office dA

Green Wall Design
Urban Farming Food Chain
Los Angeles, CA
EOA/Elmslie Osler Architects

Research Award of Excellence
Tim Carter

Civic Award of Excellence, Individual
Kerry Ross

Civic Award of Excellence, Organization
Storm Water Infrastructure Matters

Special Recognition
Celebrity Solstice – Lawn Club
Green Roof Service Expertise

Source: Green Roofs for Healthy Cities

Holcim Awards for Sustainable Construction

The Holcim Awards for Sustainable Construction encourage **future-oriented, tangible sustainable design initiatives in the building and construction industry**. The competition was created by the Swiss-based Holcim Foundation for Sustainable Construction and is conducted in partnership with some of the world's leading technical universities. Prize money totaling $2 million per three-year competition cycle encourages and inspires achievements that go beyond convention to explore new ways and means.

www.holcimfoundation.org

2009 Global Recipients

Gold
River Remediation and Urban Development
   Scheme
Fez, Morocco
Aziza Chaouni (Morocco); Takako Tajima

Silver
Low-Impact Greenfield University
Ho Chi Minh City, Vietnam
Kazuhiro Kojima (Japan)

Bronze
Sustainable Planning for a Rural Community
Beijing, China
Yue Zhang (China); Feng Ni (China)

Source: Holcim Foundation for Sustainable Construction

Lifecycle Building Challenge

The Lifecycle Building Challenge rewards **projects that facilitate and advance the eventual recovery of building systems, components, and materials through adaptation, disassembly, or dismantling.** Lifecycle thinking encompasses the idea of creating buildings that are stocks of resources for future buildings. The program is sponsored by the US Environmental Protection Agency. Winners are announced at the West Coast Green Conference.

www.lifecyclebuilding.org

2009 US Winners

Student Building
[Un] Modular Design for Deconstruction
David Fleming, University of Cincinnati

Professional Building
Bernheim Arboretum Visitors Center
Clermont, KY
William McDonough + Partners

Professional Product
Modular Temporary Construction Wall/
  Barricade
ENVY Modular Wall Systems

2009 Outstanding Achievements Awards

Best School Design
School M.O.D.
Yosuke Kawai and Ikue Nomura, University
  of Pennsylvania

Best Green Job Creation
ReAnimateLA: Center for Ecological & Urban
  Recovery
Los Angeles, CA
Hayley Stewart, California State Polytechnic
  University, Pomona

Best Greenhouse Gas Reduction
Bernheim Arboretum Visitors Center
Clermont, KY
William McDonough + Partners

2009 Honorable Mentions

Student Building
Political Ply - An Arid Zone Shade Structure
Jason Griffiths, Arizona State University

School M.O.D.
Yosuke Kawai and Ikue Nomura, University
of Pennsylvania

Professional Building
Reclaimed Space: Sustainable, Modern
Zak Hardage, Tracen Gardner, and Kimber
Reed-Barber, Reclaimed Space, Austin, TX

2009 International Winner

Student Building
The Worm Bar
Miaoling Li, National University of Singapore
(Singapore)

2009 International Honorable Mentions

Student Building
Carapace Communion
Rhys Owen, University of Westminster (UK)

CLOTHed Pavilion
Hui Ying Lim, National University of Singapore
(Singapore)

Garden Toilet
Caijin Huang, National University of Singapore
(Singapore)

Source: US Environmental Protection Agency

National Award for Smart Growth Achievement

Through the National Award for Smart Growth Achievement, the US Environmental Protection Agency recognizes **public entities that promote and achieve smart growth**, thus creating better communities and initiating environmental benefits. The competition is open to local and state governments and other public-sector entities. Nonprofit or private organizations and individuals are not eligible for the award; however, when collaborating with a governmental or public-sector entity their participation is acknowledged.

www.epa.gov

2009 Winners

Overall Excellence in Smart Growth
Envision Lancaster County Comprehensive
    Plan and Implementation
Lancaster, PA
Lancaster County Planning Commission

Built Projects
Parkside of Old Town
Chicago, IL
Chicago Housing Authority; FitzGerald
    Associates Architects; Holsten Real Estate
    Development Corporation

Policies and Regulations
The City of Charlotte
Charlotte, NC
Charlotte Department of Transportation

Smart Growth & Green Building
Tempe Transportation Center
Tempe, AZ
City of Tempe; Architekton + Otak

Source: US Environmental Protection Agency

National Green Building Awards

The National Association of Home Builders presents the annual Green Building Awards to recognize **leaders who have advanced green-home building**. With this program, the NAHB hopes to encourage builders to incorporate green practices into their developments, designs, and construction methodologies and to speed the public's acceptance of sustainable, environmentally friendly building. A jury of industry professionals selects the winners, who are celebrated at the annual NAHB National Green Building Conference.

www.nahb.org

2010 Winners

Single Family Custom/Luxury Project of the Year
Charity Works Greenhouse
McLean, VA
Cunningham | Quill Architects

Single Family Custom/Affordable Project of the Year
Cottage
Petoskey, MI
J.R. Construction Building & Design

Single Family Production/Luxury Project of the Year
Model NOGM4
Marietta, GA
New World Home

Single Family Production/Affordable Project of the Year
Rosewood Hills
Columbia, SC
Mungo Construction

Multifamily Luxury
Circle at Concord Mills
Concord, NC
Crescent Resources

Multifamily Affordable
Wingate Manor
Shiloh, IL
Gundaker Commercial Group

Green Development of the Year
Fishhawk Ranch
Lithia, FL
Newland Communities

Green Remodeling Project of the Year
Philip Beere

Green Remodeling Advocate of the Year
Philip Beere

Builder Advocate of the Year
Michael Chandler

Corporate Advocate of the Year
Pardee Homes

Individual Advocate of the Year
John Barrows

State/Local Government Advocate of the Year
Platte County, MO

New Green Building Program of the Year
Home Builders Association of Delaware Green Building Council

Program of the Year
Green Home Builders of the Triangle

Source: National Association of Home Builders

Smart Environments Awards

The International Interior Design Association and *Metropolis* magazine launched the Smart Environments Awards program in 2006 to recognize the **best design solutions from the past five years that fully integrate sustainable design strategies**. The competition is open to interior designers and architects and aims to celebrate socially responsible, beautiful, functional designs that integrate design excellence, human well-being, and sustainability.

www.metropolismag.com

2009 Winners

Twelve West
Portland, OR
ZGF Architects

The Plant: Café Organic
San Francisco, CA
CCS Architecture

Kroon Hall, School of Forestry &
    Environmental Studies, Yale University
New Haven, CT
Centerbrook Architects and Planners

*Source: International Interior Design Association
and* Metropolis

Solar Decathlon

In the biennial Solar Decathlon competition, multidisciplinary student teams from colleges and universities from around the world design, build, and operate **houses that are powered entirely by the sun**. The houses must be attractive, effective, and energy efficient and produce enough energy to power an electric car. Finalists transport their houses to the National Mall in Washington, DC, where final judging takes place under the direction of the US Department of Energy, the competition's sponsor.

www.solardecathlon.org

2009 Winners

First Place
surPLUS House
Technische Universität Darmstadt (Germany)

Second Place
Gable House
University of Illinois at Champaign-Urbana

Third Place
Refract House
Santa Clara University; California College
    of the Arts

Appliances
Gable House
University of Illinois at Champaign-Urbana

Architecture
Refract House
Santa Clara University; California College
    of the Arts

Comfort Zone
surPLUS House
Technische Universität Darmstadt

Communications
Refract House
Santa Clara University; California College
    of the Arts

Engineering
ICON Solar House
University of Minnesota

Home Entertainment
Gable House
University of Illinois at Champaign-Urbana

Hot Water
Gable House
University of Illinois at Champaign-Urbana

Lighting
ICON Solar House
University of Minnesota

Market Viability
BeauSoleil Home
University of Louisiana at Lafayette

Net Metering
surPLUS House
Technische Universität Darmstadt

Source: Solar Decathlon

Top Green Projects

The American Institute of Architects' Committee on the Environment annually selects the Top Green Projects to highlight **viable architectural design solutions that protect and enhance the environment**. Winning projects address significant environmental challenges, such as energy and water conservation, use of recycled materials, and improved indoor air quality. Responsible use of building materials, daylighting, efficient heating and cooling, and sensitivity to local environmental issues are some of the jury's considerations.

www.aiatopten.org

2010 Winners

355 11th Street
San Francisco, CA
Aidlin Darling Design

Homer Science & Student Life Center
Atherton, CA
Leddy Maytum Stacy Architects

KAUST
Thuwal Kingdom, Saudi Arabia
Hellmuth, Obata & Kassabaum

Kroon Hall
New Haven, CT
Centerbrook Architects and Planners; Hopkins
    Architects

Manassas Park Elementary School + Pre-K
Manassas Park, VA
VMDO Architects

Manitoba Hydro Place
Winnipeg, MB, Canada
Smith Carter (Canada); Kuwabara Payne
    McKenna Blumbert Architects (Canada)

Omega Center for Sustainable Living
Rhinebeck, NY
BNIM Architects

Special No. 9 House
New Orleans, LA
KieranTimberlake

Twelve West
Portland, OR
ZGF Architects

Watsonville Water Resource Center
Watsonville, CA
WRNS Studio

Source: American Institute of Architects

Top 10 Green Building Products

The Top 10 Green Building Products of the Year award recognizes the **best products added to the** *GreenSpec* **directory** during the past year as selected by editors of *Environmental Building News*. With more than 2,000 listings, the directory contains a wide range of materials, products, and equipment that can help reduce the environmental impact of a building. *GreenSpec* carefully evaluates all products; manufacturers do not pay to be listed, nor docs the directory carry advertising.

www.buildinggreen.com

2009 Winners

Project FROG Modular Green Classroom
Project FROG

Pozzotive Plus CMUs and Concrete Brick
Kingston Block

Invelope Integrated Wall Insulation and
    Rainscreen System
Invelope

Thermafiber Mineral Wool Insulation Products
Thermafiber

Baltix Recycled- and Biobased-Content Office
    Furniture
Baltix

Rheem HP-50 Heat-Pump Water Heater
Rhccm

Convia Energy-Management Infrastructure
Convia

Pentadyne GTX Flywheel Energy Storage
Pentadyne

Silva Cell Subsurface Tree Protection and
    Stormwater System
Deep Root

Mobile Solar Power Generator
Mobile Solar Power

Source: BuildingGreen

America's 11 Most Endangered Historic Places

The National Trust for Historic Preservation annually compiles a list of the **most threatened historic sites in the United States**. Since 1988, this program has highlighted more than 185 historic buildings, sites, and landscapes threatened by neglect, deterioration, insufficient funds, inappropriate development, or insensitive public policy. While being listed does not guarantee protection or financial support, the attention generated by the program has produced significant support for many of the threatened sites.

www.preservationnation.org

2010 Endangered Historic Places

America's State Parks and State-Owned
   Historic Sites
Nationwide

Black Mountain
Lynch and Benham, KY

Hinchliffe Stadium
Paterson, NJ

Industrial Arts Building
Lincoln, NE

Juana Briones House
Palo Alto, CA

Merritt Parkway
Fairfield County, CT

Metropolitan AME Church
Washington, DC

Pågat
Yigo, Guam

Saugatuck Dunes
Saugatuck, MI

Threefoot Building
Meridian, MS

Wilderness Battlefield
Orange and Spotsylvania Counties, VA

Source: National Trust for Historic Preservation

European Union Prize for Cultural Heritage/ Europa Nostra Awards

The European Union Prize for Cultural Heritage/Europa Nostra Awards promote **high standards and high-quality skills in conservation practice**. To stimulate the cross-cultural exchange of information, the program promotes skills in conservation, research, service, and education and training. The awards are granted annually by the European Commission and Europa Nostra, the Pan-European Federation for Cultural Heritage.

www.europanostra.org

2010 Conservation Winners

Nordkette Cableway Stations
Innsbruck, Austria

La Fonderie de la Société Alsacienne de
    Construction Mëcanique
Mulhouse, France

Le Collège des Bernardins
Paris, France

Sarcophagi of the Dukes of Pomerania
Wolgast, Germany

Neues Museum
Berlin, Germany

Ancient Tower and Adjacent Buildings at
    Horio-Aghia Triada
Amorgos, Greece

National Observatory of Athens
Athens, Greece

Fortifications and City Walls of 's-Hertogen-
    bosch
's-Hertogenbosch, Netherlands

Westergasfabriek
Amsterdam, Netherlands

Monastery of Santa Clara-A-Velha
Coimbra, Portugal

Roman Theatre
Cartagena, Spain

Church of Los Descalzos
Ecija, Spain

Royal Site of San Ildefonso
San Ildefonso, Spain

Sultan's Pavilion of the Yeni Mosque
Istanbul, Turkey

St. Davids Bishop's Palace
St. Davids, UK

St. Martin-in-the-Fields
London, UK

Source: Europa Nostra

Great American Main Street Awards

Each year the National Trust for Historic Preservation's National Main Street Center celebrates five communities that have demonstrated **considerable success with preservation-based revitalization**. These towns have generated support from their residents and business leaders, drawn financial assistance from both public and private sources, and created innovative solutions for their unique situations.

www.mainstreet.org

1995
Clarksville, MO
Dubuque, IA
Franklin, TN
Sheboygan Falls, WI
Old Pasadena, CA

1996
Bonaparte, IA
Chippewa Falls, WI
East Carson Street
  Business District,
  Pittsburgh, PA
Saratoga Springs, NY
Wooster, OH

1997
Burlington, VT
DeLand, FL
Georgetown, TX
Holland, MI
Libertyville, IL

1998
Corning, IA
Lanesboro, MN
Morgantown, WV
Thomasville, GA
York, PA

1999
Bay City, MI
Cordell, OK
Denton, TX
Lafayette, IN
San Luis Obispo, CA

2000
Coronado, CA
Keokuk, IA
Newkirk, OK
Port Townsend, WA
St. Charles, IL

2001
Danville, KY
Elkader, IA
Enid, OK
Mansfield, OH
Walla Walla, WA

2002
Cedar Falls, IA
La Crosse, WI
Milford, NH
Okmulgee, OK
Staunton, VA

2003
Greenville, SC
Littleton, NH
Manassas, VA
Rome, GA
Wenatchee, WA

2004
Burlington, IA
Encinitas, CA
Paso Robles, CA
Rogers, AR
Westfield, NJ

2005
Barracks Row,
  Washington, DC
Emporia, KS
Frederick, MD
New Iberia, LA
Washington Gateway,
  Boston, MA

2006*
El Reno, OK
Lynchburg, VA
Natchitoches, LA
Parsons, KS

2009
Broadway District,
  Green Bay, WI
El Dorado, AR
Federal Hill,
  Baltimore, MD
Livermore, CA
Rehoboth Beach, DE

2010
Columbus, MS
Fairmount, WV
Ferndale, MI
Lee's Summit, MO
Paducah, KY

*Awards were not granted in 2007 or 2008.

Source: National Trust Main Street Center

J. Timothy Anderson Awards

The J. Timothy Anderson Awards for Excellence in Historic Rehabilitation honor **outstanding real estate projects that rehabilitate historic buildings using federal historic rehabilitation tax credits**. Entries are judged for their overall design and quality, interpretation and respect of historic elements, impact on the community, and financial and market success. The National Housing & Rehabilitation Association named the competition in memory of Boston architect and preservation advocate J. Timothy Anderson.

www.housingonline.com

2009 Winners

Best Mixed-Income Residential
Baker Square II
Dorchester, MA
The Architectural Team

Best Market-Rate Residential
Market at Fifth
Pittsburgh, PA
Landmarks Design Associates

Best Historic Rehabilitation Project Utilizing New Markets Tax Credits
Court Square Center
Memphis, TN
CM Design Corporation

Best Commercial/Retail/Non-Residential Project
The Old Cotton Factory
Rock Hill, SC
McClure Nicholson Montgomery Architects

Best Historic Rehabilitation Project Involving New Construction
Globe Mills
Sacramento, CA
Applied Architecture

Most Innovative Adaptive Reuse
Charles H. Shaw Technology & Learning Center
Chicago, IL
Farr Associates

Best Historic Rehabilitation Project Utilizing Low-Income Housing Tax Credits, Large
Toward Independent Living & Learning
Chelsea, MA
Mostue & Associates Architects

Best Historic Rehabilitation Project Utilizing Low-Income Housing Tax Credits, Small
Fairbanks Flats Rowhomes
Beloit, WI
Gorman & Company, Inc.

Judges' Awards
Park Lane at Sea View
Staten Island, NY
Hugo Subotovsky Architects

Westin Book Cadillac Hotel & Condominiums
Detroit, MI
Kaczmar Architects; Sandvick Architects

Source: National Housing & Rehabilitation Association

Knoll Modernism Prize

The Knoll Modernism Prize is awarded biennially to a design professional or firm in recognition of an **innovative design solution that preserves a Modern landmark**. The program is also intended to inspire the preservation and restoration of other great Modern buildings, enhancing awareness of the significant role that modernism plays in our architectural heritage. The prize is sponsored by the World Monuments Fund and Knoll. Recipients receive an $10,000 honorarium and a limited-edition chair manufactured by Knoll.

www.wmf.org

2008 ADGB Trade Union School
Bernau, Germany
Brenne Gesellschaft von Architekten mbH
(Germany)
2010 **Bierman Henket Architecten (Netherlands)**
Wessel De Jonge Architecten (Netherlands)

Source: World Monuments Fund

National Preservation Awards

The National Trust for Historic Preservation annually recognizes citizens, organizations, and public and private entities for their dedication to and **support of historic preservation**. A jury of preservation professionals selects the winners of the National Preservation Awards using such criteria as the projects' positive effect on the community, pioneering nature, quality, and degree of difficulty. Special interest is also placed on projects that use historic preservation as a method of revitalization.

www.preservationnation.org

2010 Winners

Eastern Market Restoration
Washington, DC

Empire State Building Lobby Restoration
New York, NY

Fox Theater
Spokane, WA

Hanover Theatre for the Performing Arts
Worcester, MA

Historic Fifth Street School
Las Vegas, NV

King Edward Revitalization Project
Jackson, MS

Land Trust for Tennessee
Nashville, TN

Main Street Iowa
Des Moines, IA

Milwaukee City Hall Exterior Restoration
Milwaukee, WI

Montana Legislature House Appropriations Committee and Senate Finance and Claims Committee, Montana Governor Brian Schweitzer, and the Montana Preservation Alliance
Butte, MT

Nemours Mansion and Gardens
Wilmington, DE

The Royalton
Miami, FL

Rosenwald Schools Initiative
Southern United States

Save Our Bridge
St. Augustine, FL

Sengelmann Hall
Schulenburg, TX

Source: National Trust for Historic Preservation

NTHP/HUD Secretary's Award for Excellence in Historic Preservation

The Secretary's Award for Excellence in Historic Preservation, conferred jointly by the National Trust for Historic Preservation and HUD, honors **preservation projects that provide affordable housing or expanded economic opportunities for low- and moderate-income families and individuals**. Nominations are reviewed for their impact on the community, quality and degree of difficulty, unusual or pioneering nature, affordable housing and economic development opportunities, and ability to fit within a community redevelopment plan.

www.huduser.org/research/secaward.html

1998	A.T. Lewis and Rio Grande Lofts Denver, CO	2005	Umpqua Community Development Corporation Roseburg, OR
1999	Belle Shore Apartments Chicago, IL	2006	Midtown Exchange Minneapolis, MN
2000	The city of Covington Kentucky	2007	Hilliard Towers Apartments Chicago, IL
2001	Notre Dame Academy Cleveland, OH	2008	Ajo Curley School Project Ajo, AZ
2002	Hamilton Hotel Laredo, TX	2009	Fairbanks Flats Rowhomes Beloit, WI
2003	Ziegler Estate/La Casita Verde Los Angeles, CA	2010	**Crown Square Development St. Louis, MO**
2004	Reviviendo Family Housing Lawrence, MA		

Source: National Trust for Historic Preservation

UNESCO Asia-Pacific Heritage Awards

As a part of UNESCO's culture heritage program in Asia and the Pacific, the Awards for Culture Heritage Conservation celebrate the efforts of individuals and private-sector organizations to **conserve and restore structures more than 50 years old**. In addition, the Jury Commendation for Innovation recognizes newly built structures that demonstrate outstanding standards for contemporary architectural design that are well integrated into historic contexts.

www.unescobkk.org/culture/heritageawards/

2010 Winners

Award of Excellence
Hong San See Temple
Singapore

Awards of Distinction
Red Brick Warehouses
Yokohama, Japan

Gulabpur Khanqah
Skardu, Pakistan

Awards of Merit
Fu'long Taoist Temple
Sichuan, China

Chowmahalla Palace
Hyderabad, India

Old Houses in the World Heritage Fort of Galle
Galle, Sri Lanka

Honorable Mentions
Ballaarat Mechanics' Institute
Ballarat, Australia

North Xinjiao Street
Zhejiang, China

Chhatrapati Shivaji Maharaj Vastu
    Sangrahalaya (Prince of Wales Museum)
Mumbai, India

Jury Commendation for Innovation
No award granted

Source: United Nations' Educational, Scientific and Cultural Organization

World's 100 Most Endangered Sites

The World Monuments Fund's biennial list of the 100 Most Endangered Sites contains **architectural sites and monuments most in danger of destruction**. For many sites, inclusion on this list is their only hope for survival. Limited financial support is also available and is awarded on a competitive basis. The World Monuments Fund is a private, nonprofit organization that fosters awareness and preservation of the world's cultural, artistic, and historic resources.

www.wmf.org

2010 Endangered Sites

Afghanistan
Old City of Herat

Argentina
Buenos Aires Historic Center
Teatro Colón, Buenos Aires

Armenia
Aghjots Monastery, Garni Village

Austria
Wiener Werkbundsiedlung, Vienna

Bahrain
Suq al-Qaysariya, Muharraq

Belgium
Sanatorium Joseph Lemaire, Tombeek

Bhutan
Phajoding, Thimphu

Bolivia
Convento-Museo Santa Teresa, Cochabamba
Misiones Jesuíticas de Chiquitos

Chile
Churches of Arica Parinacota

Colombia
San Fernando and San José Fortresses,
   Cartagena de Indias
Santa Fe de Antioquia Historic Center

Comoros
Ujumbe Palace, Mutsamudu

Cyprus
Historic Walled City of Famagusta

Ecuador
Todos Santos Complex, Cuenca

Egypt
New Gourna Village, Luxor, West Bank
Old Mosque of Shali Fortress, Siwa Oasis

France
Hôtel de Monnaies, Villemagne l'Argentière
Parish Church of Saint-Martin-des-Puits

Greece
Churches of Lesvos

Guatemala
Kaminaljuyu, Guatemala City

Haiti
Gingerbread Houses, Port-au-Prince

India
Chiktan Castle, Kargil
Dechen Namgyal Gonpa, Nyoma
Historic Civic Centre of Shimla
Kothi, Qila Mahmudabad

Iraq
Al-Hadba' Minaret, Mosul

Ireland
Russborough, Blessington, County Wicklow

Israel
Cathedral of Saint James, Old City of
    Jerusalem
Old City of Lod

Italy
Historic Center of Craco
Ponte Lucano, Tivoli
Villa of San Gilio, Oppido Lucano

Japan
Kyoto Machiya Townhouses

Jordan
Damiya Dolmen Field, Jordan Valley

Kazakhstan
Vernacular Architecture of the Kazakh Steppe,
    Sary-Arka

Lao People's Democratic Republic
Hintang Archaeological Landscape,
    Houameuang District
Tam Ting, Nam Kong River at Ban Pak Ou

Mexico
Acueducto de Tembleque, Zempoala to
    Otumba
Las Pozas, Xilitla
Templo do San Bartolo Soyaltepec
Templo de San Felipe Tindaco, Tlaxiaco
Templo y Convento de los Santos Reyes,
    Convento de la Communidad, Metztitlán

Republic of Moldova
Assumption of Our Lady Church, Causeni

Morocco
Lixus, Larache

Pakistan
Petroglyphs in the Diamer-Basha Dam Area,
    Northern Areas
Shikarpoor Historic City Center

Panama
Colón Historic Center
Corozal Cemetery, Panama City
Mount Hope Cemetery, Colón

Paraguay
La Santísima Trinidad del Paraná, Trinidad

Peru
Chankillo, San Rafael District
Jesuit Churches of San José and San Javier,
    Nazca
Pachacamac Sanctuary, Lurín
Pikillaqta, Cuzco
Santuario Histórico Machu Picchu, Cuzco
Tambo Colorado, Humay
San Francisco de Asís de Marcapata
Santa Cruz de Jerusalén de Juli

Philippines
Nuestra Señora de la Asunción Church,
    Municipality of Santa Maria
Rice Terraces of the Philippine Cordilleras,
    Ifugao
San Sebastian Basilica, Manila

Romania
Fortified Churches of Southern Transylvania,
    Sibiu

Russian Federation
Church of the Icon of the Mother of God of
    the Sign, Podolsk District

Slovakia
Lietava Castle

South Africa
Wonderwerk Cave, Ga-Segonyana/Kuruman

World's 100 Most Endangered Sites

Spain
Historic Landscape of Sevilla
Historic Landscape of Toledo
Numancia, Soria and Garray
Old Town of Ávila
Route of Santiago de Compostela
Temple Expiatori de la Sagrada Família,
    Barcelona

Sri Lanka
Dutch Fort in Batticaloa

Tanzania
Pangani Historic Town

Uganda
Wamala King's Tombs, Nansana, Wakiso
    District

United Kingdom
Carlisle Memorial Methodist Church, Belfast
Edinburgh Historic Graveyards
Sheerness Dockyard
St. John the Evangelist Parish Church,
    Shobdon
Tecton Buildings at Dudley Zoological Gardens

United States
Atlanta-Fulton Central Public Library,
    Atlanta, GA
Bridges of the Merritt Parkway, CT
Cultural Landscape of Hadley, MA
Miami Marine Stadium, FL
Phillis Wheatley Elementary School, New
    Orleans, LA
St. Louis Cemetery No. 2, New Orleans, LA
Taliesin, Spring Green, WI
Taliesin West, Scottsdale, AZ
Taos Pueblo, NM

Uzbekistan
Desert Castles of Ancient Khorezm, Republic
    of Karakalpakstan

Venezuela
Facultad de Arquitectura y Urbanismo,
    Universidad Central de Venezuela, Caracas
Parque del Este, Caracas

Source: World Monuments Fund

10

MAKING A DIFFERENCE |

Initiatives that improve the quality of the
human environment and benefit humanity
are the subject of this chapter. Awards in
this developing genre relate to affordable
housing and other movements that
demonstrate enhanced responsibility to
social issues through buildings.

(Note: Bolded text indicates additions to the existing list.)

AIA/HUD Secretary's Housing and Community Design Award

The Housing and Community Design Award, presented by the American Institute of Architects and the US Department of Housing and Urban Development, celebrates **excellence in affordable housing, community design, and accessibility**. It also emphasizes design as integral to creating thriving homes and communities. The Alan J. Rothman Housing Accessibility Award was named for the late HUD senior policy analyst who was an expert on disability issues.

www.aia.org

2010 Winners

Community-Informed Design
Congo Street Green Initiative
Dallas, TX
buildingcommunity WORKSHOP

Creating Community Connection
Arbor Lofts
Lancaster, CA
PSL Architects

Excellence in Affordable Housing Design
Paseo Center at Coyote Creek
San Jose, CA
David Baker + Partners, Architects

Alan J. Rothman Award for Housing Accessibility
Madrona Live
Seattle, WA
Tyler Engle Architects

Source: American Institute of Architects

Design for Humanity Award

The American Society of Interior Designers grants the annual Design for Humanity Award to an individual or institution for significant design-related initiatives that have had a universal and far-reaching effect on improving the **quality of the human environment**. A committee appointed by the ASID board reviews the nominations, and the award is presented at ASID's annual national convention.

www.asid.org

1990	The Scavenger Hotline	2000	Victoria Schomer
1991	E.I. Du Pont de Nemours & Company	2001	ASID Tennessee Chapter, Chattanooga
1992	The Preservation Resource Center	2002	Cynthia Leibrock
1993	Neighborhood Design Center	2003	Habitat for Humanity International
1994	Elizabeth Paepcke and International Design Conference in Aspen	2004	Architecture for Humanity and Cameron Sinclair
		2005	Patricia Moore
1995	Cranbrook Academy of Art	2006	The Robin Hood Foundation
1996	Wayne Ruga and the Center for Health Design	2007	Katrina Cottages
		2009*	Greg Mortenson
1997	Barbara J. Campbell, *Accessibility Guidebook For Washington, DC*		HOK Community Service Project
		2010	**Ray Anderson**
1998	William L. Wilkoff		
1999	AlliedSignal, Inc., Polymers Division		

*No award was granted in 2008 when ASID adjusted the award schedule.

Source: American Society of Interior Designers

I. Donald Terner Prize

The biennial I. Donald Terner Prize for Innovation in Affordable Housing began in 2006, the 10th anniversary of the death of I. Donald Terner. Administered by the Center for Community Innovation at the University of California, Berkeley, the prize honors the **work of Don Terner, whose non-profit BRIDGE Housing Corporation has built more than 10,000 affordable housing units**. The award recognizes both projects and the leadership teams behind them.

www.communityinnovation.berkeley.edu

2009 Recipients

Winner
Maverick Landing
Boston, MA
ICON Architecture

Finalists
Civic-Morrison Redevelopment
Portland, OR
SERA Architects

Renaissance at Civic Center Apartments
Denver, CO
The Lawrence Group

St. Vincent's Gardens
Santa Barbara, CA
Lauterbach & Associates Architects

Nuevo Amanecer Apartments
Pajaro, CA
KTGY Group

East Biloxi Homes Program
Biloxi, LA
Gulf Coast Community Design Studio

Source: Center for Community Innovation

John M. Clancy Award

The John M. Clancy Award for Socially Responsible Housing encourages **excellence in the design of urban housing for underserved populations**. Named after architect John M. Clancy, whose work focused on enhancing the lives of ordinary citizens, the award honors public and private multifamily housing projects that serve diverse populations of all income levels. This biennial program is sponsored by Goody Clancy & Associates and administered by the Boston Society of Architects/AIA.

www.johnclancyaward.org

2009 Winners

Honor Awards
Intervale Green
South Bronx, NY
Edelman Sultan Knox Wood/Architects

Multifamily Affordable Housing
Gloucester, MA
Bergmeyer Associates

Project Place – Gatehouse
Boston, MA
Hacin + Associates

Awards for Design
Rheingold Gardens
Brooklyn, NY
Magnusson Architecture and Planning

Waverly Woods
Belmont, MA
Mostue & Associates Architects

Source: Boston Society of Architects/AIA

Keystone Award

Created in 1999 by the American Architectural Foundation, the Keystone Award honors **individuals and organizations outside the field of architecture that have increased the value of architecture and design in our culture**. The award's objective is to encourage leadership by all members of society, reflecting the increasingly important role design plays in our lives and communities. Recipients are celebrated at the annual Accent on Architecture Gala in Washington, DC.

www.archfoundation.org

1999	Richard M. Daley	2006	Pritzker Family
2000	Rick Lowe	2007	Save America's Treasures
2002	Joseph P. Riley Jr.	2008	Museum of Modern Art
2004	US General Services Administration, Public Buildings Service	2009	Manuel A. Diaz
		2010	*No award granted*
2005	Jeremy Harris		

Source: American Architectural Foundation

Whitney M. Young Jr. Award

The American Institute of Architects bestows the Whitney M. Young Jr. Award annually upon an architect or architecturally oriented organization that has demonstrated **exemplary professional responsibility toward current social issues**, a challenge civil rights leader Whitney Young set forth to architects. Current issues include such areas as affordable housing, the inclusion of minorities and women in the profession, access for persons with disabilities, and literacy.

www.aia.org

1972	Robert J. Nash
1973	Architects Workshop of Philadelphia
1974	Stephen Cram*
1975	Van B. Bruner Jr.
1976	Wendell J. Campbell
1980	Leroy M. Campbell*
1981	Robert T. Coles
1982	John S. Chase
1983	Howard Hamilton Mackey Sr.
1984	John Louis Wilson
1985	Milton V. Bergstedt
1986	Richard McClure Prosse*
1987	J. Max Bond Jr.
1988	Habitat for Humanity
1989	John H. Spencer
1990	Harry G. Robinson III
1991	Robert Kennard
1992	Curtis Moody
1993	David Castro-Blanco
1994	Ki Suh Park
1995	William J. Stanley III
1996	John L. Wilson
1997	Alan Y. Taniguchi
1998	Leon Bridges
1999	Charles F. McAfee
2000	Louis L. Weller
2001	Cecil A. Alexander Jr.
2002	Robert P. Madison
2003	Hispanic American Construction Industry Association
2004	Terrance J. Brown
2005	Stanford R. Britt
2006	Theodore C. Landsmark
2007	National Organization of Minority Architects
2008	Norma Merrick Sklarek
2009	Clyde Porter
2010	**Benjamin Vargas**

* Honored posthumously

Source: American Institute of Architects

Wolf Prize for Architecture

The annual Wolf Prize celebrates **outstanding living scientists and artists in the fields of agriculture, chemistry, mathematics, medicine, physics, and the arts**—the arts category rotating among architecture, music, painting, and sculpture. In 1976 Ricardo Wolf established the Wolf Foundation, and shortly thereafter the Wolf Prize, to "promote science and arts for the benefit of mankind." The prize carries a $100,000 honorarium.

www.wolffund.org.il

Architecture Recipients

1983	Ralph Erskine (Sweden)		1996	Frei Otto (Germany)
1988	Fumihiko Maki (Japan)			Aldo van Eyck (Netherlands)
	Giancarlo de Carlo (Italy)		2001	Alvaro Siza (Portugal)
1992	Frank Gehry		2005	Jean Nouvel (France)
	Jørn Utzon (Denmark)		**2010**	**Peter Eisenman**
	Sir Denys Lasdun (UK)			**David Chipperfield (UK)**

Source: Wolf Foundation

11

DESIGN RESOURCES |

Resources that enhance the understanding of landscape architecture, architecture, historic preservation, and urban planning issues are presented in this chapter. Book awards are followed by organizations: the history, purpose, and membership benefits of major national and international design associations, along with a summary listing of numerous design and building-related organizations and government agencies.

(Note: Bolded text indicates additions to the existing list.)

Abbott Lowell Cummings Award

The Vernacular Architecture Forum's Abbott Lowell Cummings Award honors **distinguished books about North American vernacular architecture and landscapes**. Books are evaluated for their level of scholarship, use of fieldwork, and research methods. A founder of the VAF, Abbott Lowell Cummings was a prolific researcher and writer best known for his magnum opus *The Framed Houses of Massachusetts Bay, 1625–1725* (1979).

www.vernaculararchitectureforum.org

1984 No award granted

1985 *Big House, Little House, Back House, Barn: The Connected Farm Buildings of New England*
Thomas Hubka
University Press of New England

1986 *Hollybush*
Charles Martin
University of Tennessee Press

1987 *Holy Things and Profane: Anglican Parish Churches in Colonial Virginia*
Dell Upton
Architectural History Foundation

1988 *Architecture and Rural Life in Central Delaware, 1700–1900*
Bernard L. Herman
University of Tennessee Press

1989 *Study Report for Slave Quarters Reconstruction at Carter's Grove*
Colonial Williamsburg Foundation

Study Report for the Bixby House Restoration
Old Sturbridge Village

1990 *Manhattan for Rent, 1785–1850*
Elizabeth Blackmar
Cornell University Press

Building the Octagon
Orlando Rideout
American Institute of Architects Press

1991 *Architects and Builders in North Carolina*
Catherine W. Bishir, Charlotte Vestal Brown, Carl R. Lounsbury, and Ernest H. Wood
University of North Carolina Press

1992 *Alone Together: A History of New York's Early Apartments*
Elizabeth Collins Cromley
Cornell University Press

A Place to Belong, Community, Order and Everyday Space in Calvert, Newfoundland
Gerald Pocius
University of Georgia Press

1993 *Homeplace: The Social Use and Meaning of the Folk Dwelling in Southwestern North Carolina*
Michael Ann Williams
University of Georgia Press

The Park and the People: A History of Central Park
Roy Rosenzweig and Elizabeth Blackmar
Cornell University Press

1994 *The Stolen House*
Bernard L. Herman
University Press of Virginia

Abbott Lowell Cummings Award

1995 *Living Downtown: The History of Residential Hotels in the United States*
Paul Groth
University of California Press

1996 *An Illustrated Glossary of Early Southern Architecture and Landscape*
Carl R. Lounsbury
Oxford University Press

1997 *Unplanned Suburbs: Toronto's American Tragedy, 1900–1950*
Richard Harris
Johns Hopkins University Press

1998 *City Center to Regional Mall: Architecture, the Automobile, and Retailing in Los Angeles, 1920–1950*
Richard Longstreth
MIT Press

1999 *The Myth of Santa Fe: Creating a Modern Regional Tradition*
Chris Wilson
University of New Mexico Press

Architecture of the United States
Dell Upton
Oxford University Press

2000 *Delta Sugar: Louisiana's Vanishing Plantation Landscape*
John B. Rehder
Johns Hopkins University Press

Cheap, Quick & Easy: Imitative Architectural Materials, 1870–1930*
Pamela H. Simpson
University of Tennessee Press

Building Community, Keeping the Faith: German Catholic Vernacular Architecture in a Rural Minnesota Parish*
Fred W. Peterson
Minnesota Historical Society Press

2001 *Vernacular Architecture*
Henry Glassie
Indiana University Press

2002 *The Patina of Place: The Cultural Weathering of a New England Landscape*
Kingston William Heath
University of Tennessee Press

2003 *Theaters of Conversion: Religious Architecture and Indian Artisans in Colonial Mexico*
Samuel Y. Edgerton
University of New Mexico Press

2004 *A River and Its City: The Nature of Landscape in New Orleans*
Ari Kelman
University of California Press

2005 *Temple of Grace: The Material Transformation of Connecticut's Churches, 1790–1840*
Gretchen Buggeln
University Press of New England

2006 *Town House: Architecture and Material Life in the Early American City, 1780 – 1830*
Bernard L. Herman
University of North Carolina Press

The Courthouses of Early Virginia: An Architectural History
Carl R. Lounsbury
University of Virginia Press

2007 *Two Carpenters: Architecture and Building in Early New England, 1799–1859*
J. Ritchie Garrison
University of Tennessee Press

2008 *A Manufactured Wilderness: Summer Camps and the Shaping of American Youth, 1890–1960*
Abigail Van Slyck
University of Minnesota Press

2009 *Baltimore's Alley Houses: Homes for Working People since the 1780s*
Mary Ellen Hayward
Johns Hopkins University Press

2010 *Delirious New Orleans: Manifesto for an Extraordinary American City*
Stephen Verderber
University of Texas Press

* Honorable Mention

Source: Vernacular Architecture Forum

Alice Davis Hitchcock Book Award

The Society of Architectural Historians has granted the Alice Davis Hitchcock Book Award annually since 1949 to North American publications that demonstrate a **high level of scholarly distinction in the field of architectural history**. The award is named in honor of the mother of Henry-Russell Hitchcock, a past president of the SAH and an international leader in architectural history for more than half a century.

www.sah.org

1949   *Colonial Architecture and Sculpture
            in Peru*
        Harold Wethey
        Harvard University Press

1950   *Architecture of the Old Northwest
            Territory*
        Rexford Newcomb
        University of Chicago Press

1951   *Architecture and Town Planning in
            Colonial Connecticut*
        Anthony Garvan
        Yale University Press

1952   *The Architectural History of Newport*
        Antoinette Forrester Downing
            and Vincent J. Scully
        Harvard University Press

1953   *Charles Rennie Mackintosh and the
            Modern Movement*
        Thomas Howarth
        Routledge and K. Paul

1954   *Early Victorian Architecture in Britain*
        Henry-Russell Hitchcock
        Da Capo Press

1955   *Benjamin H. Latrobe*
        Talbot Hamlin
        Oxford University Press

1956   *The Railroad Station: An Architectural
            History*
        Carroll L.V. Meeks
        Yale University Press

1957   *The Early Architecture of Georgia*
        Frederick D. Nichols
        University of North Carolina Press

1958   *The Public Buildings of Williamsburg*
        Marcus Whiffen
        Colonial Williamsburg

1959   *Carolingian and Romanesque
            Architecture, 800 to 1200*
        Kenneth J. Conant
        Yale University Press

1960   *The Villa d'Este at Tivoli*
        David Coffin
        Princeton University Press

1961   *The Architecture of Michelangelo*
        James S. Ackerman
        University of Chicago Press

1962   *The Art and Architecture of Ancient
            America*
        George Kubler
        Yale University Press

1963   *La Cathédrale de Bourges et sa Place
            dans l'Architecture Gothique*
        Robert Branner
        Tardy

1964   *Images of American Living, Four
            Centuries of Architecture and
            Furniture as Cultural Expression*
        Alan W. Gowans
        Lippincott

1965 *The Open-Air Churches of Sixteenth
        Century Mexico*
      John McAndrew
      Harvard University Press

1966 *Early Christian and Byzantine
        Architecture*
      Richard Krautheimer
      Penguin Books

1967 *Eighteenth-Century Architecture in
        Piedmont: The Open Structures of
        Juvarra, Alfieri & Vittone*
      Richard Pommer
      New York University Press

1968 *Architecture and Politics in Germany,
        1918–1945*
      Barbara Miller Lane
      Harvard University Press

1969 *Samothrace, Volume III: The Hieron*
      Phyllis Williams Lehmann
      Princeton University Press

1970 *The Church of Notre Dame in Montreal*
      Franklin Toker
      McGill-Queen's University Press

1971 No award granted

1972 *The Prairie School: Frank Lloyd Wright
        and His Midwest Contemporaries*
      H. Allen Brooks
      University of Toronto Press

      *The Early Churches of Constantinople:
        Architecture and Liturgy*
      Thomas F. Mathews
      Pennsylvania State University Press

1973 *The Campanile of Florence Cathedral:
        "Giotto's Tower"*
      Marvin Trachtenberg
      New York University Press

1974 *FLO, A Biography of Frederick Law
        Olmsted*
      Laura Wood Roper
      Johns Hopkins University Press

1975 *Gothic vs. Classic, Architectural
        Projects in Seventeenth-Century
        Italy*
      Rudolf Wittkower
      G. Braziller

1976 No award granted

1977 *New Orleans Architecture Vol. V:
        The Esplanade Ridge*
      Mary Louise Christovich, Sally Kitredge
        Evans, Betsy Swanson, and
        Roulhac Toledano
      Pelican Publishing Company

1978 *Sebastiano Serlio on Domestic
        Architecture*
      Myra Nan Rosenfeld
      Architectural History Foundation

1979 *The Framed Houses of Massachusetts
        Bay, 1625–1725*
      Abbott Lowell Cummings
      Belknap Press

      Paris: A Century of Change, 1878–1978
      Norma Evenson
      Yale University Press

1980 *Rome: Profile of a City, 312–1308*
      Richard Krautheimer
      Princeton University Press

1981 *Gardens of Illusion: The Genius of
        Andre Le Notre*
      Franklin Hamilton Hazelhurst
      Vanderbilt University Press

1982 *Indian Summer: Luytens, Baker and
        Imperial Delhi*
      Robert Grant Irving
      Yale University Press

1983 *Architecture and the Crisis of Modern
        Science*
      Alberto Pérez-Goméz
      MIT Press

1984 *Campus: An American Planning
        Tradition*
      Paul Venable Turner
      MIT Press

Alice Davis Hitchcock Book Award

1985   *The Law Courts: The Architecture of*
      George Edmund Street
   David Brownlee
   MIT Press

1986   *The Architecture of the Roman*
      Empire: An Urban Appraisal
   William L. MacDonald
   Yale University Press

1987   *Holy Things and Profane: Anglican*
      Parish Churches in Colonial Virginia
   Dell Upton
   MIT Press

1988   *Designing Paris: The Architecture of*
      Duban
   David Van Zanten
   MIT Press

1989   *Florentine New Towns: Urban Design*
      in the Late Middle Ages
   David Friedman
   MIT Press

1990   *Claude-Nicolas Ledoux: Architecture*
      and Social Reform at the End of the
      Ancient Régime
   Anthony Vidler
   MIT Press

1991   *The Paris of Henri IV: Architecture*
      and Urbanism
   Hilary Ballon
   MIT Press

   Seventeenth-Century Roman Palaces:
      Use and the Art of the Plan
   Patricia Waddy
   MIT Press

1992   *Modernism in Italian Architecture,*
      1890–1940
   Richard Etlin
   MIT Press

1994*   *Baths and Bathing in Classical*
      Antiquity
   Fikret Yegul
   MIT Press

1995   *The Politics of the German Gothic*
      Revival: August Reichensperger
   Michael J. Lewis
   MIT Press

1996   *Hadrian's Villa and Its Legacy*
   William J. MacDonald and John Pinto
   Yale University Press

1997   *Gottfried Semper: Architect of the*
      Nineteenth Century
   Harry Francis Mallgrave
   Yale University Press

1998   *The Dancing Column: On Order in*
      Architecture
   Joseph Rykwert
   MIT Press

1999   *Dominion of the Eye: Urbanism, Art*
      & Power in Early Modern Florence
   Marvin Trachtenberg
   Cambridge University Press

2000   *The Architectural Treatise in the*
      Renaissance
   Alina A. Payne
   Cambridge University Press

2001   *The Architecture of Red Vienna,*
      1919–1934
   Eve Blau
   MIT Press

2002   *Modernism and Nation Building:*
      Turkish Architectural Culture in the
      Early Republic
   Sibel Bozdogan
   University of Washington Press

   Marcel Breuer: The Career and the
      Buildings
   Isabelle Hyman
   Harry N. Abrams

2003   *The Chicago Auditorium Building:*
      Adler and Sullivan's Architecture
      and the City
   Joseph Siry
   University of Chicago Press

2004 *The Chicago Tribune Tower
Competition: Skyscraper Design
and Cultural Change in the 1920s*
Katherine Solomonson
Cambridge University Press

2005 *House and Home in Modern Japan:
Architecture, Domestic Space, and
Bourgeois Culture, 1880–1930*
Jordan Sand
Harvard University Press

2006 *Architecture and Nature: Creating the
American Landscape*
Christine Macy and Sarah
Bonnemaison
Routledge

2007 *Architecture and Suburbia:
From English Villa to American
Dream House, 1690–2000*
John Archer
University of Minnesota Press

2008 *The Domestic Architecture of
Benjamin Henry Latrobe*
Michael W. Fazio and Patrick A.
Snadon
Johns Hopkins University Press

2009 *A Manufactured Wilderness: Summer
Camps and the Shaping of
American Youth, 1890–1960*
Abigail A. Van Slyck
University of Minnesota Press

2010 **Michelangelo, Drawing, and
the Invention of Architecture**
Cammy Brothers
Yale University Press

* No award was granted in 1993 when the award schedule
was adjusted to coincide with the annual meeting.

Source: Society of Architectural Historians

Antoinette Forrester Downing Book Award

The Society of Architectural Historians grants the Antoinette Forrester Downing Book Award to **outstanding publications in the field of historic preservation**. Works published in the two years prior to the award are eligible. The award honors Antoinette Downing's tireless preservation advocacy efforts in Rhode Island, including her seminal book *The Architectural History of Newport*.

www.sah.org

1987　*Providence, A Citywide Survey of Historic Resources*
William McKenzie Woodward and Edward F. Sanderson
Rhode Island Historic Preservation Commission

1988　*The Alabama Catalog HABS: A Guide to the Early Architecture of the State*
Robert Gamble and HABS
University of Alabama Press

1989　*Blueprints for Modern Living: History and Legacy of the Case Study Houses*
Elizabeth A.T. Smith and the Museum of Contemporary Art, Los Angeles
MIT Press

1990　*East Cambridge: A Survey of Architectural History in Cambridge*
Susan E. Maycock
MIT Press

1991　*Somerset: An Architectural History*
Paul Baker Touart
Maryland Historical Trust and Somerset County Historical Trust

1992　No award granted

1993　*La Tierra Amarilla: Its History, Architecture and Cultural Landscape*
Chris Wilson and David Kammer
Museum of New Mexico Press

The Historic Architecture of Pitt County, North Carolina
Scott Power, ed.
Pitt County Historical Society

1994　*The Buried Past: An Archaeological History of Philadelphia*
John L. Cotter
University of Pennsylvania Press

1995　*Along the Seaboard Side: The Architectural History of Worcester County, Maryland*
Paul Baker Touart
Worcester County

1996　*The Historic Architecture of Wake County, North Carolina*
Kelly A. Lally
Wake County Government

1997　*A Guide to the National Road* and *The National Road*
Karl B. Raitz
Johns Hopkins University Press

1998　*A Guide to the Historic Architecture of Eastern North Carolina*
Catherine W. Bishir and Michael T. Southern
University of North Carolina Press

1999   No award granted

2000   *Boston's Changeful Times*
        Michael Holleran
        Johns Hopkins University Press

2001   *Preserving Cultural Landscapes in*
            America
        Arnold R. Alanen and Robert Z.
            Melnick, editors
        John Hopkins University Press

2002   *A Building History of Northern*
            New England
        James Garvin
        University Press of New England

2003   No award granted

2004   *Restoring Women's History Through*
            Historic Preservation
        Gail Lee Dubrow and Jennifer B.
            Goodman, eds.
        Johns Hopkins University Press
            and New Hampshire Preservation
            Alliance

2005   *A Richer Heritage: Historic*
            Preservation in the Twenty-First
            Century
        Robert E. Stipe
        North Carolina University Press

2006   No award granted

2007   *Earth Repair: A Transatlantic*
            History of Environmental
            Restoration
        Marcus Hall
        University of Virginia Press

2008   *Southern Built: American*
            Architecture, Regional Practice
        Catherine Bishir
        University of Virginia Press

2009   *Cinema Houston: From Nickelodeon*
            to Megaplex
        David Welling
        University of Texas Press

2010   *At the Crossroads: The*
            Architectural History of
            Wicomico County, Maryland
        Paul Baker Touart
        Maryland Historical Trust Press/
            Preservation Trust of Wicomico

Source: Society of Architectural Historians

Elisabeth Blair MacDougall Book Award

The Society of Architectural Historians established the Elisabeth Blair MacDougall Book Award to recognize **the most distinguished work of scholarship in the history of landscape architecture or garden design** published in the previous two years. Named for the landscape historian and SAH past president Elisabeth Blair MacDougall, the award honors the late historian's role in developing this field of study.

www.sah.org

2006   *The Nature of Authority: Villa Culture, Landscape, and Representation in Eighteenth-Century Lombardy*
Dianne Suzette Harris
Pennsylvania State University Press

2007   *Cultivated Power: Flowers, Culture, and Politics in the Reign of Louis XIV*
Elizabeth Hyde
University of Pennsylvania Press

2008   No award granted

2009   *Mission 66: Modernism and the National Park Dilemma*
Ethan Carr
University of Massachusetts Press

2010   **Medici Gardens: From Making to Design**
Rafaella Fabiani Giannetto
University of Pennsylvania Press

Source: Society of Architectural Historians

Lewis Mumford Prize

Every two years the Society for American City and Regional Planning History grants the Lewis Mumford Prize for the **best book on American city and regional planning history**. Selection criteria include originality, depth of research, and contribution to the field. The award is named in honor of the celebrated urban planner, historian, sociologist, and architectural critic whose influential writings addressed the effect of buildings on the human condition and the environment.

www.dcp.ufl.edu/sacrph/

1993 *The New York Approach: Robert Moses, Urban Liberals, and Redevelopment of the Inner City*
Joel Schwartz
Ohio State University Press

1995 *The City of Collective Memory: Its Historical Imagery and Architectural Entertainments*
M. Christine Boyer
MIT Press

1997 *City Center to Regional Mall: Architecture, the Automobile, and Retailing in Los Angeles, 1920–1950*
Richard Longstreth
MIT Press

1999 *Boston's Changeful Times: Origins of Preservation and Planning in America*
Michael Holleran
Johns Hopkins University Press

*Remaking Chicago: The Political Origins of Urban Industrial Change**
Joel Rast
Northern Illinois University Press

2001 *Downtown: Its Rise and Fall, 1880–1950*
Robert Fogelson
Yale University Press

2003 *The Bulldozer in the Countryside: Suburban Sprawl and the Rise of American Environmentalism*
Adam Rome
Cambridge University Press

2005 *Downtown America: A History of the Place and the People Who Made It*
Alison Isenberg
University of Chicago Press

2007 *The Plan of Chicago: Daniel Burnham and the Remaking of the American City*
Carl Smith
University of Chicago Press

*The Horse in the City: Living Machines in the Nineteenth Century**
Joel Tarr and Clay McShane
Johns Hopkins University Press

2009 *Blueprint for Disaster: The Unraveling of Chicago Public Housing*
D. Bradford Hunt
University of Chicago Press

* Honorary Mention

Source: Society for American City and Regional Planning History

Philip Johnson Award

With its annual Philip Johnson Award, the Society of Architectural Historians recognizes **outstanding architectural exhibition catalogs**. This award is named in recognition of Philip Johnson, a distinguished architect and the first director of the architecture department at the Museum of Modern Art, whose 1932 exhibit and catalog, *The International Style: Architecture Since 1922* (co-authored with Henry-Russell Hitchcock), is credited with popularizing European modernism in the United States.

www.sah.org

1990 *Los Angeles Blueprints for Modern Living: History and Legacy of the Case Study Houses*
Elizabeth A.T. Smith
Museum of Contemporary Art and MIT Press

1991 *Architecture and Its Image: Four Centuries of Architectural Representation, Works from the Collection of the Canadian Centre for Architecture*
Eve Blau and Edward Kaufman, eds.
Canadian Centre for Architecture and MIT Press

1992 No award granted

1993 *The Making of Virginia Architecture*
Charles Brownell
Virginia Museum of Fine Arts and University Press of Virginia

Louis I. Kahn: In the Realm of Architecture
David Brownlee
Museum of Contemporary Art and Rizzoli International

1994 *Chicago Architecture and Design 1923–1993: Reconfiguration of an American Metropolis*
John Zukowsky
Prestel and Art Institute of Chicago

1995 *The Palladian Revival: Lord Burlington, His Villa and Garden in Chiswick*
John Harris
Yale University Press

1996 *The Perspective of Anglo-American Architecture*
James F. O'Gorman
Athenaeum of Philadelphia

An Everyday Modernism: The Houses of William Wurster
Marc Treib
San Francisco Museum of Modern Art and University of California Press

1997 *Sacred Realm: The Emergence of the Synagogue in the Ancient World*
Steven Fine
Yeshiva University Museum and Oxford University Press

1998 *Building for Air Travel: Architecture and Design for Commercial Aviation*
John Zukowsky
Art Institute of Chicago and Prestel

1999 *The Work of Charles and Ray Eames: A Legacy of Invention*
Donald Albrecht
Library of Congress, Vitra Design Museum, and Abrams Publishing

2000   *E.W. Godwin: Aesthetic Movement
        Architect and Designer*
        Susan Weber Soros
        Yale University Press

2001   *Mapping Boston*
        Alex Krieger and David Cobb, eds.
        MIT Press

2002   *Mies in Berlin*
        Terence Riley, Barry Bergdoll, and
        the Museum of Modern Art
        Harry N. Abrams

2003   *Richard Neutra's Windshield House*
        Dietrich Neumann, ed.
        Yale University

2004   *Central European Avant-Gardes:
        Exchange and Transformation,
        1910–1930*
        Timothy O. Benson, ed.
        MIT Press

2005   *Thomas Jeckyll: Architect and
        Designer, 1827–1881*
        Susan Weber Soros and Catherine
        Arbuthnott
        Yale University Press

2006   *Raised to the Trade: Creole Building
        Arts of New Orleans**
        John Ethan Hankins and Steven
        Maklansky
        New Orleans Museum of Art

2007   *Machu Picchu: Unveiling the
        Mystery of the Incas*
        Richard L. Burger and Lucy C.
        Salazar, eds.
        Yale University Press

2008   *Eero Saarinen: Shaping the Future*
        Eeva-Liisa Pelkonen
        Yale University Press

2009   No award granted

2010   **Home Delivery: Fabricating the
        Modern Dwelling**
        **Barry Bergdoll and Peter
        Christensen**
        Museum of Modern Art

* Honorary Mention

Source: Society of Architectural Historians

Pulitzer Prize for Architectural Criticism

Joseph Pulitzer created the Pulitzer Prize to encourage **excellence in journalism, music, and letters**. The Pulitzer Prize Board currently confers 21 awards, including one for distinguished journalistic criticism. First granted in 1970, the criticism award encompasses such areas as music, film, theater, fashion, visual arts, culture, and architecture; therefore, an award for architectural criticism is not necessarily bestowed each year. Since 1980 the board has also recognized the finalists, which are included below.

www.pulitzer.org

Recipients

1970	Ada Louise Huxtable *New York Times*	1990	Allan Temko *San Francisco Chronicle*
1979	Paul Gapp *Chicago Tribune*	1996	Robert Campbell *Boston Globe*
1984	Paul Goldberger *New York Times*	1999	Blair Kamin *Chicago Tribune*

Finalists

1981	Allan Temko *San Francisco Chronicle*	2004	Nicolai Ouroussoff *Los Angeles Times*
1983	Beth Dunlop *Miami Herald*	2006	Nicolai Ouroussoff *New York Times*
1988	Allan Temko *San Francisco Chronicle*	2008	Inga Saffron *Philadelphia Inquirer*
1997	Herbert Muschamp *New York Times*	2009	Holland Cotter *New York Times*
2002	John King *San Francisco Chronicle*		
2003	John King *San Francisco Chronicle*		
2003	Nicolai Ouroussoff *Los Angeles Times*		

Source: The Pulitzer Prize Board

Spiro Kostof Book Award

Awarded to publications that promote and **educate the public about the history of urbanism and architecture**, the Spiro Kostof Award is presented annually by the Society of Architectural Historians. An architectural historian and educator, Spiro Kostof produced numerous books on architecture and urban form, especially *The City Shaped: Urban Patterns and Meanings Through History*, that are considered to have greatly advanced the profession.

www.sah.org

1994   *Architecture Power and National Identity*
Lawrence J. Vale
Yale University Press

1995   *In the Theatre of Criminal Justice: The Palais de Justice in Second Empire Paris*
Katherine Fischer Taylor
Princeton University Press

1996   *The Topkapi Scroll: Geometry and Ornament in Islamic Architecture*
Gülru Necipoglu
Getty Center for the History of Art and Humanities

1997   *The Projective Cast: Architecture and Its Three Geometries*
Robin Evans
MIT Press

Auschwitz: 1270 to the Present
Debórah Dwork and Robert Jan van Pelt
Norton

1998   *The Architects and the City*
Robert Bruegmann
University of Chicago Press

Magnetic Los Angeles
Gregory Hise
Johns Hopkins Press

1999   *City Center to Regional Mall: Architecture, the Automobile and Retailing in Los Angeles, 1920–1950*
Richard Longstreth
MIT Press

Housing Design and Society in Amsterdam: Reconfiguring Urban Order and Identity, 1900–1920
Nancy Stieber
University of Chicago Press

2000   *The Architecture of Red Vienna 1919–1934*
Eve Blau
MIT Press

2001   *The Creative Destruction of Manhattan, 1900–1940*
Max Page
University of Chicago Press

2002   *Buildings on Ruins: The Rediscovery of Rome and English Architecture*
Frank Salmon
Ashgate Publishing Company

2003   *Architecture in the Age of Printing: Orality, Writing, Typography and Printed Images in the History of Architectural Theory*
Mario Carpo
MIT Press

Spiro Kostof Book Award

Concrete and Clay: Reworking
  Nature in New York City
Matthew Gandy
MIT Press

2004   Archaeologies of the Greek Past:
  Landscape, Monuments, and
  Memories
Susan E. Alcock
Cambridge University Press

2005   The Birth of City Planning in the
  United States, 1840–1917
Jon A. Peterson
Johns Hopkins University Press

2006   Modern Architecture and the End
  of Empire
Mark Crinson
Ashgate Publishing

The Image of an Ottoman City:
  Imperial Architecture and Urban
  Experience in Aleppo in the 16th
  and 17th Centuries
Heghnar Zeitlian Watenpaugh
Brill Academic Publishing

2007   The Politics of Taste in Antebellum
  Charleston
Maurie D. McInnis
University of North Carolina Press

2008   The Formation of English Gothic
Peter Draper
Yale University Press

2009   The Modern American House:
  Spaciousness and Middle Class
  Identity
Sandy Isenstadt
Cambridge University Press

2010   **Empire, Architecture, and the
  City: French-Ottoman
  Encounters, 1830–1914**
Zeynep Celik
University of Washington Press

Source: Society of Architectural Historians

Jean Tschumi Prize

The Jean Tschumi Prize is awarded by the International Union of Architects (UIA) to individuals to honor **significant contributions to architectural criticism or architectural education**.

www.uia-architectes.org

1967	Jean-Pierre Vouga (Switzerland)	1993	Eric Kumchew Lye (Malaysia)
1969	I. Nikolaev (USSR)	1996	Peter Cook (UK)
	Pedro Ramirez Vazquez		Liangyong Wu (China)
	(Mexico)		Toshio Nakamura (Japan)*
1972	João Batista Vilanova Artigas		COMEX (Mexico)*
	(Brazil)	1999	Juhani Pallasmaa (Finland)
1975	Reyner Banham (UK)		Jennifer Taylor (Australia)*
1978	Rectory and Faculty of	2002	Manuel Tainha (Portugal)
	Architecture of the University		Elia Zenghelis (Greece)
	of Lima (Peru)		The authors of *World Architecture:*
1981	Neville Quarry (Australia)		*A Critical Mosaic* (China)*
	Jorge Glusberg (Argentina)*	2005	*QUADERNS* magazine (Spain)
	Tadeusz Barucki (Poland)*		Peter Davey (UK)
1984	Julius Posener (GDR)		Selim Khan-Magomedov
1987	Christian Norberg-Schultz		(Russia)*
	(Norway)	2008	Luca Molinari (Italy)
	Ada Louise Huxtable (US)		Escola Sert (Spain)
1990	Eduard Franz Sekler (Austria)		
	Dennis Sharp (UK)*		
	Claude Parent (France)*		

* Honorary Mention

Source: International Union of Architects

AIGA, the professional association for design

One of the oldest and largest membership associations for professionals engaged in visual communication and graphic design, AIGA, the professional association for design was founded in 1914 as the American Institute of Graphic Arts. Its more than 20,000 members include professional designers, educators, and students in traditional communication design fields, such as type and book design, as well as such newer disciplines as interaction design, experience design, and motion graphics. In addition, AIGA supports the interests of those involved in design in other disciplines, professions, and businesses who are committed to advancing the understanding of the value of design. AIGA serves as a hub of information and activity within the design community through conferences, competitions, exhibitions, publications, educational activities, and its website.

the professional association for design

Address

164 Fifth Avenue
New York, NY 10010
(212) 807-1990
www.aiga.org

Mission

AIGA's mission is to advance designing as a professional craft, strategic tool, and vital cultural force.

American Architectural Foundation

The American Architectural Foundation is a national nonprofit 501(c)(3) organization that educates individuals and communities about the power of architecture to transform lives and improve the places where we live, learn, work, and play. The AAF's programs include the Mayors' Institute on City Design and Great Schools by Design—highly regarded initiatives that help improve the built environment through the collaboration of thought leaders, designers, and local communities. Through its outreach programs, grants, exhibitions, and educational resources, the AAF helps people become thoughtful and engaged stewards of the world around them. The AAF is headquartered in The Octagon, an 1801 Federal-style home designed by William Thornton.

Address

1799 New York Avenue NW
Washington, DC 20006
(202) 626-7318
www.archfoundation.org

Mission

The American Architectural Foundation's mission is to educate the public on the power of architecture to improve lives and transform communities. The AAF is a national resource that helps provide information and best practices to communities and leaders, promotes collaboration, and encourages design excellence.

American Institute of Architects

Representing the professional interests of America's architects since 1857, the American Institute of Architects provides education, government advocacy, community redevelopment, and public outreach activities with and for its 83,000 members. With more than 300 local and state AIA organizations, the institute closely monitors legislative and regulatory actions at all levels of government. It provides professional development opportunities, industry-standard contract documents, information services, and a comprehensive awards program.

Address

1735 New York Avenue NW
Washington, DC 20006
(202) 626-7300
www.aia.org

Mission

The American Institute of Architects is the voice of the architecture profession dedicated to serving its members, advancing their value, and improving the quality of the built environment.

American Planning Association

The American Planning Association promotes good planning practices to build better communities while protecting the environment so residents have choices in housing, transportation, and employment. The group's 43,000 members include engaged citizens, planning professionals, and elected and appointed officials. The APA strives to engage all citizens in the planning process so it is open, transparent, and reflects the needs and desires of all community members. The association has offices in Washington, DC, and Chicago. It operates local chapters across the country as well as interest-specific divisions, and provides extensive research, publications, and training opportunities. The APA's professional institute, the American Institute of Certified Planners, certifies planners and promotes high ethical standards of professional practice.

Address

205 North Michigan Avenue
Suite 1200
Chicago, IL 60601
(312) 431-9100
www. planning.org

1030 15th Street NW
Suite 750 West
Washington, DC 20005
(202) 872-0611
www.planning.org

Mission

The American Planning Association is a nonprofit public interest and research organization committed to urban, suburban, regional, and rural planning. The APA and its professional institute, the American Institute of Certified Planners, advance the art and science of planning to meet the needs of people and society.

American Society of Interior Designers

The American Society of Interior Designers was formed in 1975 with the consolidation of the American Institute of Designers and the National Society of Interior Designers. It serves more than 36,000 members with continuing education and government affairs departments, conferences, publications, online services, and more. Members include residential and commercial designers; 2,700 manufacturers of design-related products and services, also known as industry partners; and 10,500 interior design students. ASID operates 48 local chapters throughout the United States.

Address
608 Massachusetts Avenue NE
Washington, DC 20002
(202) 546-3480
www.asid.org

Mission
The mission of the American Society of Interior Designers is to advance the interior design profession through knowledge generation and sharing, advocacy of interior designers' right to practice, professional and public education, and expansion of interior design markets.

American Society of Landscape Architects

Representing the landscape architecture profession in the United States since 1899, the American Society of Landscape Architects currently serves more than 17,000 members through 48 chapters across the country. The ASLA's goal is to advance knowledge, education, and skill in the art and science of landscape architecture. The benefits of membership include a national annual meeting, *Landscape Architecture* magazine, continuing education credits, seminars and workshops, professional interest groups, government advocacy, and award programs. In addition, the US Department of Education has certified the Landscape Architectural Accreditation Board of the ASLA as the accrediting agency for landscape architecture programs at US colleges and universities.

AMERICAN
SOCIETY OF
LANDSCAPE
ARCHITECTS

Address
636 Eye Street NW
Washington, DC 20001
(202) 898-2444
www.asla.org

Mission
The mission of the American Society of Landscape Architects is to lead, to educate, and to participate in the careful stewardship, wise planning, and artful design of our cultural and natural environments.

Construction History Society of America

Founded in 2007 as an independent branch of the British-based Construction History Society, the CHSA provides a forum for everyone interested in the history of the American construction industry in all its aspects. The society attracts members from all sectors of the industry. It publishes newsletters and a well-regarded journal called *Construction History*. Biennial national meetings are held and local interest groups are forming. The next national meeting will be at MIT in Boston in 2012 and the society will be hosting the 5th International Construction History Congress in Chicago in 2015.

Address
PO Box 93461
Atlanta, GA 30377
www.constructionhistorysociety.org

Mission
The Construction History Society of America's mission is to encourage the study and research of the history of the American construction industry.

Design Futures Council

The Design Futures Council is a global think tank of design and building industry leaders who collaborate through a series of regular meetings, summits, and *DesignIntelligence*, the bi-monthly journal. The group shares information among its fellows and members on best practices and new trends in order to help member organizations anticipate change and increase competitive fitness. Recent summit topics have included sustainability and innovation. Members include leading architecture and design firms, preferred manufacturers, service providers, and forward-thinking AEC companies taking an active interest in their future.

Address
25 Technology Parkway South, Suite 101
Atlanta, GA 30092
(800) 726-8603
www.di.net

Mission
The Design Futures Council is a think tank with the mission to explore trends, changes, and new opportunities in design, architecture, engineering, and building technology for the purpose of fostering innovation and improving the performance of member organizations.

Industrial Designers Society of America

Founded in 1965, the Industrial Designers Society of America is a professional association of industrial designers, educators, and students dedicated to the promotion of the profession. By fostering innovation and high standards of design, the IDSA communicates the value of design to the public and mentors young designers in their professional career development. The organization serves its constituency through the professional journal *Innovation*, award programs, an annual conference, research sponsorship, networking opportunities, and the promotion of the practice at all levels of government.

Address

45195 Business Court, Suite 250
Dulles, VA 20166
(703) 707-6000
www.idsa.org

Mission

The mission of the Industrial Designers Society of America is to lead the profession by expanding our horizons, connectivity and influence, and our service to members; inspire design quality and responsibility through professional development and education; and elevate the business of design and improve our industry's value.

International Interior Design Association

The International Interior Design Association provides a variety of services and benefits to its more than 13,000 members through 10 specialty forums, and more than 29 chapters around the world. This professional networking and educational association promotes the interior design practice to the public and serves its members as a clearinghouse for industry information. The IIDA was founded in 1994 as the result of a merger of the Institute of Business Designers, the International Society of Interior Designers, and the Council of Federal Interior Designers. The goal of the merger was to create an international association with a united mission that would represent interior designers worldwide.

Address

222 Merchandise Mart Plaza, Suite 567
Chicago, IL 60654
(312) 467-1950
www.iida.org

Mission

The International Interior Design Association is committed to enhancing the quality of life through excellence in interior design and advancing interior design through knowledge. The IIDA advocates for interior design excellence, provides superior industry information, nurtures a global interior design community, maintains educational standards, and responds to trends in business and design.

National Trust for Historic Preservation

The National Trust for Historic Preservation is a private nonprofit membership organization dedicated to saving historic places and revitalizing America's communities. Since NTHP's founding in 1949, it has worked to preserve historic buildings and neighborhoods through leadership, educational programs, publications (such as its award-winning *Preservation* magazine), financial assistance, and government advocacy. Staff at the Washington, DC, headquarters, six regional offices, and 29 historic sites work with its 270,000 members and thousands of preservation groups nationwide to protect the irreplaceable places that tell America's story.

Address

1785 Massachusetts Avenue NW
Washington, DC 20036
(202) 588-6000
www.preservationnation.org

Mission

The National Trust for Historic Preservation is a privately funded, nonprofit organization that provides leadership, education, advocacy, and resources to save America's diverse historic places and revitalize our communities.

Society for Environmental Graphic Design

The Society for Environmental Graphic Design is a nonprofit organization formed in 1973 to promote public awareness of and professional development in environmental graphic design. This interdisciplinary field encompasses the talents of many design professionals, including graphic designers, architects, landscape architects, product designers, planners, interior designers, and exhibition designers who create graphic elements to help identify, direct, inform, interpret, and visually enhance our surroundings through such means as wayfinding or maps. Resources available to SEGD members include a quarterly color magazine, a bi-monthly newsletter, an annual conference, a design award program, technical bullctins, job bank listings, and many other formal and informal materials.

Address

1000 Vermont Avenue NW, Suite 400
Washington, DC 20005
(202) 638-5555
www.segd.org

Mission

The Society for Environmental Graphic Design is an international nonprofit educational organization providing resources for design specialists in the field of environmental graphic design; architecture; and landscape, interior, and industrial design.

Society for Marketing Professional Services

Established in 1973, the Society for Marketing Professional Services is a network of over 6,000 marketing and business development professionals representing architectural, engineering, planning, interior design, construction, and specialty consulting firms throughout the United States and Canada. The society's benefits include a certification program (Certified Professional Services Marketer), an annual marketing and management conference (www.buildbusiness.org), an annual marketing communications competition, educational programs, resources, and publications highlighting the latest trends and best practices in professional services marketing in the AEC industry. SMPS is supported by 59 chapters in the United States.

Address
44 Canal Center Plaza, Suite 444
Alexandria, VA 22314
(703) 549-6117
www.smps.org

Mission
The mission of the Society for Marketing Professional Services is to advocate for, educate, and connect leaders in the building industry.

Society of Architectural Historians

Since its founding in 1940, the Society of Architectural Historians has sought to promote the history of architecture. The membership of the SAH ranges from professionals, such as architects, planners, preservationists, and academics, to those simply interested in architecture. The society produces a quarterly journal and monthly newsletter and organizes study tours and an annual conference. There are also a number of associated, although independent, local chapters. The SAH's national headquarters is located in Chicago's architecturally significant Charnley-Persky House, designed in 1891 by the firm of Dankmar Adler and Louis Sullivan. Guided tours of the house are offered.

Address
1365 North Astor Street
Chicago, IL 60610
(312) 573-1365
www.sah.org

Mission
The mission of the Society of Architectural Historians is to advance knowledge and understanding of the history of architecture, design, landscape, and urbanism worldwide.

Urban Land Institute

Formed in 1936 as a research arm of the National Association of Real Estate Boards (now the National Association of Realtors), the Urban Land Institute is an independent organization for those engaged in the entrepreneurial and collaborative process of real estate development and land-use policymaking. The ULI has more than 34,000 members worldwide and a $53-million operating budget. ULI members include the people that plan, develop, and redevelop neighborhoods, business districts, and communities across the United States and around the world, working in private enterprise and public service. The institute's activities include research, forums and task forces, awards, education, and publishing.

Address

1025 Thomas Jefferson Street NW
Suite 500 West
Washington, DC 20007
(202) 624-7000
www.uli.org

Mission

The mission of the Urban Land Institute is to provide responsible leadership in the use of land to enhance the total environment.

US Green Building Council

The US Green Building Council was formed in 1993 to integrate, educate, and provide leadership for building industry leaders, environmental groups, designers, retailers, and building owners as they strive to develop and market products and services that are environmentally progressive and responsible. The council includes nearly 18,000 worldwide organizations and 78 regional chapters with a common interest in green building practices, technologies, policies, and standards. Its most visible program, the LEED™ Green Building Rating System, is a voluntary consensus-based rating system that provides a national standard on what constitutes a green building. It also offers professional accreditation to certify individuals who have demonstrated the ability to serve on a LEED project team and provide detailed knowledge of LEED project certification requirements and processes.

Address

2101 L Street NW, Suite 500
Washington, DC 20037
(202) 742-3792
www.usgbc.org

Mission

The US Green Building Council's core purpose is to transform the way buildings and communities are designed, built, and operated, enabling an environmentally and socially responsible, healthy, and prosperous environment that improves the quality of life.

Architectural Outreach

Countless volunteer opportunities abound for architects, designers, and others interested in the built environment, ranging from disaster relief and recovery to community empowerment, restoration, and historic preservation. The following is a partial list of organizations, coalitions, and resources aimed at the coordination and operation of national and international volunteer programs that are focused on architecture, planning, design, and community development initiatives.

Adventures in Preservation (formerly Heritage Conservation Network)
1557 North Street
Boulder, CO 80304
(303) 444-0128
www.adventuresinpreservation.org

Adventures in Preservation's hands-on building conservation workshops bring people to historic sites around the world to provide much-needed labor and technical assistance to preservation projects. Participants work with and learn from experts in the field of heritage conservation; all levels of experience are welcome.

Architects Without Borders
295 Neva Street
Sebastopol, CA 95472
www.awb.iohome.net (international) or http://awb-seattle.org (local, with international information available if other website not available)

Architects Without Borders is an international coalition of non-governmental, nonprofit, volunteer humanitarian relief organizations. It supports communities in developing visionary planning, leadership, and self-determination models upon which communities can define and achieve their own aspirations.

Architecture for Humanity
848 Folsom, Suite 201
San Francisco, CA 94107
(415) 963-3511
www.architectureforhumanity.org

Architecture for Humanity promotes architectural and design solutions to global, social, and humanitarian crises. Through competitions, workshops, educational forums, partnerships with aid organizations, and other activities, Architecture for Humanity creates opportunities for architects and designers from around the world to help communities in need.

Builders Without Borders
119 Kingston Main Street
Hillsboro, NM 88042
(505) 895-5400
www.builderswithoutborders.org

With volunteers, including architects, engineers, contractors, and others in the AEC field, Builders Without Borders specializes in affordable housing, both domestically and abroad, emphasizing sustainable structures built with locally available materials. Generally, BWB provides technical assistance to improve designs.

buildOn

PO Box 16741
Stamford, CT 06905
(203) 585-5390
www.buildon.org

buildOn enhances education and empowers youth in the United States to make a positive difference in their communities while helping people in developing countries increase their self-reliance through education and the development of educational resources.

Caribbean Volunteer Expeditions

PO Box 388
Corning, NY 14830
(607) 962-7846
www.cvexp.org

Caribbean Volunteer Expeditions is a non-profit agency dedicated to the preservation and documentation of the historical heritage of the Caribbean. Members and volunteers measure and document historical plantations, windmills, and other structures to help local Caribbean agencies keep a record of their architectural heritage. Professional assistance is appreciated.

Habitat for Humanity International

121 Habitat Street
Americus, GA 31709-3498
(800) 422-4828
www.habitat.org

Habitat for Humanity International seeks to eliminate poverty housing and homelessness from the world and to make decent shelter a matter of conscience and action. Through volunteer labor and donations of money and materials, Habitat builds and rehabilitates simple, decent houses with the help of the homeowner (partner) families.

La Sabranenque

rue de la Tour de l'Oume
30290 Saint Victor la Coste
France
www.sabranenque.com

La Sabranenque works toward the preservation of the traditional Mediterranean habitat and architecture. Working with volunteers, it preserves, restores, and rebuilds sites that can range from a simple village path to a complex of buildings using traditional construction techniques while introducing volunteers to the values of vernacular architecture and traditional construction.

National Park Service

Volunteers-In-Parks Program
1849 C Street NW
Washington, DC 20240
(202) 208-6843
www.nps.gov

The Volunteers-In-Parks Program provides a vehicle through which the National Park Service can accept and utilize voluntary help and services from the public.

One Earth Designs

PO Box 382559
Cambridge, MA 02238
www.oneearthdesigns.org

One Earth Designs is a US-based nonprofit organization that helps Himalayan communities adapt to rapid environmental and socioeconomic change by promoting environmental health and incubating local innovation and entrepreneurship. It serves as a conduit through which communities can access science, engineering, and business education for long-term self-confidence and self-efficacy, technical support to address immediate needs, and the resources necessary to achieve their own balance between tradition, a healthy environment, and the way forward.

Architectural Outreach

Open Architecture Network
Architecture for Humanity
848 Folsom, Suite 201
San Francisco, CA 94107
(415) 963-3511
www.openarchitecturenetwork.org

The Open Architecture Network is an online open-source community dedicated to improving living conditions through innovative and sustainable design. Here designers of all persuasions can share their ideas, designs and plans; view and review designs posted by others; collaborate to address specific design challenges; manage design projects from concept to implementation; protect their intellectual property rights using the Creative Commons licensing system; and build a more sustainable future.

Peace Corps
1111 20th Street NW
Washington, DC 20526
(800) 424-8580
www.peacecorps.gov

Peace Corps volunteers serve in countries across the globe: Africa, Asia, the Caribbean, Central and South America, Europe, and the Middle East. Collaborating with local community members, volunteers work in such areas as education, youth outreach and community development, the environment, and information technology.

Project H Design
PO Box 12021
San Rafael, CA 94912
http://projecthdesign.org

Project H Design connects the power of design to the people who need it most and the places where it can make a real and lasting difference. Long-term initiatives focus on improving environments, products, and experiences for K-12 education institutions in the US through systems-level design thinking and deep community engagements.

Public Architecture 1% Solution
1211 Folsom Street, 4th Floor
San Francisco, CA 94103
(415) 861-8200
www.theonepercent.org
www.publicarchitecture.org

The 1% Solution program grew out of a realization that there are no formal mechanisms supporting or recognizing pro bono architectural work within the profession. The goal of the 1% Solution is to direct one percent of all architects' working hours to matters of public interest, pro bono.

Rebuilding Together
1899 L Street NW, Suite 1000
Washington, DC 20036
(800) 473-4229
www.rebuildingtogether.org

Rebuilding Together preserves and revitalizes houses and communities, assuring that low-income homeowners, from the elderly and disabled to families with children, live in warmth, safety, and independence. Its goal is to make a sustainable impact in partnership with the community.

Red Feather Development Group
PO Box 907
Bozeman, MT 59771
(406) 585-7188
www.redfeather.org

Red Feather educates and empowers American Indian nations to create sustainable solutions to the severe housing crisis within reservation communities. Red Feather teaches affordable, replicable, and sustainable approaches to home construction, working with volunteers alongside tribe members to build desperately needed homes.

Shelter For Life International

7767 Elm Creek Boulevard, Suite 310
Maple Grove, MN 55369
(888) 426-7979
www.shelter.org

Shelter for Life International is a faith-based humanitarian organization that enables people affected by conflict and disaster to rebuild their communities and restore their lives through appropriate shelter and community development programs. Shelter for Life has occasional volunteer opportunities in project management, construction, community development, engineering, architecture, and cross-cultural relations.

slowLab

c/o New York Foundation for the Arts
20 Jay Street, 7th Floor
Brooklyn, NY 11201
(212) 366-6900
www.slowlab.org

The goal of slowLab is to promote slowness as a positive catalyst of individual, sociocultural, and environmental well-being. Current and future programs include public lectures, discussions and exhibitions, a dynamic online project observatory and communication portal, academic programs, and publishing projects.

Southface Energy Institute

241 Pine Street NE
Atlanta, GA 30308
(404) 872-3549
www.southface.org

Southface promotes sustainable homes, workplaces, and communities through education, research, advocacy, and technical assistance.

United Nations Volunteers

United Nations Campus
Langer Eugen
Hermann-Ehlers-Str.10
53113 Bonn, Germany
+49 228 815 2000
www.unvolunteers.org

The United Nations Volunteers supports sustainable human development globally through the promotion of volunteerism, including the mobilization of volunteers. It serves the causes of peace and development through enhancing opportunities for participation by all people.

World Hands Project

1406 Bishops Lodge Road
Santa Fe, NM 87506
(505) 989-7000
www.worldhandsproject.org

The World Hands Project is a group of concerned citizen-activists from diverse backgrounds that works worldwide creating solutions that address the basic needs for clean water, food production, sanitation, and shelter. Through workshops and studios, participants work with communities to establish a better quality of life by combining technical knowledge and skills with the traditional wisdom of indigenous peoples.

World Shelters for Humanitarian Needs

550 South G Street, Suite 3
Arcata, CA 95521
(707) 822-6600
www.worldshelters.org

World Shelters designs, produces, and delivers temporary and permanent structures for both emergency response and long-term humanitarian needs.

Source: DesignIntelligence

Design & Building-Related Organizations

The following associations, organizations, and government agencies offer a variety of information and support for the design and construction industry.

Associations & Organizations

Acoustical Society of America
2 Huntington Quadrangle, Suite 1NO1
Melville, NY 11747
(516) 576-2360
http://asa.aip.org

Air-Conditioning, Heating & Refrigeration Institute
2111 Wilson Boulevard, Suite 500
Arlington, VA 22201
(703) 524-8800
www.ahrinet.org

Air Conditioning Contractors of America
2800 Shirlington Road, Suite 300
Arlington, VA 22206
(703) 575-4477
www.acca.org

Alliance to Save Energy
1850 M Street NW, Suite 600
Washington, DC 20036
(202) 857-0666
www.ase.org

American Arbitration Association
1633 Broadway, 10th Floor
New York, NY 10019
(212) 716-5800
www.adr.org

American Architectural Manufacturers Association
1827 Walden Office Square, Suite 550
Schaumburg, IL 60173
(847) 303-5664
www.aamanet.org

American Concrete Institute
38800 Country Club Drive
Farmington Hills, MI 48331
(248) 848-3700
www.concrete.org

American Council of Engineering Companies
1015 15th Street NW, 8th Floor
Washington, DC 20005
(202) 347-7474
www.acec.org

American Forest Foundation
1111 Nineteenth Street NW, Suite 780
Washington, DC 20036
(202) 463-2462
www.affoundation.org

American Gas Association
400 North Capitol Street NW, Suite 450
Washington, DC 20001
(202) 824-7000
www.aga.org

American Hardware Manufacturers Association
801 North Plaza Drive
Schaumburg, IL 60173
(847) 605-1025
www.ahma.org

American Horticultural Society
7931 East Boulevard Drive
Alexandria, VA 22308
(703) 768-5700
www.ahs.org

American Institute of Building Design
7059 Blair Road NW, Suite 201
Washington, DC 20012
(800) 366-2423
www.aibd.org

American Institute of Steel Construction
One East Wacker Drive, Suite 700
Chicago, IL 60601
(312) 670-2400
www.aisc.org

American Lighting Association
2050 Stemmons Freeway, Suite 10046
Dallas, TX 75342
(800) 605-4448
www.americanlightingassoc.com

American National Standards Institute
1819 L Street NW, Sixth Floor
Washington, DC 20036
(202) 293-8020
www.ansi.org

American Nursery & Landscape Association
1000 Vermont Avenue NW, Suite 300
Washington, DC 20005
(202) 789-2900
www.anla.org

American Resort Development Association
1201 15th Street NW, Suite 400
Washington, DC 20005
(202) 371-6700
www.arda.org

American Society for Horticulture Science
1018 Duke Street
Alexandria, VA 22314
(703) 836-4606
www.ashs.org

American Society for Testing & Materials
100 Barr Harbor Drive
West Conshohocken, PA 19428
(610) 832-9500
www.astm.org

American Society of Civil Engineers
1801 Alexander Bell Drive
Reston, VA 20191
(800) 548-2723
www.asce.org

American Society of Consulting Arborists
9707 Key West Avenue, Suite 100
Rockville, MD 20850
(301) 947-0483
www.asca-consultants.org

American Society of Golf Course Architects
125 North Executive Drive, Suite 302
Brookfield, WI 53005
(262) 786-5960
www.asgca.org

American Society of Heating, Refrigerating & Air-Conditioning Engineers
1791 Tullie Circle NE
Atlanta, GA 30329
(404) 636-8400
www.ashrae.org

American Society of Mechanical Engineers
Three Park Avenue
New York, NY 10016
(800) 843-2763
www.asme.org

American Society of Plumbing Engineers
2980 South River Road
Des Plaines, IL 60018
(847) 296-0002
www.aspe.org

Design & Building-Related Organizations

American Society of Professional Estimators
2525 Perimeter Place Drive, Suite 103
Nashville, TN 37214
(615) 316-9200
www.aspenational.com

American Subcontractors Association, Inc.
1004 Duke Street
Alexandria, VA 22314
(703) 684-3450
www.asaonline.com

American Textile Manufacturers Institute
5340 Fryling Road, Suite 300
Erie, PA 16510
www.textileweb.com

APA – The Engineered Wood Association
7011 South 19th Street
Tacoma, WA 98466-5333
(253) 565-6600
www.apawood.org

Architectural Research Centers Consortium
c/o Prof. Michael D. Kroelinger
Herberger Institute for Design & the Arts
Arizona State University
PO Box 872102
Tempe. AZ 85287
(480) 965-5561
www.arccweb.org

Architectural Woodwork Institute
46179 Westlake Drive, Suite 120
Potomac Falls, VA 20165
(571) 323-3636
www.awinet.org

ASFE
8811 Colesville Road, Suite G106
Silver Spring, MD 20910
(301) 565-2733
www.asfe.org

Asphalt Roofing Manufacturers Association
750 National Press Building
529 14th Street NW
Washington, DC 20045
(202) 207-0917
www.asphaltroofing.org

Associated Builders & Contractors
4250 North Fairfax Drive, 9th Floor
Arlington, VA 22203
(703) 812-2000
www.abc.org

Associated General Contractors of America
2300 Wilson Boulevard, Suite 400
Arlington, VA 22201
(703) 548-3118
www.agc.org

Associated Owners & Developers
PO Box 4163
McLean, VA 22103
(703) 734-2397
www.constructionchannel.net/aod

Association for Contract Textiles
PO Box 101981
Fort Worth, TX 76185
(817) 924-8048
www.contracttextiles.org

Association for Facilities Engineering
12801 Worldgate Drive, Suite 500
Herndon, VA 20170
(571) 203-7171
www.afe.org

Association for the Advancement of Cost Engineering
209 Prairie Avenue, Suite 100
Morgantown, WV 26501
(304) 296-8444
www.aacei.org

**Association of Architecture School
Librarians**
William R. Jenkins Architecture and Art Library
University of Houston
Houston, TX 77204
(713) 743-2337
www.architecturelibrarians.org

Association of Energy Engineers
4025 Pleasantdale Road, Suite 420
Atlanta, GA 30340
(770) 447-5083
www.aeecenter.org

**Association of Higher Education Facilities
Officers**
1643 Prince Street
Alexandria, VA 22314
(703) 684-1446
www.appa.org

Association of Pool and Spa Professionals
2111 Eisenhower Avenue
Alexandria, VA 22314
(703) 838-0083
www.apsp.org

Association of the Wall & Ceiling Industry
513 West Broad Street, Suite 210
Falls Church, VA 22046
(703) 538-1600
www.awci.org

Brick Industry Association
1850 Centennial Park Drive, Suite 301
Reston, VA 20191
(703) 620-0010
www.bia.org

Building Codes Assistance Project
1850 M Street NW, Suite 600
Washington, DC 20036
www.bcap-energy.org

Building Futures Council
800 West 6th Street, Suite 1600
Los Angeles, CA 90017
(213) 430-4662
www.thebfc.org

**Building Owners & Managers Association
International**
1101 15th Street, NW, Suite 800
Washington, DC 20005
(202) 408-2662
www.boma.org

Building Stone Institute
5 Riverside Drive, Building 2
Chestertown, NY 12817
(518) 803-4336
www.buildingstoneinstitute.org

California Redwood Association
818 Grayson Road, Suite 201
Pleasant Hill, CA 94523
(925) 935-1499
www.calredwood.org

Carpet and Rug Institute
730 College Drive
Dalton, GA 30720
(706) 278-3176
www.carpet-rug.com

Cedar Shake and Shingle Bureau
PO Box 1178
Sumas, WA 98295
(604) 820-7700
www.cedarbureau.org

Center for Health Design
1850 Gateway Boulevard, Suite 1083
Concord, CA 94520
(925) 521-9404
www.healthdesign.org

Design & Building-Related Organizations

Color Association of the United States
315 West 39th Street, Studio 507
New York, NY 10018
(212) 947-7774
www.colorassociation.com

Composite Panel Association/Composite Wood Council
19465 Deerfield Avenue, Suite 306
Leesburg, VA 20176
(703) 724-1128
www.pbmdf.com

Construction Management Association of America
7926 Jones Branch Drive, Suite 800
McLean, VA 22102
(703) 356-2622
www.cmaanet.org

Construction Specifications Institute
110 South Union Street, Suite 100
Alexandria, VA 22314
(800) 689-2900
www.csinet.org

Copper Development Association
260 Madison Avenue, 16th Floor
New York, NY 10016
(212) 251-7200
www.copper.org

Council of Professional Surveyors
1015 15th Street NW, 8th Floor
Washington, DC 20005
(202) 347-7474
www.acec.org/coalitions/COPS/

Council on Tall Buildings and Urban Habitat
Illinois Institute of Technology
S.R. Crown Hall
3360 South State Street
Chicago, IL 60616
(312) 567-3307
www.ctbuh.org

Deep Foundations Institute
326 Lafayette Avenue
Hawthorne, NJ 07506
(973) 423-4030
www.dfi.org

Design-Build Institute of America
1100 H Street NW, Suite 500
Washington, DC 20005
(202) 682-0110
www.dbia.org

Design Management Institute
101 Tremont Street, Suite 300
Boston, MA 02108
(617) 338-6380
www.dmi.org

Door & Hardware Institute
14150 Newbrook Drive, Suite 200
Chantilly, VA 20151
(703) 222-2010
www.dhi.org

Edison Electric Institute
701 Pennsylvania Avenue NW
Washington, DC 20004
(202) 508-5000
www.eei.org

EIFS Industry Members Association
513 West Broad Street, Suite 210
Falls Church, VA 22046
(800) 294-3462
www.eima.com

Electrical Power Research Institute
3420 Hillview Avenue
Palo Alto, CA 94304
(800) 313-3774
www.epri.com

Gas Technology Institute
1700 South Mount Prospect Road
Des Plaines, IL 60018
(847) 768-0500
www.gastechnology.org

Glass Association of North America
2945 SW Wanamaker Drive, Suite A
Topeka, KS 66614
(785) 271-0208
www.glasswebsite.com

GreenBlue
600 East Water Street, Suite C
Charlottesville, VA 22902
(434) 817-1424
www.greenblue.org

Hardwood Plywood & Veneer Association
1825 Michael Faraday Drive
Reston, VA 20190
(703) 435-2900
www.hpva.org

Hearth, Patio & Barbecue Association
1901 North Moore Street, Suite 600
Arlington, VA 22209
(703) 522-0086
www.hpba.org

Human Factors and Ergonomics Society
1124 Montana Avenue, Suite B
Santa Monica, CA 90403
(310) 394-1811
www.hfes.org

Illuminating Engineering Society of North America
120 Wall Street, 17th Floor
New York, NY 10005
(212) 248-5000
www.iesna.org

Institute of Electrical & Electronics Engineers, Inc.
3 Park Avenue, 17th Floor
New York, NY 10016
(212) 419-7900
www.ieee.org

Institute of Store Planners/ Retail Design Institute
25 North Broadway
Tarrytown, NY 10590
(800) 379-9912
www.retaildesigninstitute.org

International Association of Lighting Designers
Merchandise Mart
200 World Trade Center, Suite 9-104
Chicago, IL 60654
(312) 527-3677
www.iald.org

International Code Council
500 New Jersey Avenue NW, 6th Floor
Washington, DC 20001
(888) 422-7233
www.iccsafe.org

International Facility Management Association
1 East Greenway Plaza, Suite 1100
Houston, TX 77046
(713) 623-4362
www.ifma.org

International Furnishings and Design Association
150 South Warner Road, Suite 156
King of Prussia, PA 19406
(610) 535-6422
www.ifda.com

International Society of Arboriculture
2101 West Park Court
Champaign, IL 61821
(217) 355-9411
www.isa-arbor.com

International Wood Products Association
4214 King Street
Alexandria, VA 22302
(703) 820-6696
www.iwpawood.org

Design & Building-Related Organizations

Irrigation Association
6540 Arlington Boulevard
Falls Church, VA 22042
(703) 536-7080
www.irrigation.org

ISA–The Instrumentation, Systems, and Automation Society
67 Alexander Drive
Research Triangle Park, NC 27709
(919) 549-8411
www.isa.org

Joslyn Castle Institute for Sustainable Communities
1004 Farnam Street, Suite 101
Omaha, NE 68102
(402) 933-0080
www.ecospheres.org

Landscape Architecture Foundation
818 18th Street NW
Suite 810
Washington, DC 20006
(202) 331-7070
www.lafoundation.org

Light Gauge Steel Engineers Association
1202 15th Street, Suite 320
Washington, DC 20005
(202) 263-4488

Maple Flooring Manufacturers Association
111 Deer Lake Road, Suite 100
Deerfield, IL 60015
(847) 480-9138
www.maplefloor.org

Marble Institute of America
28901 Clemens Road, Suite 100
Cleveland, OH 44145
(440) 250-9222
www.marble-institute.com

Metal Building Manufacturers Association
1300 Sumner Avenue
Cleveland, OH 44115
(216) 241-7333
www.mbma.com

National Association of Environmental Professionals
P.O. Box 460
Collingswood, NJ 08108
(856) 283-7816
www.naep.org

National Association of Home Builders
1201 15th Street NW
Washington, DC 20005
(202) 266-8200
www.nahb.org

National Center for Preservation Technology & Training
645 University Parkway
Natchitoches, LA 71457
(318) 356-7444
www. ncptt.nps.gov

National Clearinghouse for Educational Facilities
1090 Vermont Avenue NW, Suite 700
Washington, DC 20005
(202) 289-7800
www.edfacilities.org

National Concrete Masonry Association
13750 Sunrise Valley Drive
Herndon, VA 20171
(703) 713-1900
www.ncma.org

National Conference of States on Building Codes & Standards
505 Huntmar Park Drive, Suite 210
Herndon, VA 20170
(703) 437-0100
www.ncsbcs.org

National Council of Acoustical Consultants
9100 Purdue Road, Suite 200
Indianapolis, IN 46268
(317) 328-0642
www.ncac.com

National Electrical Contractors Association
3 Bethesda Metro Center, Suite 1100
Bethesda, MD 20814
(301) 657-3110
www.necanet.org

**National Electrical Manufacturers
Association**
1300 North 17th Street, Suite 1752
Rosslyn, VA 22209
(703) 841-3200
www.nema.org

National Fire Protection Association
1 Batterymarch Park
Quincy, MA 02169
(617) 770-3000
www.nfpa.org

National Fire Sprinkler Association
40 Jon Barrett Road
Patterson, NY 12563
(845) 878-4200
www.nfsa.org

National Glass Association
8200 Greensboro Drive, Suite 302
McLean, VA 22102
(866) 342-5642
www.glass.org

National Institute of Building Sciences
1090 Vermont Avenue NW, Suite 700
Washington, DC 20005
(202) 289-7800
www.nibs.org

National Lighting Bureau
8811 Colesville Road, Suite G106
Silver Spring, MD 20910
(301) 587-9572
www.nlb.org

National Kitchen & Bath Association
687 Willow Grove Street
Hackettstown, NJ 07840
(800) 843-6522
www.nkba.org

National Organization of Minority Architects
c/o School of Architecture and Design
College of Engineering, Architecture and
Computer Sciences
Howard University
2366 6th Street NW, Room 100
Washington, DC 20059
(202) 686-2780
www.noma.net

National Paint & Coatings Association
1500 Rhode Island Avenue NW
Washington, DC 20005
(202) 462-6272
www.paint.org

National Preservation Institute
PO Box 1702
Alexandria, VA 22313
(703) 765-0100
www.npi.org

National Society of Professional Engineers
1420 King Street
Alexandria, VA 22314
(703) 684-2800
www.nspe.org

National Sunroom Association
1300 Sumner Avenue
Cleveland, OH 44115
(216) 241-7333
www.nationalsunroom.org

National Wood Flooring Association
111 Chesterfield Industrial Boulevard
Chesterfield, MO 63005
(800) 422-4556
www.woodfloors.org

Design & Building-Related Organizations

New Buildings Institute, Inc.
1331 Washington Street
Vancouver, WA 98660
(360) 567-0950
www.newbuildings.org

North American Insulation Manufacturers Association
44 Canal Center Plaza, Suite 310
Alexandria, VA 22314
(703) 684-0084
www.naima.org

NSSN: A National Resource for Global Standards/American National Standards Institute
25 West 43rd Street
New York, NY 10036
(212) 642-4980
www.nssn.org

Plumbing Manufacturers Institute
1921 Rohlwing Road, Unit G
Rolling Meadows, IL 60008
(847) 481-5500
www.pmihome.org

Portland Cement Association
5420 Old Orchard Road
Skokie, IL 60077
(847) 966-6200
www.cement.org

Precast/Prestressed Concrete Institute
200 West Adams Street, Suite 2100
Chicago, IL 60606
(312) 786-0300
www.pci.org

Preservation Trades Network, Inc.
PO Box 151
Burbank, OH 44214
(866) 853-9335
www.ptn.org

Professional Construction Estimators Association of America
PO Box 680336
Charlotte, NC 28216
(877) 521-7232
www.pcea.org

Professional Landcare Network (PLANET)
950 Herndon Parkway, Suite 450
Herndon, VA 20170
(703) 736-9666
www.landcarenetwork.org

Rocky Mountain Institute
2317 Snowmass Creek Road
Snowmass, CO 81654
(970) 927-3851
www.rmi.org

Society of American Registered Architects
14 East 38th Street
New York, NY 10016
(888) 385-7272
www.sararchitects.org

Society of Fire Protection Engineers
7315 Wisconsin Avenue, Suite 620E
Bethesda, MD 20814
(301) 718-2910
www.sfpe.org

Society for Marketing Professional Services
44 Canal Center Plaza, Suite 444
Alexandria, VA 22314
(800) 292-7677
www.smps.org

Steel Framing Alliance
1140 Connecticut Avenue NW, Suite 705
Washington, DC 20036
(202) 785-2022
www.steelframingalliance.com

Sustainable Buildings Industry Council
1112 16th Street NW, Suite 240
Washington, DC 20036
(202) 628-7400
www.sbicouncil.org

Tile Council of America, Inc.
100 Clemson Research Boulevard
Anderson, SC 29625
(864) 646-8453
www.tileusa.com

Tree Care Industry Association
136 Harvey Road, Suite 101
Londonderry, NH 03053
(603) 314-5380
www.treecareindustry.org

Vernacular Architecture Forum
PO Box 1511
Harrisonburg, VA 22803
www.vernaculararchitectureforum.org

Underwriters Laboratories Inc.
2600 NW Lake Road
Camas, WA 98607
(877) 854-3577
www.ul.com

Vinyl Institute
1737 King Street, Suite 390
Alexandria, VA 22314
(571) 970-3400
www.vinylinfo.org

Waterfront Center
P.O. Box 53351
Washington, DC 20009
(202) 337-0356
www.waterfrontcenter.org

Window & Door Manufacturers Association
401 North Michigan Avenue, Suite 2200
Chicago, IL 60611
(312) 321-6802
www.wdma.com

Government Agencies

Army Corps of Engineers
441 G Street NW
Washington, DC 20314
(202) 761-0011
www.usace.army.mil

Bureau of Land Management
Office of Public Affairs
1849 C Street NW, Room 5665
Washington, DC 20240
(202) 208-3801
www.blm.gov

**U.S. Census Bureau Manufacturing
and Construction Division**
Washington, DC 20233
(301) 763-5160
www.census.gov/const/www

Department of Agriculture
1400 Independence Avenue SW
Washington, DC 20250
(202) 720-2791
www.usda.gov

Department of Energy
Forrestal Building
1000 Independence Avenue SW
Washington, DC 20585
(202) 586-5000
www.energy.gov

Department of Labor
Frances Perkins Building
200 Constitution Avenue NW
Washington, DC 20210
(877) 889-5627
www.dol.gov

Design & Building-Related Organizations

Department of the Interior
1849 C Street NW
Washington, DC 20240
(202) 208-3100
www.doi.gov

Department of Transportation
1200 New Jersey Avenue, SE
Washington, DC 20590
(202) 366-4000
www.dot.gov

Environmental Protection Agency
Ariel Rios Building
1200 Pennsylvania Avenue NW
Washington, DC 20460
(202) 272-0167
www.epa.gov

Federal Emergency Management Agency
500 C Street SW
Washington, DC 20472
(202) 621-3362
www.fema.gov

General Services Administration
1800 F Street NW
Washington, DC 20405
(866) 606-8220
www.gsa.gov

National Institute of Standards & Technology
100 Bureau Drive, Stop 1070
Gaithersburg, MD 20899
(301) 975-8295
www.nist.gov

United States Access Board
1331 F Street NW, Suite 1000
Washington, DC 20004
(202) 272-0080
www.access-board.gov

International Organizations

Architects' Council of Europe
Rue Paul Emile Janson, 29
B-1050 Brussels, Belgium
+32 2 543 11 40
www.ace-cae.org

Architecture Institute of Japan
26-20, Shiba 5-chome, Minato-ku
Tokyo 108-8414, Japan
+81-3-3456-2051
www.aij.or.jp

DOCOMOMO International
Funcació Mies van der Rohe
Provença 318 pral 2
ESP-08037 Barcelona
+34 934879030
www.docomomo.com

European Federation of Landscape Architects
Avenue d'Auderghem, 63
1040 Brussels
Belgium
+32 2 230 3757
www.iflaonline.org

International Centre for the Study of the Preservation and Restoration of Cultural Property
Via di San Michele 13
I-00153 Rome, Italy
+39 06 585531
www.iccrom.org

International Council of Societies of Industrial Design

455 St-Antoine West, Suite SS10
Montreal, QC, H2Z 1J1
Canada
(514) 448-4949
www.icsid.org

International Council on Monuments and Sites

49-51 rue de la Fédération
75015 Paris, France
+33 (0) 1 45 67 67 70
www.icomos.org

International Federation of Interior Architects/Designers

317 Outram Road
#02-57, Concor de Shopping Centre
Singapore 169075
+65 63386974
www.ifiworld.org

International Union of Architects

33 avenue du Maine
F-75755 Paris cedex 15, France
+33 (1) 45 24 36 88
www.uia-architectes.org

Japan Institute of Architects

Kenchikuka Kaikan
2-3-18, Jingumae
Shibuya-ku, Tokyo 150-0001
Japan
+81-3-3408-7125
www.jia.or.jp

Royal Architectural Institute of Canada

330-55 rue Murray Street
Ottawa, ON, K1N 5M3
Canada
(613) 241-3600
www.raic.org

Royal Australian Institute of Architects

Level 2, 7 National Circuit
Barton ACT 2600
Australia
(02) 6121 2000
www.architecture.com.au

Royal Institute of British Architects

66 Portland Place
London W1B 1AD
UK
+44 (0)20 7580 5533
www.architecture.com

United Nations Human Settlements Programme (HABITAT)

PO Box 30030, GPO
Nairobi, 00100, Kenya
(254-20) 7621234
www.unchs.org

Source: DesignIntelligence

Architecture Critics

Below is a listing of the major US newspapers as well as a few magazines and online publications that regularly feature architectural writing and criticism. Some publications have a staff architecture critic while others have an art critic or critic-at-large who routinely covers architecture stories.

Arizona Republic
Richard Nilsen
Fine Arts Critic
200 East Van Buren Street
Phoenix, AZ 85004
(602) 444-8000
www.azcentral.com

Atlanta Journal-Constitution
Catherine Fox
Architecture Critic
72 Marietta Street NW
Atlanta, GA 30303
(404) 526-5151
www.ajc.com

Austin American-Statesman
Jeanne Claire van Ryzin
Arts Critic
305 South Congress Avenue
Austin, TX 78704
(512) 445-3500
www.statesman.com

Baltimore Sun
Mary Carole McCauley
Fine Arts Reporter
501 North Calvert Street
Baltimore, MD 21278
(410) 332-6000
www.baltimoresun.com

Bergen Record
John Zeaman
Art Critic
150 River Street
Hackensack, NJ 07601
(201) 646-4000
www.northjersey.com

Boston Globe
Robert Campbell
Architecture Critic
135 Morrissey Boulevard
Boston, MA 02125
(617) 929-2000
www.boston.com

Boston Herald
Sandra Kent
Arts and Lifestyle
One Herald Square
Boston, MA 02118
(617) 426-3000
www.bostonherald.com

Charleston Post and Courier
Robert Behre
Architecture Critic
134 Columbus Street
Charleston, SC 29403
(843) 577-7111
www.charleston.net

Charlotte Observer
Allen Norwood
Home Editor
600 South Tryon Street
Charlotte, NC 28202
(704) 358-5000
www.charlotteobserver.com

Chicago Sun-Times
Pending
350 North Orleans Street
Chicago, IL 60654
(312) 321-3000
www.suntimes.com

Chicago Tribune
Blair Kamin
Architecture Critic
435 North Michigan Avenue
Chicago, IL 60611
(312) 222-3232
www.chicagotribune.com

Cleveland Plain Dealer
Steven Litt
Art & Architecture Critic
Plain Dealer Plaza
1801 Superior Avenue
Cleveland, OH 44114
(216) 999-5000
www.plaindealer.com

Dallas Morning News
Pending
508 Young Street
Dallas, TX 75202
(214) 977-8222
www.dallasnews.com

Dayton Daily News
Alexis Larsen
Lifestyle Editor
1611 South Main Street
Dayton, OH 45402
(937) 222-5700
www.daytondailynews.com

Denver Post
Kyle MacMillan
Fine Arts Critic
101 West Colfax Avenue
Denver, CO 80202
(303) 820-1201
www.denverpost.com

Detroit Free Press
Mark Striker
Fine Arts Critic
615 West Lafayette
    Boulevard
Detroit, MI 48226
(313) 222-6400
www.freep.com

Los Angeles Times
Christopher Hawthorne
Architecture Critic
202 West First Street
Los Angeles, CA 90012
(213) 237-5000
www.latimes.com

Louisville Courier-Journal
Diane Heilenman
Visual Arts Critic
525 West Broadway
Louisville, KY 40201
(502) 582-4011
www.courier-journal.com

Milwaukee Journal Sentinel
Mary Louise Schumacher
Architecture Reporter
333 West State Street
Milwaukee, WI 53203
(414) 224-2000
www.jsonline.com

New York Times
Nicolai Ouroussoff
Architecture Critic
229 West 43rd Street
New York, NY 10036
(212) 556-1234
www.nytimes.com

Newark Star-Ledger
Dan Bischoff
Art Critic
1 Star-Ledger Plaza
Newark, NJ 07102
(973) 392-4141
www.nj.com/starledger

Newport News Daily Press
Mark St. John Erickson
Arts/Museum/History
    Reporter
7505 Warwick Boulevard
Newport News, VA 23607
(757) 247-4600
www.dailypress.com

Philadelphia Inquirer
Inga Saffron
Architecture Critic
400 North Broad Street
Philadelphia, PA 19130
(215) 854-2000
www.philly.com

Pittsburgh Post-Gazette
Patricia Lowry
Architecture Critic
34 Boulevard of the Allies
Pittsburgh, PA 15222
(412) 263-1100
www.post-gazette.com

Portland Oregonian
David Row
Visual Arts Critic
1320 SW Broadway
Portland, OR 97201
(503) 221-8100
www.oregonian.com

Providence Journal
Bill Van Siclen
Art Critic
75 Fountain Street
Providence, RI 02902
(401) 277-7000
www.projo.com

Raleigh News & Observer
Sherry Howe
Design Critic
215 South McDowell Street
Raleigh, NC 27602
(919) 829-4500
www.newsobserver.com

Rocky Mountain News
Mary Chandler
Art & Architecture Critic
101 West Colfax Avenue
Suite 500
Denver, CO 80202
(303) 892-5000
www.rockymountainnews.com

San Antonio Express-News
Jennifer Hiller
Arts Critic
301 Avenue E
San Antonio, TX 78205
(210) 250-3000
www.mysanantonio.com

San Diego Union-Tribune
David Coddon
Arts Critic
350 Camino de la Reina
San Diego, CA 92108
(619) 299-3131
www.signonsandiego.com

Architecture Critics

San Francisco Chronicle
John King
Urban Design Writer
901 Mission Street
San Francisco, CA 94103
(415) 777-1111
www.sfgate.com

San Jose Mercury News
Alan Hess
Architecture Writer
750 Ridder Park Drive
San Jose, CA 95190
(408) 920-5000
www.mercurynews.com

Seattle Times
Sheila Farr
Art Critic
1120 John Street
Seattle, WA 98109
(206) 464-2111
http://seattletimes.nwsource.
    com

South Florida Sun-Sentinel
Emma Trelles
Arts Writer
200 East Las Olas Boulevard
Fort Lauderdale, FL 33301
(954) 356-4000
www.sun-sentinel.com

St. Paul Pioneer Press
Pending
345 Cedar Street
St. Paul, MN 55101
(651) 222-1111
www.twincities.com

Wall Street Journal
Ada Louise Huxtable
Architecture Critic
200 Liberty Street
New York, NY 10281
(212) 416-2000
www.wsj.com

Washington Post
Philip Kennicott
Culture Critic
1150 15th Street NW
Washington, DC 20071
(202) 334-6000
www.washingtonpost.com

Source: DesignIntelligence

Bookstores

The following is a list of US architecture and design bookstores, including rare and out-of-print dealers that specialize in design titles.

ARIZONA
Builder's Book Depot
1001 East Jefferson, Suite 5
Phoenix, AZ 85034
(800) 284-3434
www.buildersbookdepot.com

CALIFORNIA
Arcana: Books on the Arts
1229 Third Street Promenade
Santa Monica, CA 90401
(310) 458-1499
www.arcanabooks.com

Builder's Book
8001 Canoga Avenue
Canoga Park, CA 91304
(800) 273-7375
www.buildersbook.com

Builders Booksource
1817 Fourth Street
Berkeley, CA 94710
(800) 843-2028
www.buildersbooksource.com

Hennessey + Ingalls
214 Wilshire Boulevard
Santa Monica, CA 90401
(310) 458-9074
www.hennesseyingalls.com

J.B. Muns Fine Arts Books
1162 Shattuck Avenue
Berkeley, CA 94707
(510) 525-2420

**MAK Center for Art and
Architecture Bookstore**
835 North Kings Road
West Hollywood, CA 90069
(323) 651-1510
www.makcenter.org

Moe's Books
2476 Telegraph Avenue
Berkeley, CA 94704
(510) 849-2087
www.moesbooks.com

Potterton Books
Pacific Design Center, G154
8687 Melrose Avenue
West Hollywood, CA 90069
(310) 289-1247
www.pottertonbooksusa.com

Sullivan Goss
7 East Anapamu Street
Santa Barbara, CA 93101
(805) 730-1460
www.sullivangoss.com

**William Stout Architectural
Books**
804 Montgomery Street
San Francisco, CA 94133
(415) 391-6757
www.stoutbooks.com

COLORADO
Tattered Cover Bookstore
2526 East Colfax Avenue
Denver, CO 80206
(303) 322-7727
www.tatteredcover.com

DISTRICT OF COLUMBIA
AIA Bookstore
1735 New York Avenue NW
Washington, DC 20006
(202) 626-7300
www.aia.org/store

**National Building
Museum Shop**
401 F Street NW
Washington, DC 20001
(202) 272-2448
www.nbm.org

ILLINOIS
**Chicago Architecture
Foundation Bookstore**
224 South Michigan Avenue
Chicago, IL 60604
(312) 922-3432
www.architecture.org/shop

INDIANA
AIA Indiana Bookstore
1200 South Madison
Suite LL20
Indianapolis, IN 46225
(317) 634-6993
www.aiaindiana.org

MARYLAND
Baltimore AIA Bookstore
11 1/2 West Chase Street
Baltimore, MD 21201
(410) 625-2585
www.aiabalt.com

MASSACHUSETTS
Ars Libri
500 Harrison Avenue
Boston, MA 02118
(617) 357-5212
www.arslibri.com

**Charles B. Wood III
Antiquarian Booksellers**
PO Box 2369
Cambridge, MA 02238
(617) 868-1711
www.cbwoodbooks.com

Bookstores

F.A. Bernett
144 Lincoln Street
Boston, MA 02111
(617) 350-7778
www.fabernett.com

MISSOURI
St. Louis AIA Bookstore
911 Washington Avenue
Suite 100
St. Louis, MO 63101
(314) 621-3484
www.aia-stlouis.org

NEW YORK
Argosy Bookstore
116 East 59th Street
New York, NY 10022
(212) 753-4455
www.argosybooks.com

Cooper-Hewitt Museum Bookstore
2 East 91st Street
New York, NY 10128
(212) 849-8355
www.cooperhewittshop.org

Hacker Art Books
45 West 57th Street
New York, NY 10019
(212) 688-7600

Neue Galerie Bookstore
1048 Fifth Avenue
New York, NY 10028
(212) 628-6200
www.neuegalerie.org

New York School of Interior Design Bookstore
170 East 70th Street
New York, NY 10021
(212) 472-1500
www.nysid.edu

Potterton Books
D & D Building, Lobby Level
979 Third Avenue
New York, NY 10022
(212) 644-2292
www.pottertonbooksusa.com

Rizzoli Bookstore
31 West 57th Street
New York, NY 10019
(212) 759-2424
www.rizzoliusa.com

Royoung Bookseller
564 Ashford Avenue
Ardsley, NY 10502
(914) 693-6116
www.royoung.com

Strand Book Store
828 Broadway
New York, NY 10003
(212) 473-1452
www.strandbooks.com

Urban Center Books
111 West 57th Street
New York, NY 10019
(212) 935-3595
www.urbancenterbooks.org

Ursus Books
981 Madison Avenue
New York, NY 10075
(212) 772-8787
www.ursusbooks.com

OREGON
Powell's City of Books
1005 West Burnside
Portland, OR 97209
(503) 228-4651
www.powells.com

PENNSYLVANIA
AIA Bookstore & Design Center
1218 Arch Street
Philadelphia, PA 19107
(215) 569-3188
www.aiaphila.org

Joseph Fox Bookshop
1724 Sansom Street
Philadelphia, PA 19103
(215) 563-4184
www.foxbookshop.com

TEXAS
Brazos Bookstore
2421 Bissonnet Street
Houston, TX 77005
(713) 523-0701
www.brazosbookstore.com

WASHINGTON
AIA Spokane Bookstore
335 West Sprague Avenue
Spokane, WA 99201
(509) 747-5498
www.aiaspokane.org

Hinck & Wall
760 Hemlock Street
Edmonds, WA 98020
(800) 561-1203
www.gardenhistory.com

Peter Miller Architecture and Design Books
1930 First Avenue
Seattle, WA 98101
(206) 441-4114
www.petermiller.com

Source: DesignIntelligence

Journals & Magazines

The following is a list of major architecture and design journals and magazines from around the world, ranging from the mainstream to the cutting edge. Whether looking for periodicals that take a less traditional approach or for exposure to the most recent projects and design news, this list is intended to provide an opportunity to explore new ideas and perspectives about design and expand your knowledge about the profession.

US Publications

Architect
One Thomas Circle NW, Suite 600
Washington, DC 20005
(202) 452-0800
www.architectmagazine.com
The official magazine of the AIA, published monthly by Hanley Wood, LLC.

Architect's Newspaper
21 Murray Street, Fifth Floor
New York, NY 10007
(212) 966-0630
www.archpaper.com
Published monthly.

Architectural Digest
6300 Wilshire Boulevard, Suite 1100
Los Angeles, CA 90048
(800) 365-8032
www.architecturaldigest.com
Published monthly by Condé Nast Publications, Inc.

Architectural Record
Two Penn Plaza, Ninth Floor
New York, NY 10121
(212) 904-2594
www.architecturalrecord.com
Published monthly by the McGraw-Hill Companies.

ASID ICON
608 Massachusetts Avenue NE
Washington, DC 20002
(202) 546-3480
www.asid.org
The magazine of the American Society of Interior Designers, published quarterly.

Common Ground
1849 C Street, NW (2286)
Washington, DC 20240
(202) 354-2277
http://commonground.cr.nps.gov/
Published quarterly by the National Park Service for the heritage community.

Communication Arts
110 Constitution Drive
Menlo Park, CA 94025
(650) 326-6040
www.commarts.com
Published eight times per year.

Contract
770 Broadway, 4th Floor
New York, NY 10003
(847) 564-8900
www.contractmagazine.com
Published monthly by Nielsen Business Publications, USA, Inc.

Design Intelligence
25 Technology Parkway South, Suite 101
Norcross, GA 30092
(800) 726-8603
www.di.net
Published bimonthly by Greenway Communications.

Journals & Magazines

Dwell
550 Kearny Street, Suite 710
San Francisco, CA 94108
(415) 373-5100
www.dwell.com
Published 10 times per year.

eco-structure
One Thomas Circle, NW, Suite 600
Washington, DC 20005
(202) 736-3353
www.eco-structure.com
Published eight times a year.

Engineering News Record
Two Penn Plaza, 9th Floor
New York, NY 10121
(212) 904-3507
www.enr.com
Published weekly by the McGraw-Hill
Companies.

Faith & Form
47 Grandview Terrace
Essex, CT 06426
(860) 575-4702
www.faithandform.com
Quarterly journal of the Interfaith Forum on
Religion, Art and Architecture.

Fine Homebuilding
Taunton Press
63 South Main Street
Newtown, CT 06470-5506
(203) 426-8171
www.taunton.com/fh/
Published eight times a year by Taunton
Press.

Harvard Design Magazine
48 Quincy Street, Gund Hall
Cambridge, MA 02138
(617) 495-7814
www.gsd.harvard.edu/research/
publications/hdm/
Published twice a year by the Harvard
University Graduate School of Design.

Innovation
45195 Business Court, Suite 250
Dulles, VA 20166
(703) 707-6000
www.innovationjournal.org
Quarterly of the Industrial Designers Society
of America.

Interior Design
360 Park Avenue South, Floor 17
New York, NY 10010
(561) 750-0151
www.interiordesign.net
Published 15 times a year by Sandow Media
LLC.

Interiors & Sources
615 Fifth Street SE
Cedar Rapids, IA 52401
(319) 364-6167
www.interiorsandsources.com
Published nine times a year by Stamats
Business Media, Inc.

Journal of Architectural Education
Association of Collegiate Schools of
Architecture
1735 New York Avenue, NW
Washington, DC 20006
(202) 785-2324
www.jaeonline.org
Published quarterly by Blackwell Publishing for
the ACSA.

Journal of Interior Design
Interior Design Educators Council, Inc.
9100 Purdue Road, Suite 200
Indianapolis, IN 46268
(317) 328-4437
www.idec.org
Published biannually by John Wiley & Sons,
Inc. on behalf of the Interior Design Educators
Council.

**Journal of the American Planning
Association**
122 South Michigan Avenue, Suite 1600
Chicago, IL 60603
(312) 431-9100
www.planning.org/japa
Published quarterly by the American Planning
Association.

**Journal of the Society of Architectural
Historians**
1365 North Astor Street
Chicago, IL 60610
(312) 573-1365
www.sah.org
Published quarterly by the Society of
Architectural Historians.

Landscape Architecture
636 Eye Street NW
Washington, DC 20001
(202) 898-2444
www.asla.org
Published monthly by the American Society of
Landscape Architects.

Metropolis
61 West 23rd Street, 4th Floor
New York, NY 10010
(212) 627-9977
www.metropolismag.com
Published 11 times a year.

Old House Journal
4125 Lafayette Center Drive, Suite 100
Chantilly, VA 20151
(800) 826-3893
www.oldhousejournal.com
Published bimonthly by Home Buyer
Publications/Active Interest Media.

Perspective
222 Merchandise Mart Plaza, Suite 567
Chicago, IL 60654
(888) 799-4432
www.iida.org
Published quarterly by the International Interior
Design Association.

Places
Center for Environmental Design Research
University of California, Berkeley
College of Environmental Design
390 Wurster Hall, #1839
Berkeley, CA 94720
(510) 642-2896
www.cedr.berkeley.edu
Published three times a year by the Design
History Foundation.

Preservation
1785 Massachusetts Avenue NW
Washington, DC 20036
(800) 944-6847
www.nationaltrust.org
Published bimonthly by the National Trust for
Historic Preservation.

Journals & Magazines

International Publications

Abitare
Via Ventura 5
20134 Milano, Italy
+39 02 210581
www.abitare.it
Monthly magazine in Italian and English.

AD (Architectural Design)
1 Oldlands Way
Bognor Regis
West Sussex, PO22 9SA, UK
+44 01243 843 335
Published bi-monthly by John Wiley and Sons,
Ltd.

AJ (Architects' Journal)
Greater London House
Hampstead Road
London, NW1 7EJ, UK
+44 020 207 728 4651
www.architectsjournal.co.uk
Published by EMAP Construct.

l'Arca
Via Antonio Raimondi, 10
Milano, 20156, Italy
+39 02 36517220
www.arcadata.com
Published 11 times a year.

**Architectural History: The Journal of the
Society of Architectural Historians of Great
Britain**
Simon Green
RCA HMS, 16 Barnard Terrace
Edinburgh, EH8 9NX
Scotland, UK
www.sahgb.org.uk
Published annually.

Architectural Review
Greater London House
Hampstead Road
London, NW1 7EJ, UK
+44 020 1858 438847
www.arplus.com
Published by EMAP Construct.

Architecture Australia
Level 3, 4 Princes Street
Port Melbourne, Victoria
Australia 3207
+61 (03) 9646 4760
www.archmedia.com.au/aa/
Official magazine of the RAIA published six
times a year.

l'Architecture d'Aujourd'hui
54/56 avenue Hoche
75008 Paris, France
+33 1 58051751
www.larchitecturedaujourdhui.fr
Published six times a year in French and
English.

Arkitektur
Box 4296
SE102 66 Stockholm, Sweden
+46 8 702 7850
www.arkitektur.se
Published eight times yearly with English sum-
maries.

a+u magazine
2-31-2 Yushima, Bunkyo-ku
Tokyo, 113-0034, Japan
+81 33816-2935
www.shinkenchiku.net
Published monthly in Japanese and English by
A+U Publishing Co., Ltd.

Blueprint
John Carpenter House
John Carpenter Street
London, EC4Y 0AN, UK
www.blueprintmagazine.co.uk
+44 020 7936 6400
Published monthly by Progressive Media
Publishing, Ltd.

Canadian Architect
12 Concorde Place, Suite 800
Toronto, ON, M3C 4J2, Canada
(416) 510-6845
www.canadianarchitect.com
Published monthly by Business Information
Group, a division of Hollinger Canadian
Newspapers, LP.

Casabella
D. Trentacoste 7
Milan, 20134, Italy
+39 02 66 21 56 31
Published 11 times a year in Italian with an
English summary.

El Croquis
Avda de los Reyes Catolicos 9
E-28280 El Escorial
Madrid, Spain
+34 91 8969410
www.elcroquis.es
Published bimonthly in Spanish and English.

Domus
Via G. Mazzocchi 13
Rozzano
Milan, 20089, Italy
+39 0282472276
www.domusweb.it
Published 11 times a year in Italian and
English.

Hinge
24/F, Empire Land Commercial Centre
81 Lockhart Road
Wanchai
Hong Kong, China
+852 2520 2468
www.hingenet.com
Published monthly.

Japan Architect
2-31-2 Yushima, Bunkyo-ku
Tokyo, 113-8501, Japan
+81 3 3816-2532
www.shinkenchiku.net
Published quarterly in Japanese and English.

Journal of Architecture
4 Park Square
Milton Park
Abingdon
Oxfordshire OX14 4RN, UK
+44 20 7017 6000
www.tandf.co.uk/journals/rjar/
Published six times a year by RIBA and
Routledge, an imprint of Taylor & Francis.

Journal of Sustainable Product Design
Centre for Sustainable Design
University College for the Creative Arts
Farnham Campus
Faculty of Design
Falkner Road
Farnham
Surrey GU9 7DS, UK
+44 (0)1252 89 2772
www.cfsd.org.uk/journal/index.html
A quarterly journal published by Kluwer
Academic Publishers in partnership with the
Centre for Sustainable Design.

Journals & Magazines

Journal of Urban Design
4 Park Square
Milton Park
Abingdon
Oxfordshire OX14 4RN, UK
+44 20 7017 6000
Published three times a year by Routledge,
Taylor & Francis Group.

Ottagono
Via Stalingrado, 97/2
40128 Bologna, Italy
+39 051 3540 111
www.ottagono.com
Published monthly in Italian and English.

Volume
Archis Foundation
PO Box 14702
1001 LE Amsterdam, Netherlands
31 20 3203926
www.archis.org
Bilingual magazine published six times each
year by Stichting Archis in association with the
Netherlands Architecture Institute.

Wallpaper
Blue Fin Building
110 Southwark Street
London, SE1 0SU, UK
+44 20 3148 5000
www.wallpaper.com
Published 10 times a year.

Source: DesignIntelligence

Museums

There are many museums around the world devoted solely to architecture and design. In addition, many major museums maintain strong design collections and regularly host architecture and design-related exhibits. The following contains the contact information for these organizations.

US Museums

A+D Architecture and Design Museum
6032 Wilshire Boulevard
Los Angeles, CA 90036
(323) 932-9393
www.aplusd.org

Art Institute of Chicago
111 South Michigan Avenue
Chicago, IL 60603
(312) 443-3600
www.artic.edu/aic/

Athenaeum of Philadelphia
219 South Sixth Street
Philadelphia, PA 19106
(215) 925-2688
www.philaathenaeum.org

Center for Architecture
536 LaGuardia Place
New York, NY 10012
(212) 683-0023
www.aiany.org/centerforarchitecture/

Chicago Architecture Foundation
224 South Michigan Avenue
Chicago, IL 60604
(312) 922-3432
www.architecture.org

Cooper-Hewitt, National Design Museum, Smithsonian Institution
2 East 91st Street
New York, NY 10128
(212) 849-8400
www.cooperhewitt.org

Heinz Architectural Center
Carnegie Museum of Art
4400 Forbes Avenue
Pittsburgh, PA 15213
(412) 622-3131
www.cmoa.org

MAK Center for Art & Architecture L.A.
The Schindler House
835 North Kings Road
West Hollywood, CA 90069
(323) 651-1510
www.makcenter.org

Museum of Arts & Design
2 Columbus Circle
New York, NY 10019
(212) 299-7777
www.madmuseum.org

Museum of Contemporary Art, Los Angeles
MOCA at California Plaza
250 South Grand Avenue
Los Angeles, CA 90012
(213) 626-6222
www.moca-la.org

Museum of Design
Marquis II Office Tower
285 Peachtree Center Avenue
Atlanta, GA 30303
(404) 979-6455
www.museumofdesign.org

Museum of Modern Art
11 West 53rd Street
New York, NY 10019
(212) 708-9400
www.moma.org

Museums

National Building Museum
401 F Street NW
Washington, DC 20001
(202) 272-2448
www.nbm.org

Octagon Museum
1799 New York Avenue NW
Washington, DC 20006
(202) 626-7420
www.archfoundation.org

Price Tower Arts Center
510 Dewey Avenue
Bartlesville, OK 74003
(918) 336-4949
www.pricetower.org

San Francisco Museum of Craft + Design
550 Sutter Street
San Francisco, CA 94102
(415) 773-0303
www.sfmcd.org

San Francisco Museum of Modern Art
151 Third Street
San Francisco, CA 94103
(415) 357-4000
www.sfmoma.org

Skyscraper Museum
39 Battery Place
New York, NY 10280
(212) 968-1961
www.skyscraper.org

Storefront for Art and Architecture
97 Kenmare Street
New York, NY 10012
(212) 431-5795
www.storefrontnews.org

Van Alen Institute
30 West 22 Street, 6th Floor
New York, NY 10010
(212) 924-7000
www.vanalen.org

Virginia Center for Architecture
2501 Monument Avenue
Richmond, VA 23220
(804) 644-3041
www.virginiaarchitecture.org

International Museums

Alvar Aalto Museum
(Alvar Aalto Museo)
Alvar Aallon katu 7
Jyväskylä, Finland
+358 14 266 7113
www.alvaraalto.fi

Architecture Center of Vienna
(Architekturzentrum Wien)
Museumsplatz 1, im MQ
A-1070 Vienna, Austria
+43 522 3115
www.azw.at

Bauhaus Archive/Museum of Design
(Bauhaus-Archiv/Museum für Gestaltung)
Klingelhöferstraße 14
10785 Berlin, Germany
+49 30 254 00 20
www.bauhaus.de

Canadian Centre for Architecture
1920, rue Baile
Montreal, QC, Canada H3H 2S6
(514) 939-7026
www.cca.qc.ca

Danish Architecture Center
(Dansk Arkitektur Center)
Strandgade 27B
1401 Copenhagen K, Denmark
+45 32 57 19 30
www.dac.dk

Danish Design Center
(Dansk Design Center)
27 H C Andersens Boulevard
1553 Copenhagen V, Denmark
+45 33 69 33 69
www.ddc.dk

Design Museum, Finland
(Designmuseo)
Korkeavuorenkatu 23
00130 Helsinki, Finland
+35 89 622 0540
www.designmuseum.fi

Design Museum, London
Shad Thames
London SE1 2YD, UK
+44 20 7403 6933
www.designmuseum.org

Design Museum at the Cultural Center of Belém
(Museu do Design, Centro Cultural de Belém)
Praça do Império
1499-003 Lisbon, Portugal
+351 213 612 400
www.ccb.pt

German Centre for Architecture
(Deutsches Architektur Zentrum)
Direktorin Kristien Ring
Köpenicker Straße 48/49
10179 Berlin, Germany
+49 30 278799-28
www.daz.de

German Architecture Museum
(Deutsches Architektur Museum)
Schaumainkai 43
60596 Frankfurt am Main
Germany
+49 69-212 38844
www.dam-online.de

International Center for Urbanism
(Centre International pour la Ville, l'Architecture et le Paysage)
Rue de l'Ermitage 55 Kluisstraat
Brussels 1050, Belgium
+32 (0)2 642 24 50
www.civa.be

The Lighthouse: Scotland's Centre for Architecture, Design & the City
11 Mitchell Lane
Glasgow, G1 3NU, Scotland
United Kingdom
+44 141 221 6362
www.glasgowarchitecture.co.uk/lighthouse.htm

Museum of Architecture in Wroclaw
(Muzeum Architektury we Wroclawiu)
ul. Bernardynska 5
PL 50-156 Wroclaw, Poland
+48 (71) 343 36 75
www.ma.wroc.pl

Museum of Estonian Architecture
(Eesti Arhitektuurimuuseum)
Arts centre
Rotermann's Salt Storage
Ahtri 2, Tallinn 10151
tel. +372 625 7000
www.arhitektuurimuuseum.ee

Museum of Finnish Architecture
(Suomen Rakennustaiteen Museo)
Kasarmikatu 24, 00130
Helsinki, Finland
+358 9 8567 5100
www.mfa.fi

Museums

Netherlands Architecture Institute
(Nederlands Architectuurinstituut)
Museumpark 25
3015 CB Rotterdam, Netherlands
+3110-4401200
www.nai.nl

National Museum of Art, Architecture and Design
(Nasjonalmuseet for Kunst, Arkitektur og Design)
Kristian Augusts gate 23
Oslo, Norway
+47 21 98 20 00
www.nationalmuseum.no

Palladio Centre and Museum
(Centro Internazionale di Studi di Architettura Andrea Palladio)
Contra' Porti 11
I-36100 Vicenza, Italy
+39 (04) 44 32 30 14
www.cisapalladio.org

RIBA Architecture Gallery
66 Portland Place
London W1B 1AD, UK
+44 20 7580 5533
www.architecture.com

Röhsska Museum of Design and Applied Art
(Röhsska Museet för Konsthantverk och Design)
Vasagatan 37-39
SE-400 15 Göteborg, Sweden
+46 31-36 83 150
www.designmuseum.se

Schusev State Museum of Architecture
Vozdvizhenka str., 5
119019 Moscow, Russia
+7-495-690-05-51
www.muar.ru

Swedish Museum of Architecture
(Arkitekturmuseet)
Skeppsholmen
SE-111 49 Stockholm, Sweden
+46 8 587 270 00
www.arkitekturmuseet.se

Swiss Architecture Museum
(Schweizerisches Architekturmuseum)
Steinenberg 7
Postfach 911
CH-4001 Basel, Switzerland
+41 61 261 1413
www.sam-basel.org

Victoria and Albert Museum
Cromwell Road
London SW7 2RL, UK
+44 20 7942 2000
www.vam.ac.uk

Vitra Design Museum
Charles-Eames-Str. 1
D-79576 Weil am Rhein
Germany
+49 7621 702 32 00
www.design-museum.de

Zurich Museum of Design
(Museum für Gestaltung Zürich)
Ausstellungsstr 60
8005 Zürich, Switzerland
+41 43 446 67 67
www.museum-gestaltung.ch

Source: DesignIntelligence

Salary and Compensation Guide

Every year *DesignIntelligence* tracks the compensation of design professionals. Its annual *Compensation and Benefits Survey* includes benchmark compensation statistics from US design firms and discussions of human resources trends. The data below is extracted from the 2010 *Compensation and Benefits Survey*. Additional salary statistics and compensation-related information can be found in this report available at *www.di.net/bookstore*. Note: the numbers below are base compensation figures, not including bonuses, if any. Where a range is indicated, it represents the mean highest to the mean lowest.

Executive Staff

Chief Executive Officer/President
Mean: $198,341

Chief Operating Officer
Mean: $154,333

Partner, owner/equity
Mean: $176,353 – $121,500

Principal, non-owner, non-equity
Mean: $183,800 – $128,917

Associate Principal, non-owner, non-equity
Mean: $135,588 – $112,389

Note: Principals typically receive a significant bonus, with the mean often ranging from 15 percent to 55 percent or higher.

Design Staff

Project Manager, 15–19 yrs. exp.
Mean: $99,630 – $85,577

Project Manager, 10–14 yrs. exp.
Mean: $87,147 – $71,586

Project Manager, 5–9 yrs. exp.
Mean: $81,619 – $62,000

Architect, 15–19 yrs. exp.
Mean: $97,767 – $73,700

Architect, 10–14 yrs. exp.
Mean: $85,361 – $66,294

Architect, 5–9 yrs. exp.
Mean: $69,711 – $54,026

Interior Designer, 15–19 yrs. exp.
Mean: $88,462 – $73,643

Interior Designer, 10–14 yrs. exp.
Mean: $76,778 – $60,875

Interior Designer, 5–9 yrs. exp.
Mean: $58,714 – $44,103

Landscape Architect, 15–19 yrs. exp.
Mean: $96,286 – $68,000

Landscape Architect, 10–14 yrs. exp.
Mean: $77,111 – $55,889

Landscape Architect, 5–9 yrs. exp.
Mean: $58,000 – $44,750

Salary and Compensation Guide

Mechanical/Electrical/Plumbing Engineer, 15–19 yrs. exp.
Mean: $110,400 – $89,375

Mechanical/Electrical/Plumbing Engineer, 10–14 yrs. exp.
Mean: $93,200 – $72,300

Mechanical/Electrical/Plumbing Engineer, 5–9 yrs. exp.
Mean: $78,200 – $59,700

Structural Engineer, 15–19 yrs. exp.
Mean: $95,750 – $79,778

Structural Engineer, 10–14 yrs. exp.
Mean: $93,250 – $78,857

Structural Engineer, 5–9 yrs. exp.
Mean: $79,500 – $59,467

Note: Design staff typically receive a mean bonus ranging from 3 percent to 8 percent or higher.

Specialized and Support Staff

IT Manager
Mean: $87,941 – $68,000

Marketing Director
Mean: $100,353 – $77,333

Marketing Associate
Mean: $72,235 – $53,813

Marketing Assistant
Mean: $50,313 – $38,615

Office Manager
Mean: $54,400 – $49,583

Administrative Assistant
Mean: $48,692 – $35,121

Note: Specialized and support staff typically receive a mean bonus ranging from 3 percent to 8 percent or higher.

Architecture Interns

Year 1
Mean: $42,107 – $37,250

Year 2
Mean: $47,407 – $40,156

Year 3
Mean: $47,407 – $40,156

Source: March/April 2010 DesignIntelligence

Note: Architecture interns typically receive a mean bonus ranging from 2 percent to 3 percent.

INDEXES | Names & Sites

Name Index

NOTE: Pages in italics refer to illustrations. See the Site Index beginning on page 583 for architectural projects, sites and works.

Name Index

Name Index

Name Index

Name Index

Name Index

E

F

F.A. Bernett, 532
Fabos, Julius, 250
Facility Design Group, 97, 169
Fainsilber, Adien, 251
Fairbanks, Bruce S., 366
Fairfax and Sammons Architects, 417
Faith & Form, 343, 534
Faithful+Gould, 233
Fanning, Ronald H., 61
Fanning/Howey Associates, 61, 169, 215
Farbor, Sam, 254
Farmer, Brent, 109
Farr, Sheila, 530
Farr Associates, 469
Farrell, David M., 103
Farson, Richard, 242
Fast Company, 244, 263, 359
Fathom, 169
Fathy, Hassan, 266
Faulkner, Stenhouse, Fryer, 380
Fazio, Michael W., 493
Fedrizzi, Rick, 242
FEH Associates, 230
Fehn, Sverre, 258
Feilden Clegg Bradley Studios, 293
Fein, Gilbert M., 387
Feiner, Edward A., 242, 265
Feitel, Arthur, 381
Fender Katsalidis Architects, 299
Fentress, Curtis, 41, *264,* 265
Fentress Architects, *40,* 41, 169, 299, 364, 367
Fentress Bradburn Architects, 365, 367, 385, 405
Fergus Garaber Group, 169
Ferguson, William, 381
Ferguson & Shamamian Architects, 170, 249, 341
Ferguson Pape Baldwin Architects, 170
Fergusson, Frances D., 262
Fergusson, James, 260
Ferraro Choi and Associates, 170
Ferrey, Benjamin, 260
Ferris, Roger, 69
Ferris Architects, 444
FFKR Architects, 403
FGM Architects, 82, 170
Field Paoli Architects, 131, 170, 216
Fine, Steven, 498
Fine Homebuilding, 534
Finegold Alexander + Associates, 170, 215
Finney, David R., 145
Fischer, Martin, 242
Fischer, Victor, 240
Fisher, Harold H., 249
Fisher, Tom, 242
Fisher Marantz Stone, 446
Fiske, Bradford, 47
Fiskum, Stephen, 45, 242
Fitts, Michael A., 265
FitzGerald Associates Architects, 170, 216, 460
FKP Architects, 60, 170
Flabiano, Mattia, 49
Flad, Harvey Keyes, 262
Flad Architects, 57, 170
Flagg, Ernest, 374
Flaming Beacon, 447
Flansburgh Architects, 144, 170, 329
Flatiron-Manson, 322
Fleener, Brian, 57
Fleischer, Joseph, 59
Fleming, David, 458

Fletcher Farr Ayotte, 170, 391
Fletcher Thompson, 97, 170, 230
Flewelling & Moody, 170
Flocos, Sabret, 142
Florian Nagler Architekt, 335
Floud, Peter, 284
Flynn, Dalton and Van Dijk, 369
Flynn, Kevin, 238
Flynn, Michael D., 67
Flynn Battaglia Architects, 421
Fogelson, Robert, 497
Fogle Stenzel Architects, 216
Follett, James, 242
Follmer, Michael D., 99
Fong & Chan Architects, 374
Fontillas, John, 123
Foor & Associates, 229
Forbes, Rob, 262
Ford Powell & Carson, 170, 343
Foreign Office Architects (UK), 310
Foreman Architects Engineers, 170
Forest, Robert, 79
Forest City Enterprises, 423
Forgey, Benjamin, 271
Formation Design Group, 359
Forrest, Deborah Lloyd, 252
Forrester Construction Company, 322
Fort-Brescia, Bernardo, 71
Forum Architecture & Interior Design, 170, 216
Forum Studio, 117, 170
Foss Architecture & Interiors, 171, 230
Foster, Lord Norman
    awards/honors, 237, 242, 246, 248, 251, 257, 258,
        261, 295
    works/projects, 288
Foster, Richard, 376
Foster & Associates, 309
Foster + Partners
    awards/honors, 310, 335, 352, 353
    staff/collaborators/associates, 242
    works/projects, 297, 298, 363, 365, 367, 377, 379, 381
Fougeron, Anne, 238
Fowle, Bruce, 73
Fox, Catherine, 528
Fox, Corinne, 240
Fox, Robert D., 142
Fox Architects, 142, 171
Fraker, Harrison, 242
Fram, Donald, 238
Frampton, Kenneth, 237, 247
Francis Cauffman, 76, 171
Frank C.Y. Feng Architects & Associates, 300
Frank L. Hope and Associates, 405
Frank O. Gehry and Associates, Inc., 309, 376, 383
Frank Williams and Partners Architects, 277
Frankel, Neil, 242, 255
Frankel + Coleman, 171, 242
Franklin, Carol Levy, 262
Franklin Associates Architects, 171
Franzen, Ulrich, 248
Franzheim, Kenneth, 379
Frasca, Robert, 35
Fraser, David Van, 281–282
Frazier Associates, 216
FRCH Design Worldwide, 171
Frechette, Roger, 242
Fred Bassetti & Co., 371
Freed, James Ingo, 248, 265
Freelon, Philip G., 253, 265
Freelon Group, The, 171, 401, 445
Freeman, Raymond L., 250

Name Index

H

Name Index

Name Index

Name Index

Name Index

Name Index

Name Index

Name Index

Q

R

Name Index

Name Index

Name Index

Name Index

Name Index

Site Index

NOTE: This is an index of architectural sites, projects and works. Entries marked with an asterisk (*) refer to plans associated with a site. Locations that are not an architectural site per se—for example, universities—can be found in the Name Index starting on page 546. Pages in italics refer to illustrations.

Site Index

Site Index

Site Index

Site Index

Site Index

Site Index

Site Index

Site Index

Site Index

About the Editors

James P. Cramer is the founding editor and publisher of the *Almanac of Architecture & Design* as well as *DesignIntelligence*, a journal on trends and strategies published by Greenway Communications on behalf of the Design Futures Council. Cramer is one of the country's foremost management consultants to the design industry and is the founder and CEO of the Greenway Group, a leading strategy consulting and business networking firm. He is the author or co-author of several hundred articles and several books, including the critically acclaimed *Design Plus Enterprise: Seeking a New Reality in Architecture* and the bestselling *How Firms Succeed: A Field Guide to Design Management Solutions*. Cramer is the former chief executive of the American Institute of Architects, a Richard Upjohn Fellow of the AIA, and a Fellow of the International Leadership Forum. He is president of the Washington, DC-based think tank the Design Futures Council and has more than 80 honors to his credit for service to the architecture and design community.

Jane Paradise Wolford, Ph.D., is an architectural historian and the editor of the *Almanac of Architecture & Design*. She is also a senior consultant with Greenway Communications and an editor for the Ostberg Library of Design Management. Wolford has a doctorate in architectural history, theory, and criticism from the Georgia Institute of Technology as well as a Master of Science degree in architectural history from there. Her doctoral thesis established the theoretical and practical framework for architectural contextualism in its definitions and aspects of construction that enable buildings to relate better to each other and encourage a more sustainable, cohesively built environment. She is a LEED accredited professional. She also studied at Westmont College in Santa Barbara, CA, where she earned her bachelor's degree in English, and the University of California Berkeley, where she received her teaching credential. She and her husband, Arol Wolford, founded Construction Market Data in 1981, a leading international construction information service. Enlightening the public about the transformational potential of architecture is her quest.

Jennifer Evans Yankopolus is an architectural historian and the editorial advisor to the *Almanac of Architecture & Design*. She works with numerous architecture and design publications as an editor. In addition to a master's degree in architecture history from the Georgia Institute of Technology, she holds a master's degree in heritage preservation from Georgia State University and a BS in business from Drake University.

östberg

Library of Design Management

Every relationship of value requires constant care and commitment. At Östberg, we are relentless in our desire to create
and bring forward only the best ideas in design, architecture,
interiors, and design management. Using diverse mediums of
communications, including books and the Internet, we are con-
stantly searching for thoughtful ideas that are erudite, witty, and
of lasting importance to the quality of life. Inspired by the architecture of Ragnar Östberg and the best of Scandinavian design
and civility, the Östberg Library of Design Management seeks
to restore the passion for creativity that makes better products,
spaces, and communities. The essence of Östberg can be
summed up in our quality charter to you: "Communicating concepts of leadership and design excellence."